HIGHER PROBABILITY

COMMODITY TRADING

A Comprehensive Guide to Commodity Market Analysis,

Strategy Development, and Risk Management Techniques

Aimed at Favorably Shifting the Odds of Success

CARLEY GARNER

COMMODITY MARKET ANALYST & BROKER AT DECARLEYTRADING.COM

dt

DeCarley Trading, LLC

HIGHER PROBABILITY COMMODITY TRADING
A Comprehensive Guide to Commodity Market Analysis,
Strategy Development, and Risk Management Techniques Aimed
at Favorably Shifting the Odds of Success

Carley Garner

ISBN: 9781942545521
Library of Congress Control Number: 2016942104

Published by DeCarley Trading, LLC
an Imprint of Wyatt-MacKenzie

www.DeCarleyTrading.com

DeCarley Trading, LLC

ACKNOWLEDGMENTS

This book is dedicated to my colleagues at DeCarley Trading, Zaner Group, TheStreet.com, Technical Analysis of STOCKS & COMMODITIES magazine, and the team at CNBC's Mad Money. Without their support and encouragement, none of this would be possible.

ABOUT THE AUTHOR

Senior Commodity Market Strategist and Broker, STOCKS & COMMODITIES Magazine Columnist, TheStreet.com Contributor, and Author

Carley Garner is an experienced futures and options broker with DeCarley Trading, a division of Zaner Group, in Las Vegas, Nevada. She is also the author of *Higher Probability Commodity Trading*; *A Trader's First Book on Commodities* (two editions); *Currency Trading in the Forex and Futures Markets*; and *Commodity Options*. Her e-newsletters, *The DeCarley Perspective,* and *The Financial Futures Report*, have garnered a loyal following; she is also proactive in providing free trading education.

Carley is a magna cum laude graduate of the University of Nevada Las Vegas, from which she earned dual bachelor's degrees in finance and accounting. Carley jumped into the options and futures industry with both feet in early 2004 and has become one of the most recognized names in the business. Her commodity market analysis is often referenced on Jim Cramer's *Mad Money* on CNBC and she is a regular contributor to TheStreet.com and its Real Money Pro service.

Carley has also been featured in the likes of STOCKS & COMMODITIES, *Futures, Active Trader, Option Trader* magazines, and many more. She has been quoted by *Investor's Business Daily* and *The Wall Street Journal* and has also been known to participate in radio interviews. She can be found on the speaking circuit.   Visit Carley at www.DeCarleyTrading.com.

Keep in touch on social media:

 @carleygarner

 DeCarleyTradingCommodityBroker

 decarleytrading

PRAISE FOR HIGHER PROBABILITY COMMODITY TRADING BY CARLEY GARNER:

"Carley has been a respected figure in the futures industry for many years. Her approach to successful markets analysis, trading, and trading education is one of keen preparation and study, continually absorbing markets knowledge, and following the basics of market analysis and trading that have propelled the most successful traders/analysts over the past 125 years." — **Jim Wyckoff, 30-year veteran trader/markets analyst JimWyckoff.com.**

"Higher Probability Commodity Trading is one of the rare cases of a book that does a great job combining fundamental, seasonal, and technical analysis. Carley Garner's latest book is a must own for anyone considering trading commodities or options on commodities." — **Russell Rhoads, CFA - Director of Education at the CBOE Options Institute**

"As someone who has been deeply involved in the commodities and derivatives markets, since the start of my career in 1989, I have read a lot of books on trading, a lot. I also have had the privilege of learning from some of the greatest traders in the world and seen an incredible number of changes in our industry over the years since then. Even as seasoned traders, we must always be open to learning and adapting to our ever-changing markets, commodities are always in an evolutionary stage. Ms. Garner has written a solid, educational, and entertaining primer on these markets, filled with insight, advice, and strategy. She has done so in a concise, easy to understand yet not placating voice, which is a rarity for trading books of this caliber. Whether you are just starting your journey into the world of commodities or are a professional trader with years of experience, there is something in this book for everyone. Without a doubt, Higher Probability Commodity Trading will give you the insight you need to make smarter, better-informed, and hopefully profitable trading decisions. While you may not utilize all of the information in this book immediately, you will certainly find what you need, for whatever stage you're at in your adventure into the world of Commodities Trading. I highly recommend this book for every trader's reading list." — **Kevin S. Kerr, President, Kerr Trading International, Frequent business news contributor**

"Amid a dearth of excellent new literature on commodity trading, Carley Garner has authored an impressive overview of concepts and techniques traders can use to "put the odds in their favor." As someone with experience as a commodity broker, trader, and analyst, I was first struck by her honesty about not only the allure, of but also the risk in trading commodities --- and then by her realistic insights into how to manage that risk. Ms. Garner writes from the perspective less of a broker than of an intelligent, well-versed teacher who wants her students to succeed. I highly recommend Higher Probability Commodity Trading to all traders from novice to experienced. Even those who have been around a while can learn — or relearn! — something." — **Jerry Toepke, Editor, Moore Research Center, Inc.**

I have been trading commodities and futures for more than 20 years, and whether you are new to trading or have been trading for a while: THIS book is for you! It's one of the most comprehensive books that I have seen on this topic. Carley covers everything you need to know: The most important indicators, Seasonalities, Commitment of Traders Report (COT), Day Trading, Position Trading and even Options Trading. My personal favorite is the chapter "Speculating in VIX Futures". And the best: Even though this book is covering all aspects of Commodities Trading, it's an easy read filled with PRACTICAL strategies, tips and tricks. In short: Get this book! — **Markus Heitkoetter, Futures Trading Veteran**

"There isn't a better book for learning how to master the art and science of trading commodities. Higher Probability Commodity Trading is a must read for the beginner or experienced trader. Carley opens the door to lesser-known tricks and strategies - this book is the only commodities book on my desk." — **Rob Booker, Host of The Booker Report**

ALSO BY CARLEY GARNER:

Commodity Options

A Trader's First Book on Commodities

Currency Trading in the Forex and Futures Markets

RISK DISCLOSURE

There is a substantial risk of loss in trading futures and options. Past performance is not indicative of future results.

The information and data contained in this text was obtained from sources considered reliable. Their accuracy or completeness is not guaranteed. Information provided in this book is not to be deemed as an offer or solicitation with respect to the sale or purchase of any securities or commodities. Any decision to purchase or sell as a result of the opinions expressed in this text will be the full responsibility of the person authorizing such transaction.

Seasonal tendencies are a composite of some of the more consistent commodity futures seasonals that have occurred over the past 15 or more years. There are usually underlying, fundamental circumstances that occur annually that tend to cause the futures markets to react in a similar directional manner during a certain calendar year. While seasonal trends may potentially impact supply and demand in certain commodities, seasonal aspects of supply and demand have been factored into futures & options market pricing. Even if a seasonal tendency occurs in the future, it may not result in a profitable transaction as fees and the timing of the entry and liquidation may impact on the results.

No representation is being made that any commodity trading account has in the past, or will in the future, achieve profits using these recommendations. No representation is being made that price patterns will recur in the future. There is unlimited risk in option selling or open-ended option spreads.

TABLE OF CONTENTS

SECTION 1: INTRODUCTION TO COMMODITY ANALYSIS AND SPECULATION

Too many beginning traders look to the commodity markets as a source of vast riches to pad their retirement, or worse, to be the solution to years of neglecting their retirement plans. Others hope their trading skills will enable them to quit their jobs and speculate online from a private island in the South Pacific. The reality, however, is the commodity markets are neither of those things. Instead, futures and options were created to offer end users a way to hedge their price risk and for speculators to accept substantial levels of risk in hopes of returning a profit. This book, and more specifically Section 1, will bring readers up to speed on the mechanics, truths, and opportunities offered by the commodity market, while offering some words of advice to shift the probabilities of success favorably. If after reading this paragraph, you are inclined to put the book down to seek literature on stock trading, I can assure you—active speculation in any arena comes with hefty risks. Yet commodity trading comes with unique advantages that potentially trump opportunities presented by almost all other asset classes.

INTRODUCTION: LEVERAGE SEPARATES COMMODITY TRADERS FROM SPECULATORS

The commodity markets are unique in that they offer participants free, and easy to acquire, leverage. There is no other market in the world that does this. Even real estate, which provides property buyers with the opportunity of high-leverage home ownership, investments, and speculation, requires a relatively stringent approval process and interest payments. In the commodity markets, the bar is set comparatively low to open and utilize interest-free leverage.

Generally speaking, an individual need only $20,000 in net worth, and a similar annual income, to get their foot in the door. As a result, commodity futures markets often attract traders with destructive mindsets focused on "get rich quick" behavior, and a lack of financial backing necessary to create an environment in which the odds of success are favorable. As is usually the case, it takes money to make money in the world of commodities. That said, the advent of ultra-small futures products such as e-micro gold and the e-micro currency futures traded on the Chicago Mercantile Exchange (CME) enable less-capitalized traders to favorably shift the odds of success in a similar manner that larger traders do with their capital. In essence, the "little guy" can now trade like the "big boys" if they are willing to exercise discipline in their product choice and conduct.

In short, the commodity markets offer opportunities for traders of all sizes, strategies, and risk-aversion levels. Yet, the manner in which a trader approaches the market will determine whether the commodity markets are a source of gambling entertainment or a legitimate investment. Contrary to popular belief, the commodity markets are not evil, nor are they any more risky than speculative stock trading. The reality is, most of the nightmarish stories depicting account-draining losses by

> "In this game, the market has to keep pitching, but you don't have to swing. You can stand there with the bat on your shoulder until you get a fat pitch."
> —Warren Buffett

commodity traders have little to do with market volatility; instead, it is almost always the result of overleveraged and overactive trading. In other words, the trader himself determines how risky his commodity trading account will be through the decisions made to utilize leverage. Most traders make the mistake of simply accepting the leverage built into the commodity markets as "normal" and proceeding accordingly, but it is possible to dramatically reduce the leverage by simply trading a smaller contract size, or adding funds to the account above and beyond the required margin. Before discussing this in further detail, let's introduce two seemingly obvious but often overlooked facts:

      Putting money to work, whether you do it as a trader or an investor, in the commodity markets is far different from doing so in traditional asset classes such as stocks and bonds.

      Trading is not investing. Understanding the difference between these two approaches is important because the allocation of your assets should be overweight in investments, and underweight in trades.

There are few, if any, activities in which individuals have the potential to do themselves such significant harm more than the commodity markets. Yet, there are even fewer opportunities capable of yielding the magnificent rewards found in futures and options trading. The difference between the two outcomes often boils down to experience, or more specifically a productive mental outlook on trading. Unfortunately, experience cannot be bought, nor can it be mimicked. Nevertheless, I am able to write this book from a unique perspective.

Most financial literature is authored by scholars and academic types with an extensive knowledge of market theory and mathematical equations. In contrast, I am armed with a more practical and hands-on basket of knowledge. The goal of this book is to provide readers with a realistic view of commodity trading intertwined with lessons I've learned throughout my commodity brokerage career, which began in 2004. I've either experienced first-hand, or witnessed, nearly all possible trading mistakes. I hope I am able to pass along some of these hard-learned lessons in a less painful way—through this book.

COMMODITIES VS. STOCKS/BONDS

The primary difference between putting money to work in the commodity markets as opposed to stocks or bonds is the absence of cash flow. For instance, stockholders often receive dividends or benefit from stock buybacks. The corresponding cash flow makes it possible for investors to profit from stock and bond holdings, regardless if the price of the security goes up. Simply put, traditional investments provide a cushion from losses through income, but commodities don't pay dividends or interest; instead, commodity traders are left to fend for themselves via market timing.

Unfortunately, this simple fact is often forgotten as eager speculators jump into the commodity markets in hopes of massive profits. For a green trader, the lack of a dividend seems to be an inconsequential opportunity cost to high-leveraged futures trading. For them, it is difficult to imagine their market predictions could be inaccurate; after all, they've been paper trading for several months with unprecedented success. Still, as all traders eventually learn the "hard way," trading with real money is an emotional game that can suddenly turn a simple practice of trend following into a seemingly impossible task. Accordingly, the lack of a risk cushion in the form of a yield or dividend is something to recognize and account for.

Further, not only do dividends pad the return potential for stock traders, their mere existence promotes an overwhelming tendency for equities to go up over time despite temporary setbacks such as the flash crashes of May 2010 and August 2015.

Another aspect to be aware of before participating in the commodity market is the nature of contract expiration. Stock traders can theoretically hold a position "forever" in hopes of a poorly timed trade eventually paying off, but a commodity trader is typically using a futures contract, or an option on a futures contract, which faces expiration dates. Although it is possible for a futures trader to roll over expiring contracts into distant contract months, there are still transaction obstacles and slippage. Those who think they are avoiding this conundrum via the purchase of exchange traded funds (ETFs) are mistaken. Although they do not see it, there are behind-the-scenes transactions taking place to avoid delivery of the underlying futures contracts. Thus, ETF holders are indirectly suffering from the inefficiencies of rolling contracts.

On a side note, ETFs are an extremely inept way to gain commodity exposure. Due to high management fees, administrative costs, fund rebalancing, the burden of internal fund transaction costs, and other inefficiencies, a product has been created that doesn't necessarily correlate to the underlying commodity. I've observed situations in which a double-digit percentage move in a commodity yields a meager 2% to 3% move in the ETF created to track that commodity. Leveraged ETFs such as the "two times" (2X) or "three times" (3X) securities are even less competent.

Commodity futures contracts can be conveniently bought or sold in any order proficiently with minimal cost or burden. If a speculator believes the price of corn is going lower, he has the ability to sell a contract with the intention of buying it back at a later date. Stock traders can do this too, but they must first borrow shares from their broker and pay interest on the transaction; these obstacles slow down the process and increase the costs. The ease of selling a futures contract before it was ever purchased or owned is made possible by the fact that futures traders are buying and selling a liability to make or take delivery of the underlying asset, as opposed to buying or selling the actual asset itself as stock traders do.

While we are at it, there are a few notable benefits of trading futures relative to trading stocks we haven't touched upon yet:

- **Futures traders enjoy expanded trading hours.** Aside from an afternoon pause, traders can easily execute orders around the clock without any inconveniences or restrictions. Stock traders are generally limited to making transactions from 9:30 a.m. to 4:00 p.m. Eastern. However, asset prices are a global phenomenon; despite the stock market being closed overnight, prices are constantly changing!
- **Low account minimums for futures traders.** Futures speculators can generally open a trading account with as little as a few thousand dollars. Buy and hold stock traders can do the same, but most brokers require $50,000 to $100,000 for active speculation.
- **It is possible to sell options without large cash outlays in the futures markets.** Depending on the brokerage firm, it might be possible to implement a premium collection strategy in a trading account with as little as $5,000 to $10,000. Stockbrokers generally require $50,000 to $100,000 in a trading account to sell options. Further, since stockbrokers require a trader to have the entire cash outlay to purchase the underlying stock should a sold option be exercised, this can be hundreds of thousands for some securities. Futures traders don't have to worry about that because the underlying asset is a leveraged futures contract; thus, it is only necessary to have the margin to hold the futures contract once exercised.

- **All futures accounts are granted portfolio margining.** This practice allows margin breaks for covered calls, option spreads, and so forth. Stockbrokers typically require at least $100,000 to provide portfolio margining.
- **Futures traders receive favorable tax treatment.** All futures, and options on futures, transactions are taxed at a blended rate of 60% long-term capital gains and 40% short-term capital gains. Stock speculators holding a position less than a year face the higher short-term capital gains rate. Further, a futures trader faces a much simpler reporting process when filing taxes. Unlike stock traders, who must report each individual stock transaction, futures traders report a single figure to the IRS from a 1099 issued by their brokerage firms.

TRADING VS. INVESTING

> "Face reality as it is, not as it was or how you wish it to be." —Jack Welch

As a long-time commodity broker, I'm often approached by individuals pledging their interest in "investing in commodities." That phrase makes me cringe, but not because I think commodity trading should be avoided. After all, I make my living providing traders with the means to efficiently and effectively trade commodity futures and options via online trading platforms or through a full-service broker. It is in my best interest to attain as many clients as possible, and I'm honored that individuals and institutions are interested in utilizing my brokerage services. Nevertheless, I'm adamant about ensuring that each prospect inquiring about our brokerage services is aware of the realities of commodity trading. I want them to understand the risks, even more so than the potential rewards. Further, I want them to understand that for most, participating in the commodity markets is not an investment; it is a trade.

To clarify the distinction, trading is an active speculation on price changes. In the commodity markets, one might go long or short a market in anticipation of relatively short-term moves. Some commodity traders enter and exit a market within minutes, or even seconds. Those shorting the market are merely placing a wager that the price of an asset will decline. Clearly, neither of these activities have anything to do with investing.

Investors, on the other hand, are the "buy and holders" whose goal is to accumulate gains on a long-term basis, namely several months or even several years. One could argue a commodity strategy in which a trader buys a crude oil contract with the expectation of holding it for a prolonged period of time in anticipation of higher prices is an investment, rather than a trade. I agree; there are some investment qualities in such a market approach, but even so it is not the same type of investment one would get in a stock or bond portfolio. We will discuss that shortly. In addition, if this strategy is being employed in an underfunded account, it is being done on leverage. In my opinion, the existence of leverage constitutes a trade rather than an investment because the profits and losses on a percentage basis are exaggerated.

Although there are no guarantees or assurances, investors typically face better odds of success in the long run than active traders might. However, they do so with expectations of relatively lower profit potential than traders hope to achieve. Naturally, savvy and experienced traders might fare better than traditional investors, but they are undoubtedly accepting higher levels of risk to do so.

In addition, commodity trading, or even low-leveraged buy and hold commodity investing, are partaking in a much more active practice than investors typically would. Annual rebalancing of a portfolio might be sufficient for an emblematic stock and bond retirement portfolio, but that is not the case with commodities due to contract expiration, the absence of dividends and interest, or even a historical pattern of price appreciation. Unlike stocks, which have continually moved higher throughout history, commodities tend to trade in long-term ranges and cycles. Aside from low levels of inflation, commodities are not necessarily expected to appreciate in the long run the way equity securities are.

To recap, traders face far less room for error and decisions tend to be less permanent. An *investor* who is early, or wrong, can simply hold a position for several months or years if necessary in an attempt to recoup losses, but a leveraged *trader* rarely considers this as an option. There is a saying in the trading business that claims that "an investment is a speculation gone wrong."

ARE COMMODITIES A TRADE, OR AN INVESTMENT?

The truth is, the commodity markets can be either a trade *or* an investment. The distinction doesn't come from the market; it comes from the manner in which the market is traded. It is common for inexperienced traders to assume the free leverage granted by the futures industry is an advantage that must be used to the fullest extent. However, experienced traders understand that leverage can work against them just as easily as it can work in their favor. Most trades, and strategies, are optimized by reducing, or even eliminating, leverage.

> "The elements of good trading are: (1) cutting losses, (2) cutting losses, and (3) cutting losses. If you can follow these three rules you may have a chance." — Ed Seykota

For commodity futures traders, this is easy...simply trade fewer lots, use mini contracts, or overfund the account. As an example, if the margin to go long a corn futures contract at $3.90 representing 5,000 bushels is $1,375, a trader can fully fund his account to eliminate leverage by trading a single lot for every $19,500 deposited into the account. Now, $19,500 represents the contract value and is figured by taking the current price of corn multiplied by the contract size ($3.90 x 5,000). Funding the account with the full amount of the contract value, $19,500 in this case, increases the room for error and, therefore, the odds of success relative to trading a corn futures contract in a minimally funded account ($1,375). To illustrate, the percentage gains and losses of a corn futures contract in a $1,375 account will be dramatic, but in a $19,500 account they will be far more manageable.

Another method of de-leveraging the futures market is trading mini-sized futures contracts when available. In the example of a corn trader attempting to mitigate leverage, it is possible to trade a mini corn futures contract representing 1,000 bushels, rather than 5,000. The 1,000-bushel contract carries a contract value of $3,900 ($3.90 x 1,000), and thus, a trader with as little as $3,900 in his account could trade a single mini corn futures without any leverage at all. Similarly, a trader with a $10,000 account balance could trade three mini corn futures to gain exposure to the price changes of $11,700 worth of corn. Such a trade would be only slightly leveraged. As you can see, it is the trader who controls the leverage, and thus account volatility, not the commodity market itself.

In the absence of extreme leverage, and when trading from the long side of the market, it is fair to consider commodities to be an investment rather than a speculative trade. Whether your money is allocated to the commodity markets as a trading vehicle or an investment is solely up to your risk tolerance and portfolio management. In my opinion, the optimal choice lies somewhere in between the two extremes.

MOST PEOPLE LOSE TRADING COMMODITIES, SO IT MAKES SENSE TO GO AGAINST THE GRAIN

I wish it weren't the case, but most people lose trading commodities. Armed with this fact, it might be reasonable to assume going *with* the grain is probably a bad idea. In essence, following the herd will likely lead to slaughter, because that is where most market participants will eventually find themselves. I realize this sounds extremely pessimistic, and even worse, counterproductive to someone like me who makes a living assisting and facilitating commodity traders. Yet, in my experience, those who find consistent trading success in commodities have started by getting a grip on reality. Simply buying or selling a commodity based on the latest news story, rumor, or tip from a friend will never end the way it was imagined.

"You don't need to be a rocket scientist. Investing is not a game where the guy with the 160 IQ beans the guy with the 130 IQ." —Warren Buffett

Throughout this book, we will deliberate the advantages and disadvantages of various trading strategies, market analysis techniques, and approaches to risk management. Regardless of anybody's opinion on the right or wrong way to trade, there really isn't a preferable way to speculate...other than identifying the perils of crowd following.

The sure way to get into trouble in trading is by being a follower rather than a leader. Don't shortchange your trading results by cutting corners, relying on the research of others, or forgoing complex trading strategies because it is uncomfortable to learn something new.

WITH UNLIMITED MONEY, IT WOULD BE HARD TO LOSE TRADING COMMODITIES

While it is certainly not easy to make money in the futures and options markets, traders with extremely deep pockets and a great deal of discipline stand to fare better than the average retail trader. In theory, a trader backed by substantial risk capital, no time limit, and the sense to mitigate futures market leverage could essentially weather any storm in the commodity markets. In other words, they theoretically would "never" lose. This is because commodities are "goods," not "bads"; unless something changes dramatically in the way we live, we will always need corn, soybeans, crude oil, natural gas, and so forth to some degree.

Further, the commodity markets go through boom and bust cycles. Even in the most trying times—think natural gas and crude oil in early 2016, or gold in late 2015—there is light at the end of the tunnel. In the oil industry there is a saying that "the cure to low oil prices is low oil prices." This is precisely how a market bust resolves itself. When prices are cheap, producers adjust their behavior in a manner that will eventually decrease supply; in addition, end users tend to consume more at lower prices. Thus, the decrease in supply and increase in demand eventually turns the bust into a flourishing boom. At the other end of the spectrum, high-flying commodities lead to less demand as consumers make alternative arrangements; producers, on the other hand, rush to bring more of the commodity to market to capitalize on higher prices. In this environment, a commodity boom quickly falls into a bust. The cycle never looks or feels the same, but the end result repeats itself continuously. However, there are always antagonistic forces that prevent prices from plunging to zero.

For example, when crude oil was above $100 per barrel in 2014, US shale oil producers were rushing to frack as much oil out of the ground as they could with little concern for budgeting or cost management. However, when crude oil fell below $30 in 2016, oil producers were aggressive in handing pink slips to employees and shutting down rigs. Each of these behaviors work toward repeating the commodity cycle. In short, when prices are high, producers rush to bring product to market and demand tapers. When prices are low, production slows and demand increases.

Knowing the nature of commodity boom and bust cycles, a trader with immense pain tolerance, financial capital, patience, and discipline to accept massive drawdowns in exchange for nearly certain trading success might "never" lose money trading commodities. Of course, assumptions aren't always realistic; reality suggests the aforementioned theory is flawed in that it ignores transaction costs, the contango (rolling contract months at unfavorable prices), the slim possibility of a commodity brokerage firm failure such as MF Global or PFGBEST, and the reasonable odds of a trader dying before prices recover from the entry price. Don't forget, commodity prices hover in long-term ranges but sometimes there can be several years, or even decades, between peaks and troughs.

In the real world, none of us enjoy the luxury of unlimited time or money. Even the largest hedge funds, institutional traders, or wealthy individual traders don't have *unlimited* funds. Further, few possess the discipline necessary to pace themselves or have the wherewithal to hold positions indefinitely. In the case of an investment fund, they are at the mercy of client redemptions that almost always come at the worst time—when the going gets rough.

With these unrealistic assumptions in mind, let's take a look at how big the drawdowns might be in any given commodity per single lot traded should a speculator attempt to ride out any adverse price move the market has to offer. Let's accept that a commodity price could lose as much as 70% of its current value, which certainly isn't impossible; ask anybody who attempted to play the long side of commodities in 2014 and 2015. We'll use a 70% decline possibility as the assumed risk of going long a long-term position trade with unlimited financial backing. If crude oil is trading at $35, the potential drawdown of going long with no other expectation, or goal, than assuming prices will eventually be higher than $35, is $24,500 per contract. In other words, should the commodity decline 70% from entry, the trade would be suffering a paper loss of nearly $25,000. This sounds steep, but it isn't; because $35 oil is trading at a massive historical discount, risk is tapered. To put things into perspective, an e-mini S&P trader could lose more than $70,000 should prices drop 70% from the 2000 level. These are substantial sums of money to lose that the coolest of heads would struggle to endure for long.

Anybody taking such a long-term view of a commodity, and willing to ride the ebb and flow necessary to capitalize on the inevitable boom and bust cycle, would obviously look to establish long positions after a market has suffered a substantial decline. Likewise, a long-term short position should only be established at significantly high prices. Buying a commodity into a massive upswing could take both your lifetime to recover *and* your kids'. Just imagine going long crude oil at $150 per barrel in 2008. Oil prices will probably see this price again, but will it be in our lifetime? It is hard to say.

Take note that individual stocks, unlike commodities, have the ability to become completely worthless. Therefore, they are not necessarily candidates for ruthless buy and hold strategies. Thus, purchasing shares of a particular company with the mindset of "It will be impossible to lose if held long enough" is an even bigger fallacy than it is in the commodity markets. I've seen companies that were once staples in our society disappear, all the while putting their shareholders through the ringer. You might recall the telephone company WorldCom, or more recently Blockbuster. I think we can all agree that in the history of the commodity markets, we've never seen a market go to zero. Even if it did, there would always be potential for a recovery, which also differs from individual stocks. If a stock becomes worthless, it is delisted, leaving shareholders with no chance of recouping lost money; yet, commodities always have a chance to redeem themselves.

Commodities aren't much better prospects for this type of "head in the sand" trading. We always have personal financial or emotional limits that any particular market trend can easily overcome. So once again, is it possible to construct a scenario in which a trader could ride out any storm? Yes. Is such a strategy more feasible in commodities than it is stocks? Yes. Nevertheless, it isn't realistic.

THERE IS NO BLACK AND WHITE, ONLY PLENTY OF GRAY

As we will discuss, when it comes to trading or analyzing the commodity markets there is no right or wrong way. Ultimately, the final verdict on your chosen method of speculation is the bottom line in your trading account. However, in the meantime the journey each trader takes will be as unique as their

> "I am not young enough to know everything." —Oscar Wilde

thumbprint. Unfortunately, for many commodity traders, the inability to operate well in an environment in which there are few rules or guidelines proves to be too much to handle. As humans we are programmed to expect a precise, and maybe even quantifiable, answer to each question, but in trading that doesn't exist.

For example, there is a plethora of methods with which commodity traders analyze the markets. Some traders focus solely on the fundamental landscape, others look to price action for clues, while some use seasonal patterns or even market sentiment indicators for guidance. However, each method of analysis need not be mutually exclusive. Each school of thought offers a potential edge to traders willing to piece the puzzle together; thus, traders should be able and willing to wear the hats of a chartist, a fundamentalist, a seasonal analyst, and a sentiment specialist.

Too often, traders peg themselves as one or the other but doing so almost guarantees they will miss something important. For instance, there are countless occasions in which market prices change direction long before fundamentals do. In many of those cases, the chart was telling the story much earlier than the general public was made aware of changes in the fundamental landscape. Further, chartists who ignore fundamental data will eventually be caught off guard as the market undergoes a repricing to account for changes in supply and demand. One of the most telling forms of analysis is market sentiment. Sometimes, clues buried deep within sentiment indicators provide insight into something brewing despite a commodity market being entrenched in a deep trend with corroborated fundamentals. Accordingly, traders can improve their odds by being mindful of various market analysis techniques as opposed to being a "one-trick pony."

> "Learn every day, but especially from the experiences of others. It's cheaper!" —John Bogle

Regardless of the method of market analysis chosen, there will never be a way to predict future price movement with exact certainty. More important, traders who determine price targets, or support and resistance areas in their market analysis, must acknowledge that no matter how precise the method of arriving at those figures was, they are still nothing more than an estimate. If chart analysis suggests support in gold futures lies at $1,090 per ounce, a market printing at $1,085 shouldn't be seen as a complete failure tagged with the assumption that prices will continue to fall. In fact, the commodity markets frequently set "bear traps" in which it appears support levels have been broken, but selling dries up quickly and prices reverse. Sometimes, when markets look their best is precisely the worst time to be a buyer; conversely, a market in dire straits can be a gold mine of opportunity.

There is no shortage of commodity market literature discussing the basics of fundamental and technical analysis, but few venture into the other arenas this book does. The goal of this book is to provide readers with tips and tricks on gathering information, interpreting it, and utilizing each of these methods of analysis. Ideally, through the combination of these techniques, readers will become more capable commodity traders and experience fewer unpleasant surprises.

CHAPTER 1: COMMODITY MARKET REFRESHER

Before discussing various commodity market strategies, it is important everyone is on the same page in regard to a basic understanding of the futures markets, futures contracts, and the options written against them. Thus, let's visit a refresher course to ensure proper understanding of the more advanced topics discussed throughout this work. In the meantime, if you feel as though you need a more in-depth discussion, particularly on the topic of calculating commodity profit and loss, I've covered these topics extensively in my book *A Trader's First Book on Commodities*.

WHAT IS THE CASH MARKET?

The cash market, also referred to as the "spot market," is the venue in which commodities are bought and sold for immediate delivery. An example of a cash market transaction would be the sale of soybeans by a grain farmer to a grain elevator operator. The price reflects only the current value of the commodity and results in an immediate changing of the hands. The cash market is in contrast to the futures market, which represents future delivery of the underlying commodity at a price incorporating the cost of carrying that commodity until the delivery date.

WHAT IS A FUTURES CONTRACT?

By definition, a futures contract is an agreement traded on an organized exchange to buy or sell commodities or financial assets at a fixed price at an agreed-upon date in the future. It is the exchange itself that determines the date, quantity, and quality of the underlying asset, but it is the traders who determine price.

> "He who is not courageous enough to take risks will accomplish nothing in life." —Mohammad Ali

Because futures contracts are agreements to buy or sell a commodity in the future, they are liabilities, rather than actual assets. As a result, they can be bought (go long) or sold (go short) in any order. Unlike equities, which require traders to borrow shares of stock from their broker and pay interest before shorting, futures traders simply click their mouse and hang on for the ride. There are no interest charges, but of course the trader must have the proper margin posted in his trading account and pay a transaction fee to his broker.

To demonstrate, a March corn futures contract expiring on March 14 listed on the Chicago Board of Trade division of the CME Group represents 5,000 bushels of corn. A trader who believes corn prices will rise from a hypothetical current level of $3.90 could simply purchase the futures contract in hopes of being able to sell it back at a higher price. Likewise, if the trader believed the price would drop, he could sell a futures contract with the intention, but not the guarantee, of being able to buy it back at a lower price.

Although most speculators don't hold the position long enough to experience the delivery consequences, anybody holding a futures contract into expiration is essentially agreeing to make, or take, delivery of the underlying commodity. Thus, a trader long March corn would be seeking to acquire 5,000 bushels of corn on March 14 at the purchase price of $3.90. The actual price of corn at the time of delivery is irrelevant because the agreement was purchased at $3.90; therefore, that price stands. Had the trader sold the March corn contract at $3.90, he would be responsible for delivering 5,000 bushels of corn at the agreed-upon price (the price the futures contract was sold, $3.90).

By offsetting, or exiting, the futures contract before delivery, the trader is also offsetting the obligation to make, or take, delivery. A trader wishing to remain long or short the corn market beyond expiration of the March contract must "roll over" his obligation by selling the March contract and then purchasing the next contract month, which expires in May. As a result, the trader can continue accepting price risk exposure without having to undergo the process of actually buying or selling the underlying 5,000 bushels of corn, or whatever the commodity traded happens to be.

Because futures contracts are priced for delivery to take place at some point in the future, the going price of a futures contract represents market expectations of change in worth between the current date and the delivery date; it also includes the cost to carry. In the case of physical commodities, it generally includes the cost of storage and insurance; the cost to carry built into pricing is known as *contango*.

This book repeatedly mentions the calculation of profit, loss and risk, in regards to the trading of futures contracts. On each occasion, the general calculation will be offered but if you are in need of an in-depth lesson on calculating in commodities, I recommend you read my book *A Trader's First Book on Commodities*.

PIT VS. ELECTRONIC TRADING

Up until mid-2015, all futures contracts were traded in two distinct arenas, via a traditional open outcry pit and via electronic execution. If you are young, and new to the trading community, you might not be aware of what trading pits or the practice of open outcry execution are. In short, the pits are designated areas in which exchange members buy and sell futures contracts through hand gestures known as *arb*. Although the transactions are communicated through hand

> Computers killed the trading floors, like streaming music killed the radio. All we can do is embrace and adapt!

movements, they are accompanied by aggressive and loud shouting and, in some cases, a degree of physicality. The process of open outcry trade execution is often referred to as "organized chaos." If you haven't seen the movie *Trading Places* starring Eddie Murphy and Dan Aykroyd, you should; it captures the essence of pit trading in all of its glory. Further, the documentary *Floored*, directed by James Allen Smith, depicts a candid story of the ups and downs experienced by those in the CME trading pits.

To the detriment of many who made a living on the trading floors in downtown Chicago, most open outcry trading pits were closed in July 2015. The only pits left as this book was going to press were options trading pits and the full-sized Standard & Poor's 500 futures.

Although the closure of the futures trading pits marks the end of an era, there is relatively little to no impact to the average retail trader. At the time the CME Group announced the pit closure, only about 1% of all executed futures contracts on the exchange were traded in the pits, meaning nearly all of CME Group trades are executed electronically, and so, most traders probably didn't notice the change at all.

Electronic trade matching, or *screen trading* as industry insiders refer to it, is an extremely quick and efficient means of order execution relative to open outcry. Yet despite the clear advantages of electronic trade matching such as transparency, speed of execution and fill reporting, and fill quality (less slippage), the disadvantages are often overlooked. For instance, up until now when the exchange, or even brokerage firms, experienced technology issues it was possible to route orders to the pit for execution. Such events don't occur frequently, but they do happen. In the absence of an alternative means of execution, it only takes a single instance of halted trade to have a dramatic impact on the integrity of the markets and work against orderly trading.

Louis Winthorpe III, the character played by Dan Aykroyd in *Trading Places*, described the futures trading pits as "the last bastion of pure capitalism." When the pits died, a little piece of the hearts and minds of industry veterans died with them. Nevertheless, we've known all along this was an inevitable and necessary step in the progression toward market efficiency. When the pits closed I mourned the death of tradition, but I also embraced the future of the industry. Change is hard, but it doesn't have to be bad.

WHAT IS THE BID/ASK SPREAD?

> Like consumers, market participants must account for the "vig." They will always pay the higher price and sell the lower one.

I suspect most readers of this book are well aware of the fact that any asset, whether it be commodity futures, options, stocks, baseball cards, or houses, has two different prices at any given time. There is a price in which it is possible to buy the asset, and one that represents the price it can be sold. In the world of commodities, the price an asset can be bought at is the "ask" (sometimes referred to as the "offer"); the price a trader can sell an asset is the "bid." The difference between these two prices is known as the "spread," or more descriptively, the "bid/ask spread."

In liquid markets, the bid/ask spread is narrow and rather inconsequential to a trader, but in illiquid markets it can be a hidden transaction cost posing as a massive hurdle to overcome. A crude oil call option expiring 30 days from now might be bid at 0.47 and offered at 0.49; in this example the bid/ask spread is $0.02, or $20 because each penny in crude is worth $10 to a trader. If you look at the same option in the overnight session when liquidity is sparse and market makers are nonexistent, it might be 0.10 bid at 0.92. In this example, the bid/ask spread is $0.82, or $820. That type of massive spread would almost ensure a trading loss if a trader was foolish enough to execute at the stated prices. Aside from waiting for more liquidity to show up, as it always does during the normal day session, a trader would want to enter an order to "split the bid." Somebody interested in buying the option would enter an order to buy it at 51, which would represent a relatively fair price because it is equidistant from the bid and ask.

I could write an entire book on options trading strategies; in fact, I already have. In my first venture into trading literature, I wrote a book titled *Commodity Options*. The book takes readers through several detailed option strategies and covers commodity option nuances from head to toe. This time, we will merely scratch the surface with the purpose of giving readers the information they need to determine whether there is a place for options trading in their speculative portfolio. I also want to offer some alternative views on how options can offer opportunities for hedging various other commodity trading strategies.

Perhaps the biggest mistake that traders make is not utilizing options to mitigate risk and volatility. Few people can enter speculative positions with perfection; despite our best efforts, we simply cannot see into the future. Thus, being savvy to the possibilities of options trading, or combining options with futures, will come in handy for position and swing traders. Not only are options extremely flexible trading vehicles enabling traders to adjust position risk, and even purpose, in an instant, but they are also an effective way to reduce the overall account volatility that comes with trading commodities. Simply put, options allow traders to de-leverage the futures markets and slow trades down to a more manageable level.

Most readers of this book are likely either proficient in options trading terminology and concepts or they have intentionally avoided options trading education due to the perceived complexity. I can assure you understating option concepts isn't as overwhelming as it seems on the surface; in fact, with a little practice it will become second nature. Unfortunately, I'm referencing the concepts, not trading results.

We'll briefly define options in this section to ensure everyone is on the same page, then in Chapter 9, "Options Trading Strategies," we will dive into the advantages and disadvantages of various approaches to the commodity markets using options as the trading vehicle or as a means of hedging futures contracts.

WHAT IS AN OPTION?

Before it is possible to understand how options can be used for speculation or hedging, it is important to know what they are and how they work. In a nutshell, there are two forms of options, and two general ways to trade them. Most are well aware of the types of options: calls and puts. And most are also familiar with the concept of being a net buyer of option premium or a net seller

> "Before anything else, preparation is the key to success." —Alexander Graham Bell

of option premium; but fewer fully understand the true risk and rewards that come with each approach.

The buyer of an option pays a premium (payment) to the seller of an option for the right, but not the obligation, to take delivery of the underlying futures contract. Such a process of taking on the underlying futures contract is known as *exercising* an option. An option exercise can only be initiated by the buyer of the option or the exchange at option expiration should the futures price be trading beyond the strike price of the option.

On the other hand, the seller of an option is interested in collecting the premium in speculation that the underlying futures price will not surpass the strike price of the option. Further, the option seller believes the value of the option will decline as time and volatility grind down. Accordingly, the financial value of an option is treated as an asset, although eroding, to the option buyer and a liability to the seller.

Ω **Call options.** Give the buyer the right, but not the obligation, to buy the underlying futures contract at the stated strike price within a specific period of time. Conversely, the seller of a call option is obligated to deliver a long position in the underlying futures contract from the strike price should the buyer opt to exercise the option or the exchange does so at expiration due to the option being in-the-money (which we'll define in a bit). Essentially, this means that the seller would be forced to take a short position in the market upon exercise.

Ω **Put options.** Give the buyer the right, but not the obligation, to sell the underlying futures contract at the stated strike price within a specific period of time. The seller of a put option is obligated to deliver a short position from the strike price in case the buyer chooses to exercise the option, or the exchange does so at expiration because the option is in-the-money (again, we'll define this soon). Keep in mind that delivering a short futures contract simply means being long from the strike price.

Table 1: Option buyers face limited risk, but option sellers face unlimited risk.

	Call	Put	
Buy			Limited Risk
Sell			Unlimited Risk

The value of any particular option is dependent on two components, the intrinsic value and the extrinsic value. The intrinsic value of the option is its true worth at any particular moment, while the extrinsic value is the worth assigned to it by market participants based on expectations of future movement in the price of the underlying commodity.   The relationship between option price and intrinsic and extrinsic value can be expressed as the following equation:

Option Price = Intrinsic Value + Extrinsic Value

INTRINSIC VALUE

The simplest way to think about intrinsic value is to view it as the worth of an option if it expired right now. To illustrate, let's discuss the difference between an in-the-money and an out-of-the-money option. Although you might often hear traders refer to an option as being "in-the-money" if it is profitable, I assure you that is not the conventional interpretation of the phrase in the industry.

If the price of the underlying futures contract is beyond the strike price of a particular option, it is said to be in-the-money. In the case of a put, this would entail the futures price to be below the stated strike price, but a call option is only in-the-money if the futures price is above the strike price. For example, if crude oil futures are at $42.00 per barrel, a $40.00 call option in oil is in-the-money by $2.00. Accordingly, the intrinsic value of that option is also

$2.00. Because each penny is worth $10 to a crude oil trader, this is equivalent to $2,000 (200 x $10). Therefore, the option price will at least be $2.00 in premium, or $2,000 at any time prior to expiration.

Knowing the definition of an option that is in-the-money, we can infer that if the futures price is not beyond the strike price of an option, it is said to be out-of-the-money and, of course, if the price of the underlying is at the strike price of the option, it is known as at-the-money. Only in-the-money options have intrinsic value; for options that are at-the-money or out-of-the-money there is no intrinsic value, but there will always be extrinsic value at any time before expiration of the option.

EXTRINSIC VALUE

Extrinsic value is the component of the option premium assigned by the market price that is not accounted for in the intrinsic value. In the previous example of a crude oil call in-the-money by $2.00, if the market price for that particular option is $3.00 in premium, or $3,000, the additional $1.00 in premium is essentially the time value that market participants have determined appropriate through supply and demand for that particular option.

> Extrinsic value includes implied volatility, which is the portion of option price accounting for market expectations of futures volatility.

Extrinsic value can fluctuate wildly as the market determines the fair price for the option based on time to expiration, market volatility, event risk, demand for the option, and proximity to the underlying futures price. As a rule of thumb, the extrinsic value of options is higher during times of high volatility, or in advance of a major economic or agricultural report in which demand for options by speculators is high. Further, an option with a strike price close-to-the-money will have a higher value than an option with the same expiration month and a deep-out-of-the-money strike price. Similarly, an option expiring the current month will always be worth more than an option with the same strike price expiring next month because the market values the increased probability of the option becoming in-the-money in a 60-day time allotment vs. a 30-day.

IMPLIED VOLATILITY

Implied volatility is the portion of an option's extrinsic value that accounts for the market's expectations of future volatility. It is the amount of exuberance that market participants price into the value of an option based on their outlook of event risk. Implied volatility can cause otherwise fairly priced options to quickly become irrationally priced. Conversely, implied volatility can disintegrate as quickly as it appears. In many cases, it is fluctuations in implied volatility that make it possible for option traders to make and lose money. As such, an option buyer will benefit from an increase in implied volatility, but a seller will benefit from a decrease in implied volatility.

Examples of the significance of implied volatility can be seen prior to the release of a significant piece of economic data or commodity fundamental report; a crude oil option trader has likely noticed oil options increasing in value on Tuesday afternoon and Wednesday morning, even in the absence of a material futures market move. This is because the market is pricing in a higher level of implied volatility ahead of the weekly inventory report. Other sources of noteworthy implied volatility are USDA reports in the grain markets. Financial futures, on the other hand, see increases in implied volatility ahead of the monthly employment reports and Federal Reserve Open Market Committee (FOMC) meetings. In each instance, implied volatility tends to get lofty ahead of the news and collapse following the news. Barring any market surprises, option strangle sellers face promising prospects by simply timing the entry of their trade ahead of the aforementioned events.

It is easy to see how knowing the implied volatility for any particular option can be useful. Unfortunately, not all futures and options trading platforms offer implied volatility readings. In fact, most free platforms do not offer this information. Those traders willing to pay platform fees will find implied volatility stats within their premium platforms, which typically run anywhere from $100 to $150 per month. A more economical source of implied volatility is Moore Research Center, Inc. (MRCI). Although I have access to implied volatility stats in my trading platform, I prefer to use MRCI.

CALCULATING THE BREAKEVEN POINT OF AN OPTION

An option held to expiration will only be profitable to the buyer if the futures price is beyond the strike price of the option enough to cover the premium paid to purchase the option. Likewise, the premium collected by the option seller acts as a buffer toward losses. In fact, at expiration, the option seller is profitable if the option is in-the-money as long as the intrinsic value does not exceed the premium collected. The point at which the buyer and seller become profitable, or unprofitable, is known as the breakeven point. Because option trading is a zero sum game, if the buyer of the option is profitable the seller is suffering a loss, and vice versa. Accordingly, the break-even point, ignoring transaction costs, is the same for both traders but the experience is inverse.

Breakeven = Strike Price +/- Premium Collected

To illustrate, a trader purchasing a soybean call option with a strike price of $10.00 for $0.25 (25 cents) in premium would need to see the futures price of soybeans above $10.25 to turn a profit. If the price is exactly at $10.25 at expiration, the trade is merely breaking even despite being $0.25 in-the-money. This is because the intrinsic value of the call option is simply offsetting the premium paid to purchase it. If the price is below $10.25 but above $10.00, the trader loses the difference between the premium paid and the intrinsic value.

Conversely, if an option seller sold the same option, he would be profitable as long as the price of soybeans is below $10.25 at expiration. If it is below the strike price of $10.00, he keeps the entire 25 cents in collected premium. If the price is at $10.10, the trader would net 15 cents before commissions and fees because, despite the option being in-the-money, the premium collected exceeded the intrinsic value of the option at expiration. Should the price of soybeans be above the breakeven point of $10.25, the trader is losing penny for penny on the trade; this is not unlike being short a futures contract from $10.25.

WHAT IS MARGIN?

Not all brokerage firms charge the same margin. Commodity exchanges set a minimum, but the broker can charge more. Be sure to choose a broker who requires the exchange minimum margin.

Again, because futures contracts are agreements to transact the underlying commodity at some point in the future as opposed to actual cash market commodity transactions, they are essentially liabilities. Accordingly, there is no actual cash exchanging hands, but to ensure market participants are "good for it," the exchange requires each trader to post a minimal amount of margin. The margin deposit is an attempt by the exchange to guarantee both sides of each transaction. Both the buyer and the seller will be able to meet their obligation when the trade is offset. Generally, the exchange sets margin at a level that they believe will be the most probable daily loss limit. For instance, if the margin set for crude oil is $5,060, it is implied that the exchange estimates the largest single trading session move in that contract would be equivalent to a $5,060 loss. In the case of crude oil, this equals a $5.06 move in oil because, as previously mentioned, each penny of price movement represents $10 ($10 x $5.06).

Thus far, I've introduced margin in a simplistic manner; however, as with anything else in commodities it is more complicated than meets the eye. For starters, there are actually two margin figures listed for each futures contract: an initial margin and a maintenance margin.

 Initial Margin

The initial margin is the sum of funds a trader must have on deposit with their commodity broker to enter into a particular futures, or short option, position. This is the most commonly referenced margin requirement and is also the most straightforward. Although the initial margin for option traders can get complicated, a futures trader can easily find the exchange minimum initial margin for each futures product listed on the exchange's website or other web sources. Keep in mind that brokerage firms have the right to charge their clients margin in excess of the exchange-stated initial margin, but they do not have the freedom to charge their clients less. Unless, of course, they are day trading; we will get into that shortly.

For instance, if the exchange requires a client to have $4,500 on deposit to trade a single contract of gold futures, the initial margin is said to be $4,500. As long as there is at least $4,500 in a trading account (exactly $4,500 is enough), a position in gold can be established.

 Maintenance Margin

The maintenance margin rate is one that identifies when a particular trade has gotten into trouble enough to justify requiring the trader to take action. The maintenance margin is a threshold that, if surpassed, will trigger a margin call in an account. Maintenance margin is generally about 80% to 90% of the initial margin, but it can fluctuate from product to product, along with market volatility. Using the gold example, the maintenance margin might be $3,750; if so, a trader starting with $4,500 in their account who sells a gold futures contract will receive a margin call if his account balance drops to $3,750. This represents a $750 loss in the futures position, or a $7.50 increase in the price of gold (each dollar price change in gold is equivalent to $100 to a futures trader).

On an important note, margin calls are not triggered intraday. Instead, a margin call is only issued if a trader's account is beneath the maintenance margin level at the official day session close. Adding to the confusion, the official closing time is that which the open outcry pits *used* to close. Because the trading pits no longer exist for most futures contracts, the closing time is nothing more than an arbitrary point of time in the trading day.

Believe it or not, commodity market margin gets even more complicated. Day traders and option traders delving into unlimited risk strategies face another set of margin requirements.

DAY TRADING MARGIN

Unlike traditional initial margin, which is set by the exchange, futures traders who employ a strategy of entering and exiting positions within the same trading day are often provided discount margins by their brokerage firm. In some cases, the discounted margin is shockingly low, which results in incredibly high levels of leverage and risk. The distinction between the exchange setting the margin and the broker setting the margin is significant because it implies the initial margin requirement faced by traders holding positions overnight is a floor existing regardless of the brokerage firm, yet day trading margins are negotiable at each brokerage and, in some cases, day trading margins vary depending on the individual broker chosen. It is possible for a client of a particular brokerage firm to be granted a day trading rate of $1,000, while a client of the same firm but a different account manager (broker) is granted a $500 day trading margin.

Not only do day trading margins vary by brokerage and individual broker, they vary by product. Stocks indices such as the e-mini S&P are typically set at lower day trading rates, while less liquid and arguably more volatile markets such as gold and silver are generally set at higher day trading rates. Nevertheless, there isn't a concrete day trading margin level for any market; it is an ambiguous figure arrived upon, and enforced, by the commodity broker.

We will go into more detail throughout subsequent chapters, but the bottom line is that day trading margin is lower, but not necessarily better for undisciplined traders.

OPTION MARGIN (SPAN)

The most complicated type of margin is SPAN, which stands for standard portfolio analysis of risk. SPAN margin is similar to the portfolio margining system in stock trading accounts in that it takes all positions into account to determine a net risk of the portfolio. Accordingly, option spreads or strategies involving antagonistic futures and options are margined at a lower rate than the aggregate total of the outright positions would be.

> If you think commission is expensive, try getting what you pay for. Discount brokers generally charge higher margin rates to option traders.

Take, for example, a trader who is short an e-mini S&P put with a strike price of 1700 and a SPAN margin requirement of $2,400. He could sell an equivalent call option without seeing an increase in margin. On its own, the sale of a 1900 call might carry a margin requirement of about $2,400 but if done in the same account with a currently open short 1700 put, the net margin will generally be about $2,400 for the combined spread. This is because the SPAN margin calculator knows the trader can only lose on one side of the trade, but not both. This is a simplistic example, but it should give you an idea of how SPAN nets open positions to provide traders with discounted margin requirements based on the true risk. Don't worry if you had a hard time following this trading example, because we'll discuss this strategy in more detail throughout this book.

In essence, SPAN is a complicated formula developed by the CME Group applying a margin requirement to the perceived risk based on factors such as market volatility, event risk, proximity of the strike prices to the current futures market price, and so on. Because of this, not only do SPAN margin requirements fluctuate from day to day, they fluctuate from minute to minute. For that reason it is sometimes difficult for traders, particularly green traders, to accurately determine their true margin requirement. On the bright side, because of the flexibility SPAN margining offers, traders can quickly and easily reduce margin via trading adjustments should things get tight. A trader near, or on, a margin call might look to buy or sell options counter to their current position to lower risk and margin without completely exiting the position or adding funds to the trading account. We deliberate this topic in Chapter 16 when we discuss risk management and margin adjustment strategies.

Not all brokerage firms offer their clients access to SPAN margin, which is essentially the exchange minimum margin requirements for options trading. Many brokers use the exchange's SPAN margin as a starting point; they apply what has been coined an upcharge to the SPAN margin rates to pad the risk of their clients' trading activities. In other words, most brokerage firms charge their short option traders more than the exchange minimum. If your broker is charging you something other than the SPAN minimum margin, you should strongly consider trading elsewhere. Chances are, this isn't the only corner they are cutting to the detriment of their clients' trading environment.

Keep in mind, SPAN only applies to clients trading options on futures, or a combination of futures and options. Those trading outright futures contracts, or even futures spreads, are subject to the stated initial and maintenance margin requirements for the contract being traded. In addition, SPAN margin calculations are kept confidential by the CME Group, so it is difficult and costly to gain access to an accurate SPAN calculator. Some, but not all, commodity trading platforms are capable of offering estimates of SPAN, but they should be used as a guide rather than the end all and be all; they aren't perfect.

ORDER TYPES

Throughout this work we will debate several trading strategies as well as order types and execution methods. It is crucial we review common order types available in most major trading platforms. There are a handful of "exotic" order types not listed here, but this will be a good refresher of those referred to frequently. Although this might seem elementary, there are seasoned traders out there who still get limit and stop orders confused.

As you sift through these order types, keep in mind these apply solely to the trading of futures contracts. Options, on the other hand, can generally be traded only with the use of limit orders. Futures exchanges typically don't accept stop-loss or market orders on option trades.

MARKET ORDER

A market order is simply an instruction to execute a given position at the best possible price at that precise moment. Traders utilizing market orders are giving up control of the fill price in exchange for a guaranteed fill. Their priority is getting a fill, not getting a particular price on that fill. In liquid markets, market orders are extremely efficient, but in illiquid markets, a market order might be filled at undesirable prices. Before venturing into thinly traded commodities, check the bid/ask spread. If it is wide, a market order is not appropriate; a limit order is a better choice.

STOP ORDER

> Stop-loss orders can be used as risk management or as trade entry. In either case, the price must get "worse" for the order to get filled.

A "stop order," often referred to as a stop-loss order, is one that becomes a market order once the stated price is reached; "reached" implies the stop price becomes part of the bid/ask spread. Because it becomes a market order, it is prone to slippage. Under most market conditions, stop orders are ultimately filled at, or near, the noted stop price. But in highly volatile markets, or in the case of a gap in price from the closing price of one session to the opening price of another, the actual fill prices could be sharply off the mark. In today's nearly 24-hour markets, this is a lot rarer than it used to be but there can sometimes be substantial differences in Friday's closing price to the Sunday night futures open.

Most traders use this order type to "stop the loss" of an open position—hence the name—but it can also be used to enter a new trade or protect profits of an existing trade. A stop order is always placed at a price that is "worse" than the current market price; if it is a buy stop, the order must be placed above the market, but if it is a sell stop, it must be placed below the market. Accordingly, when a stop order is filled it is, by nature, buying at a relatively high price and selling at a relatively low price.

An example would be a trader long gold at $1,185.00, who wishes to mitigate his risk by placing a stop-loss order at $1,180.00. Assuming no slippage on the stop fill, the trader would "stop his loss" at $500. This is because each dollar in gold is worth $100 to the trader (($1,185.00 - $1,180.00) x $100)). The same trader might trail his stop-loss to $1,190.00 should the price of gold move up to $1,195. This locks in a profit of $500. Conversely, a trader who believes gold will continue higher if it reaches a certain point might place a buy stop to enter a long contract at $1,195.00; if the price is reached, he will buy one contract in hopes of being able to sell it at a higher price down the road.

LIMIT ORDER

Unlike a stop order, which requires the futures contract price to get "worse" for it to be filled, a "limit order" is an "or better" order. It will only be filled if the price moves in the direction required for a more favorable fill price. A limit order is an order in which the trader would like to buy a contract if the price gets lower (better) or sell it if it gets higher (better).

> A limit order is an "or better" order because the price of the instrument must get better before the order will be filled.

To illustrate, if the gold trader wanted to enter the gold market on weakness to improve the entry price, he might enter a limit order to buy a contract at $1,180.00. In this case, the trader is accepting the risk of missing the trade altogether in hopes of being long from a "better" price. If the trader is filled on his limit order at $1,180.00, he might then place a limit order to sell the contract at $1,195.00 in hopes of the price reaching the desired level. Of course, there are no guarantees it will reach the desired limit order price. Further, even if it does hit the price, the order might not get filled. There is a saying in the business: "It has to go through it to do it." Meaning the trader is only owed a fill if the futures price ticks above the stated limit order price. In this case, the order is only guaranteed to get filled if the price reaches at least $1,195.10, a tick above the stated limit order price.

MARKET IF TOUCHED (MIT)

A "market if touched" order type is essentially a specialized limit order. It is based on the same concept of prices needing to get "better" before the orders will be filled, but an MIT order will be filled if the stated price is touched. Unlike a limit order, it is not necessary for the price to go *through* it; if the price is merely reached, the order becomes a market order and returns a fill to the trader. Also in contrast to a limit order, it is possible for fill slippage to occur when using MIT orders, resulting in a fill being reported at a worse price than the stated MIT price.

STOP/LIMIT ORDER

The "stop/limit order" is perhaps the most confusing order type there is. The name implies that it is somehow both a stop and a limit order, but that isn't the case. It is actually a stop order with a catch. Essentially, this is a stop-loss order in which the trader states how much slippage he is willing to accept. This might seem like a wonderful idea, but it has the ability to cause plenty of heartache.

An example of a stop/limit order might be to sell gold at $1,185.00 on a stop/limit of $1,183.00. This is a stop order to sell gold at $1,185.00 but only if the order can be filled at a price above $1,183.00. Generally, this order would be filled at a price much better than $1,183.00 anyway, but the trader is stating he won't accept slippage beyond that point.

If the futures price trades through the stop/limit price without the possibility of filling it within the trader's stated slippage "limit," the order dies. As a result, the trader who attempted to limit his stop order slippage by placing it as a stop/limit suddenly has no stop order working at all. You can imagine the horrified surprise of some traders when they check their account to find complete carnage. This order type is the equivalent of picking up nickels in front of a moving steamroller.

FUTURES AND OPTIONS EXCHANGES

Unlike equity securities, which can be traded on multiple exchanges, or the forex market, which involves the trading of off-exchange products, all futures and options are listed on a specific exchange for execution.

Each commodity futures and options contract listed on a US futures exchange must be approved by the CFTC before being made available for trading; thus, there is generally only one liquid version of each product. On the surface, knowing which exchange that corn, crude oil, or cotton is traded on might not seem necessary, but this knowledge can do wonders for locating contract specifications, keeping track of details of the delivery process and option expiration policies, being aware of opening and closing times, and for avoiding trading mishaps in which the wrong product symbol is traded.

CME GROUP

Most of the futures and options traded in the US are handled on the exchange level by the CME Group. When I entered the business in the early 2000s, there were five primary domestic commodity exchanges—the New York Board of Trade (NYBOT), the Commodity Exchange (COMEX), the Chicago Board of Trade (CBOT), the New York Mercantile Exchange (NYMEX), and the Chicago Mercantile Exchange (CME). Since then, the CME has acquired all of the aforementioned exchanges with the exception of the NYBOT.

I've listed the popular trading vehicles associated with each of the CME Group exchanges here. These are by no means exhaustive, but it should give you a good idea of what type of commodity trades on which exchange, and where to find statistics on them. Product details and information on any CME Group–listed commodities can be conveniently found at www.CMEGroup.com.

- **CBOT.** Grains and interest rates products such as corn, soybeans, wheat, soybean oil, soybean meal, oats, Treasury bonds, and Treasury notes.

- **NYMEX.** Energies such as crude oil, heating oil, natural gas, and RBOB gasoline.

- **CME.** Currencies and interest rate products such as the euro, yen, British pound, Australian dollar, Canadian dollar, Swiss franc, and others.

- **COMEX.** Precious and industrial metals such as gold, silver, palladium, platinum, and copper.

INTERCONTINENTAL EXCHANGE (ICE)

The Intercontinental Exchange (ICE) bought out the New York Board of Trade (NYBOT) in 2007. In doing so, they acquired the rights to futures and options written against soft commodities such as cocoa, coffee, cotton, orange juice (frozen concentrate), and sugar. The exchange also lists the widely quoted, but not as widely traded, US Dollar Index and the highly volatile Russell 2000.

CHAPTER 2: TECHNICAL ANALYSIS IN COMMODITIES

My favorite form of market analysis is the charting of commodity prices. The practice can be as complicated and mathematical as one would like to make it. Those seeking fancy formulas and equations will find satisfaction in technical analysis, but so will the "big picture" trader.

Because of my passion for technical analysis in commodities, I've been a frequent guest and contributor to the "Off the Charts" segment of the *Mad Money* TV show on CNBC hosted by Jim Cramer. In my opinion, charts have the ability to tell us about news or market tendencies before we ever hear it from a newscaster or read about it in *The Wall Street Journal*. This is because traders anticipate, or learn, of events and react in the marketplace faster than news can generally travel to the masses.

I'm certainly aware of the plethora of technical analysis information available in other trading publications, books, and even on the Internet. Accordingly, I won't regurgitate already well-circulated information on each of the available technical trading tools and methods; I want to take this opportunity to demonstrate how I prefer to use and interpret a handful of favored indicators. First, let's review the practice of, and various forms of, technical analysis.

WHAT IS TECHNICAL ANALYSIS?

Technical analysis is the practice of gauging past and present price action in an attempt to predict future price changes. Some commodity technicians focus on using technical oscillators, which are essentially mathematical equations used to create plotted trend or momentum lines; other technicians concentrate on drawing trend lines. There is even a brand of technical analysts who employ seemingly mystical mathematical tools such as the Fibonacci ruler and Gann fan. Although not discussed in this book, there are also technicians who believe that judicious use of astrology can help predict commodity markets.

> "Stock market bubbles don't grow out of thin air. They have a solid basis in reality, but reality is distorted by misconception." —George Soros

It took a long time for the academic financial community to recognize the benefits of technical analysis; in fact, most college finance professors still preach that technical analysis is a waste of time. I beg to differ. Although on the surface it seems silly to expect what most consider to be random price movements to find support or resistance at predetermined technical levels using formations such as triangles, head and shoulders, or even spreading fans drawn on the top of a commodity chart, the truth is it works more often than it doesn't.

Perhaps the best explanation is that technical analysis is a self-fulfilling prophecy. After all, each market participant has access to the same books and, therefore, theories on what a commodity chart should look like. Thus, if many traders see a particular pattern and act according to the most common technical theory, market prices have a high probability of following the rules set forth by the technical community.

Another logical explanation for the consistent success of technical indicators and tools is the fact that markets are simply a conglomerate of the opinions of all market participants. Although some market participants are more sophisticated, or better funded, than others they all have one thing in common—they are human. Humans are prone to repetitive behaviors and suffer from emotional decision making. Further, even though we claim to learn from our mistakes, most of us rarely do. This isn't a conundrum exclusive to the commodity markets; human fear and greed can explain the boom and bust cycles in markets of all asset classes—for instance, the tech stock bubble of the late 1990s, the real estate boom and bust of the early 2000s, and most recently the bitcoin fiasco.

In each scenario, market participants disregard the true value of an asset; instead, they irrationally bid up its price due to skewed perceptions of its worth, and fear of missing out on the next big thing. This concept is known as the "herd mentality" because humans tend to display sheep-like qualities when it comes to following the crowd. In the end, however, the party generally ends in despair when investors let greed hold them in a trade too long; or convince them to buy into an already lofty market, eventually paying dearly for their mistake. Nevertheless, it is these patterns of feast or famine for long-term investors, or buy and holders, that offer the most attractive opportunities for active traders. As a result, I put technical analysis at the top of my analytical priority totem pole.

METHODS OF TECHNICAL ANALYSIS

The first step to developing a technical analysis arsenal is to determine which approach to the market best fits your personality and risk tolerance. It is important to be honest with yourself about this because a lack of confidence and comfort in your method will guarantee trading losses at the hands of panicked decision making.

Notice that I didn't suggest that you find the optimal trading approach, just the one that works for you. This is because what works for one trader might not work for the next. Trading losses aren't generally caused by a flaw in the analysis or interpretation of the market; they are most likely an error in execution due to the emotions involved. On multiple occasions, I've witnessed traders working off of the exact same trading recommendation come up with vastly different results. In some cases, one trader was wildly profitable while the other suffered a devastating drawdown. The difference is usually that one trader jumped the gun on the entry while one of them failed to exit as recommended, or one of them liquidated the position at the worst possible time. The best way to avoid the undesirable result is to keep within your comfort zone; traders who can do this will consistently make logical decisions, as opposed to letting their emotions guide their trading.

Not all methods of technical analysis operate under the same premise, but they all have the same goal: predict future price movement successfully more often than not. It sounds simple, but unlimited complexities in free markets make this a difficult task. Among commodity market technicians, there are three primary schools of thought with substantially opposing views on the markets: trend trading, breakout trading, and countertrend trading. With the exception of option traders, or spread traders, whose strategy might profit from sideways price movement, futures traders of all time horizons will fall under one of these three umbrellas.

I'm most comfortable with a countertrend approach to technical analysis, but that doesn't mean you have to agree with me. In fact, there are some extremely successful traders who passionately believe trend trading is the optimal solution, while others believe breakout trading offers the most favorable odds of success. Again, there are no black and white answers in trading or market analysis. Each trader must do some soul searching along with trial and error to find the best fit. The objective of this section is to inspire some thought on the matter by supplying the advantages and disadvantages of each to help readers determine where their own comfort levels can be found.

TREND TRADING

The goal of trend trading is to catch the long-lasting rally or decline. These types of moves don't occur frequently, but the trend trader knows that when they happen they can be lucrative. In its simplest form, trend trading incorporates the use of a combination of moving averages and technical oscillators to create relatively slow entry and exit triggers. Some trend trading systems also involve overlay rules such as to buy after a certain number of positive closes, or to buy the first positive close after a new 30-day high. Naturally, there are an unlimited number of possible trend trading rules, but they all encompass slow triggers.

> "The four most expensive words in the English language, 'This time is different.' " —Sir John Templeton

Because of the nature of the analysis and strategy, trend traders are slow to buy into a rally, and therefore they often buy relatively high prices of a move. Conversely, they are repeatedly late sellers into a bear move, causing a tendency to sell low in hopes of the market going even lower. Simply put, trend traders require the market to move considerably before a trend can be said to be established, rather than attempting to pick tops or bottoms.

Due to lagging entry signals, trend traders face dismal odds of success on a per-trade basis. Nevertheless, the premise of the strategy lies in the expectations of eventually catching a dramatic market move in which the gains are so significant they offset the frequent losses that can take place before catching a ride in the market.

Conclusion: Trend traders experience large and frequent drawdowns in exchange for the prospects of massive long-term profits during trending market environments. Most commodity market analysts agree that prices spend about 80% of the time range trading and only 20% of the time trending. Accordingly, this is a rather low-probability strategy in the short run but for those with deep pockets, plenty of patience, and the ability to endure financial pain, the long-term prospects can be attractive. Eventually, all commodity prices experience a massive trend; those trend traders who survive could enjoy a nice payday.

A notable example is a sharp rally in gold occurring in early 2016, at a time in which gold bulls were scarce. Gold prices quickly jumped from about $1,050 to about $1,250 in a matter of weeks. This represented a move of roughly $20,000 per contract. A trend trader would have never been able to buy the low, due to the slow nature of the strategy, but it is conceivable that most trend trading methods would have gotten long somewhere between $1,080 and $1,100 to produce a gain of somewhere between $17,000 and $15,000. Nevertheless, trend trading systems rarely keep the majority of open profits due to loose stop-loss orders and slow exit signals, but it is fair to say it would have been a great trade. Unfortunately, for those utilizing such a trading method, there were several false signals prior to that move that could have easily caused thousands of dollars in damages before the strategy paid off.

Let's take a look at a crude oil chart to get a feel for what it might be like to be a trend trader (Figure 1). Because the parameters of each trading system vary dramatically, this is simply an ambiguous example to illustrate the advantages and disadvantages of this particular trading method derived from technical analysis. Each false signal might represent a loss of anywhere from $2,000 to $4,000; however, the successful signal might result in a paper profit of somewhere in the $15,000 neighborhood. In hindsight, it is easy to see the strategy was well worth the initial struggle, but things don't always work out this nicely, and the trader suffering multiple thousands in losses prior to the payday might not have the fortitude to stay in the game long enough to reap the reward.

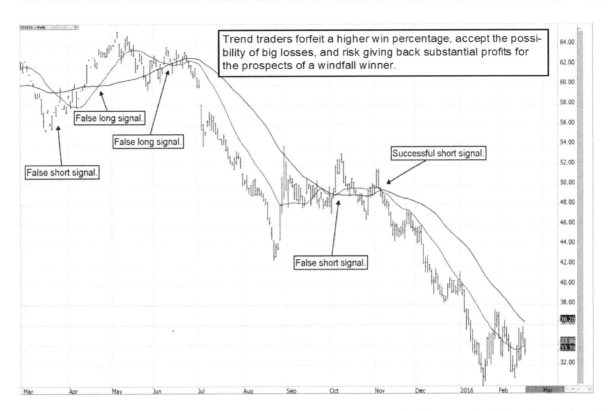

Trend traders forfeit a higher win percentage, accept the possibility of big losses, and risk giving back substantial profits for the prospects of a windfall winner.

False long signal.

False long signal.

False short signal.

Successful short signal.

False short signal.

Figure 1: Although there are an unlimited number of trend trading systems, a common signal for entry and exit is based on simple moving averages (SMA). In this streamlined crude oil example, a crossover of the 50-day and 20-day SMA produces a signal.

BREAKOUT TRADING

The trading community refers to market breakouts frequently; from this, some infer that profiting from such a pattern might be relatively easy. However, nothing is ever as simple as it seems. Breakout traders identify support and resistance levels of trading channels and attempt to establish a long or short futures position should the price of a commodity venture beyond the noted levels. The breakout trader believes if prices surpass support or resistance, market participants will react in a manner that leads to a continuation of the move in a spectacular fashion. Since breakout traders are typically indifferent to which direction prices breach the trading range, they simply seek a sharp price move.

In my experience, breakout traders are similar to trend traders in that their strategy seeks the relatively rare, but substantial, price move that could yield blockbuster returns. However, those implementing this strategy often suffer from trading droughts in which frequent losses occur on false signals. These signals occur when prices move slightly above resistance, or slightly below support, only to reverse course and fall back into the trading range. These patterns are known as *bull traps* and *bear traps*, respectively, and are the culprit for rather low win/loss ratios among breakout trading strategies.

Also similar to trend traders, breakout traders require the market to substantially move in the intended direction before an entry signal is triggered. Accordingly, this strategy comes with the same difficulty of buying at high prices in hopes of higher prices, and selling at low prices in hopes of lower prices (Figure 2). Ironically, market prices often peak or trough at levels at which breakout trades start getting interested in jumping on the trend.

Breakout traders attempt to buy or sell a commodity once it punches through support or resistance, but it is an easier trade on paper than in reality.

After mass chaos, the breakout finally materialized.

Bull trap

Bear trap

Bear trap

Figure 2: Breakout trades are never as clean as the trader would like. Bull traps and bear traps are frequent occurrences, and true breakouts often hug the technical resistance or support before making and sustaining the breakout.

Conclusion: Breakout traders accept the risk of getting caught in a bull or bear trap, in exchange for the prospect of being part of a runaway market. Because commodity markets spend most of their time trading within a defined range, breakout traders are generally provided with fewer successful trading opportunities. Nonetheless, one large winner could far outweigh the losses suffered at the hands of false breakouts from the trading range. This strategy typically involves less risk per trade than a trend-trading strategy might present, but the accumulation of several small losses can frustrate a trader and deplete a trading account.

COUNTERTREND TRADING

For those who have a psychological issue with buying an asset after it has already increased in value, or selling it on the heels of a decline, there is the technical analysis method of *countertrend trading*. This practice is also referred to as "swing trading." Although it goes against human nature, and it isn't necessarily the most popular approach, I believe that buying into large dips and selling the rips can be the most efficient means of technical analysis trading. I've often referred to this type of trading as "extreme trading," because like the thrill seekers who participate in extreme sports, countertrend traders are entering the long side of a trade while the majority of traders are heading for the exit door. Similarly, countertrend traders are selling into commodity markets at a time during which the general public is scrambling to jump on the bull bandwagon.

> "If everybody is thinking alike, then somebody isn't thinking." —General George S. Patton Jr.

As you begin scouring the charts for support and resistance levels, trading channels, and overextended oscillators, I'm confident you will find, more often than not, that prices tend to turn around precisely when the trend seems the most obvious to continue.

In other words, rather than using tools and indicators to identify a trend and go with it, traders might be better off determining overextended market conditions and trading against the tide. If the goal is to buy low and sell high (which it should be), being bullish near technical support in an oversold market, and bearish near resistance in an overbought market, should offer the best odds of success (Figure 3).

The premise, and in my opinion the appeal, of countertrend trading is simple. Most speculators lose money trading commodities; therefore, merely following the pack is probably going to produce negative results in the long run. Also, if everyone is getting overly exuberant about a current market trend, whether it is bullish or bearish, prices will ultimately reach a climax in which they violently reverse. This is because despite there being massive numbers of bandwagon traders, eventually there is a limited supply of buyers and sellers. After all, in a bull run, once all of the buyers are in, and the shorts forced out (short traders cover their positions by buying contracts back), who is left to buy? A smart trader once told me, "Buy 'em when they cry and sell them when they yell."

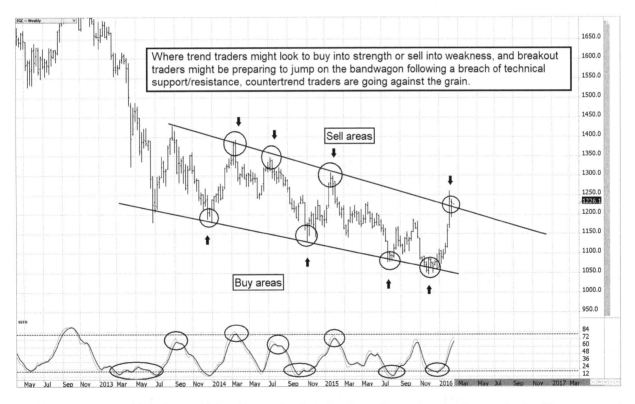

Figure 3: Countertrend traders look to establish positions against the current wave of momentum at major support and resistance areas, and where technical oscillators are suggesting the move is overdone. The gold market from 2013 to 2016 offered a great environment for countertrend trading.

Trader Peter Lynch, former manager of the Magellan Fund at Fidelity Investments, once had the following to say about trading in the stock market: "The one principle that applies to nearly all these so-called technical approaches is that one should buy because a stock or the market has gone up and one should sell because it has declined. This is the exact opposite of sound business sense everywhere else, and it is most unlikely that it can lead to lasting success in Wall Street. In our own stock-market experience and observation, extending over 50 years, we have not known a single person who has consistently or lastingly made money by thus 'following the market.' We do not hesitate to declare that this approach is as fallacious as it is popular."

Conclusion: Countertrend traders are approaching the commodity markets with an outlook opposite from what a trend or breakout trader would. Instead of looking to profit from the lower-probability outcome with the potential to return a home-run caliber trade, countertrend traders prefer to take part in the higher-probability trade even if it means implementing a less-exciting base-hit strategy.

TECHNICAL OSCILLATORS AND INDICATORS

Before computer technology, technical analysts calculated moving averages and other momentum functions by hand. Those with a fair amount of ambition actually plotted the results of the equations on a paper chart—with an easily erasable pencil, of course. Times have obviously changed. Using technical oscillators, which are simply mathematical representations of market momentum and price change, is as easy as opening a commodity chart. All futures charting software, trading platforms, and even complimentary-access websites offer dozens of technical oscillators intended to help traders identify trends, along with overbought and oversold markets. We couldn't possibly cover each of them in this brief discussion, but I'd like to touch on a few that I find helpful, and will be referenced throughout this book.

"The markets can be understood looking backward, but must be traded looking forward." —Larry Williams

Keep in mind, most futures charting packages enable traders to adjust the parameters of each technical oscillator should they believe they can improve it for their needs. Further, most offer traders the ability to create their own "magical" technical oscillators based on inputted parameters. In my opinion, spending endless hours tweaking oscillators, and perhaps even creating new indicators, is a waste of resources. The original creators of the indicator spent plenty of time optimizing it for average market conditions. In addition, because the nature of a technical oscillator is to simply plot the past, chances are, most won't be able to create a new indicator that performs any better than the existing one.

Ironically, all of this technology probably hasn't improved the unfavorable statistic suggesting 80% of commodity traders lose money. Further, computer-generated oscillators simplify market analysis but regardless of which are used, they certainly don't guarantee trading success. They are merely another helpful tool in attempting to predict price changes.

That said, don't be fooled by a low-volatility market. If a commodity market is trading in a tight range, *all* of the technical oscillators tighten up. As a result, many of them will produce false signals because they are working on recent data, which isn't representative of normal market conditions.

Although I mention a handful of indicators throughout this section that I utilize often, that doesn't necessarily mean I believe any of them offer any sort of miraculous trading edge. Instead, I do believe all oscillators perform equally in the long run. They are all providing the same thing: a visual depiction of what has already happened in the marketplace. The primary difference is that some oscillators are designed to be slower, producing fewer trading signals. Others are intended to be quicker, offering a higher frequency of trading guidance, in exchange for the likelihood of increased false signals. In my opinion, traders are best off using at least one quick indicator and one slow indicator, then using some sort of netted conclusion. Conservative traders, on the other hand, should stick to the slower indicators.

RELATIVE STRENGTH INDEX (RSI)

The relative strength index (RSI) is my "go-to" indicator for determining the technical status of runaway markets. The RSI is a momentum indicator that compares the magnitude of recent gains and losses to identify overbought or oversold market conditions. Mathematically, RSI can be expressed in the following equation whereas RS (Relative Strength) is equivalent to the average up days' closes divided by the average days' down closes. By default, the indicator uses the previous 14 closes to determine RS. Those looking to speed up the indicator could drop it a few notches, but to slow it down, it would be necessary to increase the number of closes used in the calculation.

$$RSI = 100 - 100/(1 + RS)$$

HOW TO USE RSI

You have probably quickly discovered that computerized oscillators saved hours of hard labor for chartists. Calculating and plotting the RSI manually would be a full-time job. RSI values range from zero to 100, with 100 signifying an extremely overbought market and zero an oversold market. The RSI is a relatively slow-paced and stable indicator. As is true with any oscillator, it is fallible; but I believe it is among the most useful.

In a nutshell, I look for the RSI to move above 70 or below 30. Once it breaches either of these thresholds, the current price move can be said to be near exhaustion. Futures trend traders might take this as a cue to protect profits by tightening their stop orders, selling call options against their positions, or simply exiting the trade. Swing traders, on the other hand, might take an extended RSI reading, along with other corroborative analysis techniques, as a signal to enter a new position in the opposite direction of the trend. Perhaps this involves selling out-of-the-money options against the trend, buying options intended to profit from a trend reversal, buying or selling futures contracts countertrend, or some sort of mixture of both instruments to mitigate position volatility and margin.

As you begin charting the RSI, you will find it rarely dips below 30 or rises above 70. The scarcity of a trigger is a good clue that the indicator has a slow trigger, and any signal it does provide should be a relatively quality indication for those interested in countertrend swing trading. After all, a signal is only produced in rather extreme market conditions.

In Figure 4, it is clear the RSI is proficient at identifying areas of potential inflection. This is a weekly chart of the Canadian dollar, which depicts what starts out as a range-bound market in 2011 through 2013, which is eventually followed by a profound downtrend. In the range-bound market, a reading at or near 70 or 30 in the RSI was capable of reversing the trend on a dime, but in the downtrending market, the indicator pinpointed levels of congestion before the trend resumed. In either instance, a swing trader might have been able to speculate profitably with this information.

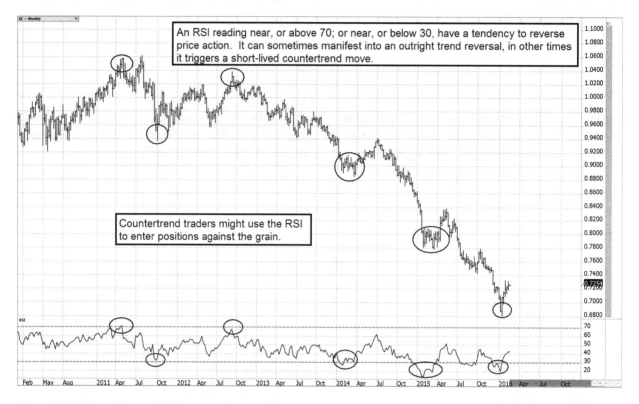

Figure 4: The RSI is proficient at identifying a market that has moved "too far too fast."

Some traders use RSI a little differently than I do; instead of using it as a countertrend signal, they use it for trend trading. For example, if the RSI crosses above 50 it can be considered a sign that a sustainable uptrend is developing. Conversely, a move below 50 might indicate trend trades should sell into the bearish momentum.

Exactly how the indicator is utilized will vary slightly from trader to trader; there isn't a right or wrong way to apply it. Nevertheless, I believe RSI to be most valuable to countertrend traders. Yet again, trend traders might use the RSI as an indication that it is time to protect profits by trailing the stop-loss order more aggressively than would normally be the case.

SLOW STOCHASTICS

Slow stochastics is probably the most written about and over-relied upon indicator. Despite the word "slow" in its title, slow stochastics is actually a rather quick indicator. As a result, it jumps the gun to signal possible reversals from overbought and oversold levels. Nevertheless, it is something I glance at to get a feel for what other traders might be looking at and to get a quick look at where the market might be in regard to fair pricing.

Specifically, the slow stochastic is a momentum oscillator comparing the closing price of a particular commodity to its price range over a given time period, usually 14 days. However, the pace of the oscillator can be adjusted by changing the time period. Obviously, decreasing the time period speeds it up, and increasing it will delay it.

The slow stochastic oscillator is composed of two lines labeled as %K and %D, which trend higher or lower, along with market movement. The oscillator is built on the premise that in an uptrending market, prices tend to close near the high, and in a descending market, closes are generally near the low.

In case you are wondering, this is what the equation for slow stochastics looks like:

$$\%K = 100\,[(C - L14)/\{H14 - L14\}]$$

C = the most recent closing price

L14 = the low of the 14 previous trading sessions

H14 = the highest price traded during the same 14-day period

%D = 3-period moving average of %K

HOW TO USE SLOW STOCHASTICS

Memorizing or even fully understanding how slow stochastics are calculated, and what exactly the two lines generated represent, isn't imperative. What you should be able to garner from the indicator is the overall direction of momentum. Those interested in active countertrend trading seeking a quick signal might consider buying when the %K line crosses over the %D line. Similarly, aggressive sellers might consider taking a position when the %K crosses beneath the %D. Consider yourself warned, because slow stochastics is quick to trigger a signal; there will be times this indicator lures swing traders into the market painfully early. Nevertheless, a crossover that occurs with the lines at values in excess of 80 or sub-20 tend to be surprisingly reliable.

When slow stochastics is working as it is intended, the results are stunning, as displayed in Figure 5. However, markets in prolonged trends tend to bring out the worst in the slow stochastics. Due to its quick nature, following this indicator without the help of other technical analysis tools could lead to large losses on the wrong side of a long trend.

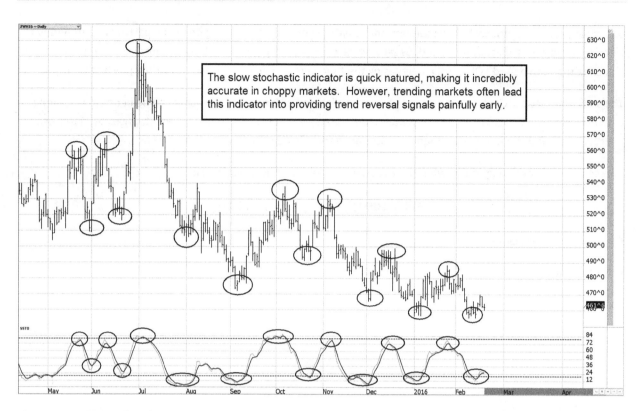

The slow stochastic indicator is quick natured, making it incredibly accurate in choppy markets. However, trending markets often lead this indicator into providing trend reversal signals painfully early.

Figure 5: Sometimes, such as the wheat market in 2015, slow stochastics makes trading look easy, but using this indicator as a primary trading trigger in trending markets will turn out equally as poorly.

MOVING AVERAGE CONVERGENCE DIVERGENCE (MACD)

In addition to being a mouthful, the moving average convergence divergence (MACD) is the one indicator capable of bringing traders back into reality. This is because it is an incredibly slow-moving oscillator that enables its users to take a step back from the chaos of today and look at the long-term trend in prices.

The MACD is known as a trend-following momentum indicator. It is essentially two moving averages, with a built-in indication of the relationship between the two moving averages. In essence, the primary MACD line is calculated by subtracting the 26-day exponential moving average (EMA) from the 12-day EMA. In addition to the MACD line, there is a nine-day EMA, which is considered the signal trigger line. This line is plotted on top of the MACD and produces signals when it crosses over the MACD line.

Some trend traders who prefer to wait for the market to essentially send them a memo stating a trend has begun will wait for the MACD line to cross above or below the zero line, which is the center value. I caution that using delayed signals like this would require a trader to trade with very deep stop-loss orders, or otherwise be willing to accept substantial ebb and flow before cutting the trade loose. Waiting for such lengthy confirmation of a trend might mean entering the market near a short-term peak or trough.

HOW TO USE MACD

There are various versions of plotting the MACD. Some charting applications plot the two EMA lines on top of a histogram, others simply display a third line, yet others leave the additional component out altogether. Regardless of format, the additional element contributes the same information; it displays the magnitude of the divergence between the two lines. In my view, it simply adds unnecessary complexity and confusion. Most people can simply look at the two MACD EMA lines to determine if they are touching or distant from each other. The idea is when the two EMA lines are wide apart, the trend is in full bloom. As the lines converge, the trend is running out of steam.

I generally use the MACD as a tool for identifying the long-term trend. I don't, however, require the MACD to portray a buy or sell signal before I make a bullish or bearish conclusion. Due to the extremely slow nature of the indicator, a trend reversal often occurs well before the indicator finally gives a signal (Figure 6).

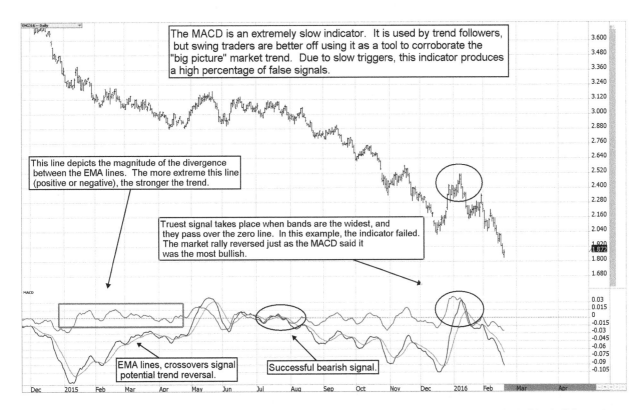

Figure 6: In 2015, natural gas futures were in an unprecedented downtrend. As a result, the MACD produced multiple false bullish signals. This is particularly true for those using a pass of the zero line as an entry signal.

WILLIAMS %R (WPR)

I've met Larry Williams at a Trade Navigator cocktail party. During our chat, he offered several trading gems that I will likely never forget. Despite this, I believe his biggest contribution is the Williams %R technical indicator. Like other oscillators, the WPR is a momentum indicator calculated using 14 days of market action, used to measure the overbought or oversold conditions of a particular commodity market.

HOW TO USE WPR

The WPR displays values from zero to -100; this traditional version of the indicator was displayed in the opposite manner than most. A reading in excess of -80 indicates a selloff could be running its course, but a reading above -20 suggests the current rally could be long in the tooth. However, I prefer to keep things as simple as possible. To save myself the hassle of looking at inverse values, I convert the indicator to a zero to 100, which inverts the overbought and oversold areas. A reading over 80 is considered overbought, while a reading under 20 is oversold (Figure 7). Apparently I wasn't the only person who prefers to work with positive figures. Most charting platforms either default to the positive integer version or give you the choice to do so. Sorry, Larry!

I once read that Larry intended the WPR to be used as a trend trading tool and not necessarily a swing trading indicator luring traders into the markets in hopes of picking a top or bottom. Nevertheless, because it is a relatively quick-triggered indicator, that is probably how the WPR is best used. I like to use the WPR in conjunction with the RSI; the WPR is the "get-set" indicator, while the RSI is the "go."

Figure 7: One of my favorite technical oscillators, Williams %R is quick to call a market turn. In this euro chart, price action was volatile but overall sideways, an ideal environment for this particular indicator.

BOLLINGER BANDS

Bollinger bands are, by far and away, my favorite technical tool. Perhaps it is because they are based on an easy to understand concept, or maybe it is because I secretly enjoyed taking statistics classes in college. In either case, Bollinger bands are simply two price bands plotted two standard deviations away from a simple moving average (SMA). By default, this SMA is usually based on 20 days of price action.

The greatest feature of Bollinger bands is their ability to conform to market conditions. Because standard deviation is a measure of volatility, the bands expand and contract as market volatility fluctuates higher and lower, respectively. When the bands are particularly narrow, it is generally a good indication that prices are on pause, but soon due for a large breakout. Conversely, when the bands are expanded to extreme levels, it is often a sign of a market that has gotten ahead of itself and is probably facing a contraction in volatility. Many option sellers look at wide Bollinger bands as a cue to prepare for premium collection ventures. We'll talk more about this in Chapter 17, "Use Commodity Market Volatility to Your Advantage with Mean Reversion and Delta Neutral Trading."

> Bollinger bands are derived from statistics and probabilities. If used properly, they might dramatically increase the odds of profitable trading.

Although the width of the bands itself can be a useful trading tool, the bands also serve as a measure of overbought and oversold. Unlike other technical oscillators, Bollinger bands are built around a statistical theory that attempts to quantify the odds of a market trading, and staying, at a price beyond the band. If you are unfamiliar with statistics and standard deviations, in the simplest version a standard deviation is a measure of how volatile, or spread out, prices are from the mean, or average. Where this information becomes extremely useful is in its implication of the bell curve of standard deviation. In theory, prices should trade within one standard deviation of the mean roughly 68% of the time, it should trade within two standard deviations of the mean roughly 95% of the time, and within three standard deviations of the mean 99.74% of the time.

HOW TO USE BOLLINGER BANDS

From a trading standpoint, the most useful aspect of Bollinger bands is the visual display of two standard deviations. A market will often trading beyond *one* standard deviation and will rarely trade beyond *three* standard deviations. Yet markets trade beyond two standard deviations somewhat frequently, but statistics suggest prices won't stay outside of the bands for long (Figure 8). Accordingly, prices often reverse, or at least pause, once they reach the bands.

Executing trades in the opposite direction of the trend, at a time during which prices are beyond one of the Bollinger bands, should theoretically pose a 95% chance of the trade working out favorably, at least temporarily. Unfortunately, it isn't quite that easy because as prices change, so does the mean and so does the standard deviation. Thus, at any given time the Bollinger bands are simply offering a snapshot of the current environment, but the standard deviation and the odds of the trade will adjust in real time and the new reality can be highly unfavorable at times. Nevertheless, I believe this is a great tool for those interested in swing trading or other countertrend strategies. In many cases, prices will bounce off the bands to reverse course and establish a new trend.

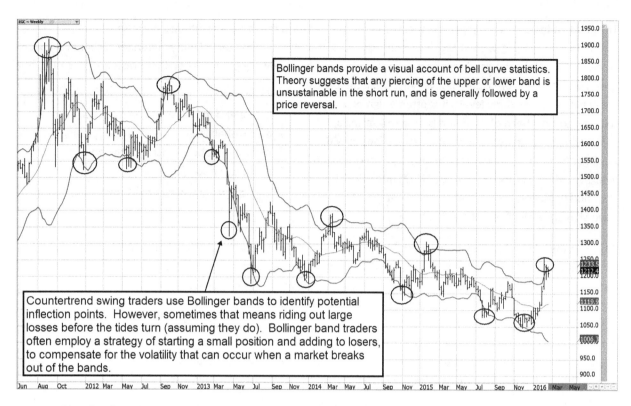

Bollinger bands provide a visual account of bell curve statistics. Theory suggests that any piercing of the upper or lower band is unsustainable in the short run, and is generally followed by a price reversal.

Countertrend swing traders use Bollinger bands to identify potential inflection points. However, sometimes that means riding out large losses before the tides turn (assuming they do). Bollinger band traders often employ a strategy of starting a small position and adding to losers, to compensate for the volatility that can occur when a market breaks out of the bands.

Figure 8: Although Bollinger bands are highly accurate in the long run, traders using them will require guts and patience. In April 2013, gold prices fell $140 below the band before snapping back; this is equivalent to $14,000 per contract to a trader.

CHARTING TOOLS

I tend to be in favor of keeping things simple. The most frequently used charting tool in my platform is a simple trendline drawing tool. It is amazing how well a few simple lines on a chart can work. However, there are a plethora of market chartists out there who prefer using more complex drawing tools such as a Fibonacci ruler, Elliott waves, and the infamous Gann fan.

These geometric charting tools, sometimes referred to as *advanced charting tools*, require interaction and active decision making by the user. In my opinion, this ambiguity creates an environment in which various analysts can come to dramatically different conclusions, despite using the same tools and theory. More so than with less interactive tools, such as computer-generated oscillators, these advanced charting tools are only as good as the trader using them.

With the exception of simple trendlines, it has been my experience that advanced tools are better at explaining what has already happened than predicting what might happen next. However, I guess that could be said of all speculative tools. The intention of this section isn't to completely negate common charting tools; but it is imperative I point out the drawbacks and ambiguity of these methods. Thus, before you pay big bucks for a trading signal service that swears by these charting tools, make sure you keep your expectations in check.

TRENDLINES, TRADING CHANNELS, AND WEDGES

Most finance professors claim market prices are random. If this were true, drawing trendlines would be a waste of time; yet they seem to find a way to work more often than not. The most reasonable explanation of trendlines working a majority of the time is because traders are trained to behave accordingly. When prices reach levels at which they have reversed course before, aggressive traders will take action, assuming history will repeat itself.

Many readers might skip over the section because they deem it to be elementary knowledge. It is; however, because it is such an obvious and simple technical analysis tool, traders often detrimentally overlook or downplay its usefulness. Also, I hope to shed light on some of the less talked about characteristics of these technical tools.

HOW TO USE TRENDLINES, TRADING CHANNELS, AND WEDGES

There is nothing magical about drawing trendlines or trading channels; a child could do it. The practice involves drawing a line across the upper edge of market highs to connect it to subsequent market highs. Such a line represents resistance. A support line can be drawn by connecting market lows. If a trendline can be drawn above and below a price pattern, it is referred to as a *trading channel*.

Obviously, the concept of constructing a trading strategy around trendlines and channels might involve identifying potential entry levels for countertrend swing traders, or they might determine the entry points for breakout traders looking to catch a ride.

A wedge price pattern is simply price consolidation. Specifically, it occurs if market highs and market lows are contracting in such a way that it is possible to draw a triangle after connecting the high points, and separately the low points. There is much debate as to the nature of wedge patterns. Conventional wisdom suggests that it is a continuation pattern in which prices are prone to resuming in the direction being traveled prior to price consolidation. However, many traders believe if the point of the triangle is pointing higher, it is a bearish development, and if the tip of the triangle is pointing lower, it is a bullish pattern. After years of observation, I'm not sure there is much of an indication either way; other than when prices break above or below the wedge, they generally continue indefinitely. In Figure 9, there is an example of a price wedge that resolves itself in a complete trend reversal. Thus, traders should view a wedge pattern as a "calm before the storm." Unfortunately, the direction of the storm itself is often difficult to determine.

Keep in mind when drawing trendlines, channels, or trading wedges that it is more of an art than a science. This should make sense because, as we know, market prices are the result of human emotions and behavior. It isn't realistic to expect hundreds of thousands, or millions, of market participants to collectively behave logically or even in the same way. In Figure 9 it is clear some trendlines must be drawn with some interpretation because drawing precise lines on what appear to have been price overshoots would alter the analysis. A small and temporary breach of any given line or pattern shouldn't affect the overall analysis. Further, don't approach trendlines as a mathematical formula to pinpoint an exact support line. In trading it is good enough, and more realistic, to identify the general area of support. Unfortunately, we never know when a "small and temporary" breach will become something much larger. This is a skill that comes only with experience; even then, there is a lot of guesswork.

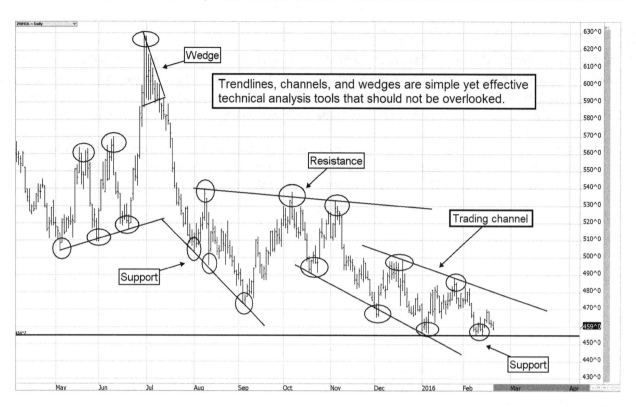

Figure 9: Drawing lines to identify support and resistance is an art, rather than a science. Drawing the lines should reflect the overall trend, not be focused on precision. Perfect trends and trendlines rarely exist.

The other technical tools we will glance at require quite a bit more imagination and faith because they are based on unconventional schools of thought. Nevertheless, whether or not you ever employ any of these analytical methods (I use them sparingly), you should know what they are and how they are used. Once again, traders are essentially competing against other market participants, so it is helpful to be aware of what they might be thinking. In addition, if you happen to frequent traders' expositions, clubs, or online forums, you will need to know these concepts.

FIBONACCI THEORY

If there ever was a charting tool that fits into the "You have to see it to believe it" category, it is Fibonacci theory. Everything logical says it shouldn't work, but it appears to have some grounds for legitimacy.

Most traders are familiar with Fibonacci rulers, but just in case you aren't, Fibonacci was the nickname for an Italian mathematician considered by many to be among the most talented western mathematicians of the Middle Ages. He was responsible for introducing what is now known as the Fibonacci sequence. In the sequence, each number is the sum of its previous two numbers, starting with zero and 1:

0, 1, 2, 3, 5, 8, 13, 21, 34, 55, 89, 144, 233, 377, 610, 987, and so forth

As the sequence progresses, two consecutive numbers divided by each other will approach what is known as the golden ratio, 61.8%; for example, dividing 610 into 987 equals 61.8%. According to Fibonacci theory, nature and therefore the markets tend to move in increments of 61.8% based on the golden ratio. Specifically, the theory suggests market moves will find support or resistance after retracing the following percentages of the initial move:

- 23.6% (found by dividing any number in the sequence by the number that is three places to the right)
- 38.2% (found by dividing any number in the sequence by the number that is found two places to the right)
- 50% (midpoint between high and low)
- 61.8% (found by dividing any number in the sequence by the number that immediately follows it)
- 76.4% (found by subtracting 0.236 from the number 1)

HOW TO USE FIBONACCI THEORY

In Figure 10, the intraday chart of the 30-year Treasury bond future depicts several encounters of support and resistance at or near levels that represent Fibonacci levels. Some might argue it is coincidence, but it repeats itself with surprising regularity. Specifically, once a declining market finds a low, it tends to find resistance at either 38.2% or 50%, or both, as it retraces the decline. Similarly, a market rally correction often gives back 38.2% or 50% of the move in normal ebb and flow. Countertrend traders might look to establish positions at the noted retracement levels in hopes of a reversal, or trend traders might be interested in using the Fibonacci support and resistance levels as guidance for stop-loss order placement.

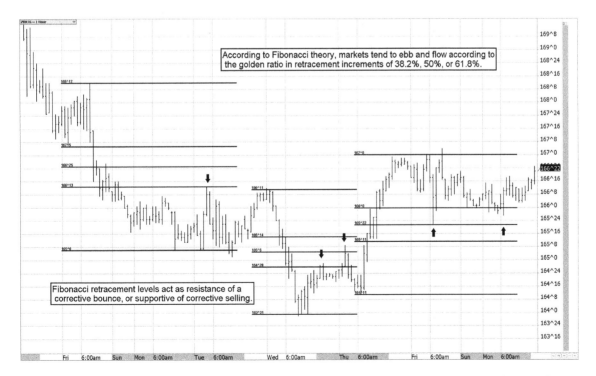

Figure 10: This intraday chart of the 30-year T-bond displays the market's tendency to retrace according to the Fibonacci ruler.

As you can see, there are several possible retracement levels, and this is grounds for criticism. For instance, by the time a trader realizes resistance at the 38.2% level didn't hold, the market is likely approaching 50%, and so on. For this reason, I look to the Fibonacci ruler as confirmation of my original assessment but not for decision making outright. With that said, I have found it to be a very helpful tool; hence, I recommend that traders at least entertain the idea of using it as an incremental tool in the trading tool belt.

ELLIOTT WAVE THEORY

Elliott wave is a popular charting method but, like economists and Fibonacci believers, each Elliott wave theorist has a relatively unique prediction. Unfortunately, in a theory as open to individual interpretation as the Elliott wave is, there are guidelines but there are also many shades of gray, and very little black and white.

"I've never met a rich technician." —Jim Rogers

Elliott wave theory was developed by Ralph Nelson Elliott and is based on the premise that market behavior is determined in waves rather than random timing. Similar to Fibonacci theory, Elliott and his theory's adherents believe that market prices rise and fall based on the golden ratio.

HOW TO USE ELLIOTT WAVE THEORY

According to Elliott's theory, the market rises in a series of five alternating waves and declines in a series of three alternating waves (Figure 11). Specifically, the market rises on the first wave, declines on the second, rallies into wave three, followed by a declining wave four and finally completes the rally on wave five. The five-wave sequence is then followed by a three-wave correction, referred to as A, B, and C.

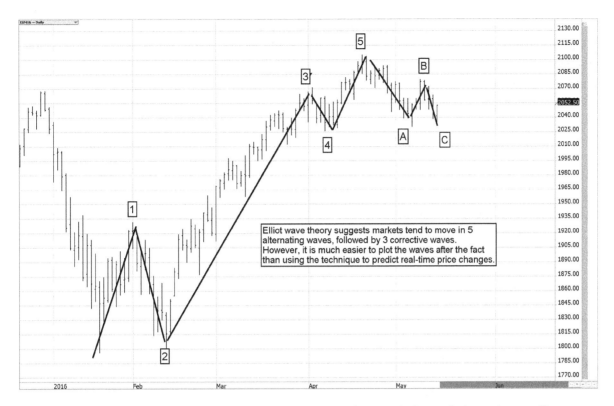

Figure 11: Elliott wave theory is prevalent in stock index trading. This chart of the Dow displays a rally that conforms to Elliott waves.

There are only three general rules to using Elliot wave theory:

1. Wave 2 cannot retrace more than 100% of wave 1.
2. Wave 3 cannot be the shortest of waves 1, 2, and 5.
3. Wave 4 can cannot overlap wave 1.

Although some traders and market analysts have made a living focusing on the Elliott wave theory, there are some glaring downfalls and the tool is open to vast amounts of subjective interpretation. The theory doesn't necessarily attempt to precisely predict the size of any of the waves and therefore it can be difficult to base entry and exit points using such a tool. Elliott wave followers use the same general principles of market retracements as Fibonacci; they believe that corrective moves will travel according to the 38.2%, 50%, or 68% tendencies. Nevertheless, even if the wave structure is intact, it can be a challenge to determine the size of the waves and the difference between the proposed wave sizes can equate to thousands of dollars to a commodity trader.

As is the case with any other trading tool, this theory should be applied in conjunction with other technical analysis instruments or indicators. In addition, there is no defined starting or stopping point. Therefore, it can be difficult to identify the proper waves until after the fact. This makes it difficult for traders to base speculative market decisions on such a theory.

GANN FAN

If you've had any exposure to commodity trading at all, you've at least heard of the Gann fan. This particular technical analysis tool has garnered a cult following in the trading world. It was originally created by WD Gann and incorporates the use of geometric angles in conjunction with time and price. Or in straighter terms, markets tend to move somewhere between a 30% to 70% angle from its starting point in the long run. As price action flows, ideally within the range of the expected angles, it will find support and resistance at specific angle intervals identified by Gann's theory. Accordingly, its followers believe the fan can be used to predict price movement, particularly at extreme levels.

HOW TO USE GANN FAN

Although charting software will allow traders to draw Gann fans in a nearly unlimited number of ways, Gann intended for the fan to be drawn with equal time and price intervals. By doing so, a rise of one price unit for each time unit is equal to a 45-degree angle. Gann fan theory suggests the ideal balance between time and price exists when prices rise or fall at a 45-degree angle relative to the time axis. Surrounding the 45-degree fan line are eight other angles that represent various levels of support and resistance (Figure 12). As the market passes through one fan line, prices should move to the next.

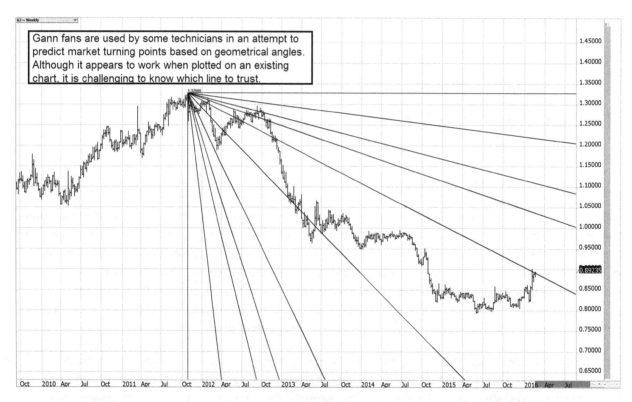

Figure 12: Multiple angle lines make for messy speculation using the Gann fan, but the overall idea that trending markets travel in a roughly 45-degree angle is reasonable, and the geometric lines tend to provide some guidance.

Gann fan analysis leaves much of the instrument drawing and interpretation to the discretion of the trader. Therefore, its usefulness is often in question. Also, because the Gann fan involves multiple lines, critics simply attribute support and resistance as coincidence. After all, if you draw enough lines on a chart, some of them are bound to hold!

CHAPTER 3: FUNDAMENTAL ANALYSIS OF THE COMMODITY MARKETS

Trading in the commodity markets based on fundamental news and analysis differs dramatically from the quick-natured technical analysis, which often requires traders to shift from bullish to bearish in the blink of an eye. Fundamental analysis provides slow-handed guidance to traders. In general, the practice of entering or exiting trades based on market

> "Understand that the right to choose your own path is a sacred privilege. Use it. Dwell in possibility." —Oprah Winfrey

fundamentals is a dawdling and tedious process, demanding massively deep pockets and patience. Imagine being a fundamentalist who identified oil as being overvalued near $100 per barrel in 2008, or on the multiple occasions oil moved above $100 from 2011 to 2013. Initially, a trader selling a futures contract solely on fundamentals would have either blown out his trading account, given up on the trade before it paid off, or suffered a roughly $50,000 drawdown before having an opportunity to profit from the correct analysis. This is because each dollar of crude oil price change equals a profit or loss of $1,000 to a one-lot futures trader. In 2008, the price of oil reached $150 per barrel before suffering from a steep decline. On subsequent occasions, the suffering would have been limited to about $10,000 to $15,000, but still a painful endeavor.

If you are familiar with the popular commodity trading book *Hot Commodities*, written by Jim Rogers, this slow-paced fundamental approach is exactly what he writes about. Not all of us have the capital to employ such a long-term view in the leveraged world of commodities, as Mr. Rogers does. Accordingly, before assuming commodity trading is as "easy" as that particular book implies, you must consider the vast financial difference in the reality of most commodity traders and the author.

Other than obtaining a big-picture consensus of the market makeup, relying on fundamental analysis alone can be a daunting task for the average trader. After all, it can take months, or even years, for traders to get their hands on absolutely accurate fundamental information. By then, the markets have already moved. Alternatively, during times in which markets are ignoring fundamentals, it can take months, or years, for prices to revert to a more equilibrium price.

WHAT IS FUNDAMENTAL ANALYSIS?

Fundamental analysis of the commodity markets involves the study of the interaction between supply and demand; with this analysis, traders attempt to predict future price movement. Specifically, the entire concept of fundamental analysis is built upon the following equations:

Demand > Supply = Higher prices

Supply > Demand = Low prices

Most analysts agree that commodity market supply and demand figures are quantifiable, yet even the diehard fundamentalists will admit accurate statistics are not available in real time. Thus, any numbers plugged into the simple and neat formulas given are relatively meaningless. If you input garbage data into the formula, the result will also be garbage. Accordingly, when an analyst runs the numbers she is almost certainly working with either outdated or inaccurate data. Fundamental analysts waiting for confirmed government supply and demand data will be calculating months after the fact. Alternatively, if they are calculating based on estimates (whether they are government or personally derived), it is nothing more than a guess.

Most recall the simple supply and demand cross charts taught in high school and college economic courses; unfortunately, this academic practice erroneously simplifies a concept that is actually highly complex. In my opinion, what appears to be the most straightforward form of commodity market analysis—fundamental—is actually the most difficult in practice.

Because of the massive complexity that comes with estimating current supply and demand details of any given commodity, the seemingly simple mathematical equation fundamentalists use to speculate on prices can be confusing at best, but misleading at worst. In addition, regardless of the time dedicated to deciphering the market's fundamental code, it can be extremely problematic for a trader to succeed using this method of analysis alone. As already discussed, I believe traders are far better off combining multiple analytical theories (technical, fundamental, seasonal, and so on).

ENERGY MARKET FUNDAMENTALS

Although the energy landscape is quickly changing, crude oil remains king. There is a saying: "Nobody has ever fought a war over ethanol." This is because there is no reason to; ethanol is derived from renewable resources. Unfortunately, more dominant forms of energy such as crude oil and natural gas are

> "Fundamentals make the market." —T. Boone Pickens

not. Nevertheless, as we learned in 2014, the world supply of fossil fuels is far greater than was believed to be the case, compliments of new technology—namely, fracking—enabling oil and gas producers, particularly in the United States, to extract oil and gas from deeper rock. The cost of fracking exceeds that of previous methods of extraction, but it has sharply increased the global supply of energy. Still, due to its eventual finite supply, for the foreseeable future, energy prices will ultimately be affected by interruptions in extraction, transportation, or distillation.

Nothing tells the story of this market better than a chart. Figure 13 paints a picture of unbelievable volatility as the crude oil market shifts from OPEC domination and supply concerns in 2008 to the realization that a global financial crisis was crippling demand for energies, to the emergence of US shale producers bringing massive, and relatively unexpected, supply to the oil market.

Figure 13: Oil fell from $150 per barrel to $30 in 2008, then again from just over $100 to $25 in 2014. These moves represented $120,000 and $80,000 per futures contract to a trader, respectively.

The price of crude oil futures peaked near $150 per barrel in mid-2008 (if you recall, many pundits at the time were calling for $200 oil in short order) and retreated to around $30 by the end of the *same year*. If you have ever dabbled in crude oil futures, you realize this is equal to about $120,000 per contract. In the midst of the chaos, most assumed the immense volatility was a byproduct of the financial crisis and was something that would never be repeated. However, a similar boom and bust cycle occurred again just a few years later. The second rise and fall took place at a slightly more reasonable pace but as a result of the slower price action, the impact of the volatility to the economy was far more intense.

SUPPLY AND DEMAND DATA

Energy traders look to the Energy Information Administration (EIA) for insight into the current stocks of oil and gas, as well as demand estimates. The EIA is a part of the US Department of Energy (DOE); the entity is in charge of accumulating fundamental energy market data and reporting it to the public. They even go as far as to make predictions, but as is the case with most analytical agencies, the accuracy of the predictions is questionable. Other significant players in the fundamental data space are Baker Hughes and the American Petroleum Institute (API).

ANNUAL FORECASTS

The EIA releases an annual forecast of crude oil prices based on extensive calculations using estimates of economic growth or contraction, demand for the product, potential substitutes in the marketplace, and inflation. Their predictions are typically long term and can span decades into the future.

Perhaps the most compelling lesson a finance major learns in college is complex equations and pricing models are only as good as the data inputted, and let's face it, economics comes down to an educated guess. Use the EIA predictions as an indicator of what *might* happen and not view it as the holy grail of price prediction.

WEEKLY INVENTORY DATA

Each week on Wednesday, at precisely 10:30 a.m. Eastern time, light sweet crude oil futures traders are scrambling to digest the contents of a government inventory report. The EIA report details refinery activity, current stockpiles, imports, and even prices at the pump.

The information on the EIA's findings is almost always met with volatility. In fact, risk-averse traders often flatten positions prior to the announcement and aggressive traders (hard-core gamblers) hope for windfall profits by positioning ahead of the EIA's inventory statement. Either way, it is important to be aware of its time of release to ensure that you are effectively managing risk exposure.

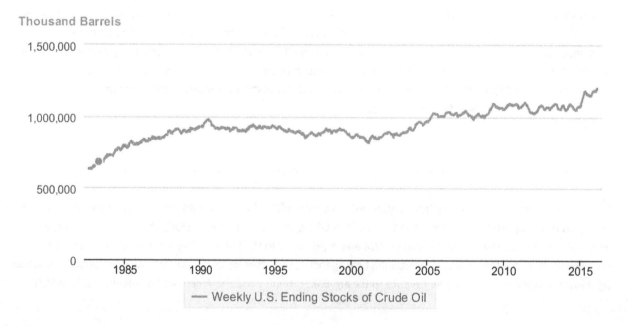

Weekly U.S. Ending Stocks of Crude Oil

 Source: U.S. Energy Information Administration

Figure 14: Weekly crude oil inventory statistics provided by the EIA portray a picture of mass oversupply going into 2016.

The meat and potatoes of the report is the US stocks figure, or inventory, which shows how much oil is available in storage (Figure 14). Many believe that monitoring inventory data will aid in the estimates of both supply and demand. For example, if the increase in crude oil stocks is more than expected, it implies weaker demand, but an unexpected draw in inventory suggests higher demand. The weekly EIA report, and a plethora of useful data, can be found on their website, www.eia.gov.

Although the EIA's weekly inventory report is considered the flagship of such data, most likely because it is available to the public at no cost, there is another inventory report available to subscribers released by the API. The API is the largest US trade association for the oil and gas industry; in fact, according to its website it is the "only national trade association."

Each Tuesday afternoon at 4:30 p.m. Eastern, the API releases its *Weekly Statistical Bulletin*, which includes its estimates of weekly oil stocks, among other statistics. As is the case with the EIA report, the focus is on crude oil stocks.

It isn't a coincidence the API version of the report is issued 18 hours prior to the government agency figures. The API report is not made available to the public; instead, it is provided to paid

> "I was very fortunate in my gene mix. The gambling instincts I inherited from my father were matched by my mother's gift for analysis." —T. Boone Pickens

subscribers of the service. The early release enhances the value to traders willing to pay for faster information. Further, some believe the API's methods of attaining their inventory data is superior to that of the EIA.

OPEC (ORGANIZATION OF THE PETROLEUM EXPORTING COUNTRIES)

Most of us are painfully aware of the Organization of the Petroleum Exporting Countries (OPEC). The oil price–controlling cartel made up of 12 countries (Algeria, Angola, Ecuador, Iran, Iraq, Kuwait, Libya, Nigeria, Qatar, Saudi Arabia, the United Arab Emirates, and Venezuela) has enjoyed the luxury of price collusion since 1965. Much to their dismay, compliments of the US fracking revolution and the subsequent oil supply glut, OPEC has far less control over energy market prices than they once did. In fact, many believe that OPEC's power has been "fracked" along with US shale.

As of 2015 the US oil field production of crude had risen to nearly 300,000 barrels of oil each month, which is double the 2008 trough. The newfound ability for the US to produce its own crude oil has opened the door to the real possibility of energy self-sufficiency. At the same time, it has all but eliminated the ability of OPEC to flex its muscles for political or economic gain. There is a fly in the ointment; OPEC's traditional method of oil extraction is much cheaper than the practice of fracking oil from US shale. When crude oil was valued in the vicinity of $100 per barrel, it seemed OPEC would be reduced to a dog begging for scraps at the table when it came to global oil demand. Knowing that US shale producers faced much higher costs of production, OPEC turned on the spigots and kept them flowing throughout the oil price collapse in hopes of forcing US shale producers out of business. Unfortunately, OPEC was moderately successful; US oil producers were forced to downsize to accommodate the supply glut.

OPEC's problems are not over with US producers. Countries such as China, India, Pakistan, and Indonesia believe they are sitting on "black gold" mines that have yet to be tapped.

In spite of a questionable future, OPEC continues to pledge the pursuit of stabilization of international oil markets, but does so in a manner that best benefits its member nations. Simply, although they are in competition with one another, each cartel member acts in a fashion that the group believes to be supportive of a steady income to the producing countries and, less important, a steady supply to consuming countries.

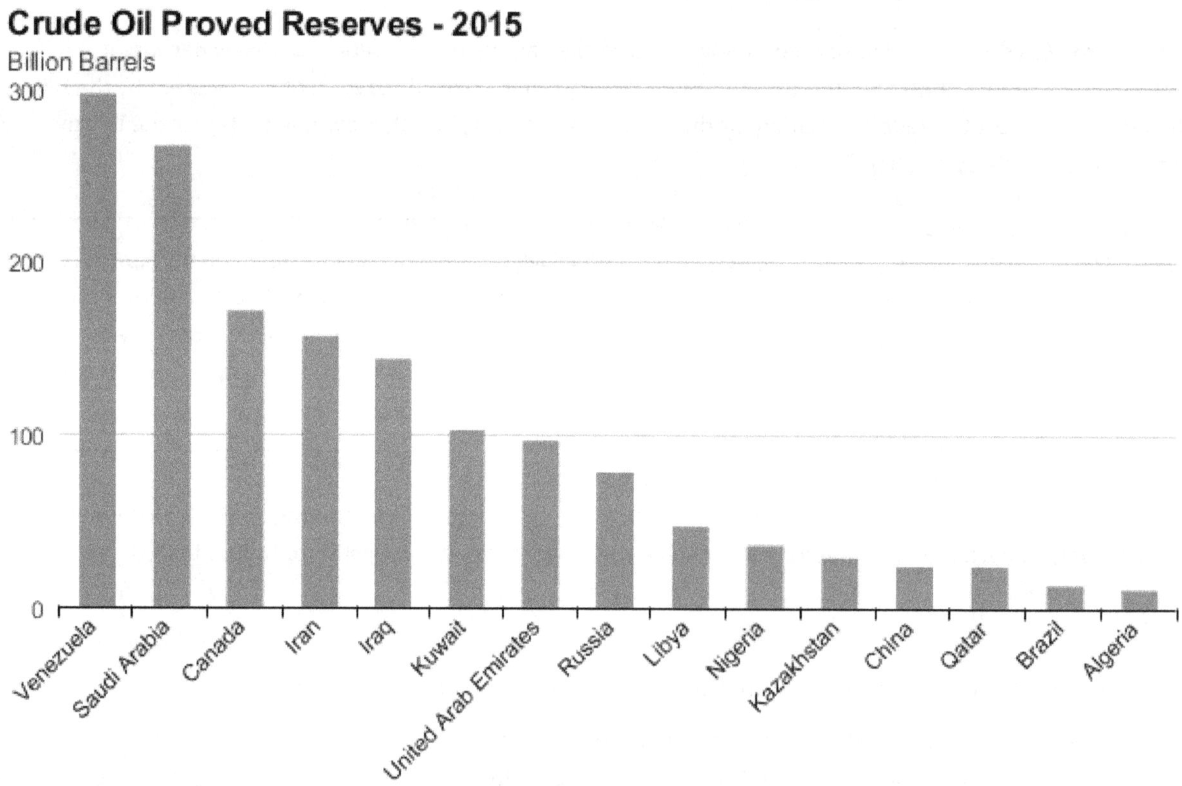

Crude Oil Proved Reserves - 2015

Billion Barrels

Figure 15: Despite internal trouble in the cartel, OPEC nations held the majority of oil global oil reserves in 2015.

OPEC nations still account for about two-thirds of the world's oil reserves and about a third of production (Figure 15). Naturally, this affords the group a considerable amount of clout. It is difficult to imagine a world in which OPEC doesn't have a strong grip on energy prices; therefore, as a commodity trader it is important to be aware of the cartel's policy, predictions, and tendencies.

US DOLLAR

Despite occasional controversy about doing so, global crude oil is quoted in terms of the US dollar. A higher US dollar tends to put downward pressure on dollar-based assets such as crude oil; conversely, a weak dollar promotes higher prices (Figure 16). This is because a cheaper dollar makes crude oil more attractively priced to overseas consumers and, therefore, increases demand for the product.

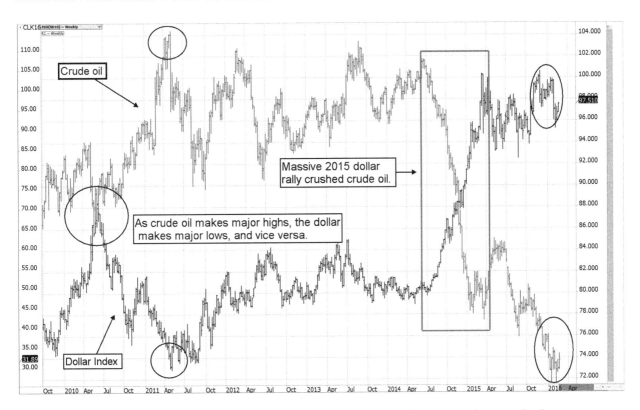

Figure 16: Oil is priced in dollars globally. Thus, fundamentals aside, a higher dollar generally equates to cheaper crude oil.

As volatile as the US currency has been, it is arguably the most stable and liquid of the denominations used by major oil players. As a result, it will likely be difficult for protestors of dollar-based asset pricing to get their way.

OIL EXPORTERS

It isn't a coincidence that oil is priced in dollars. The US is, by far, the largest importer of crude oil in the world at approximately 7 million barrels per day. Japan comes in at a not-so-close second at 4.6 million barrels per day based on the final 2014 figures. To put things in perspective in a post–shale fracking boom, in 2008 the US was importing close to 11 million barrels per day!

On the other hand, although the United States has upped its ante in the oil game, it isn't even on the map of the largest exporters. Saudi Arabia exports approximately 7 million barrels per day and Russia nearly 5 million. The remaining supply is provided by a handful of smaller exporters in the Middle East and South America. If you are wondering why the US is so low on the oil export list, it is because there are domestic laws that almost completely prohibit oil producers in the United States from exporting oil.

The oil export ban was born in the 1970s in attempt to protect US consumers from OPEC. The ban was aimed at mitigating the volatility that comes with oil price spikes, but its effectiveness is under constant question. After all, if oil producers have the ability to export oil to other countries they might have incentive, and funding, to expand operations to bring even more supply to the market. Now that the US is in a position to be a major supplier of global oil, the argument to lift the ban is at the forefront.

GRAIN MARKET FUNDAMENTALS

Those wishing to trade grain futures and options are subjected to a barrage of constant data. The US Department of Agriculture (USDA) allocates substantial resources to acquiring and compiling the usage, storage, and growing statistics of farmers and silos around the country. In an industry with so many independent operations, along with constant exposure to the uncertainty that is Mother Nature, this is no easy task.

Price pressures in the grain complex come from a nearly unlimited number of factors. To avoid analysis paralysis, traders will likely be better off narrowing their research and, better yet, knowing where to go for reliable information.

Before we look into the details of grain supply and demand, it is important to be aware of the big picture. Grain futures react to macro global economic conditions along with micro-growing environments in the primary growing regions of the US, South America, China, and India. This makes sense because grain futures traded on CME Group are based primarily on crops grown in the region but sold to overseas buyers.

Unlike mined and extracted commodities, grains are a renewable asset; supply is highly dependent on the success of the *current* crop year. Consequently, the USDA statistics on acreage planted and ending stocks are a popular gauge in measuring crop yields. Each of the USDA reports discussed in this section can be found on the agency's website, www.usda.gov, or more conveniently, the National Agricultural Statistics Service (NASS) branch at www.nass.usda.gov.

SUPPLY AND DEMAND DATA

Again, compiling supply and demand data in real time is a difficult task, but making accurate educated guesses regarding the findings is beyond impossible. Due to the complexities involved, the USDA's projected ending stocks figures are often inaccurate. Beginning traders are repeatedly caught off guard by this; most assume any data a government agency reports as gospel, but nothing could be further from the truth.

Also, it isn't uncommon for frustrated traders to express discontent over the inaccuracy of USDA data; others go as far as to suggest that the USDA could be manipulating data for their own ulterior motives. I'm not a believer in that conspiracy theory, but I can attest the practice of trading solely on the findings of the USDA is best described as financial suicide. Still, both fundamental and technical traders alike should be aware of all USDA reports and their implications. Even if you are not making trading decisions based on fundamental news, some of your competitors (market participants) are.

USDA PLANTING INTENTIONS AND ACREAGE REPORTS

Anybody who has ever traded grain futures will tell you the spring USDA reports are the most treacherous. The USDA publishes its *Planting Intention Report* in late March to provide insight into estimates of the current year's planted acreage.

The Planting Intention Report tends to get a volatile reaction. This is because prior to its March release, traders are simply relying on rumors and guesses as to what the upcoming crop year might look like. Nevertheless, even the March edition released by the USDA is nothing more than unfounded claims of the objectives of farmers. I'm not saying farmers intentionally lie about the grain they plan to put into the ground, but they are certainly free to change their minds.

It isn't until the June *Acreage Report*, which depicts how much of each grain has made it into the ground, that traders finally get to see concrete data. Of course, once the seed is in the ground the focus shifts from how much was planted, to how much grain will likely be harvested, and eventually become part of the supply stocks.

MONTHLY SUPPLY/DEMAND REPORTS

A handful of monthly reports issued by the USDA offer traders insight into the immediate fundamental environment. Included are *Crop Production*, *Monthly Ending Stocks*, and *Stocks-to-Use Ratio*.

CROP PRODUCTION

Crop production is the expected total number of bushels to be harvested in each grain. This number is generally the most important during growing seasons, but it is released each month regardless of the timing of the growing cycle. Obviously, this report garners little attention during nongrowing seasons. Generally speaking, higher numbers on the *Crop Production Report* implies higher production and theoretically lower grain prices.

ENDING STOCKS

Calculated by subtracting supply from demand, quarterly ending stocks represent the carryover into the next year—simply, how much excess grain is on hand to meet current demand. However, the USDA's monthly version of the report uses *estimates* of both supply and demand to determine what they determine the ending stocks should be. Naturally, higher-ending stocks indicate more supply and can weigh on the price of amply supplied commodities. And to point out the obvious, if the USDA is using hypothetical supply and demand figures based on their projection models to calculate the ending stocks, there is substantial room for error.

STOCKS-TO-USE RATIO

The stocks-to-use ratio is derived by dividing ending stocks by total demand. It measures how much of this year's demand can be met by existing grain. If the stocks-to-use ratio were 15%, the estimate would be that current grain supply could meet 15% of next year's annual expected demand. A higher stocks-to-use ratio tends to have a negative impact on pricing because it paints a picture of adequate supply, low demand, or both.

There are two versions of stocks-to-use ratios, the domestic ratio (Figure 17) and the world stocks-to-use (Figure 18). Most traders focus on the world figure. The global stocks-to-use ratio for corn has hovered between 30% and 12% for much of the last two decades with a comfort zone somewhere around 20%. Soybeans, on the other hand, have spent more time in the mid- to high 20% figure but maintain a similar range of 10% to 30%.

USDA SUPPLY/DEMAND US SOYBEANS	Feb USDA 13-14	Feb USDA 14-15	Jan USDA 15-16	Feb USDA 15-16
Area (M Acres)				
Planted	76.8	83.3	82.7	82.7
Harvested	76.3	82.6	81.8	81.8
Yield (Bu/Acre)	44.0	47.5	48.0	48.0
Beginning Stocks (M Bu)	141	92	191	191
Production	3,358	3,927	3,930	3,930
Imports	72	33	30	30
Supply, Total	3,570	4,052	4,150	4,150
Crushings	1,734	1,873	1,890	1,880
Exports	1,638	1,843	1,690	1,690
Seed	97	96	92	92
Residual	10	49	39	39
Use, Total	3,478	3,862	3,711	3,701
Ending Stocks	92	191	440	450
Stocks/Use Ratio	2.6%	4.9%	11.9%	12.2%

Figure 17: Domestic soybean supply and demand stats compiled by the USDA.

USDA SUPPLY/DEMAND WORLD SOYBEANS (Million Metric Tons)	Feb USDA 13-14	Feb USDA 14-15	Jan USDA 15-16	Feb USDA 15-16
Supply				
Beginning Stocks	56.22	62.43	76.93	77.08
Production	282.86	318.80	319.01	320.51
Imports	111.78	122.23	127.16	127.19
Use				
Crush, Domestic	241.31	262.67	275.35	275.86
Total Domestic	275.73	300.50	314.04	314.52
Exports	112.70	125.88	129.79	129.85
Ending Stocks	62.43	77.08	79.28	80.42
Stocks/Use Ratio	22.6%	25.7%	25.2%	25.6%

Figure 18: Global stocks-to-use ratio for soybeans tends to be more comfortable than domestic supply/demand figures.

US DOLLAR

Like crude oil, the value of the US dollar plays a role in grain valuation. This is because a stronger dollar creates an environment in which dollar-priced assets (including grains) seem expensive to foreign buyers. Accordingly, the demand for these "expensive" assets drops and often so does the price of grain. Conversely, a weak US currency enables domestic growers to market their inventory at more competitive prices, increasing demand for the products and eventually promoting higher grain prices.

Although it is easy to overlook the impact the dollar has on grain pricing, it could very well be the most dominant influence.

SOFT COMMODITIES FUNDAMENTAL ANALYSIS

The soft commodities were made famous by the movie *Trading Places*, but many novice commodity traders find it difficult to acquire fundamental research concerning the complex. If you aren't familiar with the softs, they are the food and fiber complex consisting of cotton, cocoa, sugar, frozen concentrated orange juice, and coffee. The challenge lies primarily in the fact that the softs are typically grown, cultivated, and harvested abroad and, therefore, there often isn't conveniently released data on production and demand statistics. This is unlike other commodities such as the grains and meats in which the USDA reports weekly and monthly updates on such figures.

Complicating the situation, there is a widespread belief the fundamental data seeping out of non-US producers of soft commodities such as China and South American nations is inaccurate or even manipulated in an attempt to influence market pricing. Even if their intentions are noble, most of the soft growing areas are at a technological disadvantage. Thus, the margin for error in the data is considerably high.

It isn't uncommon for this group of futures contracts to experience extreme, and many times unexplained, price moves. For instance, coffee prices soared in the second quarter of 2014 to levels only seen on a handful of occasions throughout history. However, the move was made without substantiated news of a freeze or other obstruction in supply. Nor were there any substantial changes in demand. There was a drought scare, but in the end it had little impact on the market supply. Yet the price of coffee doubled in price in a few short months!

Accessing soft market information, let alone reliable supply and demand figures, can be time consuming, but here are a few resources that will help you stay on top of the latest fundamental developments:

INTERNATIONAL COFFEE ORGANIZATION

The London-based International Coffee Organization (ICO) is a popular source of fundamental coffee news. The ICO is an intergovernmental union for coffee; their goal is to promote the consumption, quality, and efficiency of the "world coffee economy." Traders might find the organization helpful in that it compiles historical statistics and data regarding coffee fundamentals and pricing. Conveniently, the ICO offers export stats and pricing dating as far back as the 1960s on their website, www.ico.org. Further, unlike US government agencies reporting agricultural data, the ICO has a knack for packaging information in easy to understand graphs, icons, and figures. The organization is a great source of information on the big picture of coffee supply and demand.

BRAZIL'S CONAB

Companhia Nacional de Abastecimento (CONAB), which translates to "National Supply Company," has become a popular source of Brazilian coffee supply and production stats despite their mission statement: "To contribute to the regularity of supply and guarantee income to farmers, participating in the formulation and implementation of policies and agricultural supply." Some would argue that there is a conflict of interest between reporting statistics and "guaranteeing" income to farmers.

Visitors to www.CONAB.gov.br will find the latest news and statistics on the Brazilian coffee industry. Of course, it will take some work. Because it is a Brazilian site, you will either need to be fluent in Portuguese or in using a browser that is capable of effectively translating to the language of your choice. I have found Google Chrome to be extremely effective in converting the text into a format that English speakers can easily navigate.

Unfortunately, CONAB is not as effective in offering data that can be easily digested by the layman. Perhaps it should follow the lead of the ICO, rather than the USDA.

USDA

The USDA does compile periodic fundamental data on sugar, coffee, and orange juice via its Foreign Agricultural Services (FAS) branch. Although the US government might not be perfect in collecting and reporting data, the USDA is thought to be superior to most other commodity reporting organizations. Unfortunately, the USDA reports on the softs much less frequently than it does on the grains or meats, rendering it less useful for softs futures traders. Nevertheless, if you are a fundamental trader it is worth a look.

Perhaps the most valuable report on the softs issued by the USDA is that of the world supply of sugar. The report is released twice per year, in May and November. Included are estimates of production, consumption, and ending stocks. The report, entitled *Sugar: World Markets and Trade*, can be found on the FAS USDA website at www.fas.usda.gov.

To enhance the usefulness of the information, the USDA breaks down the fundamental picture for the largest sugar producers—Brazil, India, Thailand, and China—and includes comments on projected ethanol demand. Because this is a semi-annual report, traders are often starved for information prior to the release of the data. All futures markets are subject to event risk surrounding the release of a USDA report, but the lack of information on softs opens the door for price shocks. For instance, the historical 2009 sugar rally in which sugar more than doubled in value in a handful of months came on the heels of the May release of the USDA's report.

The USDA also issues a semi-annual report on coffee supply and demand statistics. The *World Markets and Trade Report* is released every June and December and offers information such as world production and export estimates broken down by country. This report can also be found at www.fas.usda.gov.

ADDITIONAL RISK DISCLOSURE FOR SOFTS TRADERS

Due to unique circumstances that soft futures and options traders face, I need to disclose a few additional notes. Aside from the aforementioned challenges in acquiring efficient fundamental data, there are other obstacles to trading markets such as orange juice, sugar, and coffee, including liquidity, explosions in volatility, and relatively high leverage. Nonetheless, you shouldn't always let these factors prevent you from participating. Instead, you should ensure that your trading strategy is appropriate for the market you are trading.

To illustrate, orange juice futures typically trade between 1,000 and 2,000 contracts in a single session. This is rather low when compared to most futures contracts; to put the volume into perspective, the e-mini S&P futures generally trade 1 to 2 million futures contracts daily, while the 10-year note and corn futures contracts each trade around 100,000 contracts in a typical session. As a result of relatively low trading volume, it is a good idea to avoid strategies that require market liquidity to thrive, such as option selling or day trading.

Similarly, sugar futures are liquid but can sometimes experience sharp bouts of volatility after prolonged inaction. This market is often favorable to synthetic trading, in which positions taken in the futures market are partially or fully hedged using long options. We discuss this concept in detail in later chapters of this book. Despite being relatively liquid, sugar is not necessarily an optimal market for option selling due to cheap option premiums.

On the other hand, coffee can sometimes be a great place for patient option sellers to capitalize due to the massive increases in premium during weather scares or other market moving events. That said, the risks of option selling in any of the soft commodities can be abnormally high, so it is imperative that traders wait for great opportunities based on historical standards as opposed to randomly selling premium.

PRECIOUS METALS MARKET FUNDAMENTALS

Speculating on the direction of precious metals based on fundamental analysis is even more challenging than it is for most other markets because at least renewable resources such as the grains enjoy frequent publications of supply and demand data. Yet similar to the softs complex, locating accurate supply and demand data for gold is much more difficult. Further, precious metals are not only an industrial commodity, but they also act in the capacity of a currency as well as a supposed hedge against economic turmoil and inflation; this makes fundamental analysis highly complex.

A popular source of fundamental data on gold is the World Gold Council. On its website, www.gold.org, you will find Excel spreadsheets lined with supply and demand data, as well as several research articles outlining trends in demand, gold mining, and so forth. It is important to note that the World Gold Council is the market development organization for the gold industry. Members are primarily gold mining companies whose interests generally benefit from higher gold prices.

Another popular source of information regarding gold fundamentals is www.Kitco.com. Kitco goes as far as to depict where the demand for gold is coming from—electronics, jewelry, and so on. Before exploring any gold fundamental website, you should accept the fact that solicitations will run rampant. Thus, make sure you are well-informed in regard to all the possible ways to participate in gold before venturing to do the research. Many informational websites generate their revenue by enticing investors to purchase gold coins or bullion. The reality is these are the only feasible choices for those with extremely long time horizons due to a gross lack of liquidity in the precious metals bullion arena. My brokerage service does offer investment in precious metals coins and bullion, but I advise most of my clients they are better off going long in the futures market due to more efficient pricing and easy entry and exit.

CURRENCY MARKET FUNDAMENTALS

Currencies change hands throughout the world for any number of reasons; any time an investor in Japan wants to put money to work in the US, he must first sell his yen and purchase US dollars. Similarly, a US corporation doing business in Europe must sell dollars and purchase euro to finance business operations. Making trading decisions based on such massive and global macro factors can be difficult. For instance, to determine the true supply and demand of a particular currency an analyst would first have to decipher all of the economic, social, and political forces that drive supply and demand...and as you can imagine, this is no easy task.

Let's take a brief (and perhaps overly simplistic) look at a handful of traditional schools of thought that currency traders will continually be exposed to and that some use to attempt to predict price movement.

INTEREST RATES

The epitome of currency market fundamental analysis is the interest rate differential. In essence, the country with the highest interest rates offered on asset deposits will, in concept, see the highest amount of buying interest. In theory, money will flow to the highest yield.

With this in mind, it comes as no surprise that currency traders keep a close eye on central bank interest rate policy. In notion, when a country raises interest rates, its currency strengthens relative to others and vice versa. Of course, trading isn't quite this artless. Markets often price in changes in interest rates before they are actually put into effect. Markets are forward looking and if the Federal Reserve, the European Central Bank (ECB), or any other central bank telegraphs its next move, the market is quick to react.

INFLATION/MONETARY POLICY

In its meekest form, inflation is an overall increase in the cost of goods and services that can be consumed within any given economy. During times of inflation, each unit of currency can buy fewer goods and services. Accordingly, inflation can best be described as erosion in the purchasing power of money. A $1 bill will always be worth one dollar, but as inflation takes hold, that single note of currency will be able to buy less and less.

Ideally, traders long a currency for speculative purposes would like to see some moderate inflation because it will keep the currency price firm. On the other hand, deflation generally keeps a currency under price pressure. If currency prices reach relatively extreme values at the hands of inflation or deflation, it might actually be the factor that reverses the currency trend.

The Fed provided a spectacular example of expansionary policy in the late 2000s by dramatically increasing the money supply and suppressing the value of the greenback to historically low levels. In essence, they were deflating the currency. However, despite a lack of inflation the cure to a cheap dollar—was a cheap dollar. From mid-2014 through the first quarter of 2015, the greenback rallied a whopping 25%!

TRADE BALANCE

As a refresher, the trade balance provides a quantitative snapshot of nations' imports and exports, and more important, the net difference between the two categories. In general, a country experiencing more imported goods and services than exported is seen as having a weaker currency. This is because in order for a country to purchase goods to import, they must convert the domestic currency (assumed to be US dollars in this example) to purchase goods in another currency. When US consumers are purchasing goods made overseas, they are in essence contributing to a lower dollar value because they are indirectly willing to sell the dollar to purchase alternative currencies needed to acquire the desired goods.

Traders in all asset classes keep an eye on the trade balance using peripheral vision, but currency traders pay relatively close attention to it. Even so, I have doubts as to whether monitoring monthly trade balance stats offer traders any type of edge in price speculation. Not only does the data severely lag reality by the time it is released, but even if it were real-time information, it would merely tell us what is already happening and not necessarily what *will* happen. In my opinion, this data point is largely priced into the markets in real time.

GOVERNMENT INTERVENTION

Throughout the last decade, government intervention, once thought of as taboo, has become the norm. Central banks around the world have been actively interfering with currency market conditions in attempt to alter, or hinder, the natural development of market cycles. In some cases, governments interfere with currency valuation indirectly through the manipulation of imports and exports, or directly with the purchase or sale of a large quantity of currency in the open market.

Government intervention is the embodiment of why fundamental analysis is difficult. When central banks intervene in the currency markets it is generally not announced. As you can imagine, the intervention operation places speculators at the bottom of the importance totem pole, but they are often the victims. Unfortunately, this is something that must be understood and accepted by anyone wishing to trade currencies in any capacity.

The most dramatic example I can recall of speculator casualties at the hands of unexpected government intervention is the Swiss National Bank's (SNB) decision to unpeg the Swiss franc from the euro in early 2015. The peg had been in place since 2011; at the time of implementation the Swiss believed their currency was overvalued because safe haven investors were flocking to the franc. Pegging the currency to the euro helped deflate the franc to ensure its exporters could compete in the global marketplace.

> "When you combine ignorance and leverage, you get some pretty interesting results." —Warren Buffett

Fast forward to 2015 and the operations that enabled the peg, which involved printing Swiss francs to buy euro, amassed an astounding $480 billion worth of euro, or about 70% of the Swiss GDP. It was clear to the SNB that it was time to rip off the bandage, so they did. The value of the Swiss franc against the dollar, as traded in the futures markets, instantly soared from about $0.97 to $1.23 (Figure 19). If you are familiar with currency futures math, you might have realized the nearly 27% gain was an instantaneous profit or loss of about $32,500 for anybody trading the franc against the dollar. Unfortunately, the move put many spot brokerage firms out of business because clients lost more money than they had on deposit and simply couldn't pay the deficit. In the futures industry, I'm not aware of any brokerage firm failures at the hands of this move, but I can assure you it put several individual brokers out on the street because brokers are held individually responsible if they have a client who loses more than is on deposit and is unable to pay their debt.

It is important to note that sudden changes in market fundamentals cannot be predicted. No amount of analysis or research could have alerted traders to imminent action by the SNB. However, government interventions tend to happen when a currency is trading at extreme levels. Governments rarely intervene with currency markets trading at mid-level valuations, but a currency being priced at historic extremes is a strong candidate. Thus, fundamental traders and trend traders, whose trading methods often involve slow reactions in the direction of the trend, are often hurt the most when governments interfere with market pricing. Yet countertrend traders stand to make substantial profits because technical oscillators are expected to be suggesting potential trend reversals at, or near, prices that become targets for intervention.

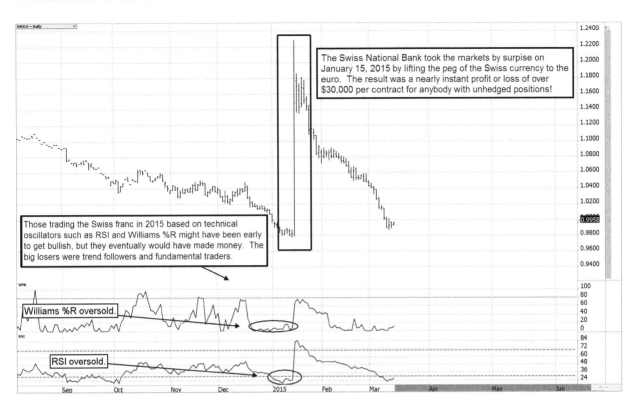

The Swiss National Bank took the markets by surpise on January 15, 2015 by lifting the peg of the Swiss currency to the euro. The result was a nearly instant profit or loss of over $30,000 per contract for anybody with unhedged positions!

Those trading the Swiss franc in 2015 based on technical oscillators such as RSI and Williams %R might have been early to get bullish, but they eventually would have made money. The big losers were trend followers and fundamental traders.

Williams %R oversold.

RSI oversold.

Figure 19: Fundamental analysis couldn't save the Swiss franc bears from a sudden change in policy by the Swiss National Bank in early 2015. However, countertrend traders might have enjoyed windfall profits.

Many may assume a simple stop-loss order would have prevented massive losses for anybody caught on the wrong side of this move, but that would be a false assumption. Because the news was completely unexpected, and the market's reaction was swift, the stop-loss slippage was intense. Most of the buy orders elected were stop-loss orders, which become market orders once reached. Further, there weren't any sellers to take the other side of the trade. Accordingly, the exchange's trade matching system seeks out the best sell limit order working to match with the triggered buy-stop orders, which was often dozens, or hundreds, of ticks above the current market price. As a result, it would not be impossible for a stop-loss order working at $1.00 to have been filled near $1.20. Assuming this was the case, the slippage alone would account for a loss of $25,000.

The Swiss franc fiasco of 2015 is an extreme example of what can happen on the heels of government intervention. In most instances, there is at least some sort of inclination of the possibility of an intervention enabling traders to prepare. Nevertheless, I felt it essential to shine light on just how volatile markets can be, and how leverage can play a part in destroying, or vastly improving, the lives of market participants. In addition, this is a great example of why stop orders might not be the best way to hedge or protect a trader from disaster. A trader with a stop-loss might have suffered a loss well into the tens of thousands of dollars regardless of where the stop-loss was placed. On the other hand, a trader *not* using a stop order with the available margin to hold the position beyond the initial reaction would have eventually seen his losses disappear. By mid-March, the Swiss franc had given back the entire move!

GDP (GROSS DOMESTIC PRODUCT)

A quick tool that currency traders can use to gauge the health of the economy backing any particular currency is the Gross Domestic Product (GDP). You are no doubt aware the GDP of a nation is the total market value of all goods and services produced domestically, including foreign businesses operating within domestic borders. In other words, it is based on geographical location rather than nationality. Generally, a higher GDP rating is considered to be favorable to the underlying currency. Thus, traders should be aware of the relative growth rates of economies associated with each currency. Once again, knowing and understanding this theory is necessary in determining market sentiment and psychology, but likely won't help you in executing profitable short-term currency trades.

INTEREST RATE MARKET FUNDAMENTALS

Interest rate traders in the futures markets look to many of the same economic points and data that a currency trader studies, as in GDP, trade balance, inflation, monetary policy, and other hints at the current strength of the economy. However, since the Federal Reserve employed a massive intervention into market rates in the mid-2000s, the one and only fundamental barometer has been the Fed itself.

Federal Open Market Committee (FOMC) meetings, Fed press conferences, and the Fed minutes, which are a written account of the conversations that took place at the FOMC meeting, have become the paramount events for fundamental bond and note traders. Further, because the Fed clearly stated a dependence on employment data when it comes to adjusting current monetary policy, the monthly non-farm payroll report offering details on how many public and private sector jobs has been added to the economy has become a circus in recent years.

NON-FARM PAYROLL REPORT

On the first Friday of each month, the government fills us in on the employment landscape of the economy. Without fail, the financial markets, and in particular interest rate–related products, begin to behave nervously on the Thursday before the announcement. The news is released at 8:30 a.m. Eastern time to plenty of emotional reaction. It isn't uncommon to see futures contracts travel thousands of dollars in one direction, and promptly reverse erasing the initial reaction to the news. Hence, caution is warranted.

Prior to Fed intervention, interpretation of the payroll report was simple. If the number was better than expected, the Treasury market would decline because investment dollars were more likely to be allocated to riskier assets with better profit potential such as stocks. Conversely, if the employment report was poor, Treasury prices would increase because nervous investors would seek the safety of government-backed fixed income securities. In today's world, however, it is difficult to determine what is good or bad. Because the Fed's interest rate policy is supposedly tied to jobs data, traders have to guess whether the news will lure, or deter, investment dollars, but they also have to determine the most likely action the Fed will take in light of this newly released data. Once again, despite the seemingly simplistic and fail-proof nature of trading based on supply and demand fundamentals, it is a complicated and, in my opinion, improbable task.

FED FUNDS FUTURES

Most interest rate speculators are trading futures and options using the 30-year bond, 10-year note, and the 5-year note futures contracts. However, there is a suite of futures contracts that can be used to speculate on the Federal funds interest rate, which is a function of monetary policy set forth by the Federal Reserve. Specifically, Fed funds futures are derivative contracts written with the FOMC's target overnight bank lending rate as the underlying asset.

Fed fund futures aren't necessarily optimal speculation vehicles for the average retail trader. However, I figured I should mention it in this section because there are a lot of media outlets and fundamental traders who use the Fed funds futures markets as a source of fundamental guidance. That said, Fed funds futures offer a low-margin and low-risk speculative vehicle. But I am not a fan of assuming the Fed funds futures market offers any amount of predictive guidance.

In a bare-bones example of how the Fed funds futures work, a trader who believes the FOMC will be increasing interest rates would sell a Fed funds futures contract; a trader who believes the Fed will lower rates would buy a Fed funds futures contract. This might sound counterintuitive, but the price of an interest rate product moves inversely to rates. Thus, if interest rates rise, bonds, notes, and even Fed funds futures contracts fall, and vice versa.

For example, if the March Fed funds futures contract was trading at 99.50. The implication is the market believes, in that moment, the Fed funds interest rate will be 0.50% at the time this futures contract expires. This is figured by subtracting 99.50 from 100.00. Fed fund futures trade like a discount bond in which the price of the contract is equal to 100 minus the interest rate. This is true unless we are in a negative interest rate environment. If the cash market Fed funds rate, not necessarily the futures rate, is negative, banks in general and even the central bank would be paid to accept deposits! Such a policy is aimed at luring banks to proactively lend funds to the general public because sitting on cash deposits represents an expense.

Many speculators look to the Fed funds futures market for answers for when the Fed might be taking action next. While most traders in Fed funds futures are highly sophisticated and are likely buying and selling these futures contracts after extensive research, they might still be wrong. Simply put, the Fed funds futures market gives us a glimpse into the expectations of other traders but does not tell us with certainty what the future will bring.

The CME Group provides a highly valuable resource to traders interested in dissecting the Fed funds futures markets known as FedWatch. By navigating to the CMEGroup.com website and searching for FedWatch, you would be able to unearth a wealth of knowledge, including the prices of several Fed funds futures contracts with various expiration months. More important, what contract values imply in regards to the probability of a rate hike at a particular point in the future.

To reiterate, the Fed funds futures contracts tell us what market participants believe the overnight bank lending rate will be at a particular time in the future. Between now and expiration, it is possible to see shrill changes in outlook. The rate may be a snapshot of today's thoughts, but two weeks from now, we might see completely different expectations blooming from the Fed funds futures market. Ultimately, nobody can predict the Fed. Not even Fed members know what the committee will be thinking or doing several months from now.

SAVE YOURSELF SOME TIME AND A HEADACHE

As you've navigated through this chapter, it may have become painfully obvious that locating and deciphering fundamental supply and demand information for each commodity market is not an easy task. In fact, anybody wishing to make trading decisions based on this method of analysis will find that it is the equivalent of a full-time job. To recap, I believe fundamental analysis should be a minimal percentage of your analysis because, in my opinion, putting a heavier weighting on findings from technical analysis is a more effective means of market prediction, and more so timing.

> "There seems to be some perverse human characteristic that likes to make easy things difficult." —Warren Buffett

Nevertheless, traders of all types, methods, and sizes must at minimum keep their peripheral vision on market fundamentals. Likewise, it is important to be aware of what other traders might be thinking. After all, predicting market price is the practice of predicting the behavior of market participants. I recommend utilizing popular commodity analysis services to simplify the process. I'm not saying you should rely solely on any newsletter or trading service, but they can provide some valuable and convenient insight.

Here are a few popular commodity trading publications that are extremely helpful in providing the information and guidance traders need without spending the time and effort required to acquire the information manually.

THE HIGHTOWER REPORT

The Hightower Report is an institution in the commodity industry. Since I can remember and long before I began work in the industry, brokers and traders have looked forward to receiving and reviewing the newsletter each morning before the trading day. David Hightower, the founder and primary writer, has more than 30 years of market experience, and it shows.

The Hightower Report newsletter offers unique insights into the fundamental and technical landscape of each major commodity futures contracts. The wealth of information contained in this daily newsletter does wonders for cutting out some of the legwork of fundamental market analysis. Specifically, according to www.HightowerReport.com, they offer the "most comprehensive daily coverage of commodity markets available." Most would have a hard time arguing the newsletter doesn't live up to its claims. Whether you are trading livestock or financial futures, *The Hightower Report* offers a brief, yet meaty, daily rundown of what to expect in the upcoming trading session.

Although the daily newsletter is the company's most distributed and utilized product, *The Hightower Report* also offers a valuable weekly newsletter highlighting any potential trend changes or fundamental red flags. They also sell an annual commodity trading guide, which includes a calendar as well as almanac-style commodity market fundamental research, including analysis featuring a big-picture outlook of each major commodity market. The guide is also handy for option and futures expiration dates, and notable agricultural and economic report dates.

For those with an actively traded commodity account, it is possible to gain access to the daily report from the associated brokerage firm. Most brokerage firms, and in some cases individual brokers, offer the daily version of the Hightower newsletter free of charge. The brokerage service is paying a bulk distribution subscription fee for the privilege of distributing it to clients. Traders without access to *The Hightower Report* via their commodity brokers can subscribe to the service on their own at a reasonable cost.

In addition to valuable fundamental market stats, the daily newsletter offers detailed trading recommendations. I am not privy to the track record or performance history of the recommendations, so I cannot offer any guidance on that particular aspect of the publication. It should also be noted that the recommendations made on the newsletter generally come with relatively high dollar risk and margin. They also tend to favor complex option spreads, or even spreads between futures and options. Casual readers of the newsletters might not be properly educated on the various trading strategies and instruments to properly employ the intended trading recommendation. Although I am a big fan of options and spread trading, readers of the newsletter should refrain from blindly following the trading advice prior to doing the homework needed to understand the risks and rewards of the strategy.

THE GRI REPORT (HELMS)

Speculators on the go might appreciate the brevity of the well-known *Helms Report*. Similar to *The Hightower Report*, the Helms has been floating around brokerage houses every morning for years. In fact, when I first entered the business the Helms was faxed to our office each morning!

Thankfully, things have changed. Nowadays, the report comes by email in an easy to read PDF format the evening before the corresponding trading session. *The Helms Report* is a great source for quick and simple market information, but categorizing it as a fundamental research tool is probably a stretch. The content focuses on the basic market premise for the day, which is generally portrayed in a couple of sentences. It also highlights certain technical analysis levels. In short, this newsletter is a quick orientation guide to each commodity trading session.

The Helms Report is issued by a research and trading firm called Global Research & Investments (GRI). GRI was formed in the 1990s through the partnership of Vitcom, Inc., and Helms Commodities. A good test to determine whether you are speaking with a seasoned commodity broker is to ask about the "GRI Report." Those who have been in the business for a considerable amount of time will probably be confused by the question. On the other hand, if you mention *The Helms Report*, the newer commodity brokers will be bewildered. For me, it will always be *The Helms Report*.

Regardless of which name you prefer to use to refer to the publication, it is a valuable resource offering a quick reference to trading tools for traders of all types and skill levels. The service has perfected the art of writing a short and sweet newsletter that covers each of the popular commodity markets.

MOORE RESEARCH INCORPORATED (MRCI)

Moore Research Inc. offers traders a wonderful and affordable alternative to the fundamental and technical focus of the Hightower and Helms reports. MRCI provides a web portal containing commodity market stats and data with a focus on seasonal analysis. We will discuss the seasonal service further in Chapter 4 regarding commodity seasonal tendencies, but I wanted to introduce the source now because it does offer some valuable fundamental tools in addition to its seasonal analysis for traders of all types.

Some of the fundamental analysis provided by MRCI includes futures and option market volatility analysis, long-term historical charts, cash market charting (as opposed to futures), intermarket correlation studies, industry report calendars, and commodity index charting such as the Goldman Sachs Commodity Index and Dow Jones–UBS Commodity Index. Traders can reach MRCI at www.MRCI.com or by phone at 541-933-5340.

CHAPTER 4: SEASONAL TENDENCIES OF COMMODITY AND FINANCIAL FUTURES

Although most commodity trading publications claim there are two primary methods of market exploration (technical and fundamental), it is worthwhile to include some less-publicized forms of market studies in your speculation. After all, if most market participants lose money trading commodities, and the most common forms of market analysis are technical and fundamental, there might be something to adding additional parameters to the mix. Simply going with the flow in any regard could lead you to slaughter with the rest of the herd.

When analyzing a commodity market, I prefer to consult multiple-chart time frames to gain an overall bias. I then glance at the latest fundamental market consensus, and after that, I look to the seasonal patterns of the market in question, the current makeup of buyers and sellers as displayed in the *COT Report*, and finally, I consider any sharp positive or negative market correlations that could affect the trade.

First, let's look at some habitual seasonal patterns that might prove to be useful in speculation. In the next chapter we'll move on to the others.

SEASONAL ANALYSIS OF THE COMMODITY MARKETS

Markets of all types and sizes undergo undeniable annual patterns. These annual cycles are not limited to agricultural commodities; annual price tendencies can be found in all commodity, stock, real estate, and even collectors' items such as art and baseball cards. Seasonal behavior is the result of many factors, but the primary drivers are annual growing cycles, weather, changes in supply and demand in anticipation of annual consumer behavioral habits, and annual political or economic events.

"Whatever happens in the stock market today has happened before and will happen again." —Jesse Livermore

The practice of identifying and attempting to profit from these somewhat predicable cycles is known as "seasonal" analysis. Similar to any other form of commodity market exploration, following seasonal patterns isn't the end-all and be-all of trading, but it is an enormously valuable tool necessary to shift the odds of success. After all, if a particular market behaves in a similar manner at a certain time of year, on most occasions, it makes sense to accommodate a trading strategy to account for the most probable direction. For instance, if a trader finds his technical and fundamental analyses are in corroboration with the general seasonal price pattern, it could give the trader justification to be slightly more aggressive. Further, if seasonal tendency is counter to other forms of analysis, it should at minimum give the trader pause. If the seasonality is strong enough, it could be a good-enough excuse to bypass the trade.

Keep in mind seasonal tendencies don't have to be bullish or bearish; there are certain times of the year in which prices in a particular market are more likely to consolidate in a sideways manner. It is also important to note that when the market trades in the opposite direction of the most common seasonal tendency, it does so with unforgiving vengeance. Thus, if you enter a trade in the direction of the seasonal tendency and it soon goes horribly wrong, don't expect it to get better. Exiting the trade and moving to the next idea is prudent; counterseasonal moves have been known to drain the trading accounts of traders who transition from "players" to "prayers."

Let's take a look at some prominent seasonal commodity patterns.

COMMON SEASONAL PATTERNS IN AGRICULTURAL COMMODITIES

Although agricultural futures contracts traded on the Chicago Board of Trade (CBOT) division of the CME Group represent a single commodity price, in reality there are dozens of related, yet separate, local cash markets with differing prices (Figure 20). CBOT corn futures might be trading at $3.95 per bushel, but a farmer in Missouri might only be able to sell his crop for $3.65; yet a farmer in Illinois might get $3.80 for his crop.

Location	Crop	Price	Last Updated
Charleston, MO (Cargill)	Corn	3.65	10/23/2015
Charleston, MO (Cargill)	Soybeans	8.91	10/23/2015
Charleston, MO (Cargill)	Sorghum	3.6	10/23/2015
Morehouse, MO (Buchheit Agri)	Corn	3.63	10/23/2015
Morehouse, MO (Buchheit Agri)	Soybeans	8.86	10/23/2015
Morehouse, MO (Buchheit Agri)	New-Crop Wheat (SRW)	4.98	10/23/2015
Mound City, IL (ADM)	Corn	3.8	10/23/2015
Mound City, IL (ADM)	Soybeans	9.01	10/23/2015
Mound City, IL (ADM)	Sorghum	3.8	10/23/2015
Scott City, MO (Consolidated Grain and Barge)	Corn	3.68	10/23/2015
Scott City, MO (Consolidated Grain and Barge)	Soybeans	9	10/23/2015
Scott City, MO (Midwest Grain and Barge)	Corn	3.6	10/23/2015
Scott City, MO (Midwest Grain and Barge)	Soybeans	8.96	10/23/2015

Figure 20: The prices of corn and soybeans in the cash market vary by market location. Thus, there are multiple prices of grain at any particular time.

The discrepancy between prices at different locales occurs at the differences in supply-demand factors for grain, as well as transportations costs, availability, cost of storage, and more. Now that we've established that there are truly several commodity markets, rather than a single nationally priced market, it should be obvious that seasonal tendencies are unique between growing markets as well. Further, crops around the world face various windows of opportunity for the optimal growing season. Although I will be simplifying the annual price patterns to guide trading decisions, I want to be clear that the markets are far from simple. Additionally, seasonal patterns are also subject to failure should something go awry in the ecosystem of any of the local markets.

Despite the complexities that come with the existence of independent local markets, as well as global growing areas, for a US-based commodity trader, the focus should primarily be on some sort of cumulative average of domestic crop cycles. In spite of everything, that is essentially the definition of the futures contract being traded and the CBOT.

The overall idea of grain seasonal trading relies on the premise that prices are expected to be low during harvest when supply tends to be plentiful. Similarly, prices are generally higher during the growing season when supplies are not readily available and the upcoming crop yield is uncertain.

CORN AND SOYBEAN SEASONALITY

Corn and soybean prices are highly correlated to one another; this is the result of having parallel planting, growing, and harvesting cycles. In my opinion, having a general understanding of these cycles might be useful to traders. With that said, because Brazil is a major contributor to the world supply of soybeans, and their growing and harvest cycles are not in sync with that of the US, there are some discrepancies between corn and soybean seasonal tendencies. We will highlight this as we discuss common patterns.

PLANTING

On any given year, the US produces roughly 30% to 40% of the world's corn and soybeans, so we'll discuss the domestic growing cycle. The exact growing cycle is dependent on local climate and weather, but in general, US corn and soybeans producers plant their crops in early April through mid-June. In a normal year (if such a thing exists), corn futures prices tend to peak in March. This is because going into planting season, market participants tend to build in a risk premium to cover any weather concerns that could delay planting. Agricultural crops are vulnerable during planting in any number of ways, but the primary antagonist is weather. Too much moisture can make fieldwork difficult or even impossible, but too little will prevent proper crop growth.

During the spring, traders are also debating how many acres farmers will allocate to each crop. For instance, most farmers have the ability to plant either corn, soybeans, or other crops, depending on which they believe will be most lucrative in that particular year. But until the seeds are in the ground, which crop farmers will choose cannot be confirmed. As planting begins and the uncertainty regarding the quantity of planted acres begins to dissipate, the price of corn and soybeans frequently relaxes in a successful planting season. However, the Brazilian soybean harvest hits the market in June or July, so the price of soybeans typically doesn't see any significant selling until this occurs. Thus, from March through July the positive correlation between soybeans and corn temporarily lapses.

GROWING

Despite eroding risk premium, the risks persist even after the US crop is planted. A lack of rain might prevent planted seeds from properly germinating, or excessive rain or freezing temperatures can result in crop loss and higher grain prices. Similarly, undue heat or a lack of precipitation will result in low pollination of the planted seeds and could result in less yield at harvest time.

HARVEST

Grain isn't valuable until it actually makes it out of the ground in usable condition. Even if planting and growing go well, weather just before or during harvest can wreak havoc on grain yields. Excessive temperatures or prolonged exposure to moisture will work against the overall goal of a successful harvest.

Nevertheless, in most years the harvest goes relatively smoothly to enable the price of corn and soybeans to reach what is typically an annual low price in October. This low is often referred as the "harvest lows" (Figures 21 and 22) by traders. Grain prices tend to be cheapest at this time of year because supply is at its highest level just after harvest, and uncertainty of that supply is at its lowest level. Once the crop is harvested, the odds of something going wrong are minimal.

CORN AND SOYBEAN SEASONAL CHARTS

During years in which there are significant weather threats, such as drought or persistent and torrential rain, there are sometimes sharp mid-summer grain rallies with enough force to create an annual high. That is more of an exception than a rule. With the exclusion of temporary weather spike rallies typically occurring in mid- to late June, in most years, the summer months see corn and soybean prices erode along with time (Figures 21 and 22). This is because the more time that passes, the less probable it will be for an unforeseen event to interfere with the growing seasons.

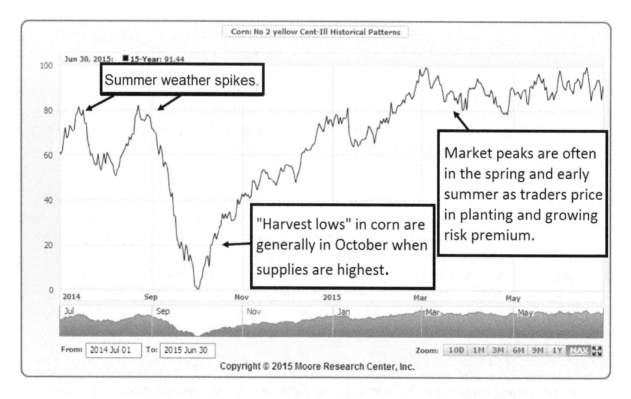

Figure 21: Corn prices are most probable to find a low around the harvest season and a peak in the summer.

You may have heard the mantra, "Rain makes grain." It is said that during the grain growing months, which usually span from May through August; the trading bias is negative if it is raining in downtown Chicago. This is because the Windy City is located in the heart of the grain belt and if it is raining on Wacker Drive, it must be getting to the nearby cornfields and this promotes higher production yields. However, even too much of a good thing can eventually have the opposite effect.

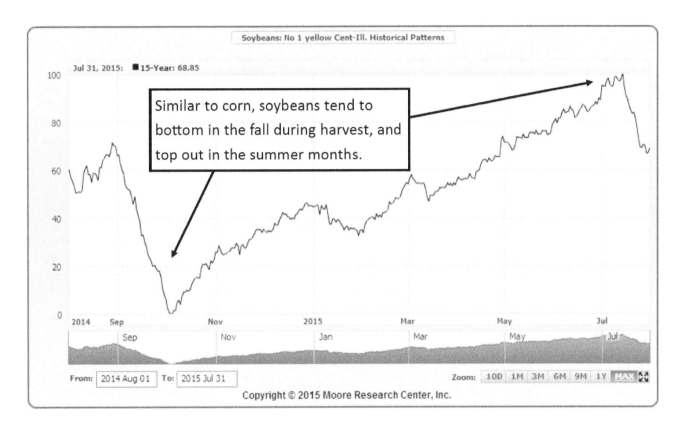

Figure 22: The soybean planting cycle, and therefore seasonality, are similar to that of corn. These two grains often trade with a high level of correlation.

THE BOTTOM LINE ON GRAIN SEASONALITY

To reiterate, the potential supply of grain is most vulnerable during the planting, pollination, and harvest stages of the crop year. During these times of year, grain prices are subject to increased levels of volatility and often incorporate a risk premium to account for the possibility of a less than perfect production cycle.

It is imperative that grain traders are aware of the fundamental market cycles and understand their implications. Without this knowledge, it is impossible to measure the risk and reward prospects of being involved in a given commodity.

GRAIN TRADING TIPS

 Perhaps the best seasonal trade in the grain complex is to look for the harvest lows in early October. In most years, the price of corn and soybeans are at their lowest level in October. Traders can feel relatively comfortable utilizing a more aggressive approach to playing the potential upside in prices such as buying futures contracts outright. It might also be a good idea to employ option spread strategies with open-ended downside risk in the form of short puts in combination of the unlimited profit potential offered by long call options.

 As mentioned, the price of corn and soybeans often taper in March. Although prices don't necessarily begin selling off immediately, they generally don't forge fresh gains after March, assuming weather conditions are favorable to the growing season. Despite a clear price pattern of weakness from March through what essentially become the harvest lows, uncertainty about Mother Nature's plan can cause unforgiving price spikes. Bearish trades during this time of year should be hedged or constructed in a manner in which the upside risk is mitigated. For example, purchasing puts offers traders limited risk with unlimited profit potential should the selling occur in a swift manner. Those looking to go short futures contracts should consider buying a call option for insurance. Being on the wrong side of a grain market weather price spike has the potential to quickly drain a trading account.

 Some traders believe it is worthwhile to purchase cheap deep out-of-the-money call options in the grain complex during the mid-summer months (late June, July, or early August) because they know if the farmers start yelling "drought," prices can quickly explode and so will the call option values. Also, traders know that the grain markets go up faster than they go down. Consequently, trading strategies with open-ended downside risk such as purchasing futures outright without protection, or selling naked put options, is generally not an ideal trading strategy this time of year because seasonal probabilities are against the trade.

ODD MAN OUT: WHEAT SEASONALITY

CBOT wheat futures represent soft red winter wheat, which is on the exact opposite harvest cycle to corn and soybeans. Wheat farmers are planting at the same time that corn and soybean farmers are harvesting. Likewise, wheat is being harvested simultaneously to the corn and soybean planting season. Despite having mirrored growing seasons, wheat prices often move in sympathy to corn and soybeans and vice versa (Figure 23). This is because many end users of grain have the freedom to substitute one for the other. For instance, a rancher might prefer to use soybeans and corn to feed livestock, but wheat is also acceptable feed. Accordingly, wheat seasonal tendencies are similar to that of corn and soybeans but have the potential to deviate greatly.

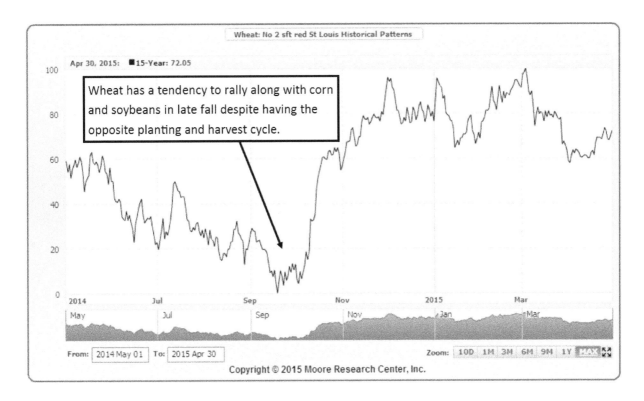

Figure 23: Wheat is planted and harvested in a cycle opposite that of corn and soybeans, but it still manages to maintain a relatively positive correlation with them.

GOLD SEASONALITY

The fact that gold prices have one of the more reliable annual patterns isn't an obvious one because it is a mined commodity. With little regard to season, or Mother Nature, the supply of gold remains relatively constant. However, the demand for gold is as seasonal as it gets. This is because gold is an asset that has little consumption value. Instead, its value is based primarily on perception. Further, the view of its value varies greatly with annual economic cycles and even holidays.

"In the absence of the gold standard, there is no way to protect savings from confiscation through inflation. There is no safe store of value." —Alan Greenspan

For instance, the demand for gold picks up prior to Valentine's Day in the US, and the wedding season in India. Specifically, gold prices often rise in December and February but taper off afterward, reaching a seasonal low in mid- to late summer. Gold then finds strength through early to mid-September prior to the Indian wedding season, which spans from October through December (Figure 24).

Elaborate weddings in India date back thousands of years and have consistently been a driver in the gold market. Traditional Indian weddings involve a bride draped in gold, helping India to become the largest consumer of gold jewelry in the world; members of the Indian population are also big fans of physical gold bars and coins. India accounts for roughly a third of global gold demand, with half of that being spent on jewelry for the average 10 million weddings held there each year.

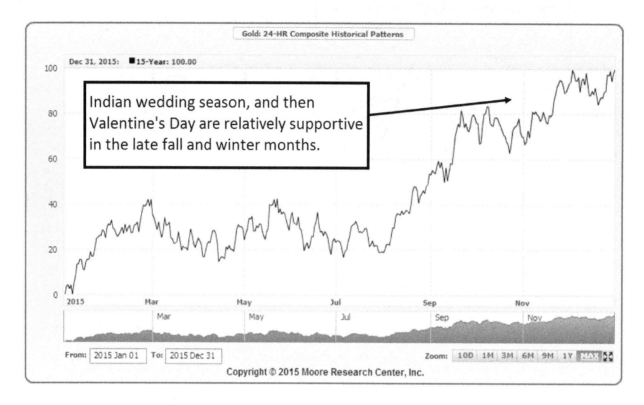

Figure 24: Gold is unique in that it has industrial value as well as perceived economic and aesthetic value. Accordingly, it regularly finds support from demand for the yellow metal during the Indian wedding season.

GOLD TRADING TIPS

 The highest gold prices are generally seen in the latter part of the year, but the buying comes early in preparation of the actual need of the gold jewelry. The most reliable seasonal trade is one that involves being bullish in gold in the early to mid-summer. Some traders are willing to begin establishing bullish positions in March, because gold often sees a large break in prices on the heels of a conclusion to the Valentine's Day demand. Early buyers must be willing to be patient and assume the risk of a drawdown before prices firm up for good. The bulls shouldn't overstay their welcome, however, considering gold buying often dries up in September to October.

 Another popular trade among commodity traders is to get bearish gold in February in anticipation of the common March break. I consider the timing of this move to be less reliable than the aforementioned summer bullish pattern because the pattern has shifted from February into March over the years. Nevertheless, being aware of this tendency might aid traders in timing, or at least help prevent painful trading mishaps.

ENERGY MARKET SEASONAL PATTERNS

I've found the energy markets to offer traders some of the most profound and reliable seasonal patterns in all of the commodity markets. However, despite this, their volatile price nature makes capitalizing on seasonal opportunities challenging. Seasonal energy traders should generally be well-funded and willing to accept elevated risks. That said, the CME Group exchange now offers mini-sized futures contracts, making it easier for smaller speculators to participate.

CRUDE OIL

Seasonal crude oil patterns are primarily made possible by changes in demand during particular times of the year. For instance, the summer driving season that takes place from May through August often sees increased consumption of gasoline. In anticipation of that consumption, refineries begin stockpiling crude oil in February and March. Similarly, once the peak driving season is behind us, the demand for gasoline, and therefore crude oil, diminishes. Accordingly, the price of crude oil has a tendency to soften in September or October (Figure 25).

CRUDE OIL TRADING TIPS

- Crude oil is the type of market with the propensity to go up with much more force than it goes down. However, those caught in bad bullish trades during the 2014 collapse might argue otherwise. Even when you are trading crude oil with seasonal probabilities on your side, this characteristic must be accounted for. Thus, any open-ended bearish trades such as naked short calls or short futures contracts should be executed with significant caution during the February through October time frame. Perhaps traders should bypass bearish plays during this time unless there are overly compelling reasons.

- The best seasonal trades in crude oil are generally bullish strategies early in the year, January and February. If prices are depressed at the time, circumstances might call for a little more aggression than would normally be taken.

- Another trade to keep an eye on is getting bearish oil in October. Should prices go into the October–November time period at lofty levels, it is often a comfortable place for bearish positions.

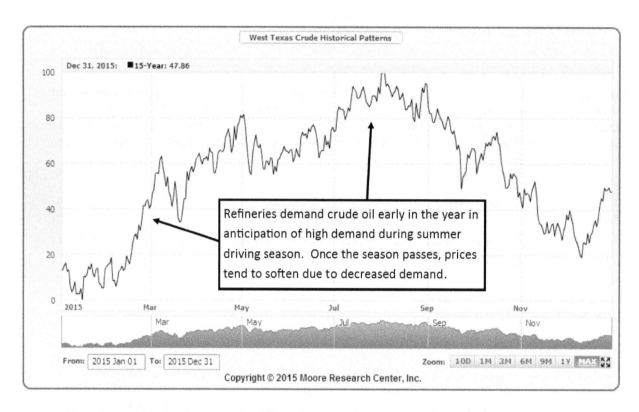

Refineries demand crude oil early in the year in anticipation of high demand during summer driving season. Once the season passes, prices tend to soften due to decreased demand.

Figure 25: The seasonal pattern of crude oil is largely dependent on the summer driving season. The strength of these moves sometimes makes it easy to forget this simple explanation for a trough early in the year and peak in mid-summer.

NATURAL GAS SEASONALITY

Many argue the seasonality of natural gas prices has diminished due to fracking. This is because the process, which injects liquid at high pressure into subterranean rocks to force open existing fissures to extract oil and gas, has flooded the natural gas market with supply. In fact, supplies grew to such levels that producers across the country actually opted to "flare" excess gas (that is, burn it) as opposed to incurring the cost of bringing it to market. This practice is the equivalent of an apparel firm designing and producing clothing only to burn it in a bonfire to save the cost of distributing it to the point of sale.

As a result of overabundant supply, there is less stress on the system during winter months and therefore less of a seasonal tendency for natural gas prices to firm up during the cold winter months. In addition, the higher consumption of natural gas during the summer months with the advent of natural gas–powered solutions to beat the heat (Figure 26) has mitigated the summer demand doldrums in this market.

Natural gas is known affectionately by speculators as the "widow maker," due to several hedge fund blowups at the hands of poorly timed positions in this particular commodity market.

Despite cries of weakened seasonal patterns, attractive opportunities remain. Even in a post-fracking world, we've seen natural gas futures explode on the heels of colder than expected weather conditions. In 2013, gas prices entered the seasonally bullish season near $3.50 and ended the bullish season with a dramatic spike to the $6.50 area!

The long-term pattern of natural gas prices has generally been an annual low price posted in September followed by a subsequent high at some point during December through February. The length and magnitude of the move is dependent on demand, or simply weather. From February through March, the price of natural gas habitually grinds lower, but generally finds support through the spring and early summer months.

NATURAL GAS TRADING TIPS

- The highest-probability annual trade, with the most potential for explosive gains, is a bullish position in natural gas from September through February. Of course, this is just a guide on the overall bias; timing of entry should be determined by other factors such as the technical setup of the chart. Further, there is generally selling pressure in late October, so simply establishing a bullish trade and just expecting to check back on it again in the late winter months won't do.

- It is never a good idea to establish bearish positions with open-ended risk such as short calls or short futures during the September through February season. Even if fundamentals appear to be highly bearish, Mother Nature is known for sharp changes in sentiment and gas prices can be highly explosive on the upside. Natural gas typically has a tendency to appreciate faster than it depreciates.

- Generally, it is a good idea to purchase cheap out-of-the-money call options in the fall in anticipation of an explosive upside move. This is nothing more than a lottery ticket strategy (low and limited risk, but unlimited profit potential). Despite unfavorable odds of success for lottery ticket plays, years in which such a strategy pays off can return substantial gains.

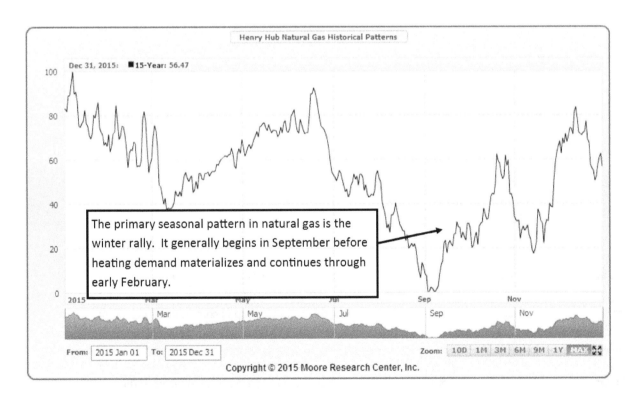

Figure 26: It is typically a bad idea to have short calls in natural gas during the winter season. Although the strategy might work in some years, a colder than expected winter can cause massive short-term supply shortages, causing prices to double or triple in short order.

One of the most extreme examples of a seasonal winter rally in natural gas took place in late 2013 and extended into the early months of 2014 (Figure 27). The move occurred due to an unexpectedly harsh winter, which increased the demand for natural gas to levels that stretched immediate supplies. Unfortunately for consumers, the true supply of natural gas was somewhat gluttonous; nevertheless, the gas wasn't available for distribution to homes and businesses. As a result, a supply shock ensued, causing prices to double in short order to account for the imbalance.

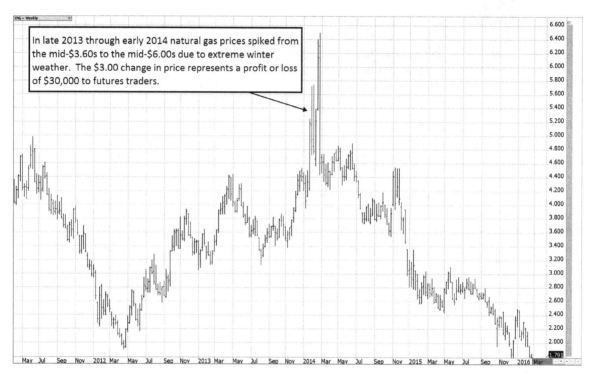

In late 2013 through early 2014 natural gas prices spiked from the mid-$3.60s to the mid-$6.00s due to extreme winter weather. The $3.00 change in price represents a profit or loss of $30,000 to futures traders.

Figure 27: In extreme price moves, the natural gas market can become relatively illiquid and explosive, particularly during the seasonally bullish time of year.

CURRENCY SEASONALITY

The average investor probably wouldn't categorize currencies as a commodity, let alone expect there to be a distinct seasonal pattern. Nevertheless, currencies are in fact a commodity traded on US futures exchanges. If you are wondering how a currency can be a commodity, the explanation is simple; commodities are simply interchangeable goods. Aside from perhaps the cleanliness or crispness of a dollar, we wouldn't prefer one over the other. They spend alike.

Currency futures differ from the spot forex market in that all currencies are priced in terms of the US dollar. Forex, on the other hand, has a complex set of rules dictating the default method of quoting currencies. For instance, the euro (EUR) is given preference over all other currencies, and thus international banking institutions always quote the euro in terms of the opposition currency—the EUR/USD, EUR/GBP (British Pound), for example.

Coincidentally, the euro futures contract is also quoted as the EUR/USD, meaning its price is the US dollar cost to purchase one euro.

Yet the yen is given priority over the dollar in forex, leading banks and spot currency markets to quote the US dollar/yen (USD/JPY). This means the quoted price is the cost to buy one US dollar in terms of the yen. In the case of the exchange rate between the two currencies, relative to forex, the futures market is quoted in opposite terms (JPY/USD). I am pointing this out because each of these seasonal patterns are based on the futures market version of the currency pair, in which the price is quoted in terms of the dollar. Thus, if you attempt to apply any of this analysis to forex, you may be working with inverted patterns. As you can imagine, it is vital to be comparing apples to apples.

EURO SEASONALITY

Aside from the dollar, the euro is undoubtedly the most popular speculative currency. It has a knack for trending well, and it also has a few distinct annual patterns that traders should be aware of. Although seasonal tendencies are mixed for much of the summer, the currency often finds some sort of bottom in, or around, July with a rally that often extends into late October. After temporary weakness in early November, the euro tends to see upward pressure going into year-end (Figure 28). The year-end buying in the euro is thought to be the moving of money away from the dollar and into the euro as multinational corporations make preparations for year-end expenses (bonuses, taxes, and so on).

EURO TRADING TIPS

 The strongest seasonal trade in the euro happens to occur at the least liquid time of year, November and December. Thus, traders should be prepared for unexpected volatility despite the normal pattern. Further, counterseasonal moves in thinly traded markets can be fierce. There is no reason for a trader to ruin her holiday over the currency market. Keep speculations at a comfortable level. The holiday season should be spent having fun with friends and family; it is not the time to load the boat (unfortunately, I speak from experience).

 Though there is a distinct pattern for a euro bottom over the summer, the timing of such a low can be highly uncertain. As a result, low-leverage strategies that leave the door open to comfortable dollar cost averaging (buying more as the market declines) are ideal. Even smaller traders can participate in such a strategy using the e-micro currency futures. At $10 per tick, traders of all sizes can adopt a buy and hold approach to currencies with the freedom to add to the position. I discuss these contracts further in Chapter 12, "The Hidden Gems of the Commodity Markets."

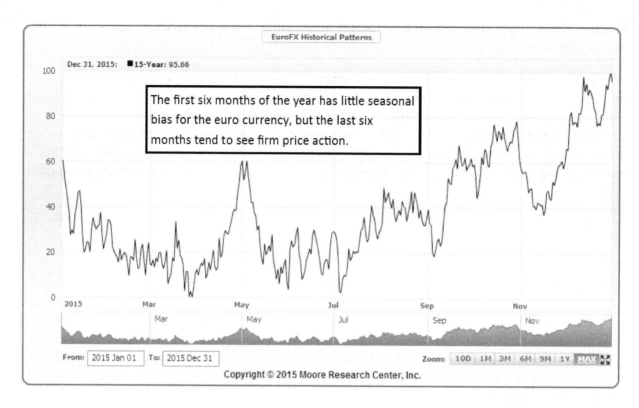

Figure 28: The euro, when paired against the dollar, often experiences end of the year strength at the hands of US dollars flowing overseas via global corporations.

DOLLAR INDEX SEASONALITY

The dollar index (DX) futures contract traded on the Intercontinental Exchange (ICE) is made up of roughly 60% euro. The remaining 40% of the index include small allocations to other major currencies such as the yen and the British pound. Accordingly, the dollar index futures contract experiences seasonal patterns that are opposite that of the euro. The DX generally peaks in the summer before it makes its way lower into year-end (Figure 29).

DOLLAR INDEX TRADING TIPS

$ The dollar index is the one currency futures contract that trades on an exchange that is not operated by the CME Group. The DX trades on the ICE on lighter volume than most CME Group currency futures. However, I like to call it the ETF of the futures world because it is essentially the value of the dollar relative to a diversified basket of currencies. Traders bullish or bearish the dollar will regularly find comfort in the DX due to mitigated individual currency risk. If something changes in Canada to drive the exchange rate between the two currencies that differs from the overall dollar trend, the trader utilizing the DX futures contract won't be as affected as one who attempted to trade the dollar via the Canadian dollar futures contract.

$ Margin requirements are generally low to trade the DX due to the inherent diversification, and thus, it is a good place for comfortable speculation relative to a high flyer such as the euro.

$ DX options are generally thinly traded and on the cheap side. They are not the best place for option sellers, but it can be a great market for those looking to speculate in currencies with long options or employing long or short futures strategies in conjunction with a long option hedge.

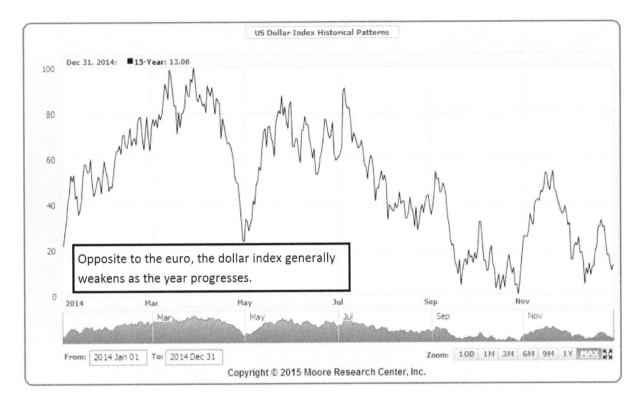

Figure 29: The dollar index generally trades inversely to the euro; thus, so does its seasonal tendency.

THE MEATS' SEASONAL PATTERNS

The meat complex isn't necessarily among the most popular venues for the average commodity speculator. Ironically, the most well-known meat product, pork bellies, was delisted from the Chicago Mercantile Exchange (CME) due to lack of trading volume. Like the aforementioned softs market, pork belly futures were made famous by *Trading Places*, perhaps the greatest trading movie of all time.

Despite questionable market liquidity, the meat futures complex features some of the most dramatic seasonal patterns in the commodity markets.

LIVE CATTLE

Live cattle prices tend to firm up early in the year ahead of the summer barbecue season in anticipation of increased demand. Oddly, the price of cattle is at its lowest when the demand is at its highest, during the summer months. The most significant seasonal move occurs in the mid- to late summer months in which cattle prices generally find a seasonal low before putting together a rally that often extends through the end of the year (Figure 30).

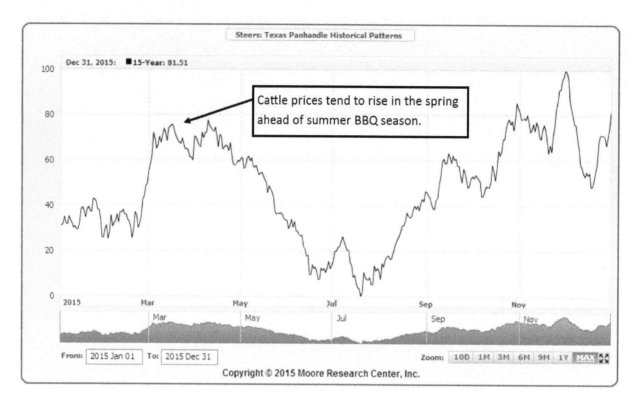

Figure 30: Cattle prices tend to be at their annual low at a time in which demand is the highest. This is because the demand for the livestock occurs well before the grocery store demand emerges for the final product.

HOGS

Some of the most volatile seasonal moves I've seen in the commodity markets have taken place in a market that rarely gets any attention—lean hog futures. Conceivably, the magnitude of seasonal moves in the hog market is directly tied to a lack of liquidity. This is because in thinly traded markets, prices can be pushed around more easily than is the case in deeper markets. For example, a large trader or hedge fund buying or selling 100 lots in the hog market could make a significant difference in short-term pricing. Yet an order to buy or sell 100 contracts in a highly liquid market such as the e-mini S&P 500 futures wouldn't have fazed the market; in fact, it is the norm.

"Money is like manure. You have to spread it around or it smells." —J. Paul Getty

The seasonal pattern followed by lean hog prices is nearly a mirror image of cattle prices (Figure 31). This isn't a coincidence; pork is a cheaper alternative to beef. Thus, consumers tend to adjust their behavior to account for price cycles. When beef prices are high, the demand for pork increases, and vice versa.

With this in mind, it should be reasonable to expect hog prices to be at their peak during the summer months, while cattle prices are at their trough. Along the same lines, hog prices are at their lowest point in the winter months.

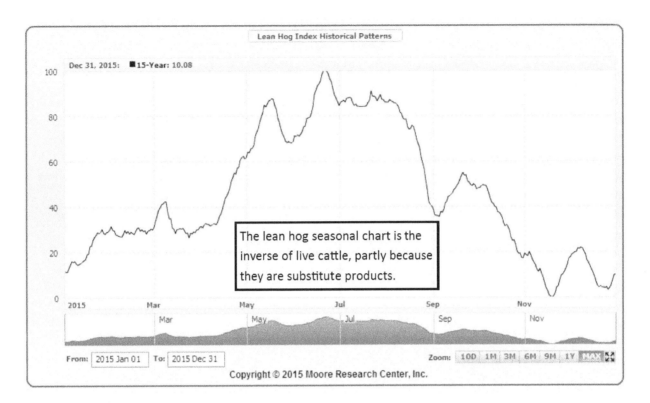

Figure 31: Demand for pork increases following a spike in beef prices because consumers are generally open to substituting pork for beef in their diets.

LIMITATIONS OF SEASONAL TRADING

Don't assume a pattern that has occurred in the past is guaranteed to occur again going forward. Similar to technical and fundamental schools of thought, seasonal analysis should be considered an asset in your trading tool belt.

Seasonality should not be the sole form of market assessment, nor should traders blindly follow annual tendencies without the help of corroborating evidence. Simply put, seasonal propensities aren't the end-all and be-all solution to successful trading, but it can be a surefire way to increase your odds of success and reduce the emotional turmoil of poor trading ventures.

There are a few complications in using seasonal data that could affect the conclusion of the analysis. It might even be prudent to cross-reference alternative seasonal sources or analysis methods before entering a position. Here are a few things to keep in mind when consulting seasonal findings:

SEASONAL CHART VERSIONS

Much to the dismay of green traders, not all seasonal charts are compiled in the same manner, nor do they always reveal the same results. To those unfamiliar with the nature of commodities, it would seem a simple task to gather and analyze seasonal price data to determine patterns. In the world of stocks, this is probably true. However, in the commodity markets, it isn't simple at all. This is because commodity futures contracts expire periodically. Each futures market differs in contract expiration dates and frequency; financial commodities such as currencies and stocks indices expire on four occasions per year (quarterly), energy commodities expire each month, and agricultural commodity futures contracts expire multiple times per year according to their growing and production cycles. With all of the various expiration dates come separate sets of data. The data for the December crude oil futures contract might differ slightly from that of the January. Similarly, the March euro currency data might have a different pattern than the December euro. As you can see, when compiling a seasonal data chart, there is plenty of room for interpretation. Some choose to use data from the front-month contract (the contract available with the nearest expiration date) until the contract expires, while others use the front month until first notice day, and yet others use the front month until some arbitrary day a week or two before first notice day.

But wait, there's more! Some traders opt to use seasonal data compiled from the cash market rather than the futures market. The premise behind using cash market seasonal charts is to mitigate the impact of the aforementioned expiring contract obstacle. Cash market commodity prices aren't expiring agreements to buy or sell; they are simply a gauge of prices that end users and producers in the cash market are willing to buy and sell at. Some believe the cash market provides more realistic price patterns. Nevertheless, using cash market seasonal charts introduces a new plethora of problems. Most concerning is the fact that there isn't a centralized cash market with a single price. Instead, there are dozens of cash markets at various locals across the country. In this book, I used cash market charts for seasonal analysis because it is most representative of reality in the long run.

TIME FRAMES MATTER

Seasonal analysts usually look at data from various time frames to ensure they aren't missing anything or being misled by outdated data. The most common sets of data are generally collected over the previous five years, 15 years, and "lifetime." You might see some seasonal references to a 20-year or 30-year sample as a replacement for lifetime. Each of the charts displayed in this chapter were compiled from data over the previous 15 years.

It is important to be aware of various time frames because seasonal patterns can and do change over time. Simply looking at the longest-term data available could mislead traders into seasonal trades that are no longer valid. In certain markets, a 20-year seasonal study might conclude the market is bullish during the summer months, but the same study conducted on the previous five years' worth of data might show a bearish tendency during the same time frame.

SEASONAL TIMING ISN'T ABSOLUTE

Too many beginning traders treat a seasonal pattern as being absolute, yet it is far from a scheduled event. Even once an annual price tendency is discovered, it is still nothing more than an estimate of when prices might see intermediate-term highs and lows—potential reversal areas. Although it doesn't seem as evident by looking at a chart, once a trade has been established, the accompanying emotional turmoil is a reminder that most seasonal reversals are long and drawn-out processes. For instance, some seasonal peaks and troughs span several weeks. Anybody who has ever traded leveraged futures contracts is painfully aware that entering a countertrend speculation within several weeks of the high or low in any given market can turn patience into a very expensive virtue.

SEASONAL TENDENCIES ARE HISTORICAL

Seasonal patterns tell us what the market has done in the past, but we can't assume that it will tell what will happen in the future. Changes in politics, weather, human preferences, emotions, and behaviors can interfere with a historical tendency. Accordingly, traders shouldn't treat their findings as being predictive but should use it to confirm, or deny, the consensus reached via other methods of market analysis.

WHERE TO FIND SEASONAL ANALYSIS

Many readers may have found themselves wondering where they will retrieve the historical price data to conduct seasonal analysis. It can be overwhelming to consider the task of sorting through it. Don't worry, there are at least two subscription services available to traders willing to do the legwork in exchange for a reasonable fee.

- Moore Research Center Inc. (www.mrci.com)—MRCI is a staple in the commodity industry. The service has been in existence since 1989 and offers subscribers an impressive amount of historical data in the form of easy to read charts and figures. MRCI is best known for its *Spread Seasonal Patterns* report and its *Seasonal Trades* report; each provides traders with insights into details of the most prominent seasonal patterns. Included are entry date, exit date, win percentage, number of winning years, number of losing years, and average profit. MRCI was the original source of all seasonal charts used in this chapter and can be reached toll free at 800-927-7259 or at 541-933-5340.

- SEASONALGO (www.seasonalgo.com)—A relative newcomer to the scene, but their superior technology makes up for their lack of fame. In fact, they consider themselves a software vendor as opposed to a commodity research firm. SEASONALGO offers interactive seasonal tools in addition to the ability to backtest strategies over historical data. They also offer easy access to subscription features via computers and mobile devices.

CHAPTER 5: THE "OTHERS"; READING THE *COT REPORT* AND INTERMARKET CORRELATIONS

We have yet to find a method of market analysis that works in all market conditions. Without the help of a crystal ball (not the Magic 8 ball you received as a birthday gift in your younger years), we will never be able to predict future market moves. However, there is one aspect of market pricing that is rather predictable: the participants. The price of any given commodity is the cumulative result of hedgers and speculators expressing their opinions, or needs, in the market via buy and sell orders. Although markets are considered to be efficient, they are far from perfect because the humans guiding price action are not. People, on the other hand, are somewhat predictable. With this in mind, I am a big fan of keeping tabs on other market participants, including the opinions they are voicing as well as expressing in their actions.

> "A market is the combined behavior of thousands of people responding to information, misinformation and whim." —Kenneth Chang

BE AWARE OF MARKET SENTIMENT AND HERD MENTALITY

As much as we would like to believe society learns from market bubbles, it doesn't. Bubble pricing dates back nearly as far as civilization itself, and I suspect they will continue to occur as long as humans are walking the planet. A bubble is a market phenomenon characterized by surges in asset prices to levels significantly above the arguable fundamental value of an asset. Bubble pricing gets so carried away that investors throw all logic and reason out the window to be a part of it.

One of the earliest examples of a market bubble is Tulip Mania, which was said to have occurred during the Dutch Golden Age in the mid-1600s. The popularity of tulips enabled the price of tulip bulbs to reach ridiculously lofty levels before collapsing. At the peak, the cost of a single bulb sold for roughly ten times the annual salary of a relatively skilled worker. At the time, consumers were so focused on their desire to possess tulips that they failed to recognize the insanity of it all.

> "You're dealing with a lot of silly people in the marketplace; it's like a great big casino and everyone else is boozing." — Warren Buffett

If this sounds crazy to you, it shouldn't; society continues to assign arbitrary values to assets that truly have little value. Think diamonds, antiques, and even gold. We've all purchased these items for prices well beyond their true worth, but we don't seem to mind because that is how we are programmed to behave. Market participants are prone to jumping on the latest bandwagon craze. Unfortunately, the majority of traders opt to take conformity action near the peaks of a bubble or the trough of a crash.

In real time, investors tend to deny the existence of a bubble, but in hindsight the clues are rather obvious. Though trend traders live and die by market exuberance, the average trader might be better served steering clear. This is because once the climax price is reached, the reversal will be sharp and swift, showing little mercy to those caught in its wrath; simply put, bubbles often precede crashes.

Each market participant is competing against all other market participants. Accordingly, being aware of what your nemesis are thinking and doing can be valuable information. In the next section, we will discuss the most complete source of such information, the *Commitments of Traders Report* (COT) issued by the Commodity Futures Trading Commission (CFTC), but there are some other telltale signs of a bubble forming or overcrowded trades. Let's start with these.

CONSULT FORUMS AND SOCIAL MEDIA FOR OVERWHELMING TRENDS OR SENTIMENTS

In today's digital world, many traders get their market news and even trading ideas from untraditional sources such as Twitter streams and Facebook groups. Then again, I would never advocate blindly following trading advice you receive from social media, since it is littered with questionable and, in some cases, downright fraudulent trading advice and sales pitches. Nevertheless, it is a great way to get a feel for what market participants might be thinking. There are large public trading groups on Facebook; a glance through the posts and comment threads might reveal which direction the trading public is leaning. One group is not a sufficient sample, but after browsing two or three, you will get a pretty good idea of the general consensus.

It is also a good idea to search Facebook and Twitter for keywords related to the market you are trading. For example, a trader considering a gold trade would probably find it worthwhile to search public social media posts for the word "gold," or its hashtag version, #gold. I'm always surprised at what I find with such searches. Most of it should be taken with a grain of salt, but every once in a while you will find a gem that you might not have discovered on your own. Not only that, you will get a feel for market sentiment.

"The riskiest moment is when you are right. That's when you're in the most trouble, because you tend to overstay the good decisions." —Peter L. Bernstein

In my opinion, the introduction to social media to the futures trading community has contributed to market volatility. It has most likely lured speculators to the commodity markets that might not have otherwise been introduced to the practice. More green traders floating around the markets tend to add to the chaos of price discovery. However, more apparent is the tendency for bandwagon traders to pile into trades.

Prior to social media, bandwagon traders were simply trend traders jumping on a market move after hearing a television piece or reading a story in the newspaper, hoping to catch a ride. In today's environment, there is far less analysis or logic applied. Traders see their cyber "friends" boasting about bullish or bearish bets in a particular market and they follow suit. Ironically, in many cases this is akin to taking investment advice from the proverbial shoeshine boy; once the crowd picks a market to target, the move can be relentless and far beyond any justifiable price point. Eventually, however, prices must revert to some sort of sustainable mean.

BARRON'S AND AAII INVESTOR SENTIMENT READINGS

For those wishing to trade stock index futures such as the e-mini S&P 500, the e-mini NASDAQ, the e-mini Dow, or the Russell 2000, it is a good idea to get a sentiment reading from a source such as *Barron's*, the American Association of Individual Investors (AAII) Sentiment Survey, or the lesser-known Market Vane service. Each of these barometers measures the percentage of investors who are bullish, bearish, or neutral on the stock market.

The general idea of an investment index is a poll is taken of various traders in regard to their expectations in the coming six months or longer, depending on the particular index.

The AAII Index is unique in that it offers those polled three sentiment choices: bullish, bearish, and neutral. Others offer only two choices, bullish or bearish. In a normal market, roughly 35% of participants are bullish, 30% are bearish, and 30% are neutral. Ironically, when bullish sentiment begins reaching or exceeding 40%, the market often begins showing signs of a top. When bearish readings creep into the high 30% mark, a market bottom is often near.

The *Barron's* Consensus Sentiment Index is a simplified version in that it simply tells us the percentage of investors polled who are bullish. A reading approaching the high 60 percents or above could be indicating all of the bulls are already participating in the market, and so prices could be near-term toppy.

PUT/CALL RATIO

Another tool for stock index traders is the put/call ratio published by the Chicago Board of Options Exchange (CBOE). The put/call ratio is a tool intended to aid in gauging market sentiment. The ratio is a simple calculation that involves dividing the number of traded put options by the number of traded call options. An increase in the ratio is a sign that traders are putting more money to work in put options than they are call options. A decrease in the ratio suggests traders are flocking to calls instead of puts. Although the ratio is telling us whether traders are bearish or bullish, in my opinion it is more useful to use this as a contrarian indicator as opposed to a signal to join the masses.

> "History must repeat itself because we pay such little attention to it the first time." —Blackie Sherrod

You will find variations of the calculation that might include all CBOE equity options traded or only those within a specific index or sector. As long as you are working with a broad-based calculation, the findings should be similar. *Barron's* focuses on the S&P 100 and the CBOE equity put/call ratios; *Barron's* is of the opinion that the former represents professional and institutional traders while the latter mostly depicts individual traders.

Look at an example of what a put/call ratio might look like. If 3,343,695 puts traded in a week on the CBOE, and 3,680,818 calls traded in the same week, the ratio of 3,343,695/3,680,818 is reduced to 91/100. There were 91 puts traded for every 100 calls. The rule of thumb is that a reading of 60/100 or higher is pointing toward a market in which sentiment is overly bearish. It might seem odd that the CBOE would record only 60 puts traded for every 100 calls, but retail stock option traders tend to be speculative bullish. The S&P 100, on the other hand, tends to represent a different type of trader, often hedgers or speculative bears, and often portrays a market in which more puts are traded than calls. If the index sees 12,061 puts traded in a particular week and only 9,103 calls, the ratio becomes 132/100, interpreted as 132 puts for each 100 calls traded. In this particular version of the put/call ratio, a reading above 125/100 indicates a market with overly bearish sentiment. In each example, the fact that traders are highly bearish in their options trading should be a red flag to indicate the market could be seeking a bottom. In short, this could be a signal to get bullish in stock index futures.

On the contrary, if the CBOE equity put/call ratio falls toward 30/100 or the S&P 100 ratio hits around 75/100, it can be considered a bearish development because it suggests that market participants are complacently bullish.

When analyzing the put/call ratio, it is important to keep things in perspective. Option traders can be fickle, so it isn't reasonable to let anything you find in the put/call ratio influence your overall opinion of the market. Don't allow yourself to be tempted to join the herd. Nevertheless, the put/call ratio will provide clues into a market that might be experiencing overzealous speculation in a particular direction. Working off the premise that most traders lose money, it makes sense to assume if the majority of traders are buying puts, the market could be nearing a low. Conversely, if traders are more interested in purchasing calls, the rally could be near exhaustion.

THE TALKING HEADS

The dream of striking it rich in the stock and commodity markets isn't a tough sell. Accordingly, there aren't any shortage of business news sources on television, investment-related magazines and newspapers, and online publications. It is easy to get caught up in the hype and fall into the habit of taking everything you read or hear as gospel, but many of the gurus on television or quoted in the newspaper aren't any better at predicting market action. In fact, many of them go with the flow. If the price of crude oil is trending lower, most analysts and commentators will dwell on bearish fundamentals and constantly seek lower prices. These analysts might, or might not, be doing their homework. Even if they are looking at factors outside of the fact that "everyone else believes," they don't have skin in the game, nor do they have crystal balls.

I've found market tops and bottoms can be found when business news talk show guests are passionate about a particular market trend. When crude oil was trading near $150 per barrel in 2008, it seemed nine out of ten talking heads were bullish. Hotshot analysts from Goldman Sachs were the parade leaders with a call for $200 crude oil. Yet in 2016 when crude was hovering in the low $30s, the majority of public analysts were calling for prices to fall under $20 per barrel!

HOW TO REACT TO AN OVERCROWDED TRADE

Human nature is to join in on the fun, but an overcrowded trade or a market bubble is a disaster waiting to happen. Once the bubble bursts, much of the money made by the bandwagon traders vanishes; even worse, those late to the party can suffer account-draining losses in the blink of an eye. Conceivably, the best description of the unwinding of an overcrowded trade was provided by Warren Buffett in 2003. "Unfortunately, the hangover may prove to be proportional to the binge."

> It is better to be on the sidelines wishing you were in, than in the market wishing you were on the sidelines!

Despite the carnage that evolves from such market events, the reality is people never learn. The markets will continue to provide examples of boom and bust trading environments, and this is particularly true in the commodity markets. If you walk away from this book with anything, I hope it is the realization that it is better to miss out on the profits of an overcrowded trade than to be caught in its whirlwind at the end. Another infamous Warren Buffett quote in regards to bubbles comes to mind: "What the wise man does in the beginning, the fool does in the end."

Using the market sentiment gauges, traders should look to either steer clear of overheated markets or at least alter the trading strategy in a manner that protects profits or limits losses should the exuberance reverse. On the other hand, aggressive and well-capitalized traders might look to such occasions for countertrend trading opportunities. Sometimes, the best traders are those who are against the grain.

ANALYZING THE *COMMITMENTS OF TRADERS REPORT*

The first thing most people think of when the Commodity Futures Trading Commission (CFTC) is mentioned is government regulation. This is because according to its website (www.cftc.gov), the CFTC is in charge of fostering "open, transparent, competitive, and financially sound markets, to avoid systemic risk, and to protect the market users and their funds, consumers and the public from fraud, manipulation, and abusive practices related to derivatives and other products that are subject to the Commodity Exchange Act." If you ask me, that's a mouthful. They are responsible for creating rules and regulations to safeguard the integrity of the futures, options on futures, and more recently forex and swaps markets. If you aren't already aware, the CFTC's enforcement arm is the National Futures Association (NFA). The NFA is in charge of making sure member firms (those required to be registered with the CFTC, and therefore regulated by them) are following the rules and regulations set forth by the CFTC.

To ensure the markets are operating as fairly as possible, the CFTC compiles data on traders holding positions above what they deem to be a threshold separating the large traders from the small. This line in the sand is known as the "reportable limit." Any trader holding a position in excess of this limit is obligated to acknowledge their identity to the agency. In addition, the broker of the trader holding a position qualifying as "reportable" to the CFTC must send *daily* reports on the positions detailing the number of contracts in the amount or in excess of the CFTC's stated reportable level. With this information, the CFTC attempts to identify potential conflicts of interest, efforts at cornering a market, or other manipulative trading behavior.

In case you are wondering what constitutes a position meeting the CFTC's criteria of a large trader, the agency claims position limits are set based on the "total open interested in each particular market, the size of the positions held by traders in the market, the surveillance history of the market, and the size of deliverable supplies for physical delivery markets."

CFTC position limits in smaller markets might be as few as 25, but in deeper markets they can be in the thousands. Most retail traders, and most readers of this book, will likely never exceed the position limits necessary to be qualified as a large trader by the CFTC. The commodity markets with position limits near 25 are markets most speculators avoid. On the other hand, popular futures contracts such as the e-mini S&P 500 will have positions limits at or near the upper end of the limit (1,000). To give you an idea, at the time of this writing the margin to hold 1,000 e-mini S&P futures overnight would be $5,060,000. Day traders would face lower margin, but day traders are not accounted for in the CFTC's position limit system because it is based on open interest at the close of a trading session as opposed to intraday. To take the discussion a step further, a trader with 1,000 open e-mini S&P futures contracts is exposing himself to the risk and reward of roughly $105 million worth of the S&P 500! This is because if the S&P 500 is valued at 2100, to find the value of each contract it is necessary to multiply the price of the index by the point value of $50. We can multiply that number by the contract size to determine the total size of the position. Remember, a trader is exposed to the profit and loss potential of the full value of the contract, but the margin required to put the position on is far less. In this example, the margin is $5,060, so a trader would need $5,060,000 to trade $105,000,000 worth of the S&P 500.

Although the CFTC is collecting and analyzing data for market integrity purposes, they release a report to the public outlining the basic structure of market participants. This report is known as the *Commitments of Traders* (COT). With the report, I believe traders can measure market sentiment to identify overcrowded trades, locate and potentially follow the so-called smart money, and even develop a contrarian indicator based on the behaviors of the small speculator. Not only will this report reveal the level of bullishness or bearishness, but unlike other sentiment readings based on polls, the COT report depicts traders actually putting their money where their mouths are! Nevertheless, deciphering the report into a credible guideline for trading takes some getting used to.

WHAT IS THE COT REPORT?

Similar to the way in which equity traders refer to SEC filings to determine the outlook of corporate officers in relation to their company stock, commodity traders look to the *Commitments of Traders* report for insight into who is buying and selling futures and options. Unlike SEC filings, the COT report doesn't reveal the names of the traders or funds holding positions in any particular commodity, but it does provide insight into the holdings of various types of traders categorized primarily by size. Simply put, the COT discloses a wealth of information on who is trading what, and in which direction. More important, it provides a glimpse into the minds and actions of certain types of traders.

> "I made all my money by selling too soon." —Bernard Baruch

The COT report is released by the CFTC every Friday afternoon, with the exception of the 2011 government shutdown, which made me realize just how much I relied on this information. In issuing the COT report, the CFTC's intent is to provide a glimpse into the makeup of the market. Despite its Friday release, the measurement itself takes place at the close of trade on Tuesday. As a result the report lags reality. Accordingly, there is some guesswork involved in the interpretation of the COT.

For a trader, it is an invaluable tool providing information on market sentiment in a quantifiable and verifiable manner. The report is a weekly snapshot of the *net* open interest on most futures contracts listed on futures exchanges. If you aren't familiar with the term *open interest*, it is simply the number of futures contracts held beyond the close of a given day session. The exact time varies per commodity, but the measurement of open interest generally occurs at 4 p.m. Central time. As a reminder, because the open interest tally occurs at the close of trade, the positions of those who are entering and exiting contracts within the same trading day (day traders) are not accounted for in these totals. As mentioned, the COT report delivers the net open interest. This means the figure reported is equivalent to the difference between the number of long contracts held minus the number of short contracts held. If there are more shorts than longs, the figure is negative. For example, if there are 650,000 total contracts open in corn futures and 400,000 are long corn while 250,000 are short, the net open interest is +150,000. Thus, traders are net long 150,000 corn contracts.

COT REPORT LINGO

There are multiple versions of the COT but in its simplest form, the CFTC determines the net position in two major categories: reportables and non-reportables. As discussed, reportables are traders whose positions exceed the CFTC's position limits. Thus, reportables are market participants trading a large number of contracts relative to the market size. Those traders categorized as non-reportables are trading a quantity of contracts beneath the set position limits. Again, most retail futures traders, and likely the majority of readers of this book, fall within the non-reportable categorization. The "reportable" designation is dominated by commodity trading advisors (CTAs) and commodity pool operators (CPOs), and even wealthy individuals. According to the CFTC, the aggregate of all reportable (large trader) positions usually represents 70% to 90% of total open interest in any given market.

The reportable category is broken into two subcategories, commercials and speculators. In English, this translates into commercial hedgers and large speculators, whereas commercial hedgers are producers or end users of a commodity seeking price stability through futures market hedges. Large speculators are referred to as the smart money because it is assumed they must have done something right to have the resources available to speculate in the quantities required to meet, or exceed, CFTC position limits.

To recap, there are three primary subcategories of traders:

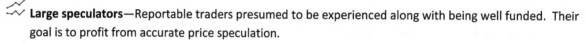 **Large speculators**—Reportable traders presumed to be experienced along with being well funded. Their goal is to profit from accurate price speculation.

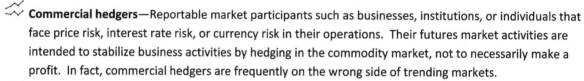 **Commercial hedgers**—Reportable market participants such as businesses, institutions, or individuals that face price risk, interest rate risk, or currency risk in their operations. Their futures market activities are intended to stabilize business activities by hedging in the commodity market, not to necessarily make a profit. In fact, commercial hedgers are frequently on the wrong side of trending markets.

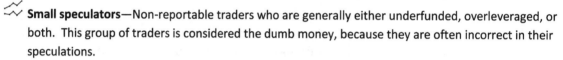 **Small speculators**—Non-reportable traders who are generally either underfunded, overleveraged, or both. This group of traders is considered the dumb money, because they are often incorrect in their speculations.

HOW TO READ THE COT REPORT

The *Commitments of Traders Report* displays the net position of each of the three categories of market participants by subtracting the number of short positions in each category from the number of long positions to determine a net figure. This net figure reveals whether speculators and hedgers are long or short the market overall, but even more important, it tells us by how much. Knowing the degree of bullishness and bearishness in each COT category can sometimes be helpful in determining whether a trend is emerging or exhausting itself.

Traditionally, traders look to computer-generated oscillators such as RSI and stochastics to identify overbought or oversold market conditions. I also like the idea of monitoring market sentiment in trading blogs, chat rooms, and news services for signs of overcrowded opinions. However, perhaps the best place to determine whether prices have been stretched too far is a quick look at the CFTC's *COT Report*. After all, actions speak louder than words and the report tells us where traders are putting their money to work.

There are three forms of guidance the *Commitments of Traders Report* provides: identifying overheated markets, identifying which direction the so-called smart money is positioned, and being aware of the contrarian implications portrayed by the holdings of small speculators.

IDENTIFYING OVERCROWDED TRADES

The herd phenomenon occurs repeatedly in the financial markets to various degrees of severity; those with their eyes open might be able to combat their greedy hearts. Years of observation have led me to believe avoiding, and enduring, the wrath of overcrowded trades is one of the most critical factors determining success and failure. Accordingly, I believe the best use of the *COT Report* to traders is in identifying markets that have accumulated overcrowding.

> "Only two things are infinite, the universe and human stupidity, and I am not sure about the former." —Albert Einstein

Once a market is overheated, it can be vulnerable to mass liquidation and this can wreak havoc on the profits of those following the herd and, worse, lure latecomers just before the trend sharply reverses. There is a well-known quip that states, "Once the last man buys, the market sells," and the COT offers a behind-the-scenes glimpse into when and where that might be.

That is exactly what happened in July 2014 in the crude oil market (Figure 32). Changes in the perception of market fundamentals and a stronger US dollar prompted large speculators to liquidate what had become the largest net long position in history. Offsetting long futures contracts requires them to sell futures, which created a price vacuum due to the lack of buyers. Although the fallout in oil was relatively predictable, the pace and size of the decline was jaw dropping.

Speculators caught on the wrong side of the move were eventually forced to sell their holdings at unimaginable prices, much of it at the hands of margin calls. Although this is an extreme example of overzealous speculation turning into panicked liquidation, it is not unlike the pattern we repeatedly see in commodity markets, as well as other asset classes. At the risk of being repetitive, the public rarely learns from its mistakes.

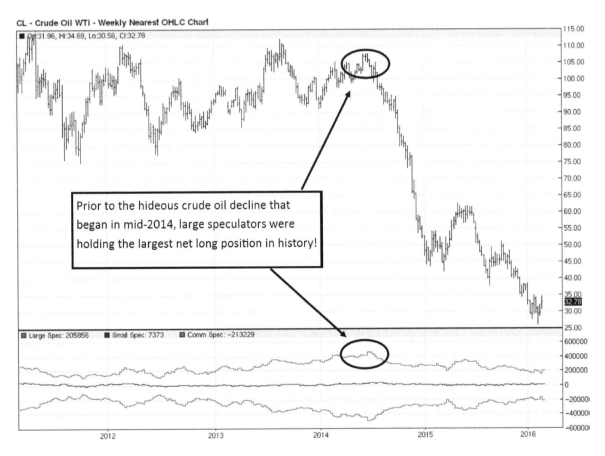

Figure 32: Sometimes when the smart money is overly invested in a particular position, it is an accident waiting to happen because they will eventually liquidate their holdings.

FOLLOW THE SMART MONEY

> "When one door closes, another opens; but we often look so long and regretfully upon the closed door that we do not see the one which has opened for us." —Alexander Graham Bell

As we know, the reportable traders that aren't legitimate commercial hedgers are known as the large speculator group. As discussed, this group of traders is considered the smart money simply because they are well capitalized and they must have known what they were doing to get into the position they are in. In addition, the smart money is prone to making the repetitive mistake of accumulating a large directional position that tends to end badly. Never forget, the trend is only your friend until it ends.

If large speculators have amassed a large net position in one direction, you've missed the opportunity to follow their lead. Instead, you should be looking for a possible trend reversal. After all, if they've already bought, the only way to exit is to sell.

Nevertheless, when the *COT Report* shows signs of a budding position among the large speculators, it can be beneficial for traders to consider jumping on the bandwagon. This is particularly true if this group of traders moves from a long position to a short position, and vice versa. Such an occurrence signals that the largest, and presumed to be most experienced, market participants have not only picked a direction but should have plenty of money to continue allocating to the trade.

Of course, it is never a good idea to blindly follow large speculators. They are only human and likely have much deeper pockets than most small speculators. Specifically, those trading enough positions to fall into the reportable category typically have the luxury of less than perfect timing due to mass amounts of capital backing their speculation. If you can't ride out adversity like the large specs, following their lead without doing your homework in other market analysis methods could mean running the risk of being forced out of the trade before it ever becomes successful—assuming it does.

In January 2015, the large speculator group of the COT began liquidating bullish holdings in the e-mini S&P 500 futures contract (Figure 33). By early March the group had gone from a net long position to a net short. Their foresight and patience paid off when in August of the same year, the S&P corrected sharply, traveling roughly 300 points, or $15,000 per contract, in less than a week. Somebody analyzing the *COT Report* might have noted the change in direction by large speculators to shift their bias to bearish. Using the report with other analytical tools, that analyst might have been lucky enough to catch the move or at least forewarned enough to avoid being hurt by it.

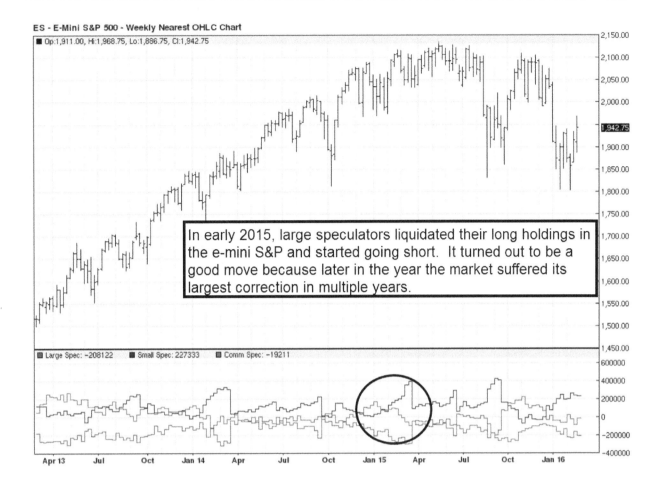

ES - E-Mini S&P 500 - Weekly Nearest OHLC Chart
Op:1,911.00, Hi:1,968.75, Lo:1,886.75, Cl:1,942.75

In early 2015, large speculators liquidated their long holdings in the e-mini S&P and started going short. It turned out to be a good move because later in the year the market suffered its largest correction in multiple years.

Large Spec: -208122   Small Spec: 227333   Comm Spec: -19211

Figure 33: Large speculators have deep pockets, and therefore the ability to hold a position longer and endure more pain than most retail traders, but they are often proven right in the long run.

FADE THE SMALL SPECS

The majority of individual retail traders fall into the small speculator category; unfortunately for them, this group of traders frequently lose money, earning the harsh title of "dumb money." Specifically, roughly 80% of all market participants may walk away from leveraged speculation with less than they started with, but they may face even more dismal odds. For this reason, many analysts, including me, look at the COT's "small speculator" category as a contrarian indicator. If COT data suggests the small speculator category is decisively net short in a particular market, it might be time to consider being bullish. On the other hand, if small speculators amass a large net long position, the best trades will likely be from the short side of the market, at least until this group of traders liquidates (Figure 34).

This might seem irrational—after all, why would you want to buy when the majority of traders like you are selling? The answer is simple. Small speculators have a history of inaccuracy and also tend to be fickle. This means they are likely to be late getting into the market and quick to liquidate once the tide turns. In addition, small speculators tend to move together and are known to chase markets and performance in the hope that previous price action will be indicative of future results. Generally, small speculators comply with human nature, which entices us to be bullish near the peaks of markets, and bearish near bottoms.

ZN - 10-Year T-Note - Weekly Nearest OHLC Chart

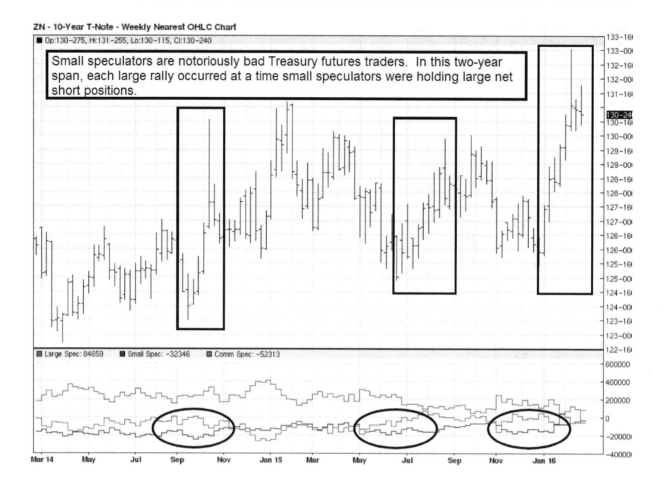

Figure 34: Unfortunately, small speculators are sometimes a better "fade" signal than they are a proper example of how and when to trade.

DON'T DWELL ON THE COMMERCIAL HEDGERS

In the world of COT, the commercials are synonymous with hedgers. This category is made up of large corporations, small businesses, and even individuals close to the action and likely to be knowledgeable on the subject. As a result, beginning traders tend to be lured toward this category in the *COT Report*. In their view, if farmers or other groups represented in the commercials category are going long corn, then they should be too. Nonetheless, traders should not attempt to follow their lead!

Although there are highly intelligent individuals making futures market decisions for members of this category, their motives are different. Commercials establish positions in the futures markets as a means of hedging their price risk. The goal of commercials isn't to predict where the market is going or even profit from trades held in the futures markets; they are simply offsetting risk of positions held in the cash market. If commercial hedgers are selling corn futures, it isn't because they believe the futures price will fall; it is because they are long in the cash market and want to hedge the risk of declining prices.

You will find commercial hedgers are perpetually long during downtrends, and short during uptrends (Figure 35). This isn't because they are rookies; it is the by-product of a hedge. If their futures hedge is losing money, their cash market operations are profitable, and vice versa.

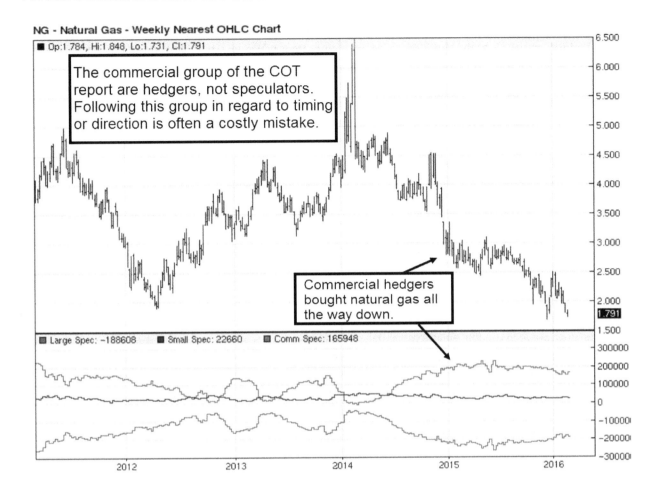

Figure 35: Commercial hedgers use the futures markets to offset price risk, not to profit. Accordingly, they are often continuously buying a downtrend and selling uptrends. Following their lead isn't advisable.

THE *COMMITMENTS OF TRADERS REPORT* DOESN'T TELL THE WHOLE STORY

Although the *COT Report* is a valuable resource to traders, it has a few flaws. For starters, the information we pore over on Friday afternoons is a snapshot of the open interest on Tuesday's close of trade. In the world of financial markets, three days can be an eternity, and so, it is very possible the net positions of all groups of traders have changed considerably by the time the report is released at the end of the week.

Accordingly, not only should any findings in the *COT Report* be confirmed with technical and fundamental analysis conclusions, but it should also be cross-referenced to the price chart to ensure the price move suggested in the report hasn't already occurred. Similarly, if you notice a clue from the report suggesting the large speculators might be getting too aggressive or could be accumulating a position, you might be able to infer confirmation by judging the difference in market price from the Tuesday data collection date and the Friday release.

Another downfall of the *COT Report* is the fact that its focus is on the open interest at the close of trade. In all fairness to the CFTC, it would be impossible to account for intraday positions held by each group. Even if they could, I'm not sure it would be any more telling than the open interest method. This is because some traders are constantly changing their position in regards to direction and quantity several times throughout the day.

In the day and age of high-frequency trading and highly discounted day trading margins, a bulk of the daily volume in many futures markets is at the hands of traders whose positions never, or rarely, show up on the report. For example, imagine a trader who lives for the thrill of being overleveraged. He might opt to take advantage of his broker's discounted day trading rates by entering his position at the open of trade and offsetting it at the close. He is exposed to the same general profit and loss potential as a trader who simply entered a contract and held it, but he doesn't have to post the overnight margin required by the exchange. Despite such a trader not being accounted for in the Commitments of Traders, those like him can have a profound impact on pricing. In fact, at times their actions can be more impactful than the buy and hold traders who *do* make it into the COT data. This is because such traders can trade massively large positions, relatively under the radar.

To put things in perspective, a trader exiting positions at the close to avoid the need to post exchange minimum margin needs a mere $500 to $1,000 on deposit in his trading account to trade a single e-mini S&P 500 futures contract, but a trader holding his position beyond the close of trade would be required to have at least $5,060 in his account per contract.

Pretending highly leveraged day traders can't affect the markets in the long term could be a financially fatal mistake. Authorities allege that the infamous 2010 flash crash was, at least in part, triggered by the actions of Navinder Singh Sarao in London, an aggressive day trader in his pajamas buying and selling e-mini S&P 500 futures from the basement of his parents' house. To be clear, the allegations aren't that Mr. Sarao forced the market lower via the positions he was taking in the market; instead, they claim that he created an automated program to generate large sell orders that were never intended to get filled. According to authorities, his intentions were to spook other market participants into selling more. He would then cancel those trades and buy at lower prices to benefit when prices recovered. This story is relevant because it exemplifies the fact that the *COT Report* is a great guide, but it is only telling us part of the story. Thus, one should never act solely on their Commitments of Traders findings.

WHERE TO FIND THE *COT REPORT*

I would venture to say the bulk of the retail trading public is unaware the *COT Report* exists; even fewer know where to find it. Luckily, the report is readily available to anyone interested in using it. The CFTC makes the COT reports available to the public free of charge on its website (www.cftc.gov), but it is also possible to register with the CFTC to have the information emailed directly to your inbox. Unfortunately, COT data directly from the CFTC is in plain text format; not unlike most government documents, it is much more difficult to decipher than it should be (Figure 36). In any case, reading the COT report can be somewhat challenging, but it could be worth the effort.

```
SILVER - COMMODITY EXCHANGE INC.   (CONTRACTS OF 5,000 TROY OUNCES)          :
CFTC Code #084691                                    Open Interest is   192,211    :
: Positions                                                                 :
:  20,867    40,455    32,074    32,894    25,034    42,214    39,843     9,944    16,595     5,694    22,530 :
:                                                                          :
: Changes from:     September 8, 2015                                      :
:  -2,025    -2,610       348    -3,455     3,034       796     5,900      -490       561       102       960 :
:                                                                          :
: Percent of Open Interest Represented by Each Category of Trader          :
:   10.9      21.0      16.7      17.1      13.0      22.0      20.7       5.2       8.6       3.0      11.7 :
:                                                                          :
: Number of Traders in Each Category                 Total Traders:   209        :
:    21        23        16         9        20        38        36        21        55        23        38 :
```

Figure 36: Although the CFTC's COT Report is a highly valuable tool for traders, the government agency doesn't go out of its way to provide its findings in a clear and convenient format.

There are a handful of software vendors and newsletter subscription services that offer the *COT Report* in an alternative format. Most traders will find those versions of the report easier to analyze. Here are a few that I've found that enable traders quick and efficient means of evaluating the net long and short positions of various types of traders.

HIGHTOWER REPORT

The Hightower Report is a popular industry publication offering daily analysis of the commodity markets. However, perhaps their most useful service is a clear and concise version of the *COT Report*. Instead of cumbersome data display, the Hightower Report strips the data down to the most important figures and color codes it to allow for immediate recognition of its meaning (Figure 37). For instance, if speculators have increased their net long net position from the previous week, the report displays the change in green; if a net long position is reduced it is red.

Commitments of Traders Analysis - Futures Only

Futures Only - 9/15/2015 - 9/22/2015

| | Non-Commercial | | Commercial | | Non-Reportable | |
	Net Position	Weekly Net Change	Net Position	Weekly Net Change	Net Position	Weekly Net Change
Combinations						
CBOT Grains	102,070	-3,580	1,238	+2,814	-103,308	+766
Crude Oil Complex	316,336	+18,400	-302,880	-9,216	-13,456	-9,184
Non-Financial	454,990	-15,686	-353,864	+51,402	-101,126	-35,716
Combined Precious Metals	115,221	+33,269	-118,867	-35,789	3,646	+2,520
Currencies						
Canadian	-38,394	+8,689	57,613	-11,719	-19,219	+3,030
Dollar	40,788	+1,034	-48,479	-2,163	7,691	+1,129
Euro	-81,033	+3,169	102,114	-296	-21,081	-2,873
Energies						
Crude Oil	259,429	+20,043	-249,771	-10,813	-9,658	-9,230
Heating Oil	-7,853	-1,537	9,506	+3,303	-1,653	-1,766
Natural Gas	-221,124	-8,825	196,157	+13,364	24,967	-4,539
Gas (RBOB)	64,760	-106	-62,615	-1,706	-2,145	+1,812

Figure 37: The Hightower Report simplifies the data in the CFTC's COT Report to help traders reach quick and accurate conclusions from the data.

BARCHART.COM

I respond better to visual data than I do to rows and columns of data. Thus, I prefer to analyze COT data from a chart. Not only does this manner of displaying the information enable analysts to judge the current environment on a historically relative basis, but it also makes it easier to identify trends in the positioning of speculators. The Barchart website found at www.Barchart.com enables traders to access daily, weekly, and even monthly charts of commodities with the *COT Report* stats depicted as line charts (Figure 38). This visual account of the report is an excellent way for traders to assess the trend of each COT group.

In contrast, working strictly from the CFTC's report or a simplified version such as the one distributed to subscribers of the *Hightower Report* requires traders to cross-reference the current week's data with that of previous weeks. As you can imagine, the process can become tedious and is error prone.

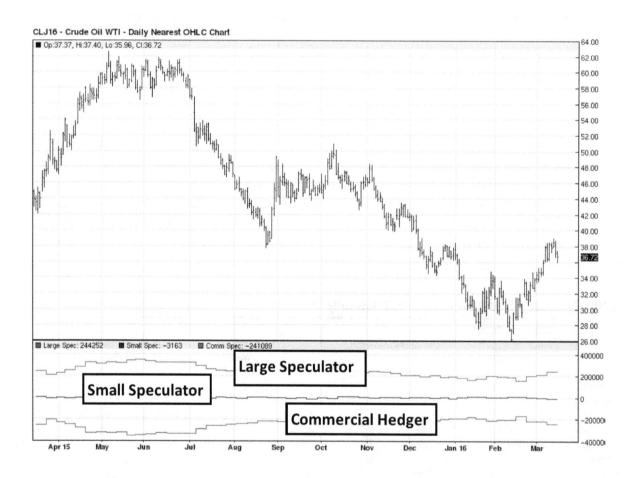

Figure 38: Barchart.com offers COT as a charting indicator displayed at the bottom of a price chart. This enables traders to visualize the current and historical net positions of various groups of traders.

INTERMARKET RELATIONSHIPS

It is naïve to assume seemingly unrelated markets move independently of each other. The reality is, the financial and commodity markets are littered with relationships that might be helpful to those attempting to speculate on price changes. Before entering a trade based on the aforementioned forms of market analysis, it is a good idea to cross-reference market correlations.

But simply assuming the historical relationship you once read about in college textbooks remains valid is a mistake. Because of government intervention, the relationship between many markets has morphed into something unrecognizable even to seasoned traders. Further, those relationships can, and will, change in magnitude and even direction as time goes on.

TO UNDERSTAND MARKET CORRELATIONS, YOU MUST UNDERSTAND PAIRS

Currency traders are familiar with the concept of trading assets in pairs, but most futures, or even stock, traders don't necessarily think of asset transactions as pairs trading. Maybe they should. Every transaction we make in the financial markets, or in daily life, involves two assets; as we make these transactions, we are essentially trading in pairs. Let's take a look at a few examples.

Prior to fiat money, transactions took place using the barter system. In today's world, the premise of an exchange is identical to the barter system, but one of the assets being exchanged is currency. It is only possible to purchase a security, or any item, by giving up something else. Further, the item being purchased merely has value relative to the asset being forfeited. When you buy a loaf of bread at the grocery store, you agree to "sell" dollars to acquire the bread. In other words, you are buying bread and selling dollars, and the store is selling bread and "buying" dollars. Keep in mind we have no way of measuring the value of a loaf of bread without comparing it to the dollar or some other currency, or asset.

Commodity trading, whether in the cash market or the futures market, is no different. When speculators buy a commodity they are essentially selling the dollar to acquire the asset. It should be obvious that changes in currency pricing can, and do, have a significant impact on other asset values. Unfortunately for speculators, there are numerous other factors determining the market price of an asset. As a result, accurately predicting market moves isn't as simple as assuming a higher greenback will automatically force all dollar-denominated assets lower. It is, however, something to keep tabs on.

THE GREENBACK AND COMMODITY PRICING

We touched on the dollar impact on commodities in Chapter 3, "Fundamental Analysis of the Commodity Markets," but I want to discuss the topic in more detail and in a broader sense. Some of the most treacherous bear markets in commodity market history were those spanning from 2014 through 2015. Although the most publicized commodity bears were crude oil and natural gas, the grain markets such as corn and wheat weren't spared. We also witnessed historical lows in markets like sugar and gold; even the meat complex finally succumbed to the commodity market curse in late 2015.

In each of these markets, there were fundamental bearish stories that percolated the trading community. They all had a common denominator; they are all priced in US dollars. In fact, gold priced in other currencies held relatively firm during much of the bear market in dollar-denominated gold. This is a sure sign that commodity markets are sensitive to currency values.

The best example of the relationship between the dollar and a commodity market may be crude oil. Analysts have debated whether the 2014 collapse in oil was at the hands of supply concerns or decreased demand expectations. The answer might be simpler than supply and demand. Another explanation could be that the value of crude oil hasn't really changed relative to other assets, yet because the world prices crude oil in US dollars, the price of oil adjusted to account for action in the currency markets. Most of the drop in crude oil could be explained by a stronger dollar. When the greenback is stronger it requires fewer dollars to purchase crude oil. This relationship is known as negative correlation. It simply means that when the dollar goes up, the price of crude has a tendency to go down, and vice versa. (See Figure 16 in Chapter 3, "Fundamental Analysis of the Commodity Markets.")

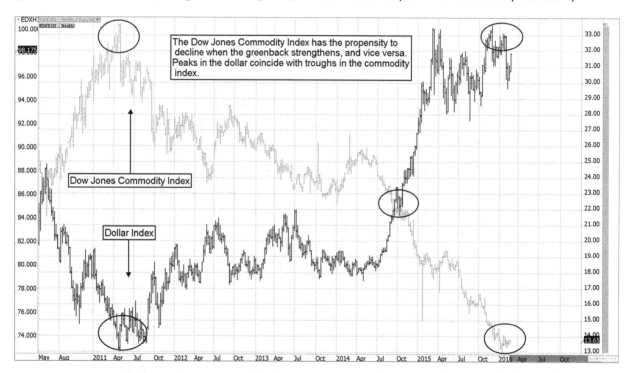

Figure 39: Commodity traders should always be aware of action in the currency market. Changes in the value of the US dollar can wreak havoc on prices of anything from crude oil, to gold, to the grains and meats.

The negative relationship between the dollar and other commodity markets is somewhat less obvious than that of gold and crude oil, but it does exist and should not be overlooked or underestimated (Figure 39). The prices of corn, wheat, and soybeans tend to move inversely to the greenback an estimated 40% to 60% of the time, but the relationship can break down during highly seasonal times of year such as during planting or harvesting.

Regardless of your market of choice, you must be aware of how it interacts with other markets. Trading is a game of odds, and of course luck. Being aware of the manner in which certain markets behave relative to others can potentially improve the probability of success. Those looking to find a bullish opportunity in crude oil, or a bearish play in Treasuries, might look to the currency market for guidance in timing.

SECTION 2: COMMODITY TRADING STRATEGY DEVELOPMENT

Most readers are already familiar with the overall concepts discussed in this section, but my goal is to shine some light on the realities of each market approach as well as play devil's advocate with the help of hindsight. Further, I believe my time as a commodity broker has provided me with an insight that other authors, or market participants, might not have.

Let's take a look at some of the basic strategies: their characteristics, their advantages, and what's more important, their disadvantages. In this section, I hope to give traders enough objective information on each market approach to enable educated guidance on developing a strategy meeting the needs of each individual. I will also provide insight on what I believe to be favorable strategies based on my observations as

> "There are so many ways to lose, but so few ways to win. Perhaps the best way to achieve victory is to master all the rules for disaster, and then concentrate on avoiding them." —Victor Niederhoffer

a commodity broker, involvements as a trader, and insights I have gained from conversations I've had with other industry participants. This is not to say I haven't been on the blunt end of a market thrashing, nor am I flawless in my analysis. I've witnessed the good, the bad, and the ugly in the markets firsthand, and I hope to share those experiences in hopes of helping you navigate the market profitably.

As we navigate and define each trading style, keep in mind that there may be as many variations in these definitions as there are market participants. This section is intended to give you a sense of these strategies and industry lingo. Hopefully, the tips, tricks, and interpretations offered here will help readers develop, shape, and fine-tune existing and future market ventures.

CHAPTER 6: POSITION TRADING IN FUTURES

Before we can define position trading in the commodity markets, we must recognize there is a dramatic difference in time frames for stock traders and futures traders. This is because the leverage involved in the commodity markets, combined with the obstacle of expiring futures contracts, tends to speed things up for traders and, therefore, shortens the time horizon. When talking about a stock trader, we can assume position trading is the purchase of a stock to be held for months or even years. However, a futures trader doesn't have the ability nor the capacity (in most cases) to hold indefinitely.

To futures traders, a position trade could be anything held longer than a day or two. The only type of trade excluded from the category of position trading is a day trade which, as I've previously mentioned, involves buying and selling a futures contract in the same trading session. Obviously, this is a widespread net being cast; some position traders are in and out of a few trades a week, while others hold for several months, which typically involves rolling over contracts to avoid expiration and delivery of the underlying asset.

Position traders, whether they are using futures, options, spreads, or some other trading strategy, generally choose between three primary forms of speculation: fundamental trading, swing trading, and trend trading. The latter two styles are derived from technical analysis strategies, while the former is the practice of entering a long-term trade anticipating of a change in market fundamentals that influence pricing. In my opinion, regardless of the charting or fundamental analysis used, traders should always consult some of the other tools we've outlined in this book such as seasonal tendencies, market sentiment, and the *COT Report*.

The primary difference between the two types of technical analysis styles is that swing traders are executing comparatively short-term countertrend positions while trend traders are attempting to trade in the direction of the trend on a relatively longer time horizon. Let's take a look at the advantages and disadvantages of each approach.

SWING TRADING

Swing trading is a style of trading attempting to profit from countertrend moves that occur in a time horizon of one to four days. A swing trader is buying into fear and selling into greed, or simply buying low and selling high. Of course, this is easier said than done!

Naturally, when it comes to speculation traders are at the mercy of the market; if circumstances call for taking a profit in the same session the trade was initiated, or if it is necessary to stick with the trade beyond the four-day mark, so be it. Nevertheless, the expectation of a swing trader upon entering the trade is for a speculative position in the time horizon.

> "I believe the very best money is made at the market turns. Everyone says you get killed trying to pick tops and bottoms and you make all your money by playing the trend in the middle. Well, for twelve years I have been missing the meat in the middle but I have made a lot of money at tops and bottoms." —Paul Tudor Jones

Swing traders might, or might not, be concerned with the fundamental makeup of the market. Either way, they are using technical analysis to time their entry. By definition they are actively and aggressively buying or selling futures contracts or trading options into predicted areas of support and resistance. Unlike trend traders, swing traders do not wait for solid confirmation of a trend; instead, they try to time market reversals.

> The premise of swing trading is to identify areas of support to be a buyer, and resistance to be a seller.

Clearly, there are an unlimited number of ways a trader could determine entry and exit points of a swing trading strategy, but most involve some sort of technical oscillator falling into oversold or overbought territory in combination with trendlines, trading channels, and other forms of support and resistance.

To reiterate, a swing trader will identify traditional areas of support and resistance and look for countertrend opportunities at, or near, support levels in conjunction with a predetermined mix of technical oscillators intended to identify potential market turns.

In Figure 40, a swing trader in the e-mini S&P 500 using the Williams %R as the *get-set* indicator and the relative strength index as the *go* indicator might have fared relatively well by selling sharp rallies and buying while others were scrambling to sell.

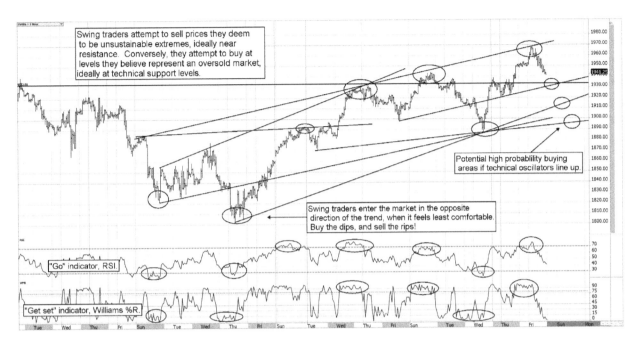

Figure 40: Swing traders are in the business of doing the exact opposite of what is comfortable—buying when others are selling, and selling when others are buying.

ADVANTAGES OF SWING TRADING

Swing trading strategies thrive in range-bound markets because as prices bounce back and forth between support and resistance, a swing trader will be exposed to a plethora of opportunity. This is a big advantage over trend trading or fundamental position trading due to the tendency of commodity markets to trade sideways a majority of the time.

> Swing traders look to buy the dips and sell the rips!

Although the stats change with market conditions, it is generally accepted as being true that markets spend 80% of the time trading in a range and only 20% of the time moving directionally to define a new trading range. Similarly, more often than not, confirmation of a trend might also mark the end of it. Once the last buyer (those seeking confirmation) is in, the market has a tendency to reverse.

There are fierce opponents to swing trading. After all, the nature of the strategy calls for entering a trade against the grain. The argument to that point is that most market participants lose money; so doing what is comfortable for most people might not be the best course of action.

In my opinion, swing trading provides traders with a relatively high probability of success on any given venture in comparison to trend traders because a profitable swing trade can occur in a typical market environment. A directionless market with various levels of volatility can result in profitable trading signals. Trend traders, on the other hand, only stand to profit in a market that experiences an abnormally large directional trend. In short, swing traders are seeking more frequent and higher-probability profits, but often give up the prospects of runaway profits should an unusually large price move occur.

DISADVANTAGES OF SWING TRADING

There is one glaring drawback involved in swing trading—when a trade goes wrong, it can go horribly wrong. Although buying a market at support and selling at resistance will work out more often than not, when it doesn't, the adverse price move could be surprisingly painful. Not only does the market move quickly and swiftly at such technical levels, but it can be difficult to identify a failure of the technical level until it is too late. Accordingly, swing traders must be market savvy and keen on risk management to survive in the long run.

In addition, swing trading is a relatively active method of speculation, and thus, comparatively high transaction costs and time dedication of implementation should be considered.

SWING TRADING INSTRUMENTS

"The trick is to make sure you don't die waiting for prosperity to come." —Lee Iacocca

The most common type of swing trading is done with the buying or selling of outright futures contracts. However, swing trading can also be effectively employed using long or short options, option spreads, and even synthetic strategies in which traders combine both futures and options to achieve a common goal. Further, it can be argued that options are better suited for swing traders than they are for trend traders, because they come with finite expiration dates. Although futures contracts also expire, they can easily be rolled into the next contract month without necessarily putting on a fresh trade with additional risk or cash outlay.

A long option trader, on the other hand, will usually have trouble executing a reasonable strategy that works in the time frame necessary for successful trend trading. The concept of swing trading is to buy low and sell high. This is in contrast to the buy high, sell higher approach to trend trading; ideally, swing option traders would be buying calls in a down market at a time in which the call options are undervalued. Swing traders would also be purchasing puts in an inclining market at a time in which put options are undervalued. Trend traders, however, would be attempting to buy calls after a relatively large rally at a time they are overpriced. As you can see, trend trading with options adds another obstacle to profitable trading that swing traders don't have to worry about—buying inflated options.

Because swing traders are relying on "normal" market conditions as opposed to uncharacteristically large trending moves, it is imperative the swing strategy is executed in a market with sufficient liquidity. A rule of thumb would be to avoid, or at least trade sparingly, any commodity market with daily trading volume of less than 20,000. If the chosen trading plan involves options, liquidity becomes an even bigger concern. Judging option liquidity can be tricky; option markets with big commercial and institutional interest, such as RBOB gasoline, might have high daily volume and open interest stats, but offer little liquidity to the average trader attempting to execute smaller lot sizes. Similarly, some option markets such as the currencies, with skimpy volume and open interest, have active market makers willing to display attractive bid/ask spreads that enable traders to enter and exit positions with ease. In essence, liquidity is measured by the ability to seamlessly trade a market, not the volume and open interest.

SCALE TRADING

Scale trading is a form of countertrend trading that typically involves a lengthy market venture in which a trader adds to losing positions. Scale trades are generally best when used as a "bottom fisher" strategy to take advantage of historically low pricing in anticipation of a reversal. It can also be used as a means of picking a market top. In any case, the goal is to utilize a dollar cost average approach with incremental position entries and exits. The practice of dollar cost averaging is common among stock traders, but due to the leverage involved in futures trading, it can be difficult to implement in commodities. If you are unfamiliar with the concept, dollar cost averaging is the technique of buying a fixed dollar amount of a particular investment on a regular schedule. In the long run, such an approach could result in more shares being purchased at lower prices and fewer being bought at higher prices. Scale trading in commodities differs in that the predetermined entry is based on price, not time or a specific dollar amount. Further, scale traders add to losing positions, but don't add to trades moving in their favor.

As a result of hefty leverage and margin requirements faced by commodity futures traders, for those of us with limited funds, scale trading is a risky endeavor because it would take a substantial amount of money to properly fund a scale trade from beginning to end. Naturally, without the ability to carry out the strategy, the results could be devastating.

The overall assumption of a scale trading strategy is it is impossible to pick a market high or low, but if a trader can get in the vicinity of a reversal, the odds of coming out ahead are good. Further, it operates with the premise that commodities are "goods," and not "bads." This means that although commodities can become cheap, they cannot go to zero.

Generally, scale traders set predetermined entry levels in advance. As market prices drift against the trader, contracts and risk are added to the equation. Likewise, if the market swings in favor of the trader, contracts added at favorable prices will be peeled off at predetermined price levels.

Most references to scale trading assume traders are using the strategy to build multimonth, or multiyear, positions. All-time lows or all-time highs are good candidates for scale trading strategies. Nonetheless, scale trading can be practiced on any time frame; swing traders and even day traders can implement a quasi-scale traded based on their technical approach to trading.

ADVANTAGES OF SCALE TRADING

Scale traders believe having plenty of risk capital and patience enables the construction of a high-probability venture if their speculation of a price reversal is even remotely accurate. Successful scale trading takes a considerable amount of discipline; simply jumping into positions and throwing good money after bad

"I will prepare and someday my chance will come." —Abraham Lincoln

as the market moves adversely isn't a sound trading strategy. In fact, doing so is a quick way to get buried in market losses.

If a trader's intention is to have a total of five futures contracts in any given speculation, opting to stagger the entry of those five contracts at various prices will almost always result in a better average entry price than simply buying five contracts at the current market price. This is because the odds of a trader picking the exact low of a move are slim.

Take, for example, a trader who wishes to go long five corn futures. The current price is $3.90; he could simply buy five at $3.90, or he could buy one contract at $3.90 and place a limit order to buy another at $3.85, and another at $3.80, and so on to $3.70. Should all orders get filed, the trader will be holding five contracts with an average entry price of $3.80. This means the trade breaks even with the market at $3.80 and makes money anywhere above it. Entering all of the contracts at $3.90 would have pegged the breakeven point at $3.90; further, if the price fell to $3.80 the trader would be losing 10 cents per contract, or $2,500, rather than breaking even as the scale strategy would have done. Likewise, if all contracts are executed, the scale trade position would be profitable at $3.90 by $2,500, but the simple one price entry would just be breaking even. The only scenario in which the one-price entry would be optimal is one in which corn prices bottom near $3.90, but most traders aren't skilled or lucky enough to successfully determine such a precise entry level.

DISADVANTAGES OF SCALE TRADING

Critics of scale trading are adamantly opposed to the idea of adding to losers. After all, the strategy calls for buying low, buying more at a lower price, and then more lower still. This goes against our programmed logic as human beings; it also contradicts the popular trading rule of "never add to losers." This is ironic because in a stock investment account, the highly touted approach of dollar cost averaging is often adding money to losing positions.

The risk of scaling into a position, as opposed to entering all at once, is the trader might not have an opportunity to execute all of the intended contracts. Using the previous example, if the low in corn turns out to be $3.78, only two of the five buy orders would have been filled. Nevertheless, if this is the case, the market is moving favorably causing little stress to the trader. Is that such a horrible outcome?

INSTRUMENTS FOR SCALE TRADING

The scale trading strategy is most efficiently employed with outright long and short futures contracts. However, some option sellers have been known to practice a version of the strategy by selling additional options at more distant strike prices, or for more premium, in a market moving against the original option sale.

In the early days of commodity futures trading, scale trading was reserved for the wealthiest of market participants. Small traders delving into such a strategy would be forced into developing much better market timing and, thus, less room for error. In essence, they ran a high risk of running out of money before the scale trade was able to turn profitable. The advent of smaller-sized futures contracts has made it possible for moderately funded, to low-funded, trading accounts to participate in scale trading. This is particularly true in the grain markets, the currency markets, and gold. The CME Group has introduced a suite of e-micro currency futures as well as an e-micro gold, which carry minuscule margin requirements and comparatively low price risk. Each of these products is a tenth the size of the original futures contract. In the case of the euro, this means that the e-micro currency futures contract size is 10,000 units rather than 100,000. Accordingly, the point value is $1.25, not $12.50; a trader long or short the market makes or loses a manageable $1.25 per tick of market movement. With these smaller contracts, scale trading is a real possibility for anyone.

TREND TRADING

The concept of trend trading plays to the heartstrings of human nature. Trend traders attempt to identify a confirmed trend and enter a speculative position intended to profit on a continuation of that trend. Trend confirmation can be attained via a plethora of technical indicators at the discretion of the trader, but the most common approach is some sort of moving average crossover, or even a signal produced by a slow moving technical oscillator like the MACD.

> Trend trading is the practice of buying high and selling higher. Or selling low and selling lower.

Unlike a swing trader who is interested in profiting as the market undergoes a trend change, a trend trader isn't interested in catching the high or low of a move; they are simply interested in benefiting from a piece in the middle.

In their quest for confirmation of a trend, trend traders often enter a market after it is already moved substantially. The strategy is designed in a manner in which trend traders are the last one to arrive at the party and the last one to leave. In the best-case scenario, trend traders miss the beginning stages of the move and leave the ending stages of the move on the table. In the worst-case scenario, the point at which they are entering the confirmed trend is the precise point the market has exhausted itself. Trend traders are frequently caught in bull and bear traps (price moves that appear to be breakouts or extensions of a trend but do not follow through on price action).

To put things in perspective, most trend trading strategies trigger buy signals in a market that is already overbought on a daily chart according to common technical indicators such as stochastics or RSI. The trading strategy then intends to follow the trend loosely, usually with deep stop-loss orders and large risks. This is because if the goal is to catch large trending moves, the market will need plenty of room to breathe. Consequently, this equals exiting the trade significantly after the trend has reversed adversely.

The most infamous trend trading strategy is known as "Turtle Trading." The original Turtle Traders, Richard Dennis and William Eckhardt, have their names forever etched in the commodity trading wall of fame. Mr. Dennis is famous for turning $5,000 into more than $100 million.

> "We are going to grow traders, just like they grow turtles in Singapore." — Richard Dennis

In the early 1980s this duo made a bet on whether *anyone* could be taught to trade well. Dennis believed it was possible, but Eckhardt was on the other side of the wager. Dennis set up an experiment in which he provided the trading capital to traders who underwent his training. The "Turtles," as they were called, were taught a specific trend-following strategy. According to former Turtle Russell Sands, as a group the Turtles trained by Dennis allegedly earned more than $175 million in only five years. This story alone has attracted trend traders to the futures markets in droves. However, most underestimate the drawdowns that can occur before the method finally pays off. The strategy also requires a massive capital outlay, not to mention trading gumption.

The exact details of the Turtle Trading strategy have been kept hidden under a rock, but some sources have leaked the supposed trading rules. In essence, the system is one that attempts to buy long-term breakouts with the intention of not risking more than 2% of the account size. A trend trading method attempting to mock the turtles might go long on a 40-day new high with an exit signal on a 20-day new low. Even the greenest of traders can see this type of trading could see massive profits *and* losses because a lot can happen in a market between a 40-day new high and a 20-day new low! Simply put, trend trading takes deep pockets and plenty of nerves to give the strategy an opportunity to work as intended. Unfortunately, most traders don't have the stomach or trading capital to implement it properly. Even those who do might see years of choppy market action and massive drawdowns before trend trading pays off.

ADVANTAGES OF TREND TRADING

Because of the lengthy process of confirming a trend and the relatively inactive style that trend trading brings to the table, it is the most comfortable strategy for most traders. After all, it is human nature to go with the flow rather than buck the trend. As a result, there might be slightly less emotional turmoil felt by traders choosing this method in relation to a swing trading approach. But the biggest advantage of trend trading is the massive and seemingly unlimited profit potential should the trader participate in a prolonged trend. A trend trader could have amassed substantial wealth during historical market moves.

> "I always say that you could publish your trading rules in the newspaper and no one would follow them. The key is consistency and discipline." —Richard Dennis

Imagine being short the e-mini S&P during the financial collapse of 2008. The market fell from nearly 1,600 in November 2007 to under 700 in March 2009. Assuming a trend trader received a sell signal somewhere in the 1,450 area and was able to ride out most of the move, it might have been possible to exit near 940 (remember, trend traders always get in late *and* get out late), and the trade would have netted $25,500 per contract. This is figured by multiplying the difference in the assumed entry and exit by the point value of the e-mini S&P 500, which is $50 (($1,450 − 940) x $50). However, this calculation ignores rollover and transaction costs, which could be material.

Keep in mind, the margin on a single e-mini S&P futures is roughly $5,000, but to implement a trend trading strategy it is necessary to have relatively deep pockets and an overfunded account. Thus, a trader would be wise to hold at least four times the required margin per contract; in this case, we will assume a starting balance of $20,000.

As great as a $25,500 profit in a $20,000 account sounds, it is an ambitious assumption and it wouldn't have come without some gut-wrenching drawdowns. We'll take a closer look at the details in the disadvantages of trend trading.

DISADVANTAGES OF TREND TRADING

Trend trading is the type of strategy that looks flawless on paper, but in reality it can be a nightmare. It takes a special kind of person to successfully trend trade; not everyone is willing to suffer painful drawdowns, leave boatloads of money on the table in both the entry and exit, agonize over the frequent and expensive false signals, and exercise the patience necessary to successfully implement the strategy. Even if the trend trading rules accurately identify a trend and provide sound and fruitful guidance throughout the process, the trader might not have the wherewithal to follow his own trading rules to benefit from the positive outcome. Trend trading is an extremely difficult strategy to employ and requires excessively deep risk capital to be put at risk.

To illustrate my point, let's consider the example in which a trend trading method called for a short in the e-mini S&P 500 at 1,450 in late 2007 and an eventual exit at 940 in early 2009, using a beginning account balance of $20,000. On the surface, a strategy capable of catching such a magnificent move appears extremely desirable. But there is a dark underbelly that traders must recognize before partaking in trend trading. For simplicity's sake, we will round prices to the nearest 10.00 S&P points and assume the trading rules were written and followed in such a way that would have kept the trade continuously active. This would have been possible with a trend trading system operating on an exit plan in which a position would be liquidated if the market posted a fresh high on the weekly chart, meaning a trend of lower highs is interrupted by a higher high. Had such a strategy existed, it would be one with extremely deep risk and have required nerves of steel. Nevertheless, it is a great example of the roller-coaster ride that is trend trading.

> Trend trading requires a great deal of discipline. Traders must forgo overwhelming desires to exit profitable trades before the method rules suggest. Most trend trading methods see profits evaporate quickly in order to give positions a chance to catch the really big move.

Using the presumptuous entry price of 1,450, the trader would have initially gained comfort in seeing prices float lower toward 1,410, at which point the trade would have been producing a paper profit of $2,000 ((1,450 – 1,410) x $50)). However, the market abruptly reversed and made its way toward 1,530. As a result, the trade went from a winner of $2,000 to a loser of almost $4,000 ((1,450 – 1,530) x $50)).

By nature, a true long-term trend trading method designed to catch the 2008 collapse would not have taken profits at 1,410; this is a swing for the fence approach to trading. Further, most trend trading systems would have allowed for the drawdown of $4,000 (or $6,000 if you count the account balance peak of $22,000). Had the strategy been configured in a manner that would have locked in profits on the initial move or prevented the large drawdown on the second move, it probably wouldn't have caught the substantial money making move that was just around the corner.

Another important point is our assumption that the trader fund the account with quadruple the minimum margin required by the exchange is actually aggressive. One of the rules thought to be in place for the Turtle Traders was to never accept a loss of more than 2% of the account balance on any particular trade; in this case, the rules would call for limiting risk to $400 (or eight e-mini S&P points). Accordingly, a Turtle Trader under those circumstances and account size would not have survived the ebbs and flows of the market to participate in the enormous gains that eventually followed. Of course, Turtle Traders were probably funding accounts much more liberally. Had a Turtle Trader funded the account with $200,000 per one lot

> Being a good trend trader is easier said than done. Most traders don't have the mental stability to see the strategy through to the end due to large drawdowns, which greatly reduces the odds of it succeeding.

of e-mini S&P 500 traded, the strategy could have absorbed the move to 1,530 without triggering an exit rule. Once again, the minimum exchange margin for an e-mini S&P 500 futures contract is a mere $5,000; I don't know of many futures traders who fund an account as heavily as the Turtles did. As a result, the 2% loss limit rule applied to Turtle Traders probably isn't feasible for the average trader. After all, funding an account with $200,000 to trade a single e-mini is actually de-leveraging the position; with the S&P 500 valued at 1,500, a single e-mini futures contract represents $75,000 worth of the S&P 500. This is the equivalent of funding an account with $200,000 to purchase $75,000 worth of stock. I don't know about you, but this seems counterproductive.

Let's get back to our example (Figure 41). Supposing a trader with a $20,000 account sold an e-mini S&P at 1,450 in November 2008. After a move to 1,410, then back up to 1,530, the market finally sold off. This time, the market made its way to 1,250 by mid-January! At 1,250, a 1,450 sell in the e-mini would be profitable by $10,000 ((1,450 – 1,250) x $50)). This is a 50% return in the trading account in less than three months, enough to make a trader salivate at the idea of taking profits, but a true trend trading system designed to catch a move of this magnitude would let it ride.

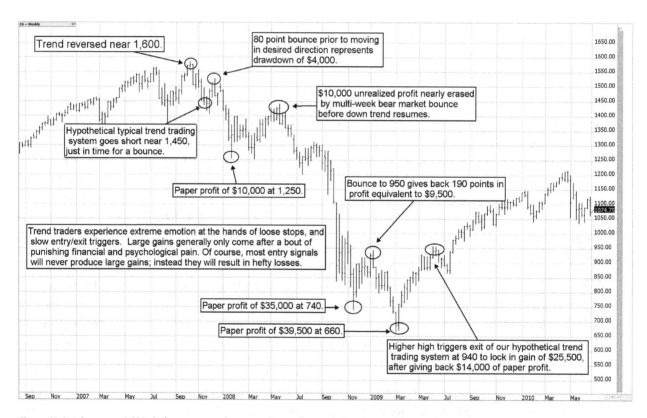

Figure 41: It takes a special kind of person, or at least massive trading capital, to be a trend trader.

After posting the 1,250 low, the e-mini S&P 500 spent the first half of 2008 retesting the 1,430 area. This trader would have watched most of the $10,000 profit evaporate before the tides turned in his favor again. Once the selling commenced, the market fell almost continuously through late 2008 to find a temporary low in November near 740. At this juncture, the paper profit would be 710 S&P points, or $35,500 ((1,450 – 740) x $50)). Once again, the market would bounce but fail to make a higher high. This time the bounce peaked near 930, which means the trade would have given back 190 points in profit, the equivalent of $9,500 (190 x $50). The S&P 500 futures eventually bottomed out near 660 in March 2009; at that point, this simplified version of the trade would have been yielding a paper profit of a whopping $39,500 ((1,450 – 660) x $50)). But as trend trading methods do, $14,000 of the gains were given back on a rally from 660 to what would have been the exit signal for this simplified system at 940 (the point on the weekly chart that ended the pattern of lower highs). In summary, the trade was profitable by $25,500 ((1,450 – 940) x $50)) before considering rollover slippage and transaction costs.

We would all agree that this is a smashing success of a trade. However, in order for this to have been possible it would have taken one of the largest one-directional moves in the history of the stock market, an initial account drawdown of $4,000 (20% of the starting account balance), and multiple intratrade five-digit drawdowns. It is fair to say the average trader probably couldn't, or wouldn't, have stuck it out to the end. Even given this winning strategy and circumstances, most traders probably would have either lost money by exiting prematurely following the initial trade entry or broken even after seeing the first $10,000 in profits wiped out. Humans simply aren't equipped to emotionally cope with these types of massive account swings without straying from the original plan. Of course, we also cherry picked this setup; the same trading method applied to the e-mini S&P to the months preceding the eventual fall from grace would have resulted in at least one, and perhaps two, mistimed entries and conceivably several thousand dollars in losses before catching the big one.

Now that we've discussed an example of what might have been the best trend trading opportunity of all time, let's get back to reality. Markets rarely see the massive moves we witnessed in 2008; even when they do, it is much easier to write about how to trade them after the fact than it would have been to have participated in the move. In more normal market conditions, trend trading methods can be extremely challenging.

As mentioned, trend traders are willing to accept the lower probability of success on any particular trade and the risk of massive drawdowns for the chance to catch the potentially life-changing market move. More often than not, what appears to be a confirmed trend quickly reverses to cause sharp losses to trend-trading strategies. Even in the previously discussed example, what was eventually a successful venture started out as a 20% drawdown.

The thing about tables is, they *always* turn. The same can be said of market trends.

Another common occurrence in trend trading is a prolonged trend allowing for substantial unrealized profits, concluding with a massive price reversal erasing most, or all, of the paper profits. This became glaringly obvious to me early in my career as a commodity broker as I followed the trading history of an interoffice trend trading strategy. The tracking of the method displayed all currently open positions in a table; all new entry signals and exit signals were listed separately. The currently open positions table almost always displayed blockbuster profits, yet the actual track record of the trading method was financially challenged (at least at that particular time). I noticed that all of the large unrealized profits the trend trading system was creating were dwindling away before the system called for an exit, at which time those trades dropped out of the open position table. Even worse, the trades that didn't work out and sustained large losses from the get-go were exited in dire circumstances and removed from the open positions table. The closed positions that represented the realized gains and losses were astonishingly horrible, and all the while the open positions were almost always displaying impressive profits. The bottom line is trend trading methods can be deceptive in that they are capable of large gains, but only in extraordinarily large and long trends do those gains actually become realized profits. Unfortunately, this is relatively normal with trend trading methods. In average market conditions, the trading method not only struggles to make money, but it struggles not to cause traders to lose their shirts! The trend is only your friend until it ends. That said, when trend trading works and the trader employing the strategy has the personality and discipline necessary to stick to the plan, it can be remarkable.

INSTRUMENTS USED

Unlike swing trading that can be accomplished via options, futures, or a combination of both, trend trading is generally best served through simple outright long or short futures contracts. Because the time horizon for trend traders is so lengthy, commodity options aren't a viable alternative to futures contracts. Not only are long-dated options expensive, they are also relatively illiquid and suffer from time value erosion. Not surprisingly, an expensive and thinly traded derivatives market translates into a deplorable trading environment. Further, if the goal of trading is to buy low and sell high, buying puts in a downtrend or selling calls in a downtrend are counterproductive actions—at least on paper.

> "I've missed more than 9,000 shots in my career. I've lost almost 300 games. Twenty-six times, I've been trusted to take the game winning short and missed. I've failed over and over and over again in my life. And that is why I succeed." —Michael Jordan

To put this into perspective, in late November 2015 crude oil was trading in the low $40s after falling from the $50 price level. Most trend trading strategies would likely begin triggering sell signals because they would deem the trend as being confirmed. A trader interested in keeping his risk limited might look to purchase a put option, as opposed to selling a futures contract or selling a call option. However, such a trading style would generally require an option with at least three months to expiration. As is always the case, the more time to expiration, the more expensive it is to buy an option. In addition, an option positioned in the direction of the trend tends to see higher demand from speculators and, therefore, carry a higher price. As a result of traders bidding up the price of puts in a downtrending market, in November 2015 the crude oil options with a March expiration were astronomically priced. A trader wishing to buy a put option with an at-the-money strike price would be facing a price tag of nearly $3.50 in premium (equivalent to $3,500). This is figured by multiplying the premium by the point value in crude oil, which is $1,000 per $1 of crude ($1,000 x $3.50).

At a glance, $3,500 for three months of limited risk in crude oil might not seem like a bad idea, but it is a low-probability venture. Not only does the market have to continue moving lower, it must do so in a finite time frame and to a magnitude that covers the cost of the option (in this case $3.50) just to break even. In short, if a trader buys a $42 put for $3.50 in premium ($3,500), at expiration he is merely breaking even if the price of crude oil is $38.50 ($42 - $3.50).

On the other hand, an option seller attempting to trade the downtrend would be selling a call option while it is on sale, as opposed to doing so at a time that might fetch top dollar. On balance, when a market is trending lower, the calls are cheaply priced because market participants believe the trend will continue. Conversely, if a market is trending higher, put options tend to be relatively cheaply priced. Thus, it can be a dangerous game to sell options in the direction of a prolonged trend. Although it appears to be an optimal strategy to many traders, it is also one with the potential to devastate a trading account in a very short amount of time.

Now imagine being short a crude call in a downtrending market. Not only was the option sold at a price that is the equivalent of being on sale, but sudden turmoil in the Middle East, or a supply disruption, can quickly turn the tides in the other direction, causing sharp losses in a matter of minutes. Call options that were once cheap are repriced by the market to account for the new trend. In this scenario, it is not uncommon to see call option prices explode exponentially. I've seen crude oil call options trading at $300 one day, worth $2,000 to $3,000 in a matter of days. Such a move could result in a loss to the option seller of $1,700 to $2,700! You might be thinking to yourself, "If this is true, wouldn't it be a good idea to buy these cheap calls each time crude oil prices become depressed?" The answer to that is a resounding *Yes!* However, that strategy falls into the countertrend swing trading bucket, not trend trading.

Unfortunately, there aren't many ways around it. If the goal is to be a trend trader, the most efficient means to the end is to employ a simple long or short futures contract position and use your seatbelt, because the swings will be stomach churning.

FUNDAMENTAL TRADING

Fundamental commodity trading is a type of position trading that either ignores technical analysis or at least considers it a low-priority factor influencing trading decisions. This method of trading calls for establishing positions in a commodity market when there is some sort of opportunity portrayed in the supply/demand environment for that particular commodity. As discussed in Chapter 3 examining fundamental analysis, traders attempt to estimate a fair market price for a commodity using the stocks to use ratio, or some other appropriate fundamental measure of supply and demand.

> "The market is always wrong. I can assure you of that." —Jim Rogers

As a reminder, in my opinion, trading commodities with a purely fundamental approach is extremely difficult. For starters, the fundamental analysis used to derive a supply and demand model attempting to predict a true commodity value is based on delayed data with questionable accuracy. Further, even access to real-time and highly accurate supply and demand information ignores the fact that market pricing is subject to volatile emotions and the human desire to predict the future. Market prices are forward looking, not backward looking, or even representative of the present.

The most well-known fundamental trader is Jim Rogers, who was mentioned in an earlier discussion regarding fundamental market analysis. He is the author of the infamous book *Hot Commodities*, subtitled "How Anyone Can Invest Profitably in the Word's Best Market." The title itself says a lot about Jim's approach to the commodity markets. The word "invest" is a bit of a stretch when referring to putting money to work in the commodity markets, but in this case I believe it applies. In summary, this book simplifies fundamental commodity trading to a simple buy and hold strategy. If prices are relatively cheap, and supply/demand fundamentals are favorable, go long until you make money.

To be fair, the book was published during the commodity boom of the mid-2000s when such a strategy could have survived. However, the commodity collapse of 2014 and 2015 proved there might be more to it than simply "investing" in commodities and hoping inflation and increased demand from developing nations would pave the road to riches. Even in an environment in which this method of trading works, extremely deep pockets are required to ride out the ebbs and flows. The average retail commodity trader does not have the wherewithal to trade a fundamental approach as suggested by the now-notorious Rogers book.

ADVANTAGES TO FUNDAMENTAL TRADING

Fundamental traders argue that the only true determinant of price is supply and demand. They will tell you that short-term deviations in price that contradict fundamentals is temporary and will eventually succumb to the supply and demand of the commodity in question. This style of trading is one that fundamental analysts find comfort in. After all, it is easier to be bullish in a market if the available data confirms a supportive fundamental picture.

DISADVANTAGES TO FUNDAMENTAL TRADING

Despite the warm and fuzzy feelings that come with a fundamentally sound trade, it takes an incredible amount of patience, trading capital, and emotional stability to make this approach work. An example that comes to mind is the Treasury market throughout most of the late 2000s and early 2010s. On the heels of the Federal Reserve's quantitative easing programs designed to artificially hold interest rates low, Treasury futures speculators were eager to sell bond and note futures under the logic that market fundamentals were changing in a fashion that would cause interest rates to rise and Treasury securities to fall. Years and thousands of blown-up accounts later, traders were still waiting for that fundamental market move that would begin to bring interest rates back toward normalization.

From a fundamental perspective, these traders' actions were sound. Never before have we seen interest rates near zero, and once the government quantitative easing programs that enabled the interest rate anomaly expired, it made sense to assume prices would revert to a more historically congruent environment. However, as of early 2016 it hadn't. Eventually it will, but even if it does, there might not be any bearish fundamental traders left to enjoy the fruits of their labor.

> Fundamental traders must understand and accept that markets can be irrational longer than most can stay solvent.

Another drawback of developing a purely fundamental trading style is that markets are all-knowing and predictive. Savvy traders tend to anticipate changes in the fundamental landscape and behave accordingly. The result is a change in price to reflect the new fundamentals before any fundamental data could possibly confirm the change. On the other hand, this goes both ways; sometimes the market predicts fundamental changes incorrectly, causing an undesirable price movement and substantial losses for fundamental traders. Rational or not, the market is always right.

INSTRUMENTS USED

Fundamental traders can conceivably deploy any number of strategies to capitalize on their analysis. However, the most efficient will be a simple long or short futures contract. This is because fundamental traders, like trend traders, are generally establishing their position for the long haul. They might not view the burden of option expiration as acceptable for their needs. Of course, not all traders have the capital or mental wherewithal to hold a trade established for a fundamental reason long enough to enjoy the benefits of a profitable trade. For less-capitalized fundamental traders, or even for those with moderate- to low-risk tolerance, the use of e-mini futures and e-micro futures could be an optimal choice. We discuss the advantages of these product suites in Chapter 12.

CHAPTER 7: DAY TRADING AND ALGORITHMIC TRADING IN FUTURES

Whether you like them or hate them, day traders and algorithmic system traders, commonly referred to as "algos," are here to stay. Both groups of traders bring additional liquidity to the marketplace, which is a positive. However, some would argue that the baggage they bring with them isn't worth the additional liquidity. It is no secret that highly day traded markets such as the e-mini S&P experience additional volatility throughout the last hour of the trading session as day traders square their positions. In addition, it is difficult to deny that algo traders haven't created a marketplace that sees severely abnormal prices at a relatively higher frequency. Nevertheless, the new challenges posed by aggressive day traders and high-frequency traders via computer algorithms aren't all that different from the obstacles faced by traders during the heyday of open outcry trading; the antagonists are simply wearing a different mask.

DAY TRADING IN FUTURES

During my time as a commodity broker, I've noticed the strategy bringing the most traders to the futures markets is day trading. The appeal of the strategy is the prospect of hypercharged trading profits, but it also comes with low barriers to entry, a lack of overnight position risk and, let's face it, it *is* exciting. Traders generally use the same technical indicators and oscillators for day trading as they would position trading, so if you have a winning strategy, why wait weeks for the outcome? Instead, traders can determine whether they have what it takes to make money within a single trading day.

Most people assume day trading only entails trades that span the traditional opening and closing times of the official e-mini S&P 500 futures day session, which is 8:30 a.m. through 3:15 p.m. Central. But that isn't necessarily true; day trading is the practice of entering and exiting futures positions within a single trading session. In today's nearly 24-hour world of futures trading, a day trade might actually be held overnight. The distinction can be found in when the position was initiated, and whether it was still open at the close of trade. Most of the financial futures markets open in the afternoon prior to the official day session and trade through the end of the day session. As a result, it is possible to hold a day trade nearly 23 hours per day. If a trader is flat at the close of a trading session, anything done during that particular session is considered a day trade.

Of course, there are some things to be aware of. Not all brokerage firms allow their clients to trade overnight; those that do might levy a small fee for holding their position. Further, many brokerages offer day traders discounted margin rates. These margin discounts are frequently only granted during the exchange's official day session (8:30 a.m. Central to 3:15 p.m. Central). On a side note, my brokerage service (DeCarley Trading) is more liberal than most, since we grant day trading margins around the clock. Some brokers go so far as to force liquidate accounts at the close of each day if the client doesn't have enough money to meet the exchange's state initial margin requirement. Not being aware of the rules and characteristics of a brokerage is a mistake capable of destroying an otherwise attractive day trading strategy.

Brokers' efforts to reduce the risk of day traders isn't because they don't want their clients partaking in the strategy. In fact, it is the opposite. Day traders tend to execute a high quantity of trades, which pads the pockets of brokerage firms. After all, the more a client trades, the more commission he pays to the broker. Accordingly, brokerage firms work hard to promote day trading via discounted margin rates and lower commission for the highest-volume day traders. They also encourage automated trading systems, which are inclined to be high-volume trading strategies. Further, risk managers at brokerage firms love the idea of their clients being flat overnight. As you can imagine, this takes much of the stress away from monitoring their client positions throughout the night. Don't forget, futures trade nearly 24 hours per day; you might be resting on the couch or fast asleep, but that doesn't mean the markets are. Global events and sentiment sway asset prices in real time without any regard to what traders in the US might be doing at the time. Likewise, US traders buy and sell futures contracts throughout their day session without thinking twice about the Europeans, who are slumbering.

I've been a commodity broker since early 2004 and have had the privilege of having a front row seat to the game of retail trading. Based on my observations, day trading is one of the most difficult strategies to employ successfully. Yet with difficulty comes potential reward for those capable of managing emotions and willing to put the time in to pay their dues. Traders able to uncover a way to make consistent profits might discover the reward is not only lucrative but also extremely convenient. They have the ability to sleep well at night and literally choose their own trading schedule.

There is an unlimited number of strategies that day traders might opt to apply, so discussing that aspect in a single chapter is unrealistic. Any market approach deliberated in Chapter 6, "Position Trading in Futures," and market analysis techniques debated in Chapter 2 with respect to technical analysis can be applied to a day trading strategy. But over the years I've noticed a few factors that play a big part in determining day trading success and failure. Hopefully, you will walk away from this section with a better understanding of risks, rewards, and reality.

COMMON MISTAKES MADE BY DAY TRADERS

Day traders face modest barriers to entry, but they also face the worst odds for success. However, much of the dismal performance by day traders can be mitigated by avoiding a few common mistakes. Unfortunately, many of the items on this list are easier said than done because, for many, they contradict some of the advantages of day trading luring them into the markets in the first place. Failing to take these steps shifts the odds of success away from the trader and toward his competition, the trading public.

BEING UNDERCAPITALIZED

As a reminder, margin requirements for intraday trading are set by the brokerage firm, not by the exchange. As previously mentioned, because brokers generate revenue based on volume commission, they have incentive to entice traders to participate in day trading strategies with low margin rates. It isn't uncommon for brokerage firms to advertise day trading rates for the stock indices such as the e-mini S&P 500, the e-mini Dow, and even the mini Russell 2000 for as little as $300 on deposit as a good faith deposit. So assuming his broker was granting him a $300 day trading margin, a trader with $3,000 in a futures account could buy or sell 10 stock index futures contracts at a time, as long as his intention is to exit by the close of trade. To green traders, this sounds like a fabulous proposition, but to those with experience it is a clear death sentence to a trading account.

With that said, in the wake of financial crisis volatility, day trading margins have increased. It is still possible to find $500 day trading margin rates for stock indices, but most brokerages have increased it to $1,000 or above. This might appear to be a disadvantage and may frustrate a few traders, but the reality is a far more reasonable amount of leverage. In addition, it is still more than enough leverage to produce large profits and losses in a trading account. To put a $500 day trading margin into perspective, we know each point in the e-mini S&P 500 is worth $50, so with the e-mini S&P valued at 2,000 a single futures contract represents $100,000 (2,000 x $50) worth of the underlying S&P 500. It is easy to see how a trader buying or selling an e-mini S&P contract worth $100,000 with as little as $500 on deposit could get into trouble. If you've done the math, in such a circumstance the trader is putting up a mere 0.5% of the contract value to partake in the profits and losses produced.

This type of leverage doesn't give traders an advantage; it gives them an incredible burden and a dismally low probability of success. Adding salt to the wounds of overleveraged day traders, many discount brokerage firms offering low margins are quick to liquidate client positions should their account equity dip (even slightly) below the stated day trading margin rate. This too adds to the likelihood of failure. A trader with $5,000 in a futures account being granted $500 day trading margins could buy or sell as many as 10 futures contracts to enter a position. However, if the market goes against the trade, even slightly, the brokerage will often liquidate the position. Each firm has slightly different risk rules, but most begin to take action if the trader has less than $400 per contract. Simply put, if the e-mini S&P moves adversely by 2.00 points, the trade might be force liquidated. Even worse, brokers often charge a liquidation fee of $25 to $50 per contract. Anyone who has traded the e-mini S&P before will tell you that 2.00 points are nothing more than random ebb and flow. Without the help of luck, a trader's entry price will have to endure more than a 2.00-point drawdown before moving in the desired direction. Day traders using this much leverage rarely survive the trade long enough to see profits.

> Day trading with high leverage is no different than spinning the roulette wheel in a Las Vegas casino.

To review: a trader starting with $5,000 and going long 10 e-mini S&P futures, as would be allowed by a $500 day trading margin, could see his position offset by the risk managers of his brokerage firm once the loss reached $1,000 ((2.00 x $50) x 10) or 2.00 points in the e-mini S&P. Further, the losses would be exacerbated by a forced-liquidation fee levied by the broker in an amount as high as $500. This trader would have lost 30% of his account in a matter of minutes on nothing more than quiet market flow. It should be clear by now that day trading futures in high quantities relative to account size or on a shoestring budget is equivalent to playing craps in Las Vegas. Traders can increase their odds of success by mitigating leverage through sufficient account funding, or at least trading minimal quantities. As a rule, it is a good idea to trade a single stock index futures contract per $10,000 on deposit in a trading account.

> "Investors operate with limited funds and limited intelligence; they don't need to know everything. As long as they understand something better than others, they have an edge." —George Soros

Aside from the leverage factor, lightly capitalized accounts might not have the means to hold positions overnight when necessary. This does traders a massive injustice because it prevents their trading strategy from adequately giving each entry signal the time necessary to work out. Stock index futures might close at 3:15 p.m. Central, but that doesn't mean your technical setup has had a chance to play itself out. For instance, a trading strategy could conceivably trigger a sell signal an hour before the close, but the restricted time frame might not allow for the anticipated price change to materialize. Thus, it might be crucial to hold positions into the overnight session, or even the next trading day, to give your strategy a fair chance to succeed. Trading sessions might be on timers but markets and technical indicators are not. If a trader is forced out of a trade at the close of the day session, it is possible he is forgoing the success of the trading signal. Most trading strategies struggle to turn profits on 50% of trades; if you are limiting the performance of each signal to the day session, it is possible the win/loss ratio will be greatly reduced.

OVERTRADING

Sometimes, to their own detriment, those drawn to day trading tend to have hyperactive personalities, and this often has a negative impact on their trading results. Rather than exercising patience, many day traders force trades out of boredom, or they rush their trading signals. The best traders are able to develop the discipline necessary to delay entry into the market until their trading strategy returns a verified signal. Further, trading on a whim or a gut feeling in the absence of a true trading signal according to the set parameters is generally a horrible idea. This is because the venture is likely a low-probability prospect to begin with, but because a trade was entered on something less than a detailed strategy, there probably isn't a sound exit strategy either. Further, it is doubtful the trader will be able to keep detrimental emotions under wraps; on balance, if the trade is entered based on emotion not logic, the psychological stress is higher. Poor decision making breeds more poor decision making. If you find yourself in the midst of a string of bad decisions, it doesn't mean you are an inept trader. It simply means you are human; even the most experienced traders will have cold spells. What differentiates the successful from the unsuccessful is the reaction to hard times in the market.

Traders who are overactive and trade without justification from a defined set of rules not only face potential peril from market losses, but they end up with a hefty commission bill that eats away at their trading account. I often find myself in conversations with traders who assume if they enter a position, and the market fails to move in the desired direction right away, they will just get out. Similarly, beginning day traders frequently express their desire to cut their losses by exiting a trade if it goes against them by a few ticks. Although the desire for risk management is admirable, the result is relatively predictable. This type of trading activity might not create large losses on each individual trade, but over time the transaction costs and small losses produced by the strategy can be substantial. Day traders using overly tight leashes to manage the risk of their trades will soon find small losses eventually leading to a big loss because the market will rarely move in the desired direction without some sort of adverse price move. A day trader cutting losses on a trade after a few contrary ticks faces a very low probability of catching a move in the desired direction. Brokerage firms love this type of trader. Not only do they pose little risk to the firm, they often pay a substantial amount of their account toward transaction costs.

To prevent overtrading, most traders must adjust the way they think about the market and the day trading opportunities it presents. Green traders look at being flat the market (being without a position) as a missed opportunity. But traders should see it in the opposite light. Those on the sidelines are not losing money, nor are they *at risk* of losing money. In addition, they are in a much better position to take advantage of a promising opportunity should it come along.

Traders often grow bored with a quiet market and execute a small trade to lessen the pain of watching paint dry. The problem with this is that quiet markets have a tendency to become abruptly volatile without any advance notice. Perhaps there is a new announcement or simply a large group of stop orders triggered to force prices outside of the narrow band of trading. In any case, a sudden change in volatility can be a painful lesson but also pose significant opportunities for those on the sidelines.

USING STOP ORDERS

Listing stop-loss orders as a common mistake that day traders make probably has readers' minds reeling. The majority of trading books, courses, and forums teach traders to always use stop orders. In fact, if you've ever trolled any of the popular social media trading groups, you've probably noticed a daily meme regarding the perils of not placing stop-loss orders. When dealing with leveraged futures contracts and theoretically open-ended risk, you may find it preferable to protect a trading account from catastrophic losses. However, stop-loss orders might not be the best way to accomplish this task.

In fact, in my opinion, the use of stops often increases the odds of trading failure. Anybody who has experienced their stop order being filled just before the market reverses understands the emotional turmoil it can cause, not to mention the financial ding to a trading account. Not only was that particular trade a failure but it can have a negative effect on trader psychology going forward, so it could affect future trades as well.

The assumption regarding premature stop-loss triggers is that "someone" could see the traders' stop order and went for it. The truth is, unless a trader is executing hundreds of contracts at a time, there wouldn't be any incentive for a trader with pockets deep enough to be capable of taking advantage of a temporary stop running price spike to pay attention to the order, let alone take action.

Most retail traders aren't swinging enough size to get onto the radars of the "big fish" in the market. Thus, if a stop order is filled just before the market reverses to a favorable direction, the trader isn't a victim; he simply placed the stop-loss order at an inopportune place. Unfortunately, this occurs frequently. Ironically, the very order intended to protect traders from large losses can easily become the *source* of the large losses. In the end, several highly certain small losses will eventually add up to crippling amounts. We will debate the use of stop-loss orders and offer alternative risk management techniques further in Chapter 16.

POSITION SIZING

Once again, futures brokerage firms offer "cheap and easy" leverage. Unfortunately, novice traders often assume $500 day trading margin for the e-mini S&P is a reasonable amount of leverage. In my opinion, utilizing the maximum leverage offered is a horrible idea, inevitably leading to massive losses. Traders are far better off trading with less leverage than is available to them. Yet, I would venture to say that most day traders execute quantities in excess of what is ideal based on available trading capital.

> When it comes to position sizing, less is usually more.

Brokerage firms are partly to blame for overleveraged futures day traders, but in the end, it is the trader's choice whether to use it. It is easy for traders to get sucked into the mindset that the more contracts traded, the more money made. They rationalize, "If the trade setup is a good one, and the belief is the market will move in the desired direction, why not trade as many contracts as possible?" Regardless of the strategy, the trader never knows which ventures will be winners and which will be losers until after the fact. Even the best trade setups can go awry. Actually, sometimes trades that look the best on paper are the trades that fail to work. On the other hand, trades that comply with the signals but not the trader's "gut feeling" often work out the best. Accordingly, a strategy of loading up on risk on any particular trade is a poor one. The more contracts traded in a single outing exponentially reduces much needed room for error. In this game, it is important to have some breathing room; no trading method is perfect.

In addition to the mathematical disadvantage of lower-success probabilities at the hands of being overleveraged, trading a high number of contracts adds to the emotional turmoil a trader will experience. The avoidance of aggressive position sizing is key to keeping harmful emotions in check such as fear and greed. If you are holding 20 contracts in a $10,000 account it would take a mere ten-point move in the e-mini S&P to blow out your trading account. Further, it would only take a five-point move to lose 50%. If you've followed the e-mini S&P intraday, you know that it can move five points in the blink of an eye. One might argue trading such size leaves the door open to double an account on a single trade. This is true, but the odds are highly against it. Even the most sophisticated and experienced traders require room for error in their trading.

How many contracts you trade at a time should be based on personal risk tolerance and available capital. However, I recommend traders initiate a position with a one-lot of a mini stock index futures contract per $10,000, or most other commodities (gold, crude oil, the grains, currencies). Of course, you can easily day trade ten or more times this amount with the given account size, but just because you can doesn't mean you should.

Sound boring? Look at it this way: an average profit of $50 per day equates to $1,000 per month and $12,000 per year. Assuming you were skilled enough to do this and started with a $10,000 account, you would have more than doubled your money in a year. It doesn't take 10 lots of any commodity futures contract to make $50 per day, but trading 10 lots dramatically increases your odds of depleting an account. To illustrate, a trader going long 10 e-mini S&P 500 futures stands to lose 10% of his trading capital for each point the contract goes against him. In a market that generally sees 10.00- to 15.00-point ranges on any given day, it would be relatively easy to cause detrimental harm to a trading account by executing too many contracts.

FAILURE TO AVERAGE PRICE

Most people will tell you not to add to your losers. Nevertheless, for those with well-capitalized accounts, I believe adding to a position as a means of adjusting your breakeven point makes sense because it increases the odds of obtaining a better average entry price.

Traders who follow the previous guideline of keeping position sizing reasonable to avoid the stress and risk that comes with overleveraging have the ability to price average. Price averaging for day traders is similar to the act of scale trading for a position trader. The premise is to nibble on futures contracts incrementally rather than buying or selling the entire desired position in a single transaction. If the plan is to go long crude oil with as many as five futures contracts, a day trader might start with a single contract and enter limit orders to buy the other four contracts at lower prices, perhaps 20 to 40 cents lower. In some scenarios, doing so will prevent the trader from getting all of the contracts filled, but it will also avoid being filled on all five in a declining market at what later turns out to have been an inopportune entry price. Once the trade is deeply underwater, emotions flare, leading to ill-advised trading decisions. Averaging the entry price will almost always lead to a more achievable breakeven point, and thus, less stress.

> "Maybe when it gets so bad that you want to puke, you probably should double your position." —Martin Schwartz

Yet the practice of price averaging is something you should treat with care. It doesn't mean you should buy another crude oil futures contract each 20 cents it drops against you without any other considerations. However, if the price of oil falls substantially beneath your initial entry, perhaps that is something to consider. Naturally, it would be wise to peel contracts off at various prices should the market turn in your favor. If you scale into a trade, it is often best to scale out of it, too.

DAY TRADING TIME FRAMES

Day trading is a broad term that can be used to describe a nearly unlimited number of strategies. It is conceivable that the most important decision a day trader makes when developing a trading plan is which time frame to use to chart the futures market—will the technical rules be applied to a chart using one-minute price bars, 60-minute price bars, or something in between? There are even some day trading platforms and charting software packages that offer traders the ability to chart futures contracts using line charts produced by plotting data points for each and every trade executed on the exchange independent of time. Others have the ability to chart price intraday using 90-minute price bars; a 90-minute chart would produce a price bar each hour and a half. Each of these examples rely on extremes, but most traders work with something in the 10- to 30-minute range. With that said, I prefer to look at a 60-minute chart. In my opinion, a 60-minute futures chart provides day traders with a "bigger picture" view of price action, which can help prevent being lured into the market on noise, rather than a valid trading signal.

The exact time frame a trader chooses should reflect his personality and risk tolerance. The shorter the time frame used, the more active the strategy will be and the higher the frequency of false signals. Conversely, longer time frames tend to experience less activity, fewer false signals, and less deceptive price moves. Yet, most technical trading strategies applied to charts with longer price bars will come with higher risks relative to a shorter bar. This is because those playing with stop-loss orders will be required to place stops deeper when using a 60-minute chart than they might with a 10-minute chart. Accordingly, there is a tendency for traders utilizing 10-minute price bars to trade larger quantities than those using 60-minute price bars. This is because the profit and loss potential per trade is generally smaller using a 10-minute trading trigger. In my opinion, day traders are better served trading less; consequently, using 60-minute bars help to tame the trader.

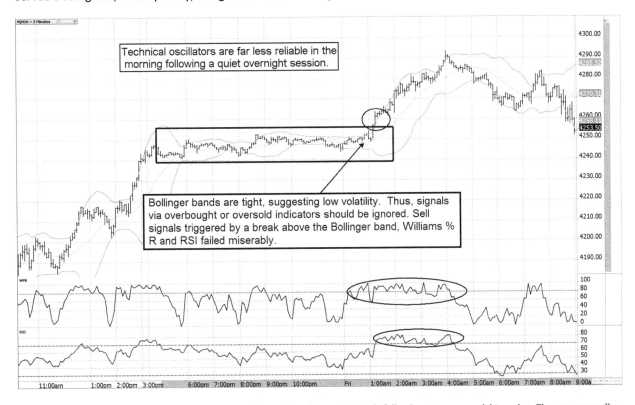

Figure 42: Beware of signals produced by technical oscillators in early morning trade following a tame overnight session. They are generally unreliable.

Most assume all technical indicators will work similarly among various time frames and during all times of the trading day, but that isn't the case. Technical oscillators are least reliable in the early morning hours (Figure 42); this is because they are being calculated based on what is often tight range trading in the overnight session. As a result, it is common to see indicators created to identify overbought and oversold market conditions produce false countertrend trading signals. Even worse, during this time of day, the indicator can easily reach highly saturated levels, giving traders a false sense of reliability.

Oscillator inaccuracy doesn't have to be early in the morning; it can happen at any time. It is far more common when using short time frames. This is because the price data used to calculate each five- or 10-minute price bar isn't necessarily a representative sample of the overall trend. Some traders think such charts will provide information that the 30- or 60-minute chart won't display for quite some time, but the overactive nature of short time frames encourages overtrading, breeds stress, and often massive losses.

The use of a five-minute chart, relative to a 60-minute chart, will undoubtedly result in a higher number of day trading signals (Figure 43). However, the goal of any trading strategy should be to locate and execute quality trades; focusing on quantity is a common misstep. Because shorter time frames disguise market noise as something significant, traders will likely fall victim to a large number of false signals. Even if the trader manages to keep losses on these high-frequency trades in check, excessive trading volume can quickly result in an expensive commission bill regardless of how low the trader has managed to negotiate his trading fees. The bottom line is, the trader's behavior plays a much bigger part in controlling transaction costs than the actual commission rate paid to his broker. We will discuss the reality of commission in Chapter 15, "Understanding the Implications of Trading Cost Decisions."

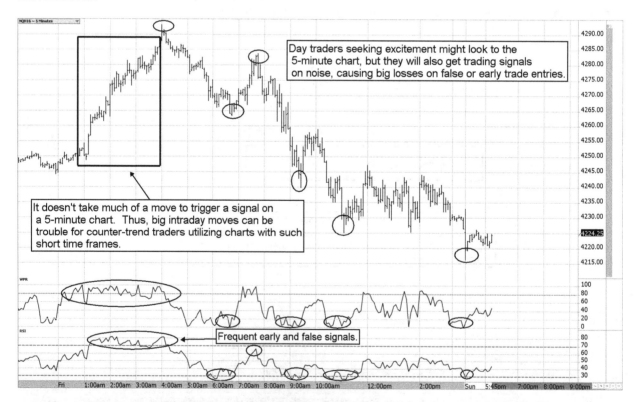

Figure 43: A five-minute chart offers day traders a higher number of trading opportunities, but the quality of the signals produced suffer relative to a longer time frame chart, such as the 30- or 60-minute.

Using charts based on short time frames, such as the five-minute chart, requires traders to place tighter stop-losses and therefore increases the odds of being stopped out of the trade prematurely. Nevertheless, because five-minute charts are so quick to generate signals, it is paramount that the trader keeps risk in check. This is because in low-volatility markets, the five-minute chart might generate a buy signal for countertrend swing traders with a mere 3.00-point decline in the e-mini S&P. However, we all know the S&P 500 is capable of moving 15 to 20 points in a minute or two. Thus, reacting to a shallow dip because the five-minute chart calls for it could put the trader into a massive losing position should he be in the wrong place at the wrong time. On the other hand, a swing trader acting on signals produced by a 60-minute chart might not receive a countertrend trading signal unless the S&P drops 15 to 20 points. Such a trader is still facing substantial risk, but on most days the S&P doesn't fall more than that. Accordingly, the odds of getting stuck with a massive loser can be mitigated.

STOP-LOSS ORDERS OR WEEKLY OPTIONS?

In Chapter 16, on deliberating risk management, we will debate the use of stop-loss orders and long options to protect futures positions from losses. It is worth mentioning in a discussion of day trading because the difference between success and failure is largely dependent on where, and how, stop-losses are used or not used.

Despite widespread chatter suggesting that one should never trade without stops, it might be the sole reason most traders lose money. Whether traders place stops too tight or too loose, stop-loss orders elected prior to favorable market movement is a common occurrence that can devastate trading accounts as well as trader psychology. Nothing hurts more than losing money on a trade despite being right about the market direction.

Day traders operating on the premise of quality over quantity by utilizing 60-minute charts, or perhaps even 30-minute charts, are generally aiming at higher profit targets than someone initiating positions based on five- or 10-minute charts. As a result, it might be worth their while to skip the practice of using stop orders and instead purchase cheap protection via weekly e-mini S&P options or e-mini NASDAQ options. If you are unfamiliar with weekly options, they are those listed by the futures exchange that expire on a weekly basis rather than a monthly basis, which has traditionally been the norm.

There are also weekly options on some commodities such as the grains and crude oil, but most day traders are applying their efforts to the stock indices due to favorable liquidity. Those trading markets that don't offer weekly options might look to the traditional monthly options if they happen to be expiring soon (two weeks or less). If it is possible to get a reasonably close-to-the-money weekly expiring call option in the e-mini S&P for less than $500, it might be worth the cash outlay to protect a short futures position for the day while protecting the trade from losses without the risk of premature stopout.

This approach might not make sense for those traders utilizing extremely short time frames with small profit targets. Obviously, if a trading signal provided by the five-minute chart calls for a long position with a profit objective of three points, it doesn't make sense to spend five or six points to protect it. Again, we will tackle this issue in more detail later on, but I wanted to introduce the idea here because it is relatively unconventional, despite being potentially helpful to a day trading strategy.

Believe it or not, in many instances and environments and when using options for protection isn't feasible, I believe not using a stop order at all is preferable. Stop-loss orders have the ability to cause more harm than good to countless traders.

SCALPING FUTURES CONTRACTS

Futures exchanges love scalpers. Their high-volume, high-frequency strategies result in massive exchange fees paid by the trader.

Those who scalp futures contracts are seeking to profit from small market moves that seem inconsequential to most trading strategies. Scalpers believe because a market never sits still, they can profit from the ebb and flow that occurs as each market participant buys or sells a futures contract. In many cases, scalpers are targeting a mere tick or two in price movement. This is equivalent to different dollar values in each commodity market but is generally somewhere around $10. A scalp that nets one tick would provide a $10 profit to the trader before considering transaction costs, while a two-tick winner would generate $20 in gain. However, unlike position traders or even day traders using longer time horizons, who find transaction costs to have little impact on their bottom line, a scalper could easily pay 30% to 50% of his profits to transaction costs. Suddenly, the $10 per tick in profit per contract is cut in half.

Because of the relatively low-profit potential per trade, scalpers are playing a volume game. They are rarely trading one or two contracts at a time. In order to make a scalping strategy worthwhile, it is necessary to trade high quantities of contracts in a clip. As you can imagine, this strategy is a dream come true for those benefiting from the trading costs of a scalping account.

Contrary to what most would believe, the futures exchange itself reaps most of the rewards from the transaction costs paid by scalpers because exchange fees are constant regardless of how much commission is paid to the broker. Yet the broker often accepts a scalping account at a discounted commission rate to help better the client's odds of making money. As a result, the broker often makes pennies per trade; even the most active scalpers don't pad the pockets of his broker as much as he thinks he is. Instead, he is probably paying anywhere from $2 to $4 per trade to the exchange. So if you are a scalper and the CME reports better than expected earnings, you should know you played a part in that.

Most scalping strategies involve attempting to buy the ask and sell the bid in any particular futures market. This goes against the norm. A trader placing an order to buy a futures contract at market price would receive a fill at the current ask price, if he placed an order to sell a futures contract at the market he would receive a fill at the current bid price. As covered in Chapter 1, the difference between these two prices is known as the bid/ask spread, and it is accepted as a normal cost of doing business in the commodity markets.

Scalp traders must recognize the relatively hidden transaction cost of trading built into the bid/ask spread. A trader entering a futures contract at the market price is immediately sustaining a paper loss in the amount of the spread and the transaction costs. For simplicity's sake, let's assume a scalper is paying a total of $5 per round turn for commission and

"There is only one side of the market and it is not the bull side or the bear side, but the right side." —Jesse Livermore

exchange fees, most of which goes directly to the exchange. By going long a crude oil futures contract, the trader is incurring a $5 transaction cost plus the spread between the bid and ask, which is generally a tick, or $10 in crude oil. Thus, upon entry, the trader is in the hole by one and a half ticks ($15). To turn a net profit of a measly $5, the scalper must pick up two ticks in crude oil.

This is easier said than done. To further illustrate, to make $50 the trader would need to execute 10 contracts and offset the scalp at a one-tick profit in addition to overcoming the one-tick hidden cost of the bid/ask spread. On the other hand, if the trader loses two ticks in the market, the total loss on 10 contracts is a quick and painful $250

(($20 + $5) x 10)! From a purely mathematical standpoint, it is difficult to justify a scalping strategy. Yet some traders with quick fingers or computer programming prowess swear by it.

A scalper thinks he can find a way to collect the bid/ask spread rather than pay it, as all other market participants do. To do this, he might place a limit order to sell a contract at the ask and buy at the bid to profit from market ebb and flow. Predicting the ability to do so often stems from judging the working limit orders of other market participants via a depth of market (DOM) panel. If you are unfamiliar with a DOM panel, it is a price ladder displayed within most futures trading platforms offering its users a glimpse into the currently working limit orders in a particular market. For instance, it will display the best 10 bids (working buy limit orders) and the best 10 asks (working sell limit orders). Accordingly, traders can see which prices within immediate reach of the market might have the most buying or selling interest. An often-overlooked drawback of DOM panels is they don't display stop orders placed by market participants, and they don't account for market orders. This makes sense, because a market order is filled immediately. Nonetheless, market orders are done by the most motivated buyers and sellers and often have the biggest impact on price.

In general, if there are more sell limit orders working than buy limit orders, the scalper assumes he will be able to buy the bid as those seller orders are filled and prices are temporarily depressed. Likewise, if a trader spots a market with more buy limit orders immediately under the market, he might believe he can sell the ask as those orders are filled and prices are temporarily boosted.

Some scalpers take the opposite approach. They believe if the DOM panel is displaying more sellers than buyers, they will be able to sell a contract and buy it back a tick or two later after the sell orders are filled and prices have fallen accordingly. Similarly, if the DOM panel suggests more buyers at prices near or a tick below the market price, a scalper might go long in hopes the filled orders will cause prices to tick higher.

Once again, you can see there is more than one way of looking at market conditions and signals, and there are even more strategies attempting to exploit them. One again, there isn't a proper or improper way to trade. The only judge is the bottom line of a trading account statement. It is also worth noting that, although these two approaches to scalping involve a vastly different thought process, both methods could work. We cannot deny that even in directionless markets, prices tick up and down as time goes on. This is all scalpers need to potentially profit. Scalping is a much more refined skill than it appears to be on the surface.

Due to extremely high transaction costs and relatively aggressive position sizing, scalpers can make or lose a substantial amount of money quickly. If your preference is to employ a conservative trading strategy, look elsewhere. Despite low monetary risk per contract for most scalping strategies, the price action in such a narrow time frame is largely random, and high transaction costs are a difficult burden to overcome. In addition, the practice of scalping in the traditional sense requires more nimble fingers than the average trader likely has. In today's world of super computers, most scalping strategies have been developed into automated, or algorithmic, trading systems.

ALGORITHMIC TRADING SYSTEMS

Often referred to as algorithmic trading systems, or "algos," an automated futures trading system is a defined set of technical rules

"You must automate, emigrate, or evaporate." —James A. Baker, GE

and parameters that ultimately determine entry and exit points for a given contract. In the event that all of the stipulated technical events occur, a buy or sell signal is created and a trade is automatically executed without human intervention. Simply, it is trading on autopilot.

The media generally portrays the algorithmic trading community as being flush in profits at the expense of the average retail trader. I'm not convinced this is the case; for every good trading system out there, there are more bad ones. I view the advantages some electronic trading systems enjoy as being akin to the edge those trading in the open outcry pits used to enjoy prior to their closure.

Floor traders in the commodity pits provided liquidity for orders coming in from traders from all over the world. As compensation for the liquidity they provided, they were able to pocket the bid/ask spread. Thus, pit traders could buy a contract and immediately sell it, or vice versa, for a small profit in normal market conditions. In doing so, they accepted the risk of the market quickly moving away from them, or not being able to offset their trade in a timely manner. During times of high volatility or at a time in which they opt to accept the risk of holding the position, they stood to make or lose more money than some people make in a year...or longer.

Those who were good at making markets and reading the emotions of other pit traders made an unbelievably good living, but there are far more stories of pit traders who lost it all. In some regretfully surprising frequency, some failed pit traders committed suicide under the pressure. I can almost guarantee you, there are some algo traders out there having the same dismal experience. It isn't all peaches and cream. If you are interested in learning more about this dynamic, particularly the stories of success and failure, I recommend you watch the movie *Floored*, directed by James Allen Smith.

WHAT IS AN AUTOMATED TRADING SYSTEM?

Although purely technical trading methods have been in existence for decades, the trading technology boom of the late 2000s has brought algorithmic system trading to the masses. Prior to this development, technical trading systems were executed manually by humans. In my early days as a commodity broker, it was fairly commonplace for a client to purchase trading signals from a third-party service and instruct their full-service broker to execute the trades on his behalf. At the time, signals could even have been transmitted by fax, since they weren't necessarily electronic communications. As time went on, most system vendors began issuing their technical trading signals via electronic means, but it was still necessary for a broker to intercept the signal and manually place the trade. Or it was possible for clients to receive and execute signals without the help of a broker, but in a less-convenient day and age, it was a significant burden. These days, traders enjoy the simplicity of subscribing to an automated trading strategy or even creating their own via computer programming languages, and letting the computer execute the generated trading signals without human intervention. Obviously, this makes for a much more efficient and timely process.

The terms "trading system" and "algo trading" can have various and very different meanings. They all involve the use of specific technical ingredients and circumstances that come together to generate entry and exit signals in a particular futures market. The vast majority of automated trading systems operate in the

> Trading is like the game of golf. The harder you try, the worse you get.

realm of futures trading; it would be rare for such an approach to be applied to options trading. Further, although algorithmic trading systems can be used by either day traders or position traders, they are generally used as day trading strategies.

Algos most commonly involve moving averages, stochastics, and other computer-generated oscillators. Along with technical indicators, many of "the computers," as they call them, are trained to scour the news headlines for keywords that are then incorporated into the buy or sell triggers.

The ultimate results of an automated trading system are highly dependent on how well the algorithmic rules perform in various market conditions. System developers spend an extensive length of time optimizing the system to manage risk and increase the odds of profitable results in any environment. But market conditions are always changing, so finding a system that works in yesterday's markets according to backtesting doesn't guarantee it will work in today's markets. As is the case with any trading venture, there are never any guarantees, and past performance is not indicative of results.

WHY USE AN AUTOMATED TRADING SYSTEM?

Automated trading systems aren't perfect, but nothing in trading is. Nevertheless, for those traders with emotional personalities or are short on time, a hands-off approach is ideal.

Eliminate emotion. Most unsuccessful traders are the victims of fear and greed. Their negative results don't necessarily have anything to do with the trading strategy itself. An automatic trading system reduces the impact of human emotion and, therefore, eliminates human nature from the equation. A trading system will execute all trading triggers and exit all trades based on the preset parameters; there is no risk of holding on to losers beyond the system threshold, taking premature profits, panicked exit, or overzealous entry. Instead, the strategy is traded exactly as intended.

Save time. System traders can comfortably carry on a normal life (have a day job and/or the freedom to step away from the computer during market hours). Trading rules are predetermined and execution is automatic, whether or not you are watching. Of course, this in no way insinuates system trading strategies are easy money; there are few automated strategies that can stand the test of time. Nevertheless, most algos experience cycles of feast and famine.

Convenience. Let the computer do the work for you. Once a particular system is created, or subscribed to, and implemented, the trading account is on autopilot. The only obligation is to keep an eye on the statements at the end of each day to ensure satisfaction with the results. Remember, the purpose of automated trading is to let the strategy run as intended. Interfering with the strategy by skipping trades, or exiting early, will almost certainly hinder the performance. If the system was sufficiently backtested, and you are comfortable with the parameters, human intervention is counterproductive.

Like markets, systems can be "traded." Speculators can actively trade a futures system performance by implementing and ceasing trading of the system based on the peaks and valleys of returns. For example, it may be an opportune time to begin trading a system that is experiencing a drawdown, or call it quits after a good run. This is because market conditions often fluctuate in cycles in which the performance of technical futures trading systems will also fluctuate. Unfortunately, many system seekers have a tendency to chase performance, but the hot system in the current market environment rarely stands up to changes in market conditions. If the markets move from trending to a narrow sideways channel, certain systems will benefit and others will suffer. We've yet to find a system that works in all conditions—most likely because it doesn't exist.

DRAWBACKS OF USING AUTOMATED TRADING

Although automated system trading puts a futures account on autopilot, it doesn't necessarily translate into automated profits; nor does it guarantee stress-free trading. Some traders will discover that automated trading creates more stress and anxiety than being in the driver's seat would.

- **Automatic trading systems lack common sense.** Because algorithmic systems are driven by technical analysis rather than human discretion, they will habitually generate signals that could be considered low-probability trades. A system may generate a sell signal in a market that is at an all-time low or a buy signal at, or near, a contract high. The trend is your friend but when it ends, it can be a trader's worst enemy.

- **Benefits of backtesting are limited.** Systems are often developed through a process known as "backtesting." However, backtesting just gives you information on what the system would have done if implemented in the past. It isn't reasonable to infer that the same results will be obtained in real time or at any point in the future. Unfortunately, the decision to employ most systems is based on hypothetical backtested results. As a result, sometimes even the best-performing systems in backtests can get off to a shockingly rocky start.

- **Markets are dynamic, not static.** Similar to the flaws of backtesting, system performance at any given point may or may not reflect its ability to operate profitably throughout time. This is because market conditions are dynamic but system parameters are typically constant. While system developers can tweak the parameters in order to enhance performance, considerable losses may be sustained prior to recognition of a need to adjust parameters.

- **Automated trades might be contrary to your opinion.** System trading eliminates the emotions involved in entering or exiting a market, but it can be challenging to watch the system execute a long trade in a market in which you are personally bearish, or a short trade in a market in which you are bullish. Thus, for some traders, system trading might lead to the sleepless nights this market approach was employed to avoid.

DO AUTOMATIC FUTURES TRADING SYSTEMS WORK?

Let's face it. If making money in the markets was as easy as quitting your day job and buying or leasing a trading system, then everyone would do it. Unfortunately, it is far more complicated than that. There are a seemingly unlimited number of futures trading systems and enough software sales representatives willing to do whatever it takes to convince you their product is capable of consistent returns in all types of

> If the advertised profits of an automated trading system are too good to be true, they are. Don't waste money and heartache chasing a pipe dream.

market scenarios. However, we have yet to find such a holy grail of trading. As you can imagine, if a system developer managed to discover the magic formula to relatively low-risk and low-stress profitable trading, he would probably keep the secret to himself. There is far more money to be made in the markets than there is in software sales. Besides, take it from me—making sales calls is a horrible existence.

Beware of trading systems that promise spectacular returns. When it comes to futures system trading, if it sounds too good to be true, it most likely is. Many of the system creators and sellers aren't required to register with the National Futures Association (NFA), and as a result, they enjoy freedom of speech without accountability. Not all system vendors abuse the privilege, but some do, and you owe it to yourself to get the facts before putting your money on the line. As a consumer, you must know who you are dealing with and what is realistic in terms of performance.

With that said, there are legitimate systems that have proven to be productive over time and in the right conditions. Many hedge funds and institutional commodity traders have adopted system trading as their primary method of speculation, so they can be useful in the right circumstances.

For those with relatively savvy computer skills and market knowledge, there are many opportunities to develop and implement an automated trading system. Futures trading platforms are far more advanced than they were a decade ago; no longer is the practice of automation reserved for the wealthy or highly experienced computer coders. Most platforms offer the ability to create and backtest systems to be applied to an account of any size, or by traders with only minimal programming knowledge. Nevertheless, as a relatively tech-savvy Generation X-er, the task is probably out of reach for now—but software is becoming more and more intuitive as time goes on.

HIGH-FREQUENCY TRADING

Not many aspects of the futures markets have garnered quite as much attention in recent years as algorithmic trading, in some forms referred to as *high-frequency trading* (HFT). HFTs are a type of algorithmic system trading characterized by lightning-fast speeds, quick entry and exit, high quantities, and in some cases high cancellation rates of orders.

> "I was afraid of it [the Internet]…because I couldn't type." — Jack Welch

In early 2014, a book written by Michael Lewis titled *Flash Boys* took the industry by storm. The best-selling book alleges the world of HFT is rigged in favor of the middle men. Soon after the book's release, our brokerage received several inquiries as to the impact these HFTs have on their futures accounts. The truth is, this book describes the practices of HFTs in equities, not futures. There is a *big* difference. For starters, all futures contracts are traded on a centralized exchange; this is far different from stocks in which traders might be buying or selling securities from their own brokerage firms' inventory or via various exchanges around the country. In futures, all trading takes place in a single market with high levels of transparency. Many of the allegations of HFTs scalping the orders of retail traders to skim profits out of the market doesn't necessarily apply to the commodity markets. In April 2014, the Commodity Futures Trading Commission (CFTC) responded to Lewis's book. Mark P. Wetjen told reporters, "I don't have the impression at the moment that futures markets are rigged."

Nevertheless, HFT trading exists in the futures markets; it is simply in a different capacity from that outlined in *Flash Boys*. A significant portion of futures trading volume on a daily basis is at the hands of HFT traders, some small but mostly big and well financed. It has been argued that due to close proximity to the Chicago Mercantile Exchange's computer server, HFTs have managed to find a way to receive data milliseconds before most market participants. To human traders, this is inconsequential, but to computers this is enough of an edge to take action ahead of the herd, said to be a potentially lucrative practice when performed in high quantities. Proponents argue these computerized trading systems are adding liquidity to the market, but the opposition says that it puts the average retail trader at a disadvantage. Those who have been in the commodity business for any length of time will tell you that before HFTs, or other forms of algorithmic trading, the disadvantage placed on retail traders was at the hands of floor brokers. Although we've seen the advantage move from floor brokers to HFTs, the average retail trader probably isn't any better or worse off.

Be that as it may, I believe that price action has changed since HFTs were introduced to the futures markets. Because HFTs process massive amounts of technical and fundamental data and combine that with a strategy of reading the tape, not much human nature is built into the system. As a result, market prices seem to be more likely to reach abnormally extreme intraday levels. Prices are expected to go farther and faster than they would have gone if human traders were manning the wheel.

In extreme cases, the result can be catastrophic. It is believed that the May 2010 flash crash in the e-mini S&P was exaggerated by HFT activity. The HFTs were programmed to detect weakness in the market bid, so when the buyers simply stepped away from their trading terminals, it created a vacuum in which the "computers" were selling heavily into a market with few buyers to take the other side of the sell orders. The result was an unfathomable price decline in a matter of minutes. Again, in August 2015 the e-mini S&P experienced a slightly less dramatic flash crash, which spanned over a handful of trading sessions; in less than three days, the e-mini S&P 500 fell nearly 270 points, or about 13%.

HFTs probably haven't ruined the game for speculators; they've just changed it. Floor traders are no longer skimming dollars from the market; now it is the HFTs doing so. If regulators shut down HFTs, either market liquidity would dry up or the advantage would be shifted to some other party. The biggest issue I have with HFT trading in the futures market is the practice of "spoofing," creating the illusion of a particular market sentiment to bait other traders into reacting. In its simplest form, a "spoofer" might enter a very large order to sell a commodity, making it appear as though there is unusually large bearish interest, but the spoofer cancels the order before it is filled. The intention of placing the trade isn't to sell the market at all; the goal is to entice other traders to sell contracts to force the price down, enabling the spoofing trading to purchase those contracts at lower levels. Naturally, a spoofer could also enter large orders to buy a commodity to trick other traders into buying contracts to bid the price of the commodity higher. Once the price ticks up, the spoofer will sell futures at a higher price than would have otherwise been possible had he not created artificial buying interest. This is an obvious deception in the marketplace and is not tolerated by futures exchanges or regulators.

Although it took some time for market regulators to catch on to the practice, spoofing is now considered a serious offense. Under the 2010 Dodd–Frank Act, spoofing is defined as the "illegal practice of bidding or offering with intent to cancel before execution." The best-known case of spoofing was carried out by Navinder Singh Sarao. I mentioned the case of Sarao in Chapter 5. Massively discounted day trading margins, healthy trading capital, and keen sense of market behavior netted him millions in the markets and also landed him in a UK prison, awaiting extradition to the US to face charges (estimated to be in late 2016).

CHAPTER 8: FUTURES SPREAD TRADING

Futures spread trading is the strategy of taking opposite positions in related futures contracts that are believed to be offsetting, or counteract one another. Specifically, a spread is defined as the purchase of one or more futures contracts and the sale of one or more antagonistic futures contracts. This definition intentionally leaves the door open for a nearly unlimited combination of spreads because the practice involves a plethora of strategies with various levels of aggression and complication.

In their simplest form, futures spreads are meant to provide traders with hedged speculative ventures into the futures markets. By nature of a spread, one leg of the trade will generally make money as the other loses. In most scenarios, essentially, spread trading involves taking a primary position in one contract and a secondary position in another contract that should counteract negative movement in the primary position.

Further complicating the practice of spread trading, the trader experiences profits and losses as the difference in the value between the two contracts changes. This concept goes against human nature because it doesn't necessarily involve being bullish or bearish in a particular market. Instead, a spread trader is only speculating on the difference in price from one contract to the other; more specifically, they are looking for the spread between two futures contracts to either narrow or widen, but in most cases, the overall direction of the underlying commodity is somewhat irrelevant.

Futures spread traders can utilize fundamental, technical, or seasonal analysis to identify trading opportunities, but spread trading is one market approach that likely involves more fundamental and seasonal analysis than technical analysis.

There are two primary forms of futures spreads—intercommodity and intracommodity. It is easy to get hung up on the difference between *intra-* and *inter-* commodity spreads, but the distinction is relatively simple. The prefix *intra* denotes that the spread is within the same commodity; conversely, the prefix *inter* is used to identify spreads between related, but different, commodities.

INTRACOMMODITY SPREADS

Intracommodity spreads, often referred to as *calendar spreads*, are the most common form of futures spreads. An intracommodity spread is one that involves the purchase of a futures market in a given delivery month, and the simultaneous sale of a contract in the same futures market but a different delivery month. Agricultural commodities are generally the most common products that intracommodity spread traders target. This is because of the differences in fundamentals from one production year to the next. For instance, an intracommodity spread trader might go long March 2016 corn and sell December 2017 corn because he believes there is a fundamental difference between these two delivery months that will result in the old crop (March contract) outperforming the new crop (December), or he is simply bullish corn prices overall and knows that the contract with the nearest expiration date tends to lead those contracts with distant expiration dates.

Intracommodity futures spreads are great in that they generally come with lower margin requirements and reduced risk relative to merely purchasing a futures contract outright. Nevertheless, it can sometimes be very difficult to make money in such spreads. This is particularly true in the slower-moving markets such as corn and soybean oil. Even during times of impressive market moves, the spread between two specific contracts might not be as lucrative as the trader had hoped for. Further, spreads can hover near breakeven for months before making a sudden and violent move (Figure 44). For those on the wrong side of the trade, the results can quickly become devastating.

Figure 44: Don't let your guard down when trading spreads; they can be extremely volatile. In this example, a spread trader might have gone several months without making or losing more than $600 on the spread, only to suddenly be in a position to make or lose a few thousand in short order.

BULL VS. BEAR INTRACOMMODITY SPREADS

An important concept to be aware of when implementing an intracommodity spread strategy is the different characteristics of ags vs. financials. Specifically, traders treat agricultural and financial markets differently in regard to creating a spread with a bullish or bearish tilt. When dealing with agricultural commodities such as corn, soybeans, or livestock, it is assumed the contract expiring sooner will experience more volatility than the back months. Therefore, the trader's primary position should be in the front month in such contracts; the antagonistic position in the back-month contract is simply a hedge against being wrong. A trader bullish soybeans might purchase a contract expiring in July and sell a contract expiring in November, for example. If he is right about soybeans moving higher, the July contract should generally rally more than the November. If so, the trader makes the difference between the profit in the July contract and the loss in the

> Ag spread traders take their primary position in the front month, and their hedging position in the back month. Financial spread traders do the opposite.

November. However, spread trading isn't always all it is cracked up to be. There are times in which extraordinary fundamental changes in supply and demand cause the historical relationship between front and back months to change. If that is the case in the soybean example, it might be possible for gains in the November contract to outpace those of the July contract. This can cause a loss to the trader despite his correct assumption of rising prices in soybeans.

Calendar spread trading in financial futures, such as currencies, stock indices, and Treasuries, is less common than doing so in agricultural commodities due to a lack of liquidity in the back months. Nevertheless, it is a common strategy in one financial contract in particular; Eurodollars. Eurodollars are not to be mistaken with the EUR/USD (referred to as the euro/dollar) currency spread; Eurodollars fall into the interest rate category. Specifically, they are US dollar deposits overseas collecting interest; they can be thought of as a Treasury bill or CD in that they are short-term discount bonds. Unlike most financial futures markets, Eurodollars have plenty of liquidity in contracts dating out several months, and even years in some cases. Accordingly, they are good candidates for intracommodity spread trading. Unlike agricultural commodities, interest rate financial products tend to see bigger reactions to market changes in the long-dated futures contracts. As a result, a trader who believes interest rates are going higher might look to sell the back month of a Eurodollar futures contract (primary position) and purchase a front-month futures contract (secondary position) as a hedge. Remember, interest rate securities decline as interest rates increase and vice versa.

WIDENING VS. NARROWING INTRACOMMODITY SPREADS

Keep in mind, a futures spread trader can still make money if he is wrong about the direction of the market. If he is long the spread, which entails purchasing the contract with the higher price and selling the contract with a lower price, as long as the distance between the two contracts widens, the trade can be profitable. This occurs if the contract the trader is long goes up more than the contract he is short, or it can occur if the contract the trader is long goes down less than the contract he is short. Conversely, the seller of the spread merely needs the spread to narrow, regardless

> A trader "buying" an intracommodity spread buys the higher-priced contract and sells the lower-priced contract. Selling the spread involves selling the higher-priced contract and buying the lower-priced one.

of the overall direction of the market. To summarize, a spread trader is trading the relationship between two contracts, as much or more than he is speculating on the overall direction of a commodity price.

Traders expecting interest rates to rise in early 2016, the equivalent of expecting the value of the Eurodollar interest rate futures contract decline, sold the December 2017 contract and bought the December 2016 contract. Because the Eurodollar is a financial, their primary position (short) was taken in the back month (December 2017), and their hedging position (long) was taken in the front month (December 2016). At the time, the 2017 contract was trading at a lower price than the 2016, so these traders *bought* the spread because they were buying the higher-priced leg. Accordingly, those traders wanted the spread between these two contracts to widen. Unfortunately, it did the opposite (Figure 45) as expectations of multiple Fed rate hikes in 2016 diminished.

Figure 45: Just like outright futures contracts, when a particular spread gets "too popular" and traders turn out to be incorrect in their speculation, liquidation of the spread can be fierce.

INTERCOMMODITY SPREADS

An intercommodity spread consists of purchasing a futures contract in a given delivery month and simultaneously holding a short position in a related commodity market in the same delivery month. Some of the better-known intercommodity spreads involve the crack spread (buying crude oil while selling unleaded gasoline and heating oil, or vice versa), the crush spread (buying soybeans and selling soybean oil and soybean meal, or vice versa), and the TED spread (spreading between 10-year notes and 30-year bonds).

Intercommodity spreads can be extremely complex. Unfortunately, it isn't a topic that could be given justice in a few short paragraphs, so I won't even try. However, if you are interested in learning more, the CME's website (www.CMEGroup.com) offers several educational articles focused on popular intercommodity spreads.

QUOTING, CHARTING, AND TRADING FUTURES SPREADS

Beginning traders are often surprised to learn trading futures spreads isn't necessarily as simple as it seems on the surface. In addition to the complexities of finding a way to make money with futures spreads, there might not be an efficient means available of trading them in all trading accounts. Further, not all genuine spreads are granted discounted margins by the exchange. However, those *that are* offered discounted spread margins by the futures exchanges are said to be "exchange-recognized spreads." Such spreads not only enable speculators to trade them without the burden of being charged full margin on both of the futures contracts involved in the spread, but they are also available using a strategy symbol on most trading platforms. Spreads that are not exchange recognized might be legitimate spreads, but they require holding double margin, or at least the margin required for each contract individually. Without the help of what is generally costly trading software capable of creating synthetic spreads, it is necessary to leg into any non-exchange recognized spread on separate order entry tickets.

For example, some traders believe that purchasing an e-mini Dow futures contract and selling a mini Russell 2000 futures contract is a bona fide spread because each of these instruments are likely to travel in the same direction in the long run. But that isn't necessarily how it works because each of these products trade on different exchanges. The e-mini Dow is traded on the CBOT division of the CME Group, while the mini Russell 2000 is traded on the International Continental Exchange (ICE). Accordingly, they charge full margin on both sides of this particular "spread"; thus, if the initial margin listed on the e-mini Dow is $4,290, and the margin on the mini Russell 2000 is $5,940, a trader must have roughly $10,000 to execute the spread. Most would likely deem this a rather inefficient use of funds. In addition, the only way to enter the spread in most basic platforms would be to buy an e-mini Dow at the market and sell a mini Russell 2000 at the market, using separate orders. In the end, the resulting position will be what was desired but in fast-moving futures. This method is subject to some price slippage on entry and exit.

Luckily for spread traders, the CME Group owns the exchange rights to most US futures contracts, which means there are substantially more exchange traded spreads today than there were prior to the CME Group acquisition of previously independent futures exchanges (NYMEX, COMEX, and CBOT).

To illustrate the convenience of using exchange recognized spreads, as opposed to non-exchange recognized spreads, a recognized spread will act as a single instrument with a single quote despite the fact that it involves multiple contracts. This is significant, particularly for those trading multileg intercommodity spreads such as the crack spread because the alternative is executing each leg separately.

Here's an example. If July wheat is trading at $5.50 per bushel and December wheat is at $6.00, a trader bullish the market could either enter an order to buy a July wheat futures at $5.50 and another order to sell a December contract at $6.00, *or* he could enter an order to buy the July/December spread for $0.50. The end result is relatively the same, but in the latter method of entering the spread, the trader has much more control in the price he pays to enter the spread in that he can name the exact price he is willing to pay for the package, rather than naming a price of each contract separately.

In the former method, the trader runs the risk of being filled at his price on one order, then being forced to execute at the market price for the other, which could be at a relatively unfavorable fill. He could also have entered a market order to execute each leg individually, but in this case he will likely see moderate slippage on the spread due to the time it takes the trader to enter the second order once the first is filled. The difference in profit and loss on the trade relative to one entry method vs. the other is inconsequential, but these types of things can go a long way toward unsettling a trader's emotional stability. Thus, those planning on doing some spread trading should ensure the trading platform they choose will fulfill the needs of futures spread trading; not all of them do.

ADVANTAGES OF FUTURES SPREAD TRADING

The primary advantage to trading futures spreads is the perception of lower volatility. After all, holding antagonistic positions in a related commodity, or the same commodity but a differing expiration month, should provide the trader with an inherent hedge. Under normal circumstances, one leg of the spread will be profitable while the other will be suffering losses. The key is to ensure the primary position makes more than the secondary position loses, or at least loses less than the secondary position makes. This also adds appeal to the strategy because the trader doesn't necessarily have to be correct on the direction of the market; it is only necessary that the spread between the two contracts behaves in the desired manner.

Due to the inherent hedge built into a spread trade, exchanges generally offer margin discounts to spread traders. A trader who opts to go long March corn and short December corn will find the margin requirement to be dramatically less than it would be to trade the contracts individually in separate accounts. It is worth noting, however, that the exchange offers discounted spread margin on futures as well as options, regardless of whether the order is entered as a spread. If a trader buys March corn on one order entry ticket, then sells December corn on a subsequent order entry ticket, or even in another trading session, the account is charged discounted margin despite the fact that the trader legged into the position.

DISADVANTAGES OF FUTURES SPREAD TRADING

Futures spreads often lull traders into believing there is little to no risk exposure. Yet, there are times in which market conditions abruptly shift. Whether it is a change in central bank policy, a natural disaster, or a change in the economy, the markets sometimes undergo sudden and unexpected repricing that ravages the accounts of spread traders. Thus, sometimes the complacency of spread traders eventually leads them into a pinch.

> "If you are in a poker game and after 20 minutes, you don't know who the patsy is, then you are the patsy." —Warren Buffett

There are nearly unlimited futures spread capabilities, giving traders the ability to construct futures spreads of a conservative or highly aggressive nature. Thus, in some instances traders are executing spreads with very little profit potential, while in other instances traders are assuming their position is relatively safe, when in reality it is capable of causing massive fluctuations in account balances.

Although I am not necessarily a fan of prolonged paper trading, I believe those looking to employ a futures spread trading strategy should paper trade them using various contract months to get a feel for how quickly, or slowly, different forms of spreads can move. This is because sometimes it can be quite different to gauge spread volatility without actually experiencing it.

Another drawback of spread trading is the potential lack of directional bias. Most traders desire to have an opinion in market direction, or at least a realistic idea of what needs to happen for their trades to turn a profit. In my opinion, spread trading often feels like playing the penny slot machines in my home town of Las Vegas. The risk is mitigated, but it isn't always clear which icons aligned will turn a profit. Instead, we just pull the handle and hope the machine will tell us we've won.

SEASONAL SPREADS

A popular approach to commodity trading is the use of seasonal spreads via computerized stat crunching, or the less intensive method of subscribing to a service like MRCI. This service has been offering spread traders high-probability, but never guaranteed, ventures for decades. Their computer programs scan various spreads, both intercommodity and intracommodity, to locate particular opportunities that have paid off repetitively throughout history.

In this example taken from the MRCI service, it is suggested that in the previous 15 years, buying the May soybean meal futures contract and selling the December soybean meal futures contract has yielded a profit in 14 of the previous 15 years (Table 2). Obviously, there is no guarantee this pattern will continue, but the odds certainly seem to favor it.

Table 2: This is an example of a seasonal spread that has hypothetically worked in 14 of the last 15 years.

Seasonal Strategy	Entry Date	Exit Date	Win %	Win Years	Loss Years	Total Years	Average Profit
Buy May Soybean Meal Sell December Soybean Meal	2/1	3/1	93%	14	1	15	$555

It is important to note that this particular information is compelling, but it doesn't tell the entire story. Although it clearly displays an entry and exit date, and the associated profits yielded from trading on these particular days, it doesn't tell us what happened between entry and exit of the trade. Thankfully, MRCI offers the ability to display the details of each of the previous 15 years (Table 3), but not all seasonal spread services are so transparent. In this particular example, digging deeper reveals the losing year resulted in a drawdown of just under $1,800; also, there was a point at which the trade suffered a paper loss of roughly $2,000. Even some of the profitable years saw moderate drawdowns before the trade finally paid off. The moral of the story is to make sure you do your homework regarding the details of the history of a particular seasonal spread. I've seen some seasonal spreads with highly profitable historical stats and seemingly high probabilities of success come with magnificent drawdowns between the stated entry and exit dates. Nevertheless, the attractive odds offered by seasonal spread trading are generally a great way to get involved in the markets with relatively mitigated risk exposure.

Table 3: This is an example of the yearly hypothetical results of a seasonal spread tracked by MRCI. Traders must be aware of drawdown potential—in this case, one bad year engulfed profits from four average years.

Year	Entry Date	Entry Price	Exit Date	Exit Price	Profit	Profit Amount	Best Equity Date	Best Equity Amount	Worst Equity Date	Worst Equity Amount
2015	02/02/15	10.70	02/27/15	14.50	3.80	380.00	02/24/15	390.00	02/09/15	-230.00
2014	02/03/14	71.10	02/28/14	93.30	22.20	2220.00	02/28/14	2220.00		
2013	02/01/13	54.90	03/01/13	75.50	20.60	2060.00	02/21/13	2630.00	02/12/13	-10.00
2012	02/01/12	4.90	03/01/12	11.30	6.40	640.00	03/01/12	640.00	02/09/12	-580.00
2011	02/01/11	34.60	03/01/11	16.90	-17.70	-1770.00			02/28/11	-1990.00
2010	02/01/10	9.10	03/01/10	9.60	0.50	50.00	02/22/10	1090.00	02/03/10	-40.00
2009	02/02/09	21.50	02/27/09	24.50	3.00	300.00	02/12/09	1390.00	02/20/09	-300.00
2008	02/01/08	20.50	03/01/08	44.20	23.70	2370.00	03/01/08	2370.00	02/21/08	-50.00
2007	02/01/07	-12.10	03/01/07	-11.70	0.40	40.00	02/14/07	220.00	02/28/07	-80.00
2006	02/01/06	-7.50	03/01/06	-7.10	0.40	40.00	02/17/06	370.00	02/02/06	-30.00
2005	02/01/05	-8.90	03/01/05	-4.60	4.30	430.00	02/28/05	520.00	02/02/05	-110.00
2004	02/02/04	57.40	03/01/04	65.30	7.90	790.00	02/20/04	1660.00	02/13/04	-240.00
2003	02/03/03	14.00	02/28/03	20.60	6.60	660.00	02/26/03	850.00	02/07/03	-220.00
2002	02/01/02	0.60	03/01/02	1.50	0.90	90.00	02/28/02	90.00	02/19/02	-140.00
2001	02/01/01	2.40	03/01/01	2.60	0.20	20.00	02/09/01	230.00	02/14/01	-0.00
Percentage Correct		93						Protective Stop		(721)
Average Profit on Winning Trades					7.21	720.71		Winners		14
Average Loss on Trades					-17.70	-1770.00		Losers		1
Average Net Profit Per Trade					5.55	554.67		Total trades		15

CHAPTER 9: OPTIONS TRADING STRATEGIES

Not unlike futures, or any other market for that matter, options trading is essentially a zero-sum game, after ignoring transaction costs. For every buyer, there is a seller; therefore, for every winner there is a loser. Not surprisingly, option buyers and option sellers enter the trade with opposite expectations and inverse risk and reward profiles. Option buyers are paying for the underlying right while sellers are selling that right. If necessary, you can review the basics of options in Chapter 1, "Commodity Market Refresher." The most important thing to remember is that option buyers are exposed to risk limited to the amount of premium paid while option sellers face theoretically unlimited risk. Conversely, option buyers have the possibility of potentially unlimited gains while the profit potential for sellers is limited to the amount of premium collected.

Let's take a look at the advantages and disadvantages of both schools of thought, but before we do I'd like to point out there are some gray areas in option strategy. Although most beginning option traders prefer the simplicity of buying or selling calls and puts outright, there are significant advantages to becoming familiar with the practice of option spread trading because it takes the best of both worlds.

By definition, an option spread is the combination of two or more different types of options or strike prices to attain a common goal. This definition is intentionally broad, because it refers to a theoretically unlimited number of possibilities. For example, an option spread might involve the purchase of both a call and a put with the same strike prices, or it could be the purchase and sale of two calls with different strike prices. Further, it could be the purchase of a call and the sale put, or any other imaginable combination. It wouldn't be feasible to discuss all of the variations and implications of option spreads, but if you are interested in learning more, you might want to pick up a copy of my book *Commodity Options*.

LONG OPTION STRATEGIES

The act of purchasing options, or purchasing option spreads falls within the category of long options. In a nutshell, if a particular strategy involves purchasing calls or puts outright or the purchase of a spread in which the cost of the long options is higher than the premium collected for the short options, it is generally considered a long option strategy. In the industry, traders refer to the premium paid for an option, or option spread, as a *net debit*; if the option trade collects more premium than is paid out, it is referred to as a *net credit*.

Another distinctive feature of long option strategies is the benefit of limited risk. That said, it is possible to construct an option spread in which the net premium is a debit but the risk is theoretically unlimited due to at least one naked, or uncovered, short option. If this is the case, even if the premium is a net debit

> Option sellers have the exact opposite intentions as the option buyer. They also have the opposite profit and loss diagram.

(cost to the trader), the strategy is categorized as a short option strategy. Thus, any option strategy involving a one-to-one ratio of long options of the same type (call or put) comes with limited risk. On the contrary, any option spread involving more short legs than long legs in a particular option type exposes the trader to unlimited risk and is typically lumped into a short option strategy because of the risk exposure. Short options that aren't covered by a long option are naked. This means they involve unlimited risk exposure once they are in-the-money.

For instance, a common long option spread strategy is the vertical spread. The buyer of the spread purchases the option with a strike price that is closer to the current futures market price, then sells an option of the same type that is distant from the current price of the underlying futures contract. Because the option with the proximal strike price is more desirable (more likely to pay out), it is always priced higher than the distant strike. Accordingly, the net premium is a debit; and because there is one long option to offset each short option, the risk is limited. If the same trader bought one call option and sold two call options in the same market, it would come with theoretically unlimited risk and would be referred to as a *short option strategy*.

Now that we have the basic terminology out of the way, let's discuss the opportunities that long and short options trading bring to the proverbial table. Many traders assume they should adopt either a long option strategy or a short option strategy but not both. However, I believe there is a time and place for each.

ADVANTAGES OF OPTION BUYING

Beginning traders tend to flock to long option trading due to the comfort of having limited risk. It is nice to know that regardless of how wrong the speculation or how poor the timing, the maximum damage is the cost of the option, or option spread, being purchased. Even better, the premium paid for the call or put gives the trader the "option" to buy or sell the futures contract at the stated strike

> Options are an eroding asset for the buyer, but they are an eroding liability to the seller.

price. As we know, futures contracts come with theoretically unlimited profit potential. Thus, an option buyer sleeps well at night, knowing the potential of his long option has no limits. This is true—unless, of course, the trade is a long option spread in which a short option caps the profit potential of the long option. In any case, it is a comfortable strategy until you consider the relatively dismal odds of success.

DISADVANTAGES OF OPTION BUYING

> If you've ever purchased an option and watched the value erode no nothing, the seller had the opposite experience.

The bottom line is, options are priced to lose. After all, there has to be somebody willing to sell the option at a particular price before a trader can actually purchase it. The trader selling the option has likely done their homework in regard to the probability of it paying out and has priced the option accordingly. Making the prospects for option buyers even worse, options are eroding assets. Thus, despite the comfort of limited risk and unlimited profit potential, there is little appeal to option buying unless a trader has absolutely keen timing, or is simply lucky. I often compare buying options to the experience of purchasing a car; once the car is driven off the lot, its value erodes quickly, eventually becoming a worthless asset. However, in option trading the process is much quicker. In quiet markets, the erosion of an option is slow and steady, each passing minute making the option slightly less valuable to own; yet in volatile markets both the explosion and subsequent implosion of option premium can be rather shocking.

For example, at the time this book was being written, crude oil was hovering near historic lows in the mid-$30s. Naturally, traders were attempting to pick a bottom in a market that rarely traded at such depressed levels. The cheapest way to go about this type of speculation was to purchase deep-out-of-the-money calls. It was possible to purchase a $47 call with about 30 days to expiration for $350 (Figure 46). Unfortunately, less than a week later the option was only worth $50 because oil futures had softened up in price by a few dollars. Given this example of a nearly 85% premium erosion in a few short days, it is easy to see how small and limited risk ventures can add up to big losses. On the flip side, there are rare occasions in which an option buyer exercises precise entry and sees a $300 option turn into a few thousand dollars. Those types of outcomes are few and far between, but they make for good conversation. In fact, it is relatively common for a long option trader to make an accurate directional speculation and still lose money. This is because a long option is only profitable at expiration if the underlying futures price travels beyond the strike price of the option, in the specified time limit, and to a magnitude in which the cost of the option is covered. It isn't enough for the market to go the right way, nor is it enough for the futures price to simply reach the strike price of the option. As you can imagine, option buying is a difficult venture.

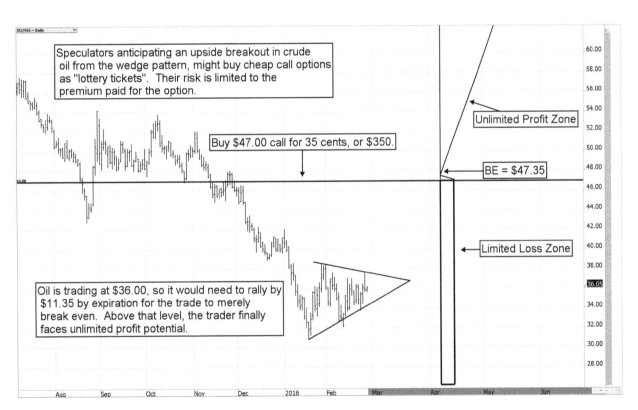

Figure 46: To be a profitable option buyer, impeccable timing and an accurate speculation of direction is necessary. Although option buyers are facing limited risk, they are also facing low winning percentages.

Keep in mind I've simplified the conversation by only discussing the outcome of the trade at expiration. At any time before option expiration, the profit and loss prospects are far more complicated. This is because option values are made up of market opinion, emotion, volatility, and time value. Those things are impossible to predict; so any guesses at a change in option price should a particular move occur is simply that, a guess.

A redeeming quality of long options trading is the fact that it is possible to make money on an option even if the underlying futures price never reaches the strike price. Yet, for this to happen, the futures price must make a substantial move in the direction of your trade on high levels of volatility. This too is somewhat rare but if it happens to you, don't get greedy. Take the money and run.

WHEN OPTION BUYING IS MOST APPROPRIATE

Some traders employ a long option-only approach to trading, and a few of them probably manage to do so profitably. But in my opinion, it is an extremely difficult way to make money in the commodity markets. That doesn't mean you should never buy options. Although the example of the eroding crude oil call didn't work out as planned, it was probably the best way to go about gaining exposure in a volatile oil market. Trading a futures contract outright comes with a margin requirement of roughly $5,000, and an average daily equity balance swing of $2,000 to $800 per contract traded. Despite the outcome, a $350 call option providing a month of upside exposure in crude oil wasn't a bad play.

I often refer to this type of cheap, long option strategy as a lottery ticket play. Similar to playing the state lottery at your local convenience store, buying a cheap countertrend option opens the door for massive profit potential for a small and limited risk. Of course, also similar to playing the lottery, the odds of a big payday are rather grim. Nevertheless, I think we can all agree that a deep-out-of-the-money option buyer has far more control of his destiny than does a lottery player, and probably faces slightly better odds of success.

USING LONG OPTIONS FOR PORTFOLIO, OR COMMODITY TRADE INSURANCE

Perhaps the best use of long options isn't for speculation at all; they might best serve as a means of hedging. Whether the intention is to buy insurance against your long stock portfolio by purchasing e-mini S&P 500 puts or hedging your e-mini S&P 500 futures day trade, long options can be a valuable tool. Of course, insurance isn't free. If you purchase an e-mini put to protect your stock portfolio, expect to pay up. Further, like auto or home insurance, the likelihood of it paying off is somewhat slim; then again, if we get another flash crash or financial disaster it will be nice to have.

In my view, commodity futures day traders can benefit greatly from short-dated "cheaply" priced options. Through the use of weekly expiring options, or monthly options in which the expiration date is nearing, it might be possible to purchase insurance in the form of a call or put against any speculative position taken in the futures market. This topic is discussed in

> Buy options when volatility is low, premiums are cheap, and nobody is watching.

more detail in Chapter 16, but as a preview, on the day prior to option expiration, slightly-out-of-the-money e-mini S&P 500 options are often going for about 6.00 points, or $300 (6.00 x $50). This creates an opportunity for a trader to enter a futures trade with potentially unlimited profit potential with the luxury of relatively cheap insurance against being wrong. Similarly, commodity traders can purchase puts and calls to protect long and short futures positions.

On a side note, in addition to hedging purposes, these short-dated options can be great short-term option trades. Again, when traded in this manner, they should be viewed as the equivalent of lottery tickets, but markets sometimes move big on expiration days so a small outlay of cash could pay off nicely if the speculation is accurate.

SHORT OPTION STRATEGIES

Short option strategies generally involve outright sold calls and puts, but it can also refer to option spreads that a trader has collected more premium on short legs than was paid out for long legs. In other words, the trade was executed at a net credit. Most short option strategies involve theoretically *unlimited risk*, and those short option strategies with *limited risk*, such as vertical credit spreads, generally carry risks that far outweigh the rewards. A vertical credit spread is simply a market approach in which an option seller takes a position and simultaneously purchases an option to limit the risk of that position. More often than not, the insurance purchase goes to waste.

> Home runs typically attract all of the attention, but over and over again it is the base hits that win the game. In the world of trading, premium collection can be considered a base-hit strategy.

In short, an option seller, or premium collector, is in the business of selling options in the hopes of time value erosion, along with favorable price movement, in the underlying futures market resulting in the loss of option value. Not unlike trading stocks, futures, or other assets, the purpose of option trading is to buy low and sell high. However, option sellers are doing so in the opposite order; they hope to sell what they believe to be high-priced options and seek the opportunity to buy them back at a lower price, or in some cases let them expire worthless.

ADVANTAGES OF OPTION SELLING

There is truly only one advantage to option selling, and that is the odds of success on any individual trade are largely in your favor. This is a compelling-enough reason for me to personally favor this strategy over most others. Nevertheless, it is far from easy money and it has been known to cause unexpected heartache. It is not for the faint of heart, nor is it for lightly capitalized trading accounts.

> Egotistical traders normally don't make good option sellers because they are constantly seeking the "big one."

There are a few features of an option selling strategy that put it at the top of the list when it comes to the probability of profitable trading. For starters, there have been numerous studies, one of which was conducted by the CME, suggesting anywhere from 60% to 80% of all options expire worthless. Armed with this knowledge, it can be assumed that a trader automatically has similar odds of success on each sold option. This assumption has a significant flaw, which will be discussed shortly; nevertheless, it is a reasonable premise.

> Option selling offers traders the most favorable odds of success on a per-trade basis, relative to all other speculative strategies.

Another aspect of option selling shifting the odds in favor of the trader is the abundant room for error. Unlike option buyers, who require the market to move in the desired direction in the time frame allotted and in a necessary and predetermined magnitude, option sellers merely need to not be *really* wrong. It is possible for an option seller to walk away from a trade profitable if he is right or wrong in regards to the market direction. Yes, that's right—an option seller can be wrong and still make money. I don't know of any other strategy that offers that amount of room for error. Of course, there are no free lunches. Even if an option seller makes money on nine out of 10 trades, there is potential for that one losing trade to do substantial damage to a trading account. This is because option sellers only lose money if they are exceptionally wrong; when such an occurrence comes to head, punishing volatility could lead to a ruinous explosion in option prices.

In Figure 47, a trader sells a natural gas put at a strike price of $1.50 on the heels of a precipitous decline. The premium collected for the put was equivalent to $400 before considering transaction costs, representing the maximum achievable profit. Thus, regardless of how well timed the trade ends up being, or how far the market rallies after the trade is initiated, the trader will only make $400. The appeal in this strategy is the fact that natural gas can drop another $0.30 (30 cents) by expiration before the trader is put in a losing position. Simply said, he can be wrong by roughly 17% on the price of natural gas, and still profit from the trade!

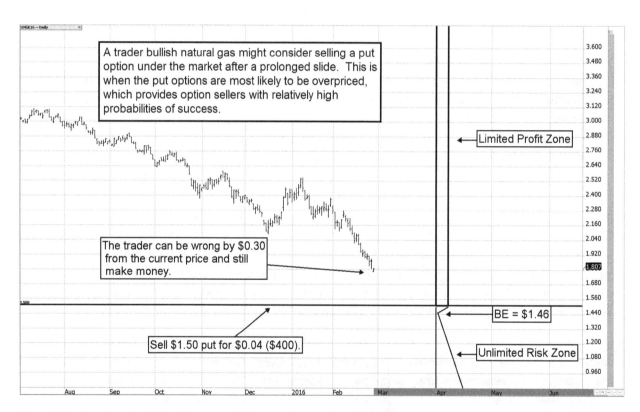

Figure 47: Option sellers face the opposite payout diagram as a buyer. They also face higher winning percentages, in exchange for unlimited risk.

If some characteristics of option selling remind you of your insurance agent, you are right. Insurance companies operate on the same premise as commodity option sellers; both are in the business of collecting premium in exchange for paying the buyer of

Option buyers can be *right* and still *lose* money. Option sellers can be *wrong* and still *make* money.

the policy, or option, in the event of a specific event occurring. Should the specified event fail to materialize, the seller of the policy, or option, keeps the entire premium. Nevertheless, option sellers and insurance companies understand that there will be very large claims to be paid out on occasion.

DISADVANTAGES OF OPTION SELLING

The frustrating disadvantage of option selling is that there is limited profit potential. In the relatively rare instance that a trader displays perfection in price speculation and timing, the most he can make on the trade is the amount of premium collected to sell the option. Imagine picking the precise low of a market, selling a put option for $600 to capitalize, then watching an unprecedented futures market rally. Futures traders, or long call traders, with the same trading idea might walk away with thousands in profits, but the option seller's profit potential is maxed out at the premium collected. This profit cap is the opportunity cost of enjoying higher success probabilities and more room for error. More often than not, this is a small price to pay.

Obviously, the elephant in the room is the theoretical unlimited risk that comes with option selling. Should an option seller discover his market analysis, and corresponding trade, to be dramatically wrong, the losses can be fast and swift. On a few occasions, I've had experiences in which a sold option worth roughly $500 on a Friday afternoon close could be trading for a few thousand dollars on the following Monday morning open due to some weekend surprise. For a short option trader, this type of explosion in option premium can be devastating and take a considerable amount of time from which to recover. Nor are surprises restricted to weekends; it is possible for an energy inventory report, an FOMC meeting, or a USDA report to shake things up midweek. Anybody interested in implementing a premium collection strategy should understand these types of unpredictable and unpreventable disasters will happen from time to time.

Beginning traders often say things like, if the option gets to a certain price or my loss exceeds a certain amount, I'll exit the trade. Obviously, it is a great idea to have such a plan in place when entering a short option speculation, but in swift moves, an option value can change so quickly that exiting at your predetermined price might be impossible. Further, it is not possible to place stop-loss orders on commodity options; the exchanges don't accept the order type because it would likely lead to massively unfortunate fill prices. This is because, as you know, a stop-loss order becomes a market order once the stated price is hit. In the case of options that aren't traded fluidly, there are times at which the bid/ask spread becomes wide and could erroneously trigger stop-loss orders, causing unnecessarily enormous losses to some trading accounts. This could occur in the overnight session when market makers are absent, or it could happen during the day session during high levels of volatility or event risk in which market makers pull their bids and asks, leaving option quotes to the best bid and offer working by retail traders. Without the additional liquidity provided to commodity option markets by market makers, the bid/ask spread can be, as a trader said once to me, "wide enough to drive a truck through."

> "Once I made a decision, I never thought about it again." —Michael Jordan

Imagine being short a natural gas put option with a theoretical value of 40 ticks, or $400. During normal trading, market makers might be quoting the option at 39 bid, ask 41. But if the market maker removes his bid and offer, the bid and ask shift to working limit orders placed by other traders. There might not be many retail trader orders working in this particular strike at that particular time; in some cases, the best offer might be some guy who has placed a good until canceled order to sell his $400 option (40 ticks) at $10,000 (1,000 ticks). Obviously, selling this option at 1,000 ticks is nothing more than a pipe dream, but the trader who placed it must like to fanaticize about the prospects of his commodity option lottery ticket. If the exchange accepted stop orders on options, such an order would automatically be filled because it essentially represents the market price! If this happened, the CME would be erroneously shifting wealth (about $9,600) from the seller of this option to the buyer—and thus, the reason exchanges won't accept stop orders for option.

Most enter short option trades with the idea that as long as the futures price doesn't surpass the strike price of the sold option to become in-the-money, the speculative position will be profitable. This is because at expiration, if the futures price isn't beyond the strike price of the option, the option expires worthless and the seller of that option keeps the premium collected. However, this is a simplified assumption because it ignores anything that occurs before expiration and it fails to account for the component of option pricing that values volatility, demand, and trader sentiment. It is quite possible for an option to increase in value subsequent to it being sold regardless of whether the futures price gets anywhere near the strike price. In fact, it is relatively common for traders to exit short options at large losses without the option ever becoming in-the-money.

All that is necessary to equate to a significant paper loss is an uptick in volatility along with an antagonistic move in the underlying futures price. For example, during the massive 12% correction that took place in August 2015 in the e-mini S&P 500, there were options with strike prices of 1500 and 1600 that increased in value from the vicinity of $4.00 in premium ($200) to $60.00 in premium ($3,000). Prior to the explosion in pricing, the futures market was hovering around the 2,050 area, so selling 1600 puts, which were 450 S&P 500 points out-of-the-money, seemed like a near-guaranteed profit to some. Yet, in a matter of a few days what appeared to be an ultra-high probability venture into option selling soon transitioned into a $2,500 loss per contract. In this example, the e-mini S&P 500 hit a low of 1,825, well above the strike price of the option of 1,600. Despite this, anybody who sold this particular option at that particular time would be suffering massive losses. Ironically, just a few days later, the S&P recovered, and the option values returned to their previous levels. Had a trader held to expiration, the trade would have reached its maximum profit potential, but I would venture to say the majority of traders couldn't have held on to their position due to feelings of panic and anxiety, they lost their trading conviction and turned bearish, they reached their pain threshold, or they simply ran out of margin money.

WHEN OPTION SELLING IS MOST APPROPRIATE

Ironically, option selling is most appropriate when it seems like it is least appropriate. For instance, option prices tend to be inflated during times of high volatility, or prior to potentially market moving announcements. This is because when event risk and market volatility is high, option traders place a higher value on options. Not only does the increased demand for the options drive up the price, but the market believes there is a higher potential for any particular option becoming in-the-money. Accordingly, options tend to be overpriced during such times. Option selling is like any other

> An option seller isn't concerned about where a market will go, but where it will NOT go.

business; you want to be a seller while prices are high, and a buyer when prices are low. Selling cheap options in low volatility is like a retailer selling items from the discount rack; it usually isn't a profitable venture. On the other hand, receiving top dollar for an option favorably shifts the breakeven point and increases profit potential.

BEING AWARE OF IMPLIED VOLATILITY AND TIMING

No option selling discussion is complete without mentioning the implications of volatility and timing of option selling. Too many option selling publications, books, and courses simply mention the concept of being a net option selling in times of high volatility, and a buyer of options in low-volatility markets, without pointing out the blatant consequences of ignoring these factors.

Some believe it is more likely that a long option strategy will have an opportunity to pay off in a volatile market. I argue this is a false perception because options on futures buyers must overcome their cost of entry before turning a profit; the higher the price of the option on the way in, the bigger the obstacle to being profitable will be.

In the beginning of pursuing an option selling strategy, it is easy to fall into assuming it is unlikely the strike price of a deep-out-of-the-money option will never be seen; therefore, timing shouldn't matter. That is a fallacy that will undoubtedly lead a new option seller to an emotional meltdown. As we've already highlighted, the simple goal of trading, whether it is futures or options, is to buy low and sell high; selling an option at a discounted price on low volatility is akin to taking a step in the opposite direction. Doing so opens the door for a scenario in which the option explodes in value exponentially. The trader put into this predicament can choose to hold the position if he firmly believes the strike price will never come into danger, or he can buy the option back in hopes of stopping the pain. In most cases, traders end up doing the latter and regretting it because deep-out-of-the-money options generally do expire worthless despite their potential for mass increases in value.

As the e-mini S&P short put example portrays, the problem for option sellers is it can behave wildly between entry of the trade and the eventual worthless expiration, forcing the undercapitalized and unprepared to realize massive losses.

Keeping tabs on implied volatility, and adjusting the trading strategy accordingly, is imperative for survival as an option seller. Those selling premium in markets experiencing historically low implied volatility will eventually regret it. Traders must be aware of the historical and current implied volatility of the market they intend to sell options in. If the implied volatility is low, the trade should be either passed, implemented on a light scale through minimal quantities, or in conjunction with some sort of long option hedge. On the flip side, if the implied volatility is at a historically high level, high probability trading opportunities exist, and for those with plenty of margin and fortitude, it might be a time to get slightly more aggressive in option selling ventures.

QUALITY VS. QUANTITY

A decision all option sellers will have to make at some point is whether to sell quality options for higher premium, or low-quality options that bring in less premium but are further from the current market price. Some option sellers prefer trading options at- or near-the-money to collect thousands of dollars per lot traded, while others prefer selling options with extremely distant strike prices for premiums as low as $50 per lot traded. Of course, to make the strategy worthwhile, the trader selling the low-quality option at a very low premium must establish a position using several contracts; this is where trouble often arises.

A common mistake among option sellers is to trade with a high concentration in a particular market, and even more so a high quantity of sold options. On the surface, it seems like selling deep-out-of-the money options with lottery-type dismal odds of success is a good idea, but it can quickly backfire on anybody who gets carried away or doesn't have the large trading capital necessary to successfully employ the strategy. As I've attempted to make perfectly clear, although the overall bet an option seller is making is the price of the commodity will not surpass the strike price of the option, an open short option can certainly sustain unbearable paper losses in the event of an increase in volatility, particularly in the adverse direction for the option itself.

When chaos ensues in an option market, it is the deep-out-of-the-money options that bear the brunt of the insanity. Thus, those trading higher quantities of such options could easily blow out their entire trading account if they failed to leave adequate margin excess. To give you an idea of what I'm talking about, I've seen traders design a strategy in which they sell crude oil options at insane strike prices for the smallest increment of premium. In their minds, they are merely printing money in their trading account because it is highly unlikely the strike price will ever be seen. Unfortunately, some of them don't last long enough to enjoy the reward of their strategy.

Imagine a trader in January 2016 who believed it would be "impossible" for the price of crude to see $10 per barrel by June. He might be tempted to sell the June $10 puts for $10 a piece (one cent in premium). The margin on this trade is very low, so he could theoretically sell 100 of them in an account as small as a few thousand dollars. If the trade is held to expiration, and the price of crude oil is above $10, the trader keeps $1,000 minus transaction costs.

Next, imagine that the minimum incremental tick for an option is $10. So the absolute lowest price the trader would be able to buy the options back at any point before expiration would be $20, a loss of $1,000. The only way this trade makes money is if it is held to expiration because buying the option back at the best-case scenario of two cents would result in a large loss. That might not be so bad, except most traders wouldn't have the ability to see the trade through. These nearly worthless options can jump from $10 to $50 or $100 on a single trading day; all it would take for this to occur is a $2.00 drop in crude oil within a single trading session. In fact, on January 13, that is exactly what happened to that option. Anyone short 100 of the June $10 puts would have immediately suffered a $4,000 drawdown at the hands of relatively "normal" market action; in other words, we aren't talking about a market crash causing this type of damage. A few moderate down days were enough to do the trick.

The practice of selling 100 nearly worthless put options in a historically wild market like crude oil is an extreme example, and in my opinion it is absolutely irresponsible for anybody trading less than a six-figure account. Nevertheless, I see traders attempt similar strategies frequently, but they rarely pan out. It isn't the trade itself that does them in, but the quantity.

If your goal is to collect $1,000 in premium, you are better off finding a strike price going for $200 to $500, which allows a trader to meet their premium collection goal with two to five contracts. Of course, this means trading closer-to-the-money options, but they won't be quite as susceptible to the explosive price changes that occur in the overly cheap options. Think about it. If you are a speculator working with small amounts of cash but would like to be involved in the market, which option strike prices will you choose? The answer is probably the cheaper options; in turn, they bid the price of the cheap options up to illogical prices. For anybody short those options, it is an unfortunate lesson to learn. So when volatility makes its way into the markets, or even the expectation of such, it is the deep-out-of-the-money options that experience the largest percentage balloon in value. This concept is known as the *volatility smile*, and it is defined as the visual display of the difference between the implied volatility in the out-of-the-money options vs. in-the-money options (Figure 48).

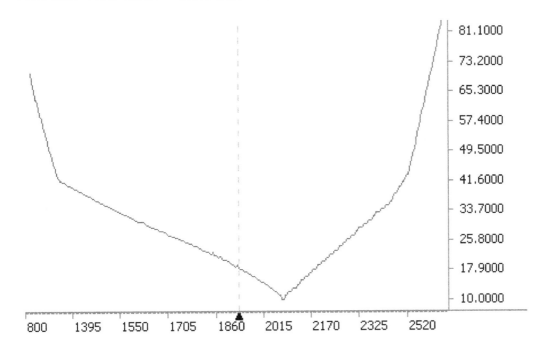

Figure 48: Implied volatility tends to get exponentially higher as the strike price gets further from the market. At-the-money options have the least amount of implied volatility built into their price. This is called a volatility smile. In this graph, the lower axis represents strike prices of options, while the right axis represents implied volatility.

NOT ALL BROKERS ALLOW CLIENTS TO SELL OPTIONS

It is a surprise to beginning traders who wish to sell options to discover the difficulty in finding a conducive brokerage relationship. The practice of option selling is a controversial strategy throughout the commodity brokerage industry. Many brokerage firms outright forbid the practice. Others allow it, but there are often strings attached. For example, some of the big-name brokers limit the particular markets its clients can sell options in, and they narrow it down even more by limiting the contract months that can be sold. Additional restrictions come in the form of higher than exchange minimum margin requirements, quantity trading limits, and other broker-imposed handcuffs.

There are a limited number of brokerage services recognizing that despite the challenges of option selling, the strategy offers the highest long-term prospects for successful trading. My brokerage service, DeCarley Trading, specializes in optimizing the trading environment for short option traders. Not only can we provide a restriction-free home for option sellers, we are experienced in the strategy and are capable of offering peripheral services such as margin call management, efficient trade adjustments, and so forth. I'm sure there are other brokers out there willing to do similar things for their option selling clients, but it is important to understand they are few and far between. If you truly want to give option selling a fair chance at success, it is imperative you find a broker who is on your side. Nevertheless, even with the optimal brokerage relationship, option selling is far from an easy-money venture and on occasion comes with excessive risk. There is a reason many brokerage firms shy away from option selling.

WHY DO SOME FUTURES BROKERS DISCOURAGE OR FORBID SHORT OPTIONS TRADING?

The concern that most brokerage firms claim to have with option sellers isn't that such traders face unlimited risk. If that was the only issue, they wouldn't allow futures trading either (futures traders also face theoretically unlimited risk). The unease that brokers experience with short options trading is option market liquidity during highly volatile market conditions. The option market is not nearly as liquid as the underlying futures market; because of this it can sometimes be difficult to accurately value positions and account balances of option trading clients. Even worse, in extreme market conditions options can quickly become irrationally overpriced with wide bid/ask spreads, leaving option sellers and their brokerage house facing considerable danger.

If a brokerage firm has a client trading futures in danger of losing more money than is on deposit in his trading account, risk managers of the firm can easily assess the situation to determine if forced liquidation of positions is necessary. This is because they can see the exact price of the futures contracts and conclude the client's account balance quickly and precisely. Ideally, any necessary forced liquidation would occur before the account balance falls into negative territory, but that isn't a guarantee.

Keep in mind that brokerage firm risk managers have the capability to place stop-loss orders to manage risk of overleveraged futures trading clients. In a similar scenario with an option-selling client, the risk manager might not have access to reasonable valuation or pricing to determine the client's true account balance, nor does he have the ability to place a stop-loss order to prevent losses from getting out of hand. Not only does the lack of clear position valuation pose risk to the client and broker, it also requires more brokerage firm manpower and experience to manage the risk than futures trading account would. When naked short options are involved, risk management is no longer a simple calculation to determine risk of an account going negative; instead, it is a somewhat time-consuming task, with plenty of educated guesses. More so, offsetting a client's futures contract to meet a margin deficit can be done quickly and conveniently with a market order, but option orders must be placed as limit orders, which exposes the process to higher risk of error, slippage, and uncertain pricing. This is particularly true when bid/ask spread are wider than usual.

We saw a punishing case of excessive bid/ask spreads during the August 2015 downturn in the e-mini S&P 500 futures options. Toward the end of a precipitous four-day decline, the bid/ask spread in most e-mini S&P options was 10.00 points, or $500 (10 x $50), in contrast to $0.50, or $25, in normal market conditions. For a trader short a handful of options, this wide bid/ask spread would be highly annoying but possibly survivable. For those trading extremely high quantities, the spread between the price that the option could be bought and the price it could be sold was equal to tens of thousands of dollars lost in what is essentially execution price slippage. A trader short 100 December 1600 puts quoted as 25.00 bid at 35.00 offered would have hypothetically suffered an additional loss of $25,000 to $50,000 due to illiquidity. In more normal market conditions, the quote would have likely been 20.00 bid at 20.50, with a probable fill price at 20.25. But on that day, it might have been possible to buy the options back at 30.00. More realistically, for traders desperate to exit their positions, it would have been necessary to pay the ask price of 35.00. Ouch!

In addition to the burden of the bid/ask spread, option prices were increasing exponentially without reasonable limits. Those clients trading short options in high quantities could have easily seen tens of thousands of dollars vanish in an instant. Because the possibility of the spreads and option premiums blowing up, as it did in this scenario, housing short options trading clients requires far more brokerage firm risk management resources than futures traders do. As a result, traders selling naked options should expect to pay moderately more in commission for their option trades than a futures trader would.

In light of the difficulties and risk that arises in extreme market volatility when housing short option traders, deep discount commodity brokers cannot afford to let clients sell options freely; this is because their profit margin is so tight. A potential gross profit of pennies per trade, in addition to the extra work and potential of a client losing more than he has on deposit, makes it difficult to justify allowing clients to sell options under these circumstances without major restrictions.

> Don't trip over dollars chasing pennies. Choose a commodity broker who can provide a supportive environment for option selling. Trying to save pennies in commission can add up to thousands of dollars in market losses due to option selling restrictions, higher margins, and forced liquidation.

If you are trading with a discount futures broker allowing option selling, you had better be aware of the fact that your positions are prone to heavy-handed forced liquidation at the first sign of trouble. I'm frequently told stories of clients whose short options were offset by their broker without any sort of notification or opportunity to rectify any margin shortfall. In fact, some brokerage firms routinely liquidate the short option positions of clients in the absence of a margin deficit; all that is required is a little discomfort from the risk manager.

Premature and unnecessary liquidation of positions is a massive disadvantage to an option seller. After all, the strategy is based on the premise suggesting most options expire worthless. If short options are bought back before the trade has a chance to prove itself, the strategy is reduced to a surefire way to lose money. Be aware of your broker's policy and "friendliness" to option selling before getting started. Not doing so could easily be the primary difference in the overall outcome of your trading results.

HERE ARE A FEW WAYS TO INCREASE THE ODDS OF AVOIDING THE BIG LOSS

On average, option sellers will make money on more trades than they will lose on. If they don't, they are unfortunate to be grossly against probabilities. Nonetheless, the trades that sustain losses must be held in check. An option seller who isn't careful, or even one who is cautious but happens to be at the wrong place at the wrong time, might see a year's worth of gains wiped out on a single loss. What is frustrating is such a move can occur in a very short period of time—days, not weeks. Let's look at a few tips on how to avoid the account-draining loss capable of negating the benefits of an option selling strategy.

UNLESS THERE IS AN OBVIOUS DIRECTION, SELL STRANGLES

A short option trader doesn't necessarily need to have an opinion on the direction on the market. Instead, for option sellers, it isn't about what the market will do; it is more about what the market will *not* do. Thus, a popular option selling approach is one in which the market outlook is neutral. The most popular strategy for neutral option sellers is a short strangle, which involves the sale of both a call and a put.

The short strangle is a method of increasing the premium collected, while arguably increasing the chances of triumph. Favorable probabilities of a short strangle come from the fact that the trade can only lose on one side but preferably neither. Further, risk exposure on one side of the strangle is partially hedged by the additional premium collected on the other side of the strangle.

When a trader is selling both a call and a put, the breakeven point is shifted outward, compliments of the extra premium, making it less likely for the trade to lose money (all else being equal). For this reason, the underlying futures market would have to move considerably more in one direction or the other to get the trader into trouble than it would if only one side of the strangle was sold. To clarify, the breakeven calculation of a strangle is as follows:

Short Strangle Breakeven = (Call Premium + Put Premium) +/- Strike Price

Despite the benefits of collecting additional premium, and constructing a neutral position that stands to profit from time value erosion, not all market conditions are ideal for option strangle selling. For instance, a market trading at an all-time low is prone to massive buying should the trend change. Likewise, a market at an all-time high probably isn't the place for a strangle either. Once the extended rally ends, the premium collected on the put will seem minuscule in comparison to the mounting losses as the market seeks a more sustainable price level. The ideal market to sell an option strangle is one that is neither at support nor at resistance, is not overbought nor oversold, and has a relatively equal probability of going either way. More important, it should be a market displaying a considerable amount of volatility; as previously mentioned, selling options in a quiet market is a sure way to get into trouble.

USE 50% OR LESS OF YOUR AVAILABLE MARGIN

Option sellers are essentially trading volatility, or more specifically implied volatility. Implied volatility is the result of human emotions run amok and at times can lead option prices to irrational extremes. More often than not, the option market realizes it got carried away, and the implied volatility implodes within a few short days. In short, the option market frequently prices in the worst, then asks questions later.

At the hands of this exploding implied volatility, or adverse futures market movement, option sellers can experience large drawdowns whether or not the futures price ever reaches the strike price of their short option. Because these spikes in option value and volatility are often quick and temporary, riding out the ebbs and flows requires extra funds in a margin account. Those attempting to sell options using the entirety of their account balance could find themselves forced out of positions prematurely and unnecessarily. The most successful option sellers I've encountered are keeping their margin to equity ratio at 50% or less. In other words, they are only using half of their account toward margin. The other half of their account balance is there to defend against temporary spikes in option prices.

WAIT FOR BIG SPIKES IN IMPLIED VOLATILITY

At the risk of being repetitive, if you have ever read a book on trading commodity options, you're likely aware of the simple rule of being an option buyer when volatility is low and a seller when volatility is high. Unfortunately, traders often underestimate the value of this rule. Selling options during times of high volatility equates to collecting more premium than is possible in a low-volatility environment, or selling similar premium using options with relatively distant strike prices than would be the case in a low-volatility environment. Each of these scenarios increase the probability of a favorable outcome relative to a comparable strategy in a quiet market because it would require the futures price to move further to create a losing scenario.

To illustrate the importance of waiting for high levels of volatility, let's take a look at the value of some euro currency futures options on December 2, 2015, and the comparable options on December 7 just a few days later, but after a historical volatility spike.

On December 2, 2015, a trader could have sold a strangle using the March $1.00 puts and $1.12 calls, each roughly six cents away from the current market price of $1.06 for a net credit of 120 ticks, or $1,500 (120 x $12.50) because each tick in the euro is worth $12.50 to a trader. At the time, implied volatility was exceptionally elevated in anticipation of a European Central Bank meeting, and a Federal Open Market Committee (FOMC) meeting a few days later, making this a relatively ideal time to sell options. On December 3, the euro currency rallied roughly five cents in a single trading session. After finding a low near $1.0540 it reached a high of $1.1010. This was the second-largest one-day increase in the history of the euro currency. At the close, the short option strangle had increased in value moderately to about 160 ticks, or $2,000 (160 x $12.50). As a result, the strangle seller would be suffering a mere paper loss of about $500 (40 x $12.50) (Figure 49). Looking back, this trade would have been even better if executed following the central bank meetings, and the resulting massive price change in the euro. Nevertheless, a trader selling a strangle immediately preceding the meeting, or one who sold immediately after the news event, most likely fared far better than a trader who sold a strangle in the weeks prior to the spike in implied volatility.

Figure 49: Selling options at times of high implied volatility, not necessarily market volatility, can do wonders to increase the odds of a successful trade.

In light of the historical move, the option market reaction was likely disappointing to most option buyers who were expecting riches. Yet on December 7, a few days after one of the largest euro currency price changes in history, the strangle had already dwindled to 80 ticks, or $1,000. At this stage, the trade would be profitable by 40 ticks, or $500 ((120 – 80) x $12.50). A $500 profit might not be anything to brag about, but it is certainly a better scenario than a trader who either sold the strangle early in a quiet market, didn't have the margin to hold the position, or didn't have the gumption. Further, this is a great example illustrating that profits and losses are highly dependent on how a trader plans for and reacts to volatility explosions, to ensure they are still in the trade to benefit from the impending implosions.

SELL OPTIONS WITH STRIKE PRICES BEYOND SUPPORT AND RESISTANCE

Essentially, an option seller is collecting a premium in exchange for the risk of the underlying futures market trading beyond the strike price of the short option. The option strangle buyer is wagering money on a bet that futures market prices will be above the strike price of the call or below the strike price of the put. The seller of the strangle is accepting that wager and will principally "pay up" should either of the options be in-the-money at expiration. Thus, placing the strike price of any sold options beyond known support and resistance sounds like an obvious strategy, but it tends to be overlooked as traders seek more premium and disregard risk. Nevertheless, proper strike price placement is a very effective way of shifting the odds favorably (Figure 50).

Figure 50: Selling options based on their premium is a mistake. Instead, traders should identify technical levels that are most likely for price reversals, and sell options with strike prices beyond those futures prices.

KNOW THE VOLATILITY TENDENCY

Most markets have a particular direction in which they are capable of the most explosive moves. For instance, the stock market tends to take the stairs up and the elevator down. As a result, put options tend to be relatively expensive when compared to calls in the e-mini S&P 500. Even more so, S&P puts are prone to massive panic pricing in a volatile downturn. I've seen e-mini S&P puts with strike prices 300 points out-of-the-money balloon to irrationally high prices. However, S&P calls generally don't have an explosive pricing nature.

> In the excitement of a big trend, traders often behave emotionally rather than logically. As a result, they exuberantly bid up the prices of low-probability options to shocking levels.

Crude oil and the grains are typically the opposite; they have the potential to move higher faster than they can move lower. Knowing this, extra caution should be warranted when selling puts in a quiet S&P environment, or calls in a quiet grain market, or oil. On the other hand, selling grain or oil calls after a massive rally can be an attractive venture; similarly, being a put seller in the e-mini S&P 500 at a time in which the stock market is in a deep trough often provides favorable odds of success. This is because these scenarios generally produce unsustainable increases in option pricing. Nevertheless, countertrend option selling, although appealing, is a stressful undertaking. It might be necessary for anybody employing such a strategy to keep a puke bucket next to the trading desk.

SELLING COUNTERTREND OPTIONS (CAREFULLY) CAN IMPROVE ODDS

Aside from selling options in a low-volatility environment, the largest mistake that beginning premium collectors make is selling options in the direction of a prolonged trend. Conventional wisdom suggests "the trend is your friend," but to an option seller, collecting premium in the direction of the trend is akin to a car salesman getting rid of last year's model off the lot via deep discounts. On the contrary, selling an option against the trend generally provides a trader with enhanced profit potential because they are in effect selling it when demand is high.

If you do opt for a trend trading style option selling program, just be sure to enter your trades on a day in which the market is trading countertrend. For instance, in an inclining equity market, e-mini S&P 500 option sellers might be interested in selling puts. If so, they will likely have a better end result if they wait to enter their short put position on a day in which the S&P 500 is down heavily. Selling stock index puts on an "up" day, or a quiet day, lowers the profit potential and arguably the risk because the odds of an increase in implied volatility causing losses on the position is much higher than relative to selling stock index puts on a "down" day. In Chapter 17, "Use Commodity Market Volatility to Your Advantage with Mean Reversion and Delta Neutral Trading," we'll discuss this concept in greater detail.

IT TAKES MONEY TO MAKE MONEY

More so than perhaps any other strategy, option sellers must be properly funded. Those who aren't properly funded find they are unable to ride out temporary spikes in implied volatility. Not too many brokerage firms allow option selling in small accounts; in fact, many of them require tens of thousands or hundreds of thousands of dollars on deposit. With that said, it isn't necessary to have a six-figure trading account to sell options with an option-selling friendly broker. At DeCarley Trading, we allow clients of nearly all sizes to sell options as long as they are doing so within reasonable levels of risk, and of course within SPAN minimum margin requirements. Nevertheless, the goal should be to keep risk in check in regards to position sizing and margin.

POSITION SIZING FOR SHORT OPTIONS TRADING

Each short option trader has his own idea of what the appropriate position size, or margin usage rate, should be. Naturally, the decision is determined by risk tolerance, faith in the particular trade, and risk capital available. Still, in almost all circumstances the axiom "Less is more" applies. As I've attempted to emphasize, a paramount aspect of a short options trading strategy is to have the financial and mental wherewithal to withstand unfavorable spikes in price and volatility. The best way to prepare for market turmoil is to trade conservatively.

As a rule of thumb, I believe that each moderately out-of-the-money option sold should be backed by roughly $10,000 in trading equity. In low-margin markets such as the 10-year note, or the slower moving grains, it might be appropriate to sell two for every $10,000 on deposit. In a higher-margin option market such as gold and crude oil, it probably makes sense to have a little more money in the account per single lot traded.

Another way to determine the appropriate account and position size is excess margin. Generally speaking, it is a good idea to utilize 50%, or less, of your account when trading short options. If your account size is $10,000 you should aim for trades that require a margin of $3,000 to $5,000. On the flip side, the excess margin listed on the bottom of your statement should be between $7,000 and $5,000.

Some might look at the funds not being used toward margin as a missed opportunity or a waste of risk capital. However, nothing could be farther from the truth. Undercapitalized commodity option sellers will almost undoubtedly get into trouble. Even those employing either school of thought in their option selling accounts will find that intentions might not be enough to create reality. Sharp temporary price moves have the ability to dramatically increase margin requirements and decrease account liquidity in a matter of days, or hours in some cases. These occurrences are exactly why option sellers must keep large margin reserves to survive.

A lack of capital dramatically increases the odds of a margin call, which can result in premature liquidation of an option trade. If the situation is dire enough, or if you are trading with a broker ill-equipped to house short options trading accounts, the liquidation might be at the hand of your commodity broker, an unpleasant experience for all parties.

THE BOTTOM LINE ON OPTION SELLING

Option selling is not for everybody due to the prospects of theoretically unlimited risk. Yet it is a strategy that everyone should consider in light of the high probability of success on any particular trade.

Before choosing to implement an option selling strategy in the futures markets, you must first realistically assess your ability to accept the prospects of unlimited risk and margin calls. Not everyone is capable of managing the emotions that come with these two characteristics of the strategy; and even those who are will have moments of weakness. As a seasoned commodity option broker, I can attest that the markets are capable of making a grown man cry. Failure to keep trading emotions in check could mean letting losers get out of hand or panicked liquidation at unfortunate prices. Either scenario could be psychologically and financially devastating to an option selling strategy.

The most counterproductive result of such an increase in volatility is the need to buy overpriced short options back to meet a margin or liquidity deficit. Often, but not always, option values deflate nearly as quickly as they ballooned as market participants realize they overreacted. Like anything else, selling options low and buying them high is a tried-and-true recipe for losses.

APPROPRIATE MARKETS FOR OPTION SELLING

Because option liquidity is, to some degree, hit or miss, not all futures markets are viable contenders for option selling. Accordingly, I'd like to offer a guideline for choosing appropriate markets for an option selling strategy.

STICK TO LIQUIDITY AND MONITOR BID/ASK SPREADS

Without liquid option markets, speculating leans toward outright gambling. This is because trading in a market without ample liquidity takes away any ease of entering and exiting positions. Instead, traders might find themselves trapped in a position longer than they prefer, or be forced to buy and sell instruments at highly unfavorable pricing. Thus, traders should be aware of market liquidity before, during, and upon exit of a particular option contract.

Appraising a commodity market for sufficient liquidity isn't as simple as looking at daily volume and open interest stats, but it's a good start. Ample volume and open interest in the particular strike price being traded is necessary to ensure the ability to enter and exit the position at a fair price under normal market conditions. Nevertheless, during times of high market stress it might be difficult to find ample liquidity in any market or strike price; thus, even the most prudent option traders might temporarily get stuck in a trade. Those types of events are relatively rare now that electronic option trading has increased the efficiency and transparency of the market.

Back to identification of option market liquidity. If execution of the desired positions results in the trader being a majority of the open interest (the number of contracts outstanding), it is generally a poor trading vehicle. Although there could be market makers providing reasonable bid and ask quotes to execute the position on the way in, there may not be the same liquidity on the way out. Each contract is different about what constitutes enough liquidity but, ideally, you will want to see active daily volume and hundreds of contracts tallied in the open interest column of the particular option in question.

There are certain markets that appear to be sufficiently liquid but aren't. For example, heating oil options often have open interest in the hundreds, or even thousands. Most trading volume and open interest in this market is in the hands of large institutional traders hedging, or speculating on, hundreds to thousands of contracts at a time. Thus, the average retail traders attempting to execute smaller orders often face the obstacle of illiquidity simply because other market participants aren't always interested in taking the other side of low-quantity orders.

Perhaps a more telling account of market liquidity is the spread between the bid and the ask price. The difference between these two prices is a good measure of market liquidity. If severe enough, markets with wide spreads between the bid and the ask price can create a scenario in which it is nearly impossible to make money, despite accurate speculation and timing. In a less dire circumstance, a wide bid/ask spread acts as a massive drag on options trading profits. In essence, it is a hidden transaction cost that is often underestimated.

For example, at the time of this writing, an April $1.20 heating oil call option expiring in 40 days and roughly 10 cents (0.10) out-of-the-money was bid at 327 and offered (ask) at 400. You could sell this option for 327, equivalent to $1,373.40 because each tick in heating oil is worth $4.20 (327 x $4.20). Or it could be bought at 400, equivalent to $1,680 (400 x $4.20). Selling this option at the quoted bid, and immediately buying it back at the quoted ask, would produce a loss of $306.60. I don't know about you, but paying the market over $300 just to play doesn't sound that attractive. Of course, traders can opt to enter a limit order to execute a trade at a price between these two figures, but they certainly wouldn't be guaranteed a fill. This type of built-in transaction cost can be extremely difficult to overcome. In a more practical example, a short option trader desperate to buy back the position might feel forced to pay the ask price. If so, he or she might have been likely to pay a few hundred dollars above a "fair" price, had liquidity been more reasonable.

The option in this particular example had an open interest of 560 contracts. Although that wouldn't be considered wildly liquid, it is enough to lure inexperienced traders into believing it is a viable candidate for speculation. Despite healthy open interest, wide bid/ask spreads create a highly illiquid environment. In our view, most traders will find markets with unreasonable bid/ask spreads, such as heating oil, are better left untouched.

PREFERABLE OPTION SELLING MARKETS

Market characteristics—and speculator interest in them—are ever changing. Nevertheless, it has been my experience that the option markets offering the most favorable liquidity, and best trading conditions, are the following:

- Ω **Stock indices.** The e-mini S&P is at the top of the list due to favorable liquidity. There are effective market makers offering efficient bid/ask spreads nearly 24 hours per day. Although options in the e-mini NASDAQ and the e-mini Dow are far less active than the e-mini S&P 500, they are certainly worthy of consideration. To a lesser degree, the Russell 2000 is a candidate for aggressive speculators. Don't be lured to Russell 2000 options for the "fat" premium, unless you are ready for stomach-churning volatility. There is a reason Russell options are priced high: risk.

- Ω **Treasuries.** Both the 10-year note and the 30-year bond offer highly fluid option trading with tight bid/ask spreads around the clock. That said, the 30-year bond options can become highly volatile with little warning; thus, it is imperative to wait for high levels of volatility prior to entering a short option in this market. Most traders are better served selling options in the 10-year note to take advantage of lower margin requirements and lower position volatility.

- Ω **Currencies.** The euro offers speculators highly liquid options and is by far the preferable currency for option traders. However, the yen, British pound, Canadian dollar, and Australian dollar are markets to consider but should be traded in a less aggressive manner. The US dollar index, unlike the other currencies that trade on the CME, trades on the ICE. The dollar index trades in abbreviated hours, the options volume is sparse, and option premium is generally low. I believe the dollar index options are attractive to option buyers but aren't a wise choice for option sellers.

- Ω **Grains.** Corn, soybeans and, to a slightly lesser extent, wheat, are enormously liquid commodity option markets. However, soybean speculation can be highly volatile and often proves to be overly difficult for green traders to handle. Wheat options are also a good "option." Beginning traders tend to look to soybean oil and soybean meal for affordable speculations relative to soybeans, but each of these markets come with liquidity issues and should be traded relatively sparingly.

VIABLE OPTION SELLING MARKETS TO USE SPARINGLY

Ω **Meats and softs.** Both of these complexes tend to suffer from light trading volume (with the exception of sugar). These markets are certainly tradable, but because of the disadvantage of liquidity they should be used less aggressively and less frequently by options sellers than the aforementioned markets. Further, as we discuss in Chapter 15, the softs (sugar, orange juice, cocoa, and coffee) are traded on the ICE, which charges hefty fees for access to real-time price data.

Ω **Gold.** Gold options are liquid enough to trade, but they can be treacherous, so caution is warranted. Nonetheless, high option values make gold options attractive for option sellers with a high risk tolerance.

OPTION SELLING MARKETS TO AVOID

Ω **Silver.** Although gold and silver are both precious metals, I didn't want to lump them into the same category, due to vast differences in liquidity. Due to speculator interest, I also didn't want to lump silver into the group of copper, lumber, and oats (discussed next). In my opinion, silver options shouldn't be touched by the average retail trader. Although there are plenty of option traders in the arena, the exchange lists strike prices for every nickel. As a result, the liquidity for each individual option is typically thin; consequently, the bid/ask spread is excessively wide and difficult to overcome. Silver options are not ideal candidates for option sellers.

Ω **Copper, lumber, oats.** Each of these option markets is sparsely traded, leading to wide bid/ask spreads. As a result, option sellers face exaggerated risks and mitigated rewards. I've seen cases in which an option sold on a particular day is followed by multiple trading sessions of favorable price action, yet due to the bid/ask spread it was not possible to offset the short option at a profit. Illiquidity prevents traders from exiting a position before expiration with a respectable profit. Yet, it exposes traders to theoretically unlimited risk throughout that time.

Making money in trading is challenging enough. There is no reason to dabble in markets so thin that traders must dig their way out of a hole to break even.

OPTION SPREAD STRATEGIES

An option spread strategy is simply a strategy in which traders combine long and short calls and puts to accomplish a common goal. Generally, option spreads involve a primary position being hedged by antagonistic positions in related options. A common example of such a spread is what is known as a *bull call spread*, involving the

> "I don't look to jump over seven-foot bars; I look around for one-foot bars that I can step over." —Warren Buffett

purchase of a closer-to-the-money call option and the sale of a further-from-the-money call. However, in other cases each leg of the option spread strategy is a hedge; a strangle trader selling both a call and a put might not have a primary position, but he does have a position that carries an inherent hedge on both sides of the market.

The number of option spread possibilities is endless. Not only can traders determine the overall strategy, but they choose the strike prices of the spreads and the ratio of the spread. A trader might convert the bull call spread into a ratio spread by selling two calls for every call purchased. In addition, the spread can be done in any number of contract months and strike prices. As a result, option traders have access to highly customizable tools enabling them to take on as much, or as little, risk as they are comfortable with.

If you are interested in learning more about various option strategies such as their mechanics, their purpose, calculating profit and loss, and when they might be appropriate to use, please refer to my book *Commodity Options*.

COVERED CALLS AND SYNTHETIC TRADING STRATEGIES

The greatest benefit of being option savvy is the ability to apply that knowledge to aid in the speculation of futures contracts. As previously mentioned, it is often possible to purchase or sell options against futures contracts to mitigate, or at least hedge, price risk. Options sold against long or short futures positions are referred to as covered calls or covered puts, depending on whether the futures contract is long, or short, respectively. Synthetic strategies are those in which options are purchased to limit the risk of a long or short futures contract outright. This strategy can be used as a substitute for placing stop-loss orders in a futures position because it eliminates the risk of premature liquidation of the trade. We touch on such strategies throughout this book, but for a more complete discussion, my aforementioned *Commodity Options* is a great source.

CHAPTER 10: MANAGED FUTURES AND CONSTRUCTING A COMMODITY PORTFOLIO

Not everyone has the time to properly construct and employ a commodity trading strategy. Further, even those who do find the time have a difficult time attaining success. Accordingly, some interested in allocating a portion of their portfolio to commodities opt for a managed futures product. As is frequently the case in the world of finance and investments, there are smoke and mirror obstacles to overcome. In this chapter I will introduce the various managed futures products available, along with key characteristics of program types, and how to choose an allocation that might be favorable to long-term growth of a commodity portfolio.

MANAGED FUTURES

A managed futures account is just as it sounds; it is a futures and options account traded by a third party. Ideally, that third party should be capable of making better trading decisions than the account owner, but that isn't always the case. Before handing the reins over to another trader, it is important to fully understand the risks taken by the account manager. Further, past performance is not indicative of futures results. This is always true, of course, but perhaps in reference to managed futures products it is even more relevant, because the best performers one year are very often the worst the next. This is because for the high-flying managed futures programs to post stellar returns, they are likely taking on a substantial amount of risk. Eventually, that risk taking will backfire to cause massive drawdowns.

WHY MANAGED FUTURES?

Most managed futures participants are investors seeking commodity exposure without having to do the legwork or are simply interested in diversifying their portfolio away from traditional holdings such as stocks and bonds. Many academic studies have concluded that a quality balanced managed futures program has the potential to reduce the overall risk in an investment portfolio because of the negative correlation, or lack of relationship, between managed futures programs and stocks and bonds. Ideally, managed futures programs perform independently of the stock market; if stocks are declining, it is possible a managed futures program is profiting, or at least losing less. This diversification helps to smooth over a portfolio's returns and can make managed futures a popular landing place for speculative fund allocation. Nevertheless, not all managed futures products are the same; and many are not worthy of providing the diversification that investors seek due to excessive risk taking.

Growth in managed futures products has skyrocketed, and this is attributable to the benefits of diversification and the ability to easily spread exposure across several asset classes. In 2002, it was estimated that more than $50 billion was under management by commodity trading advisors (CTAs); in contrast, by the end of 2015 that number had grown to roughly $330 billion (source: BarclayHedge). However, as the commodity and financial markets have continually reminded investors, just because something is popular doesn't mean everyone should flock to participate.

Managed futures is a complicated investment venue; there are various types of managed products, a vast array of strategies, and substantial variations in the amount of risk each managed futures product accepts. Accordingly, some managed products can see intense profit and loss results, while others are rather boring, netting or shaving off a few percentage points a year. Thus, we shouldn't assume picking a managed futures investment program is anywhere near as simple as choosing a mutual fund; they are worlds apart in regard to potential consequences.

TYPES OF MANAGED FUTURES PROGRAMS

Generally speaking, there are two types of managed futures programs, CTAs and commodity pool operators (CPOs). In theory, one could say merely asking your futures broker to manage your account could fall into this category, but the truth is it doesn't. If a futures broker is willing to take discretion over your trading account, he is doing so as an additional service but he might not be officially designated as a commodity trading advisor. He won't have an official track record to comfort you, nor will he have any sort of specific binding agreement, other than he will act on your behalf in the best way he knows how. I am not saying you shouldn't participate in this type of arrangement, but chances are such a managed account leans far more toward pure speculation than achieving the goal of portfolio diversification through noncorrelated trading with moderate risk taking. If you are looking for less of a gamble and more of a diversification tool, you should be looking into formal managed programs.

COMMODITY TRADING ADVISORS

In general, when referring to managed futures we are speaking of commodity trading advisors registered as such with the National Futures Association (NFA). These are formal managed futures programs that are regulated and face strict rules dictating the methods of reporting performance to the public. Of course, you shouldn't confuse being registered and regulated as being vetted, successful, or a safe investment. When regulators audit a CTA, they aren't looking at their trading strategy, nor are they concerned with whether the trading methods are inclined to produce profits. Instead, regulators simply want to make sure the CTA is accurately reporting its performance figures to the public, offering an up-to-date disclosure document, and acting within the confines of industry rules set forth by the Commodity Futures Trading Commission (CFTC). If you are unfamiliar with disclosure documents, they are essentially contracts between a client and a CTA disclosing the risks of participating in the program, as well as some basic information regarding the trading program such as assets under management, commissions, fees, historical performance, and other pertinent information.

Some are surprised to learn CTAs aren't required to have any trading experience under their belt to become registered as such with the NFA; they must merely pass a proficiency exam written by the NFA and pay annual dues to attain the CTA designation. Simply put, you shouldn't let yourself become impressed by the CTA title because it doesn't imply any skill or experience level; it is simply an easily attainable regulator designation.

When it comes to analyzing CTA performance figures, there is more than meets the eye. In some cases, performance figures are calculated on higher than typical transaction costs, causing reported statistics to be lower than reasonable expectations. In others, performance might seem better than reasonable expectations due to random factors such as untypically favorable market conditions. Thus, don't judge a book by its cover. If you truly want to know how a CTA has performed in the past, get prepared to pull out the calculator and do some figuring.

Even after you've done your homework, there is no guarantee the success of the program will continue. As market conditions shift, CTA performance will also shift. For instance, in 2006 and 2007 volatility in the equity market was at historic lows. As a result, option selling CTAs were hot. Not only was money flocking to take part, but most of it seemed to be churning easy profits as option sellers. However, we all know what happened next. The financial collapse of 2008 wiped out nearly all of the option selling programs, some of them with near-complete loss of funds under management. Those who survived were working with pennies on the dollar in trading capital. This is a good example of just how quickly things can turn, and more important, how painful being a performance chaser might be.

A distinction unique to CTAs is the fact that each investor account is traded separately. To clarify, if you opt to invest money in a particular CTA program, you will open an account at a brokerage firm recommended by the CTA. The funds in the account would be held in the same manner any other trading account would be, in the name of the account holder, not the name of the CTA. Similarly, only the account holder would have the authority to move funds out of the trading account; the CTA merely has trading authorization over the account. All trades entered on behalf of the investor are directly allocated to the trading account where profits and losses accrue, and transaction costs such as commission and exchange fees are charged directly to the investor within the trading account. As we will discuss, CPOs and funds operate on a different format.

COMMODITY POOLS

Commodity pools are essentially the mutual funds of the futures industry. By definition, a commodity pool is a private investment structure, typically a limited partnership, which combines the contributions of multiple investors to be used in futures and options trading. A commodity pool is a fund that operates as a single entity to speculate in the futures markets on behalf of the funds multiple investors. Another way to look at it is a commodity pool is a specialized hedge fund dealing only in futures, or options on futures, traded on organized futures exchanges and is registered as such with the US regulators. A similarly organized fund capable of trading stocks, bonds, real estate, or any other asset class is referred to as a hedge fund rather than a CPO. Nevertheless, the overall concept is the same; it is just the assets being speculated on that differ.

The term *commodity pool* is a legal word assigned to this type of fund by regulators. Similar to CTAs, commodity pools are regulated by the CFTC and the NFA. This is in stark contrast to traditional mutual funds, or even hedge funds, which answer to the Securities Exchange Commission (SEC). A CPO is the person or entity responsible for managing the commodity pool assets. He is also in charge of the pool's trading activity.

> A commodity pool is essentially a hedge fund that only deals in futures, and options on futures.

A commodity pool differs greatly from a CTA in the manner in which client funds are allocated and traded. As previously discussed, CTAs trade within initially established accounts of their clients, but a CPO pools client deposits to form a fund used for trading within a single trading account. Trades are executed within the commodity pool account, with profits and losses allocated to participants based on the size of their contribution to the fund.

Investors allocating money to commodity pools are extending total trust to their CPO. They do so with the understanding they will not have access to monitor their balance, or trading activity, in real time. However, they do so for the benefit of accessing markets and strategies they couldn't otherwise afford to participate in. Thus, a pooled structure enables investors to share market risk with other investors, making it a viable manner for smaller investors to participate in relatively high-risk trading strategies. The pool investor's risk is generally limited to the amount of his or her contribution to the fund, but any venture into such an arrangement should include confirmation of risk details.

Keep in mind that although the purpose of a commodity pool is to combine investor funds to create a large pool of money to participate in the commodity markets, the funds often state minimum requirements for new pool participants. Some are surprised to learn the minimums can easily be in the hundreds of thousands, but there are certainly pools available to those who would like to get involved on a smaller scale.

Commodity pools can be appealing for small investors interested in getting involved in the futures and options markets with relatively little trading capital, but there are some glaring drawbacks to pooled arrangements relative to a more traditional CTA-managed account. This is even more troubling because of the manner at which pools are structured, they are prone to fund misappropriation, and even misuse.

TRANSPARENCY ISSUES WITH COMMODITY POOLS VS. CTAS

Commodity pools involve complex accounting of client funds, trading activities, and fund expenses. As a result, not only are investors in the pool splitting the risk and reward of trading ventures, they are also sharing the burden of management and administrative costs. Because of the convolution of comingling pool participants' funds, there is little transparency in the process of when, how, and where client funds are being traded. Simply, it is the CPOs' world, and pool investors are just financiers who happen to be living in it.

> Commodity pools are hotbeds of fraud due to their organizational structure and a lack of transparency.

To clarify, a trader opting to use a CTA, as opposed to a pool, for their managed futures allocation would open a futures and options trading account, fund it, and then hand the reins over to an account manager to implement a chosen trading program. From there, a CTA investor receives daily statements displaying trading activity and account balances. In contrast, an investor in a commodity pool simply writes a check and hopes the pool operator acts with integrity. Other than a periodic statement issued by the pool itself, often quarterly, there is little information available to track trading activity and ensure the money is being used according to the pool agreement. As a result of the lack of transparency, commodity pools are hotbeds for fraud. While most CPOs operate with high levels of honor, investment Ponzi schemes and other types of deceit often use commodity pools as their vehicle. Not surprisingly, many of the commodity firms that industry regulators, namely the NFA, shut down are commodity pools. I'm not saying that all pools are improperly managed, but before investing in such a fund, it is imperative that you do your homework and know what you are getting into!

POOL INVESTORS LACK CONTROL RELATIVE TO CTA INVESTORS

Pool participants have very little control over the trading in their account, the administrative fees incurred on their behalf, or even the brokerage firm the funds are being held at. In a post–MF Global and PFG world, the brokerage firm holding your commodity trading funds is a crucial decision. If you aren't familiar with the MF Global or PFG fiascos, a quick Google search will enlighten you, but in a nutshell both of these futures brokers failed to properly segregate their client margin deposits from firm funds. As a result of bad investments and pilfering, client funds went missing. Improved industry regulations and transparency, reduce the risk of a repeat of either PFG or MF Global to "slim-to-none," in my opinion. Yet, for the sake of peace of mind, the ability to choose the brokerage firm is a welcomed luxury.

In contrast to pool investments, managed futures programs via a CTA typically enable clients to choose their brokerage firm and are not normally subject to administrative fees (but will pay CTA management fees), and in some cases might be granted some discretion in the risk/reward profile applied by the account manager.

> Regretfully, I was featured on an episode of *American Greed* as a victim of the PFG brokerage fraud. Yet, I believe the industry has taken the steps needed to avoid a repeat.

Most important, unlike CTA investors who are generally free to withdraw funds as they wish, or at least quarterly, commodity pool investors are generally locked into their pool investment for several months, or even years, after the initial investment is made. Along with the lack of transparency, the control that commodity pools deny investors is another feature that opens the door to fraudulent behavior of CPOs. Again, I'm not suggesting that all pools are mishandled; nor am I saying that all investors should avoid pools. I'm simply saying the organizational structure allows for inappropriate handling of funds much more conveniently than the CTA model does. Thus, pool participants must be aware of the big picture and exercise additional due diligence prior to risking their hard-earned money.

MANAGEMENT AND INCENTIVE FEES FOR CTAS AND CPOS

Managed futures products are commonly in business to generate management and incentive fees from clients. In essence, management fees are those charged to CTA clients or a commodity pool investment to cover day-to-day operational expenses. Management fees are charged regardless of performance of the trading program and are typically about 2% annually. Incentive fees, on the other hand, are only charged to clients if the trading performance is making progress. The most common calculation of incentive fees involves a high watermark, which prevents CTAs from charging their clients incentive fees on the same profit.

For example, if an investor starts with $100,000 in a commodity account and hands the reins over to a CTA who charges a 2% management fee and a 20% incentive fee due quarterly, he might expect to pay roughly $500 per quarter to simply have the account up and running ($100,000 x 2% x 0.25). Of course, the exact fee will vary with the balance; if the balance drops to $90,000, the quarterly management fee will be closer to $450, but if the account balance increases to $110,000, the management fee will be in the ballpark of $550.

If the account increased in value to $110,000 from $100,000 after all transaction fees and management fees are deducted, the investor must pay incentive fees on his profits, in this example 20%, or $2,000 (($110,000 - $100,000) x 20%)). However, if in the next quarter the account suffers a drawdown of $5,000, the client will be subject to the quarterly management fee, but he won't pay another incentive fee until the account gets above its all-time high quarterly balance of $110,000. Should the third quarter see the account balance move up to $115,000, the incentive fee charged would be based on 20% of the incremental increase from the high watermark of $110,000. In this example, the incentive fees would be charged on the $5,000 above the previous account level in which incentive fees were charged, which equals $1,000 (($115,000 - $110,000) x 20%)). Keep in mind, these fees are only charged and calculated on the last day of the quarter, or whichever date the trading program has specified in their disclosure document. In regard to fee calculation, the account balance between measurement dates is irrelevant.

If you have done the math, you already know after three quarters of trading, the account would have paid $1,500 in management fees and $3,000 in incentive fees to harvest a net profit of $8,500 at the end of the third quarter (keep in mind the last batch of management and incentive fees have been taken off the top at this point). On the surface, paying roughly $4,500 in fees to a CTA to return $8,500 to your trading account isn't such a bad deal. But if you consider the fact that the investor is putting up the trading capital and accepting all of the risk, it would be difficult for some to swallow. Remember, CTAs don't always make money. In fact, many CTAs lose money. Thus, the costs and risk of participating in such a program are substantial, so be sure to understand the overheads before putting your hard-earned money on the line.

CONSTRUCTING A COMMODITY PORTFOLIO

Although some traders are lured to the commodity markets with dreams of hitting it big, most have realistic expectations and are simply looking for diversification from their traditional investments. Ironically, the same diversification seekers fail to properly allocate their trading capital in the commodity markets in a diversified manner. Unlike stock or bond investments, commodity traders aren't necessarily going long the underlying asset and holding for the long haul. Instead, they are navigating the market with much more speculative strategies and trading programs. Accordingly, it is necessary to diversify *within* a commodity portfolio as well.

There are some CTAs and automated systems specializing in a long-only approach to commodities, but most futures and options trading programs seek to make money on both sides of the trade. They are not always successful, but in theory they are indifferent to a bull or bear market. Nevertheless, similar to the importance of diversifying among multiple asset classes, it is imperative to allocate money to various market strategies. I've yet to find an approach that works in all market environments, so it is best to have eggs in multiple baskets. After all, the big commodity strategy in one year is rarely the best for the following year.

For example, a commodity investor with $100,000 might be best served allocating $33,000 to a futures trading system, $33,000 to an options trading CTA, and the remaining $33,000 toward a self-directed account to trade as he sees fit. The idea of doing so is based on the premise that one method of trading might be overperforming while at the same time one of the other trading methods is underperforming.

Most traders believe they can produce better returns for themselves than an algorithm developed by a third party or an account managed by a CTA. As a result, they fail to properly diversify their commodity investment allocation. Nevertheless, in my opinion, anybody wishing to put six figures toward commodity trading should strongly consider giving a portion to established trading programs.

Here are a few things to keep in mind when choosing where to park funds earmarked for commodity trading:

ALLOCATE BETWEEN MANAGERS

Even professional traders with decades of experience are human beings, and therefore, they are subject to the same emotional mishaps anybody else is. When choosing where to allocate funds within a commodity trading portfolio, it probably isn't enough to put trading capital in different programs offered by the same account manager. For instance, some CTAs have option selling programs in addition to futures trading programs; it might be a mistake to put money to work in both programs because they might end up being somewhat correlated despite the difference in trading method. Of course, the goal is to find trading programs that are not correlated to aid in diversification.

ALLOCATE BETWEEN TIME FRAMES

Perhaps the most crucial act of diversification in a commodity portfolio is to choose trading programs, whether it is a managed account by a CTA, an investment in a commodity pool, or an automated trading strategy, with differing time frames used to derive entry and exit signals. It might be a good idea to pair a long-term futures or options trading strategy with a shorter-term approach. This might mean allocating a portion of the funds to a day trading program and a portion to a swing trading method; or a swing trading option selling program and a position trading futures trading program. There isn't a correct or incorrect answer, but each strategy in the portfolio must offer logically uncorrelated profits and losses. Correlation between asset prices, as well as commodity strategies, can be unpredictable. During times of extreme volatility, it isn't uncommon for all markets to move as one. As a result, trading strategies of different time frames, and even market approaches, can move together. Nevertheless, keeping money spread among what are normally uncorrelated programs should keep drawdowns mitigated.

DON'T CHASE PERFORMANCE

> Hot trading programs can turn cold on a dime. Look for programs with good long-term track records, but are currently in a slump.

The most common disclosure printed on financial market pamphlets, magazines, books, and commentary is "past results aren't indicative of future performance." Yet most people continue to make financial investment decisions according to the latest and greatest strategy posting blockbuster performance figures. You can't blame them, of course; they have little else to go on other than what the fund or program has done in the past, but unfortunately, the better the program has done historically might actually indicate rough times ahead. As I've mentioned, trading strategies go through boom and bust cycles, not unlike the commodity and financial markets themselves. The good times never last, but the bad times generally don't either.

With this in mind, it is important to keep track of how the fund or program has fared in the long run. Too often investors want to jump into a trading program that is hot now but has a short track record. If a trading program has less than five years of history, extra caution is warranted. I've seen programs that began trading in the e-mini S&P in 2013 or 2014 while volatility was extremely low post attractive historical performances, but once volatility returned in 2015, the seemingly flawless strategy appeared to blow up. Market cycles last five to 10 years, so to get a true picture of how a strategy will behave in various market conditions, it is desirable to have lengthy track records to consider.

Perhaps the ideal trading program might be one with a lengthy track record displaying stable to positive results but is currently experiencing a current drawdown. In other words, try to buy the program performance "low" and sell it "high."

CHAPTER 11: HEDGING PORTFOLIO AND BUSINESS OPERATIONS RISK WITH FUTURES AND OPTIONS

I t is easy to forget the futures markets were created to enable members of the economy to hedge price risk of the goods and services they either produce or utilize. Farmers and other agricultural producers and end users are subject to substantial risk, and sometimes reward, in business operations as the price of commodities such as corn and oil fluctuate. Likewise, both institutional and individual investors often use the futures markets to hedge price risk in their portfolios using futures and options in the stock indices, Treasuries, and even currencies.

Because the purpose of the commodity markets is to shift price risk to speculators through futures hedges or option positions, it is the most efficient arena of hedging price exposure. However, don't mistake efficient for cheap; in all walks of life, insurance is an expensive luxury. Further, even the most efficient suites of hedging vehicles in the world can have flaws. Let's take a closer look.

WHAT IS A HEDGE?

Having been a futures broker for more than a decade has enabled me to meet all types and sizes of hedgers. I can attest that although most come to the commodity markets with the intention of hedging, many end up speculating—at least in part. It is human nature to have an opinion, and to want to make money on that opinion. Thus, whether the goal is to hedge a portfolio or a true commodity, there is a strong tendency for market participants to implement a strategy that might be more speculative in nature than a bona fide hedge tactic. Nevertheless, a true hedge is one in which a position is taken in the futures and options market that is opposite in nature to the hedger's cash market circumstance. This makes sense because only an antagonistic futures trade will counteract any price change in the cash market.

For example, a corn farmer with a field of corn planted in the spring will look to sell his harvested crop in the fall. In order for a farmer to properly budget his operation, it is necessary to know the price he will be able to sell his corn. However, in the meantime, the price of corn can change dramatically. Thus, a farmer wishing to lock in a sales price for his crop would need to sell a futures contract to take the opposite position of his long cash market position. In other words, the farmer is said to be long corn in the form of his planted crop and must take a short position in the futures market to offset his price risk. If the price of corn goes up, he is making money in the cash market but losing it in the futures market, and vice versa. Conversely, he might decide to forgo a futures hedge; purchasing a put option instead essentially places a floor on the price of corn in exchange for the premium paid.

INSURANCE IS EXPENSIVE

Ignoring complex multileg option spread strategies or futures spreads, there are two primary instruments used to hedge price risk in the commodity markets—futures and options on futures. The use of either will provide price protection to hedgers, but it always comes at a relatively high cost because of the cost burden and opportunity cost of forgoing favorable cash market price changes. I know several ranchers and farmers who opt to be "cash market speculators" as opposed to hedging their price risk. In reality, the best course of action is somewhere in the middle through the use of a partial hedge.

COST OF HEDGING WITH OPTIONS

In the simplest form, long options provide traders and hedgers with the ability to purchase insurance against the price risk of any particular asset listed on the futures exchanges. An investor wishing to protect the value of his portfolio against a potential downturn might consider purchasing put options in the e-mini S&P 500. Doing so will provide portfolio protection from a broad-based selloff in stocks in exchange for a significant fee in the form of option premium. Or those looking to keep costs low, in exchange for less protection, can opt to purchase catastrophic insurance for a less intrusive fee. This is no different from choosing health insurance policies. Consumers can purchase low-deductible insurance with less out of pocket expense risk at a higher premium. Or they can opt for cheaper insurance premiums in exchange for high deductibles.

To illustrate the costs and benefits of purchasing options as portfolio insurance, we are going to turn to an asset class most readers likely own—equities. However, any strategy or topic discussed in regard to stock indices can be applied to those interested in hedging commodity price risk in the energy sector, metals, grains, and so on. With the S&P 500 valued at 1,900, each contract traded on the CME has a value of $95,000; as a reminder, this can be figured by multiplying the point value of $50 by the value of the index (1,900 x $50). An investor wishing to achieve the highest level of protection offered by the option market over the next 60 days would seek to purchase an at-the-money put option expiring in two months.

The cost of such insurance varies based on market volatility and perceived value in such protection by market participants, but one thing is for sure—it isn't cheap. Consequently, traders should look to purchase put options to hedge price risk at levels they believe to be near a peak, not after sharp selling has forced them into

> Hedge when you can, not when you think you must.

taking protective action. Those buying puts after the market has already declined substantially will most likely be throwing good money after bad.

With our example, we'll assume the cost of an at-the-money put (1900 strike) with 60 days to expiration is 60 points, which is relatively realistic should the volatility index (VIX) be hovering between 20 and 25. Keep in mind, the VIX spends most of its time below 20, so the premium examples provided will be on the higher side of history, but still reasonably accurate. Sixty points equates to $3,000 (60 x $50).

In an environment in which the VIX is higher, a similar put would cost considerably more; and if the VIX were depressed it might cost much less. In any case, as is evident by this example, this type of ambitious hedge becomes expensive. In fact, if a stock investor laid out $3,000 every two or three months to protect $95,000 worth of stock holdings, he would essentially be paying anywhere from 12% to 18% annually for insurance! Obviously, employing continuous and aggressive hedging strategies doesn't make sense from a math perspective. An investor doing so could easily guarantee himself a losing proposition.

The same portfolio hedger might decide to attain a more reasonable amount of risk coverage by simply purchasing a cheaper deep-out-of-the-money put to ensure protection against catastrophic loss. Given the same level of volatility and time horizon as the given example, a trader might be able to purchase an 1800 put for 30 points, or $1,500 (30 x $50), a 1750 put for about 23 points ($1,150), or a 1700 put for 15 points ($750).

Despite the out-of-the-money option strikes being far more economical than the at-the-money hedge would be, I think we can all agree portfolio insurance is extremely expensive. Even the cheapest scenario of a 1750 put would cost anywhere from 2% to 5% of the portfolio value on a yearly basis. Even more discouraging, the insurance only pays off after a 10% decline. For these reasons, for most people, portfolio insurance is more attractive as an idea than it is in practice. Nonetheless, later on, we'll offer a few ideas to hedge a portfolio on the cheap, which might make more sense for the average equity market hedger.

COST OF HEDGING WITH FUTURES

Unlike hedging with options, which requires a cash outlay that will likely never be returned, a futures hedger's cost isn't necessarily monetary. A futures hedger is paying an opportunity cost to alleviate price risk. In essence, he is forgoing any favorable market movement in exchange for price certainty. There will be times the hedge pays off tenfold, such as the infamous Southwest Airlines hedge of fuel costs just before crude oil surged to over $100 per barrel in the late 2000s. Thanks to futures contracts purchased, the airline was essentially making enough money on their futures hedges to cover the increased cost of purchasing fuel in the cash market.

However, imagine an airline that established a futures hedge of their fuel costs in 2014 with oil over $100. All of the savings incurred in the cash market at the hands of cheaper fuel was eaten up in losses in the futures market hedges. In other words, a futures hedger is guaranteeing his price and eliminating uncertainty, but giving up the possibility of beneficial price changes. In my opinion, it makes sense for hedgers to implement a partial hedge during times that they believe cash market prices will move favorably. A portfolio hedger holding $200,000 worth of stocks might use a single e-mini S&P 500 position to protect half of his portfolio if the index is deemed to be lofty in value. Conversely, if the S&P 500 is trading in a trough, the investor likely missed his opportunity to properly hedge price risk; on the heels of a market selloff, the market might be closer to a bottom than a top making a hedge strategy less desirable.

THERE IS NO SUCH THING AS THE PERFECT HEDGE

Buying or selling a futures contract that is antagonistic to a cash market position is the more pure form of hedging relative to options; yet, there will never be a perfect hedge. In regards to commodities, factors such as variants in local cash market prices relative to the futures, as well as inaccurate predictions of accurate crop yields, and so forth, all work against a perfect hedge.

Shifting focus back to portfolio hedging, because it will be useful to most readers, the efficiency of a hedge is compromised by differences in portfolio value relative to the contract values available for hedging. The e-mini S&P futures enable traders to hedge roughly $100,000 worth of stocks with a single contract, depending on the value of the S&P at the time, but a portfolio containing $350,000 could only be partially hedged using $300,000 worth of the e-mini (three contracts), or overhedged, using $400,000 of the e-mini (four contracts). In addition, the majority of market participants don't hold the equivalent S&P 500 portfolio. Instead, they own an array of equities covering multiple asset classes and even countries. Even so, the e-mini likely offers the best solution available to portfolio hedgers.

There is something else to be aware of when hedging a portfolio: the implementation of a full futures hedge roughly limits portfolio gains to dividends. This is because, in essence, a trader selling one e-mini S&P futures contract for each $95,000 invested in broad-based stocks is simply long in one arena and short in the other. Aside from dividends, any gains or losses will be circumstantial based in differences between the value of the S&P 500 and the actual stock portfolio allocation. As you can imagine, once the hedge is implemented, it can be frustrating to see higher stock prices because the trader no longer participates in the gains, but hopefully the stocks in the portfolio are high yielders.

It is difficult to justify a full futures hedge under most circumstances. Even a market trading near multiyear highs might not be a candidate for an aggressive hedge to this magnitude. As mentioned previously, partial hedges can be a great way to get the best of both worlds. A trader with a $300,000 stock portfolio could sell a single e-mini S&P futures contract to provide a cushion against a large equity market decline. In this scenario, the futures hedge would shave off about 30% off of any stock market gain, but it also turns a 10% market decline into a more manageable 7%. Not only would the hedge mitigate losses in a downturn, but it would go a long way toward managing the emotions of such an event while enabling the portfolio to collect 100% of the dividends as usual. Obviously, it is in the investor's best interest to implement the hedge on a market upswing and liquidate the hedge on a downswing.

In any case, unless a stock investor is holding his entire portfolio in an ETF or mutual fund that mimics the S&P 500, it is highly unlikely that there will be 100% correlation between the stock portfolio and the e-mini S&P. Thus, even if the intention is to provide a 30% hedge with the purchase of one e-mini S&P for every $300,000 in a stock portfolio, the final outcome might be moderately skewed.

A BETTER WAY TO HEDGE?

We've discussed the mechanics and flaws of using a long option hedge, as well as a futures hedge. Now let's focus on a less talked about method of hedging using a combination of long and short options. We'll also discuss the importance of timing hedges properly. After all, a hedge only benefits the investor if the proceeds are actually realized. In short, temporary paper profits resulting from a hedge are comforting, but in the end, they only count if the cash register is rung.

STRAY FROM CONVENTIONAL PRACTICES

There might only be two hedging vehicles, options and futures, but that doesn't mean there aren't other methods of hedging price risk. In fact, there are nearly unlimited strategies with varying levels of aggression, all made possible using combinations of these two instruments.

We've already acknowledged a hedge that offsets *all* of the price risk isn't always necessary, nor is it feasible due to extravagant costs. Instead, hedgers should focus on a method of price risk

> "Doubt is the father of invention." — Galileo Galilei

management keeping the outright, and opportunity, costs at manageable levels. Failure to do so fundamentally defeats the purpose of being in the market at all.

I believe a more logical approach to hedging can be derived by getting creative in cost control methods. For example, a strategy known as a risk reversal can be an effective way to cheaply and effectively hedge a portfolio.

Imagine the ability to purchase a put option in the e-mini S&P without the burden of paying a hefty option premium.

At a time in which the S&P 500 is trading at 2,000, a single put option would protect $100,000 (2,000 x $50) of a stock portfolio from a down draft. As we know, on its own, the purchase of such protection is outrageously expensive and acts as a massive obstacle to a profitable portfolio. However, a trader employing a risk reversal strategy would sell a call option to pay for the put option aimed at protecting the stock portfolio. Depending on how the trade is structured, it might result in "free" insurance in regards to out of pocket expense.

Let's take a look at an example. Assuming the VIX is near 20 and the S&P 500 is near 2,000, it might be possible for a hedger to purchase an 1800 put option for 21 points, or $1,050 (21 x $50). Doing so would protect the investor for a decline in excess of 10%, but not only would it fail to hedge a shallow correction, it would incur a substantial cost for the peace of mind. To cut the cost of insuring his portfolio, the investor could sell a 2100 call for 20 points; the proceeds pay for the cost of purchasing the 1800 put. The result is free portfolio insurance against a 10% drop on $100,000 worth of equities with an S&P 500–type allocation.

It is imperative to be aware of the opportunity cost involved in a risk reversal hedging strategy. Although selling a call option results in relatively free insurance from a cash expenditure point of view, the investor's cost is in the form of potentially forgoing profits should the market rally above 2100. In this example, the short 2100 call limits gains on the stock portfolio to 2,100, or 5%. This is because as the market moves above 2,100, any gains on the portfolio are offset by losses in the short 2100 call option. Generally speaking, a 5% rally per quarter is far above the average return, so under normal market conditions, it should be an opportunity cost worth accepting. Using the example above, a trader is giving up any gains in the S&P 500 above 2,100 to spare himself from the stress of a dip below 1,800.

TIMING IS EVERYTHING: HEDGES ONLY WORK IF YOU LOCK IN THE PROCEEDS

Whether the goal is to hedge commodity price risk or a stock portfolio, the end goal of a hedge should be to provide monetary benefits in addition to the luxury of stress reduction. With that said, a hedge will only provide a financial benefit if the timing is right and there are some profits locked in along the way. An investor who purchases an e-mini S&P put option for portfolio protection at a time the equity market is trading near an all-time high might eventually find his stock portfolio under pressure and his option hedge making a substantial profit.

> "It wasn't raining when Noah built the ark." —Warren Buffett

Nevertheless, if the investor simply rides out the wave of stock market destruction without ever taking a profit on the protective put, it is highly probable the market will recover to render the once-profitable insurance policy worthless. Failure to take profits on the long put lands the investor in a worse position than he would have been in without hedging his portfolio at all because he has now surrendered the cost of the put option, and possibly sustained moderate losses in the stock portfolio. Remember, the insurance only pays off on a decline in excess of 10% in this example. Thus, a decline of anything less than that results in a loss in stock value and the loss of insurance premium. On the flip side, despite a lack of monetary benefit for a hedger who fails to take profits on the hedge, he might have at least prevented the disaster of a panic liquidation of the stock portfolio. Of course, taking profits on the long put leaves the portfolio unprotected, but barring any sharp collapse, the net result should be favorable relative to either not having a hedge or failing to take profits on a hedge that pays off.

The bottom line is a hedge works best when implemented at a time in which the price and circumstance are right, not when it seems necessary to thwart disaster. If a hedge is being employed after a substantial adverse price move, it is too late. Employing a hedge when you can, not when you have to, ensures the risk reversal can be executed favorably because the sold call option would be overpriced and the long put underpriced. Attempting to execute the same strategy after a stock market plunge will force traders to do the exact opposite of what is required of traders to make money, buy low and sell high.

Similarly, if the investor chooses to use a simple long put to insure his portfolio, he will be able to get more bang for his buck in a low-volatility environment with stock prices at lofty levels. Attempting to buy a protective put after the equity market has tumbled will require the investor to pay too much for the insurance, which is counterproductive. It is naïve to assume that a hedge will perform similarly in any environment, because timing does matter!

SECTION 3: THINKING OUTSIDE OF THE BOX FOR PRODUCT SELECTION, STRATEGY DEVELOPMENT, AND RISK MANAGEMENT

Trading in the commodity markets is more of an art than it is a science. When developing a trading game plan, it is vital to explore all possibilities by viewing the markets as an open canvas of creativity. Too often, traders flock to what is easy and convenient, such as trading outright futures or options, but in doing so they are overlooking opportunities to shift the probability of successful speculation in their favor. In Section 3, we are going to build on the base of information accumulated thus far and, ideally, open minds to the endless possibilities of strategy aggression and risk management.

CHAPTER 12: THE HIDDEN GEMS OF THE COMMODITY MARKETS

Unfortunately, the highly leveraged and volatile nature of the commodity markets has a tendency to lure traders into dreams of windfall profits. Yet the net result of most trading accounts is inevitable losses. In most circumstances, traders are simply overleveraged or undercapitalized. The lack of available margin simply leaves too little room for error to facilitate potential trading rewards. However, an often-overlooked manner of alleviating the disadvantage of being a smaller trader is the use of the CME Group's suite of e-micro futures contracts and the mini grains.

Although there aren't options listed on e-micro and mini grain complexes, the smaller contract size should be sufficient in keeping risk and margin low for nearly all traders. To clarify, some of these products come with margin requirements as low as $200, and point values as low as $1! Let's take a brief look at this group of contracts.

E-MICRO GOLD

Gold is the epitome of a commodity market, but it can be one of the most treacherous futures markets to participate in, making it out of reach for many speculators. The precious metal's price is capable of volatile price swings that can make even the soundest of traders look foolish. Even those trying to mitigate volatility by trading options find the cost and risk to be extremely high. For some traders, the standard-sized gold futures contract of 100 ounces listed on the CME Group's COMEX exchange is simply too big for comfortable speculation. Consequently, many small to moderately sized retail traders have given up on the idea of speculating in the yellow metal. Alternatives such as ETFS, on the other hand, despite being more manageable in regards to risk, are highly inefficient instruments for commodity speculation due to the necessity of fund rebalancing and administrative fees. In spite of all this, most traders venturing into the commodity markets yearn for the excitement of gold.

For those traders with low risk tolerance, or a preference for sound sleep, there is a way to participate in the pure speculation that futures markets offer with manageable risk: e-micro gold futures. The e-micro eliminates many of the challenges the original-sized gold futures pose. For instance, the margin needed to trade a single contract of the original 100-ounce gold futures overnight ranges between a hefty $4,500 to $8,500 (depending on volatility), but the 10-ounce e-micro version of the futures contract can be traded for as little as $400 to $900. Similarly, although a 100-ounce contract produces a profit or loss of $100 per $1 change in the price of gold, an e-micro trader experiences an account value change of only $10. Obviously, due to the reduced contract size, the e-micro gold offers little value to day traders. Yet, for those looking to buy and hold or the opposite, for days, weeks or months, the e-micro is a great option.

E-MICRO CURRENCIES

The e-micro currency suite was introduced by the CME Group as an answer to the popularity of trading in the forex markets. If you are unfamiliar with the term *forex*, it is an acronym for "foreign exchange" and is used to identify the spot currency market. Many beginning traders fail to understand, or even recognize, the differences between trading currencies in the futures market relative to the spot forex market, but they are profound. If you are interested in learning more about this topic, you might find value in my book *Currency Trading in the Forex and Futures Markets*. In summary, forex transactions take place on a synthetic market created either by individual brokerage firms or a group of liquidity providers such as banks and other financial institutions. In my opinion, these synthetic markets are a potential disadvantage to forex traders. I believe currency traders are better off speculating in the futures markets

Prior to the advent of the e-micro currency futures, the sole advantage to trading forex over currency futures was the ability to gain access to small contract sizes and margins. However, the CME recognized they were losing market share in this arena and responded with e-micro futures.

Currency speculators seeking cross-pairs, which is any pair of currencies that doesn't include the US dollar such as the popular British pound vs. Japanese yen (GBP/JPY), won't find what they are looking for in the e-micro futures suite. Nonetheless, for those looking to trade the major currency pairs such as the euro vs. the dollar (EUR/USD), the e-micros are an untapped resource.

The margin required to establish a position in the e-micro futures contracts varies from about $170 to $500, depending on the pair chosen. The most popular EUR/USD e-micro contract generally carries a margin requirement of about $300 to $400 and a point value of $1.25 per tick. Thus, for every penny in price movement, such as from $1.10 to $1.11, a trader makes or loses $125. I think we can all agree that this is an affordable alternative to the full-sized contract, which typically carries a margin requirement of anywhere from $2,500 to $5,000 and a point value of $12.50 per tick, equivalent to $1,250 per penny in price change in the currency pair.

If you've done the math, you probably realize the e-micro is a tenth of the regular contract. The original EUR/USD futures contract represents 125,000 euro, but the e-micro contract size is a mere 1,250 units.

Obviously, you will never get rich trading e-micro currencies, but meager or moderately capitalized traders might find them extremely useful in scale trading strategies, or even less-structured dollar cost averaging strategies.

MINI GRAINS

The mini grain futures complex were among the first of the commodity mini-sized contracts. At the time they were introduced, corn was trading well under $5.00 per bushel, probably closer to $2.00. And soybeans were hovering in the $5.00 to $8.00 range. The thought of "beans in the teens" was more of a pipe dream than a realistic trading idea. Thus, their small contract size and risk reward prospects were almost laughable. Little did we know that in just a few years, mini grain futures would be an attractive alternative to trading larger contracts in a historically volatile grain market.

Similar to the e-micro futures, there are no options listed for the mini grain contracts, but the futures contracts themselves are sized in a manner enabling relatively comfortable speculation for traders of all sizes. There are three mini grain contracts listed by the CME Group: mini corn, mini wheat, and mini soybeans. Even though liquidity in the mini grain complex leaves something to be desired, they can certainly be efficiently traded, thanks to proficient market makers. Market makers are willing to "make a market" in the lightly traded mini complex because they can easily use guidance from the full-sized contract to gauge price and even hedge their risk if necessary. Although due to the small risk involved, I would assume most market makers are willing to execute orders "naked," at least momentarily.

Each of the mini-sized grains come with a contract size of 1,000 bushels of the underlying commodity, a point multiplier of $10, and an initial margin requirement ranging between $200 and $500. This is exactly one fifth the size of the original contract, offering traders the ability to easily manage a dollar cost averaging trading approach in nearly any account size.

USE SMALL CONTRACT SIZE TO YOUR ADVANTAGE: DOLLAR COST AVERAGE

Too many speculators bypass e-micro and mini contracts as being either boring or a complete waste of time. However, I argue they are an extraordinary step in leveling the playing field for market participants. Simply said, not all traders have the risk capital to establish a long-term scale trade. Nor do they have the wherewithal to ride out normal ebb and flow in the commodity markets. As a result, they are often forced out of trades before their analysis has a chance to prove itself.

Trading smaller contract sizes, which essentially mitigates the leverage involved, creates an opportunity in which there is greater allowance for inaccuracy. Even the best of fundamental or technical analysts will fail to predict prices with any precision. In a perfect world, we would all buy the lows and sell the highs, but anybody who trades will tell you this is nearly impossible. Relatively accurate speculation in the direction of a commodity market might not be enough to avoid drawdowns in a trade before the market finally moves in the desired direction. Thus, it makes sense to enter a position trade with a nibbling strategy as opposed to entering the market all at once. We first introduced this idea in Chapter 6. Such an approach is much easier to implement with e-micro and mini contracts than would be the case using the full-sized version.

To illustrate the benefits of smaller futures contracts, assume a trader wants to be long 100 ounces of gold. He has the option to buy a full-sized contract at the market price; we'll assume it is $1,150, and hope he was savvy enough to pick a good entry spot. Alternatively, he might look to buy an e-micro gold futures contract at $1,150 while placing an order to buy another at $1,145, another at $1,140, and so on. Doing so permits traders to possibly improve their average entry price and mitigates the odds of the mental anguish of a large drawdown. In addition, a lower average entry price creates a scenario in which the price of gold must appreciate less to turn a profit to the trader. Previously, this type of entry technique was reserved for large speculators.

Of course, a trader intending to dollar cost average his price on the way into a speculative trade is accepting the possibility of not executing the entire trade. If gold immediately rallied upon entry of the initial purchase at $1,150, the trader misses out on the benefits of holding a larger position into the favorable price move.

Even traders whose intent is to be long gold in smaller quantities can benefit from the comfort of the smaller contract size. At a margin requirement typically far less than $1,000, a small retail trader can get long gold futures on a long-term basis with reasonable risk. To put the difference in leverage between the e-micro and the full-sized contract in perspective, a trader purchasing the traditional 100-ounce futures contract at $1,150 with the intention of being in the trade for the long haul would see a drawdown of $5,000 if prices make their way to $1,100. This would be enough for most retail traders to shed a tear or two...or at least lose some sleep. Conversely, an e-micro trader would be suffering a loss of a mere $500 and likely be eager to add a contract to the position as a means of favorably averaging his entry price. It is easy to see how the mental state of each of these traders might be dramatically different. In addition, I think it is fair to say most prefer the latter.

SMALLER FUTURES CONTRACTS TO WIN THE MENTAL GAME

It is no secret that opting to trade e-micro futures over the full-sized version equates to far less profit potential. However, I'd like to point out that most speculative traders lose money. Thus, perhaps trading smaller with similarly smaller profit potential directly equals smaller risk, and arguably, higher probabilities of success. Because e-micro and mini contracts are undeniably less stressful than their full-sized counterparts, it is reasonable to assume their use is a step toward winning the mental game of trading.

> "Trading is a psychological game. Most people think they are playing against the market, but the market doesn't care. You're really playing against yourself." —Martin Schwartz

I've always believed success and failure at most tasks in life boils down the mental toughness, focus, and dedication, as opposed to native talent. Accordingly, I firmly trust that the difference between making and losing money in the futures markets is largely dependent on the trader's ability to remain calm in trying situations, and avoid the ego that comes with large profits. I think we can all agree that it is easier to keep your wits about you when the risk and reward is smaller. Similarly, the higher the leverage and volatility in your account balance, the more prone to panicked and detrimental decision making you will be. Opting for e-micros and minis are a great way to keep destructive emotions at bay.

E-MICROS AND MINIS "BUY" YOU TIME

Although day traders might argue otherwise, it is generally easier to correctly speculate on the direction of futures prices on a long-term or intermediate-term basis. Attempting to predict what might happen in the next few hours, or days, is a difficult proposition. For some traders, the margin burden and risk of a full-sized contract simply doesn't facilitate the ability to comfortably establish positions intended to be held weeks or months. After all, although somewhat rare, gold prices have been known to move $50 to $100 per ounce in a single trading session. A rise or fall of $100 in gold for a full-sized futures trader equals a profit or loss of $10,000; yet an e-micro trader would see a much more manageable profit or loss of $1,000. In a nutshell, it is much easier for a trader to commit to their research and game plan with the luxury of time and reasonable profit and loss fluctuations.

E-MICRO FUTURES OPEN THE DOOR TO OPPORTUNITY TO ALL TRADERS

I suspect some readers have either skipped this chapter or are reading it wondering why they would trade smaller futures contracts, given their interest in commodities in the first place was the dream of making their fortunes. The truth is, most traders participating in the futures and options markets won't see large profits by trading full-sized contracts either. At least trading smaller contracts with more tolerable risk will pose a higher probability of taking money out of the commodity markets, as opposed to simply making a deposit. In addition, you should look at the opportunity with optimism; it might take a considerable amount of time, or a gross lack of effort, to go bust trading a single lot of the e-micro gold. Full-sized gold traders cannot say that (at least not with a straight face).

Again, a trader could theoretically double a $10,000 account in a year with a profit of just $50 per day. It doesn't take a 100-ounce gold contract to meet that goal; one would likely have better odds of achieving the goal with a much smaller and comfortably sized contract. Of course, although making $50 per day in a $10,000 trading account sounds easy, I assure you it is not.

CHAPTER 13: SPECULATING IN VIX FUTURES ISN'T FOR EVERYBODY

I n a *Trader's First Book on Commodities*, the focus was to teach readers all they needed to know about the commodity markets before considering market strategy. I went into detail about each of the popular commodity markets and guided traders on how to calculate profit, loss, and risk, in each commodity market. However, a market that regrettably wasn't discussed but has quickly become a popular topic in the trading community is the Chicago Board of Options Exchange (CBOE) listed volatility index, more commonly known as the VIX. Because of its exclusion from other books I've written, and the fact that I receive countless inquiries from my brokerage clients about trading it, I feel compelled to outline some of the advantages and disadvantages of trading the VIX. In addition, it is a unique product that isn't offered at all futures brokerage firms. Thus, anybody interested in speculating in the VIX will want to keep this in mind when shopping around for a commodity broker.

> "It's not whether you're right or wrong that's important, but how much money you make when you're right and how much you lose when you're wrong." — George Soros

The CBOE describes the VIX as a "key measure of market expectations of near-term volatility conveyed by S&P 500 stock index option prices." Because the VIX value is derived from the implied volatility (the portion of an option price attributed to expectations of future volatility) in S&P options, it is commonly referred to as the *fear index*. The VIX was introduced by the CBOE in the early 1990s and is often considered to be the benchmark barometer of investor sentiment and market volatility. Because the VIX is so widely watched and mentioned, it is only natural for futures traders to get involved. What started out as an informational index at the CBOE eventually became a highly popular, yet unique, leveraged futures trading instrument.

In essence, VIX futures give speculators an opportunity to directly trade human emotions, specifically fear and complacency. Those interested in attempting to profit from changes in investor sentiment will likely find the VIX a convenient trading vehicle. Yet it is also requires a brassy attitude.

Nonetheless, there are some aspects of the VIX futures market that traders should be aware of before risking their trading capital. Trust me when I say, along with being among the most lucrative futures contracts available to trade, it is also the most unforgiving. There are unique attributes of VIX futures that should be known and largely work against speculators, but there are times in which the VIX offers relatively predicable opportunities for those with strong stomachs for risk. Let's take a closer look.

THE VIX IS NOT AN INVESTMENT VEHICLE, IT IS A TRADING VEHICLE

Unlike traditional stock and bond investments, the VIX doesn't pay dividends or interest, nor does it provide ownership of an underlying asset that holds value. Instead, the value of the VIX is purely derived by human opinion, emotion, and perception. Playing the VIX is highly speculative, even more so than any other commodity because the underlying is not an asset, it is an opinion. In contrast, commodity futures contracts are similarly leveraged and without income-producing elements, but their redeeming quality is being backed by tangible goods.

Nonetheless, despite the lack of a concrete asset, there are times in which the odds of success in trading VIX are eye catching, making it an (occasionally) attractive arena.

THE VIX TRADES INVERSELY TO THE S&P

Although the word *volatility* generally refers to extreme price movement in any direction, in reference to the VIX and its value, volatility is highly directional. The VIX goes up when stocks drop but it goes down when stocks rise. This is the case even if the stock market is soaring higher at an unusually quick pace. For this reason, traders and investors should look at bullish speculations in the VIX, as being a bearish stance in the equity market, and vice versa. They should not assume that a highly volatile bullish breakout in the S&P will increase the value of the VIX.

THE VIX, AND MORE SO VIX FUTURES, ERODE WITH TIME

Newbie traders to VIX futures have been known to opt for going long the VIX as a substitute for purchasing a put option on the e-mini S&P 500. On paper, it appears to be sound logic; unlike a long put option, which exposes traders to the obstacle of time value decay, a futures contract shouldn't see time value erosion. Yet, in the case of the VIX it does—and it can cause substantial losses to a trading account. Like long options, the VIX often wears away in value every day that lacks conviction selling in the S&P. If you've ever bought an option, only to watch the value of it dwindle to nothing while you were waiting for the market to move, you've experienced what I'm referring to.

In other words, a trader looking for the equity markets to sell off in the near future might consider buying the VIX as a hedge against their stock portfolio or as a speculative play. However, if we see a week or two of sideways action, the VIX will likely have lost value because traders then adjust their expectations of future volatility to lower levels.

In such an instance, the trader wasn't necessarily wrong about the direction of the S&P; they simply weren't immediately right. In the VIX, that is enough to lose money. VIX bulls typically have less capacity for miscue than bulls in other markets might, due to the erosion factor, shown in Figure 51.

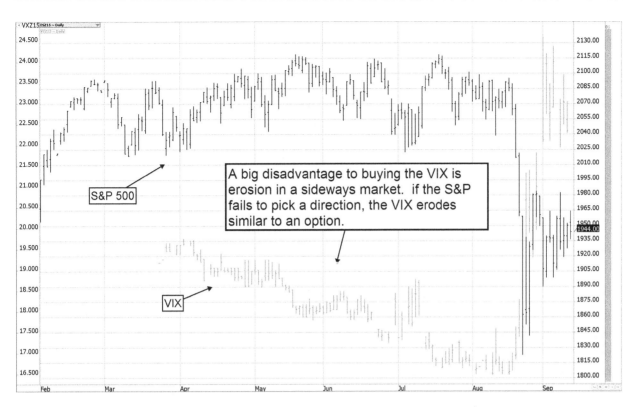

Figure 51: The VIX futures contract erodes over time if the S&P 500 doesn't decline because, like options, the market generally builds expectations of future volatility into its price.

THE VIX ISN'T A COMMODITY, BUT IT HAS A "CONTANGO"

Contango is a term used frequently but understood rarely. The term is exclusive to the commodity industry and is used to describe the relationship between the cash market of a commodity and the futures market. It is also commonly used to identify a scenario in which the value of futures contracts expiring in the near future are discounted relative to contracts with distant expiration dates. In essence, contango is an environment in which people are willing to pay more for a commodity at some point in the remote future than the actual expected price of the commodity in the proximate future. To clarify, a corn futures contract expiring in March 2016 might be trading near $3.70, but the futures contract representing delivery of the same underlying asset in September 2016 would reasonably be valued at $3.85. In agricultural products such as corn, the price discrepancy is related to the cost to carry such as storage and insurance. However, in the VIX futures, the contango is due to the uncertainty of human emotions and expectations. As time goes on, uncertainty dissipates.

In most cases, the CBOE's published VIX value (cash market) for purposes of market analysis is listed at a discount to the front month futures price, which is a tradable asset (and I use that term loosely). Similarly, the next expiring futures month is typically higher than the front month. Because the VIX trades at a contango, if all else remains equal a trader long the VIX will lose money as time goes on because the futures price and the cash market price will converge.

Table 4: The cash market volatility index is generally lower than each of the distantly expiring futures contracts. The farther the expiration date of the futures contract, the higher the VIX value; this is similar to contango in the commodity markets.

VIX Cash Index	16.50
January VIX Future (VXF6)	17.50
February VIX Future (VXG6)	18.20
March VIX Future (VXH6)	18.60
April VIX Future (VXJ6)	19.00

THE VIX GOES UP QUICKLY AND DOWN SLOWLY

One of the redeeming qualities of the VIX is its capacity to rally sharply but decline slowly. Even more so, there has been a relatively solid floor in the VIX in the low teens (Figure 52). Because of this trait, it can make an attractive speculative play for bottom fishers. If the VIX is hovering near all-time lows, it appears to be a scenario in which the downside risk, albeit significant, is far less than the upside potential. In addition, if you happen to be skilled, or lucky, enough to get in just before a large spike in volatility, it is possible to realize an exceptionally bulky profit in a short period of time. Of course, this alone doesn't negate the risks discussed previously.

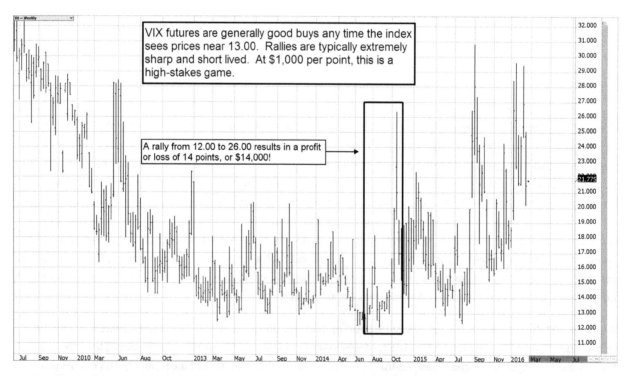

Figure 52: VIX futures trade violently in both directions, but rallies are often where the momentum is.

BEFORE TRADING THE VIX, YOU MUST KNOW WHAT YOU ARE GETTING INTO!

I can't think of a futures contract that comes with as much heartache and risk as the CBOE's VIX contract. However, I also can't think of a futures market that has the type of potential to return abnormally generous returns to those who manage to get on the right side of a trade. It is imperative traders are fully aware of the risk and reward prospects that come with being engaged in VIX trading before getting the idea to buy or sell the futures contract. Unfortunately, inexperienced traders often casually go long or short the VIX without fully understanding the intensity of their position. Before the realization of risk comes to the forefront, the trade might already be thousands of dollars underwater on a single contract. In this section, I'll focus on the bottom line in VIX trading; how to calculate gains and losses, and an example of the emotional roller coaster that is VIX trading.

VIX FUTURES CONTRACT SPECIFICATIONS

As we know, the VIX futures are traded on the CBOE. This is a significant fact because the CBOE is traditionally an equity product exchange, not a futures exchange. Even so, they own the rights to VIX futures, which trades there nearly 24 hours per day. On weekdays, trading in the VIX begins at 3:30 p.m. Central time and closes at 3:15 p.m. on the following day. There is a 15-minute pause from 3:15 p.m. to 3:30 p.m. to match that of the Chicago Merc's e-mini S&P 500 futures contract.

Each tick in the VIX is worth $10 to a trader; thus, if the VIX moves from 13.00 to 13.01 a trader has made or lost $10. The minimum tick, or price movement, for this contract is 0.01, but you will rarely see the VIX move in one-tick increments. The spread between the bid and ask in this market tends to be five ticks ($50), much wider than most futures contracts. Accordingly, prices have a tendency to fluctuate five ticks at a time. Oddly, the wide bid/ask spread isn't due to a lack of liquidity; VIX futures trade tens of thousands of contracts per day.

Naturally, if the VIX moves from 13.00 to 14.00, traders long the market have picked up $1,000 ($10 x 100) in paper gains, but those short would have an equivalent unrealized loss. A tip for calculating risk and reward in commodities is to always work with a positive figure. Therefore, you will always be subtracting the higher price from the lower price and then multiplying by the tick value (in this case, $10). The result will then be an absolute figure that must then be categorized as a profit or loss. Of course, if you bought the lower price and sold the higher, you made money, and vice versa.

As discussed, the VIX generally trickled down but has the ability to go up quickly. With this in mind, a VIX hovering at, or near, long-term lows can be an attractive place for aggressive traders to speculate. Although the risk is rather large, some view it as being relatively limited while offering seemingly unlimited profit potential.

Because the VIX isn't a CME product as the e-mini S&P 500 and most other futures contracts are, trading of the futures contract is vastly different. The two most common hiccups new VIX traders experience are the massive bid/ask spreads and accepted order types. For instance, due to liquidity concerns the CBOE doesn't accept market orders during their designated extended trading hours (3:30 p.m. through 8:30 a.m. Central the following day). In short, VIX traders cannot buy or sell the contract at the market price in the overnight trading session. Instead, they must place limit orders in which they name the price they are willing to buy or sell. This alone isn't a big deal, but try telling that to a trader attempting to liquidate a trade gone bad, who is receiving rejection notices every time he enters an order to sell his long VIX contract at the market. During my time as a futures broker, I have received plenty of phone calls from panicked clients wondering what was wrong with the trading platform, or the brokerage firm's order entry server, when in reality the client simply didn't fully understand the VIX futures contract before endeavoring to trade it.

Similarly, the CBOE doesn't accept traditional stop-loss orders. This too can quickly trigger a feeling of panic for anyone who has entered a VIX futures contract with a plan in place to implement a stop-loss order to limit risk on the trade. Attempts at placing stop-loss orders are met with rejection notices upon entry of the order. VIX traders can, however, enter stop-limit orders, which is a type of stop order that limits the amount of slippage the trader is willing to take. To refresh your memory, a stop order is one that is placed by a trader to buy a futures contract at a price that is higher than the current, or sell a contract at a price that is lower than the current, should the market reach the stated level. Once the stated stop price becomes part of the bid/ask, the order becomes a market order for immediate execution. Nevertheless, because the CBOE cannot necessarily guarantee their futures market will be liquid enough for stop-loss orders, which become market orders once elected, to produce a fill at a reasonable price, they prohibit the order type. A stop limit, on the other hand, becomes a market order if the stated stop price is reached but only if it is possible to fill the order within the stated limit price. If it isn't possible, the order simply dies. This can be a nightmare for traders on the wrong side of a big move because their stop order goes unfilled, leaving them open to unlimited risk. In short, if the exchange is unable to fill a stop-limit order within the trader's stated parameters, the trader simply does not have a stop-loss order at all and faces the risk of runaway losses. The inability to place a traditional stop-loss order only applies to the VIX and the mini-sized (not e-micro) gold and silver contracts traded on non-CME exchanges, which are more inept at facilitating trading in equity products than futures.

THE BOTTOM LINE ON THE VIX

As discussed, the VIX generally trickled down but has the ability to go up quickly. With this in mind, a VIX hovering at, or near, long-term lows can be an attractive place for aggressive traders to speculate. Although the risk is rather large, some view it as being relatively limited while offering seemingly unlimited profit potential.

SECTION 4: IMPLEMENTING WHAT YOU'VE LEARNED

If you only walk away from this book with one realization, I hope it is that there is not a wrong or right way to trade commodities. There have been millions of dollars made and lost using all possible variations of trading strategies an analytical tool. As difficult as it is for some to come to grips with, the markets have little to do with math and science; they have everything to do with psychology and artistic expression.

Making money is as simple as finding an approach to trading that enables an environment of comfort and confidence as opposed to stress and panic. Only those that can conquer the mental challenges that come with trading will find success, regardless of the trading method utilized.

We all know trading, particularly on leverage, is a difficult venture. Consequently, the peril of committing mistakes can easily outweigh the rewards of a great trade. Keeping costly mishaps to a minimum does more for your bottom line than an occasional profitable trade might. It took some time, but I eventually realized that making money is more about how much you don't lose than how much you make!

CHAPTER 14: TIPS AND TRICKS TO LIVE OR DIE BY

Over the years, I've compiled a few dos and don'ts I believe will be helpful in keeping destructive emotions at bay. Although there isn't a holy grail strategy or method guaranteeing trading profits, I believe following these simple guidelines has a significant positive impact on trading results.

NEVER CHASE MARKETS

I've both made, and witnessed, plenty of mistakes during my time as a commodity broker. By far and away, the most common mishap that traders make is chasing markets. First and foremost, chasing price is an emotional venture that tends to breed stress and poor decision making, which extends beyond the fill of the current speculation.

Humans despise uncertainty; trading and investing alike will always come with some level of blindness in regard to what the future might bring for any market venture. I often hear traders seeking confirmation of a market move before they would like to get involved. In essence, most traders wish to become bullish *after* a market has already nearly exhausted a rally and bearish while prices are in despair. To the point, these traders are chasing prices higher before buying, or lower before selling. The results can be devastating if the trend reverses once they finally decide to enter the trade.

> "It is awfully hard work doing nothing."
> —Oscar Wilde

The theory behind the behavior of buying high and hoping to sell higher, or selling low with the intention of buying it back even lower, is trend validation. Nearly any trading book you pick up will have the phrase "the trend is your friend," so it isn't surprising we are trained to chase prices. For most, it is far more comfortable entering a trade knowing that market momentum is moving in the preferred direction before they commit their hard-earned money. However, doing so can easily translate into an experience in which a trader consistently buys high and sells low, which is clearly the opposite of the desired action. As a discussed disadvantage to trend trading in Chapter 2, "Technical Analysis in Commodities," if the trader's confirmation process is lengthy, it is quite possible that just when they feel the most comfortable buying is exactly when they should be looking to sell, or at least remain on the sidelines. This is an unfortunate cycle that occurs over and over again in markets of all types. Some notable cases are the 2006 real estate bubble, the 2009 S&P 500 trough, the gold and silver boom of 2011, and most recently the oil bust of 2014. I am certain that there will be no shortage of such examples going forward; market participants seem to be blinded by greed.

Ironically for price chasers, the commodity markets have an inexplicable way of reversing at a price point that will cause the maximum amount of pain to the highest number of traders. Sometimes, human emotion causes traders to disregard logic in hopes of amassing large profits. In July 2015 the major stock indices were trolling all-time highs; at the time bullish sentiment was through the roof and money was flowing into the long side of the market. Conversely, as the slowing China story heated up in August, retail speculators began to liquidate their bullish trades and initiate fresh short positions in e-mini S&P 500 futures despite the fact that the market had already fallen nearly 300 S&P points, in excess of 10%, in a few short days. Not long after, the market made a nearly full recovery! Imagine the pain suffered by the latecomer trend traders who bought near the highs and sold near the lows. Although we'll never know exactly what occurred, monitoring price action and the CFTC's *COT Report* reveals that is exactly what many traders did.

The problem with getting into a market near historically extended prices, such as the long side of the e-mini S&P in August 2015, is the price has already moved considerably to reach such heights. Once it does, it is quite possible that all of the bulls have already acted (bought), and the bears have already thrown in the towel (bought back short positions to close). Eventually, prices reach a climax in which there simply isn't anybody left to buy; it is then that the doors are open to a dramatic trend reversal. This is precisely what happened in the aforementioned S&P 500 example. Soon after what some refer to as a "mini crash," we saw the opposite phenomenon; selling dried up, and prices reversed to the upside.

After sifting through industry chatter and in trading forums, it was evident that a large number of traders were caught with bullish trades during the plunge, and bearish trades during the miraculous recovery. You can see the pain in the chart; on the way down, margins calls and panicked liquidation forced prices dramatically lower, but once the dust settled, traders were caught short by a continuation in an upward projection. Although it was a slower process on the way up, it was clear margin troubles and the need to end suffering forced prices higher, rather than fresh bullish buying. The S&P likely ruined many of the same lives on the way up, as it ruined on the way down.

Here is the bottom line. Once a commodity story or market opinion goes mainstream, the futures market has already reacted and reflects the mindset accordingly. Trading isn't as easy as executing a speculative trade based on a *Wall Street Journal* article. If you see it in print, hear it on the news, and notice your friends talking about it, it is most likely too late to try to join in on the move. It is far less painful to miss a trade than it is to be in the market in the wrong direction. Just ask those who went short the e-mini in the 1800s on news of slowing growth in China in August 2015 (Chapter 5, Figure 33).

IF SEEKING A TREND REVERSAL, GIVE IT A CHANCE

On the other hand, traders who don't chase markets often find themselves early to participate in a potential trend reversal. It is unreasonable to assume it's possible to pick market turns with precise accuracy, yet that is exactly what swing traders attempt to do. Unlike those waiting for excessive confirmation prior to entering a trade, swing traders run the risk of being early, or worse, being outright wrong. Obviously, either scenario can be a frustrating and expensive experience. Such traders must plan accordingly; whether their strategy is to enter the trade with a hedge (long or short option), or with a tactic that allows for a wide margin of error, such as a short option or the use of micro futures, it is imperative to allow for the speculation to work. Too many swing traders make the detrimental mistake of either not being willing to ride out an adverse move enough to let the trade work itself out or they hold onto losers too long. Ironically, in doing so the inevitable conclusion is to bail on the trade at precisely the worst time. Warren Buffett said it best: "Be fearful when others are greedy, and greedy when others are fearful." Yet emotion entices us into doing the opposite.

We cannot control the markets, but we can control how we react to market action. The first step toward ensuring we are capable of making intelligent decisions is constructing a strategy that is assembled in a way that enables the market speculation to play out, rather than tempting the trader to cut it short out of fear of loss or poor preparation.

DON'T LOOK A GIFT HORSE IN THE MOUTH

It is easy to chalk up a winning trade to hours of hard work laboring over commodity charts, stats, and literature, but the truth is all good trades are made possible, at least in part by luck. Nobody can predict price movement with exact certainty. Instead, we are all making educated guesses in an attempt to beat the market; as we know, the odds of doing so are not necessarily favorable. As a result, a trader who happens to be in the right place at the right time, to catch a substantially favorable market movement in a short amount of time, is generally best served to take the money and run. At the very least, the trader should take action to protect profits such as placing a breakeven stop if it is a futures trade, or selling an antagonistic option against the position to cushion the blow should the windfall profits begin to disappear.

> "Get in, get it done right, and get out."
> —Donald Trump

Ego will often argue that there could be additional monies to be had, but the fact is, markets can take profits away as fast, or faster, than it gives them. Don't overthink your position; take a profit and walk away. I once witnessed a trader during the financial collapse of 2008 take a $10,000 trading account to roughly $500,000 in a matter of weeks through the purchase of deep-out-of-the-money puts in the e-mini S&P 500. At the time of the purchase, I believed he was essentially wagering $10,000 on what amounted to little more than low-probability lottery tickets, but as it turned out his prediction of an unprecedented stock market collapse was spot on. Sadly, the same trader quickly gave back all of the profits, and even the original investment. This might be an extreme example, but unfortunately, the lesson is a common one. Just as you should walk away from the blackjack table in Vegas after a good run, you should walk away from the markets if you are lucky enough to experience windfall profits.

SELL OPTIONS AGAINST WINNING POSITIONS

Some traders have a hard time locking in profits because they can't stand the idea of leaving money on the table. The reality is, a trader will never enter the market at the best possible level, nor will he exit at the optimal price. Offsetting a trade early or late is to be expected. However, a trader can essentially take the best of both worlds by selling antagonistic options against a winning trade. Doing so caps the profit potential, but it also brings in some premium as income to act as a buffer against adverse price movement from that point. The act of selling an option against a winning trade is not unlike a covered call strategy. The trader is willing to give up unlimited gains for the comfort of knowing he has taken action to ensure he will come out of the position in the plus column, or at least considerably reduce the risk of participating in the position. This strategy stems from the concept of never turning a winner into a loser.

This technique can be used by trading long options, or either long or short a futures contract. To illustrate, imagine a trader short a gold futures contract from $1,200. Assuming the current market price is $1,150, the trader is profitable by $50 in gold, or $5,000 in trading profits. This is figured by multiplying the point value in gold of $100, by the change in price ($50). The trader could either offset his position by buying back the gold futures contract to lock in a profit, or he could place a stop-loss order at a level that locks in a gain but also attempts to give the market enough room to keep the trade active should it continue lower.

Of course, we all know the risks and complications that come with using stop-loss orders. Another alternative would be to purchase a call option to protect the profits from a potential sharp reversal, but as we know, this type of price insurance can be costly. In my opinion, the best strategy to protect a profitable position while still leaving profit potential should the trend continue is to create a married put (the same strategy as a covered call, but utilizing a short futures contract and a short put). In gold, it is sometimes possible to sell an at-the-money put for $40 to $50, or $4,000 (40 x $100) to $5,000 (50 x $100), in premium depending on volatility. In this example, an at-the-money put equates to the $1.150 strike price. The premium that is collected acts as income to the trader, but it also acts as a risk buffer for the futures contract. It is a win/win!

Assuming the trader in this example manages to sell an $1,150 put option for $5,000 ($50) he is essentially locking in all of the open futures profits of $50. If gold rebounds to trade at $1,200, the original entry price on the day of expiration, the trader would still be profitable by $5,000, ignoring transaction costs. This is because although all of the profits on the futures contract were given back to the market, the trader keeps the premium collected on the put option sold to hedge the trader's futures contract profits. If gold continued lower to settle at any price below the strike price of the put, $1,150, on the day of expiration the trader would be profitable by $10,000. This is calculated by adding the $5,000 in futures profits earned as the market declined from $1,200 to $1,150 ((1,200 – 1,150) x $100 = $5,000), and the premium collected for the $1,150 put ($5,000). The reason the trader doesn't earn any more profit on the short futures contract below $1,150 is because the intrinsic value of the short put increases dollar for dollar with the short futures contract under the strike price. Simply, gains on the short futures contract is offsetting losses on the short put beneath $1,150. However, the trader gets to keep the extrinsic value of the premium collected. Despite the intrinsic value of the option gaining value, the extrinsic value erodes to zero at expiration. To illustrate, if gold is at $1,100 at expiration, the put option has an intrinsic value of $5,000 ((1,150 – 1,100) x $100), but the extrinsic value would be zero. Thus, the trader benefited from the extrinsic premium erosion; all the while, the risk of gaining intrinsic value was offset by the short futures contract. This statement would be true whether gold was at $1,100 at expiration, or $100. I think we can agree that walking away with an additional $5,000 for selling the put to mitigate risk is a pretty attractive proposition.

Of course, if gold rallies above $1,200, the hedge provided by the short put runs out of benefits, so the position reverts to a naked short futures contract. Nevertheless, if gold is at $1,200 on option expiration day, the trader still makes $5,000; the short futures contract is merely breaking even, but the option sold for $5,000 would be worthless!

Because of the risk of a sharp reversal that leaves the short futures position without a hedge, the technique of selling premium against a winning trade is a little more effective for those attempting to protect long options that pose limited risk. Had the trader in the previous example purchased an at-the-money put, as opposed to going short a futures contract, he would likely be far less profitable but would be provided a nice opportunity to convert the position into a risk-free trade. Assuming the trader purchased a $1,200 put for $50, or $5,000 (50 x $100), he would likely see a profit of about $3,000 on the option should the futures price drop to $1,150 and there be considerable time to expiration. If this were true, the option would be worth $80, or $8,000 (80 x $100). If you are wondering why the put buyer is only making $3,000 on the same move the short futures contract made $5,000, it is because of time value erosion and the burden of paying premium for the put option.

> If timed correctly, an option buyer in a profitable trade can sell an antagonistic option to convert the strategy into a FREE TRADE!

The put buyer could simply sell the option to lock in a $3,000 gain before commission and fees, or he could sell the $1,150 put for $5,000 to create what is essentially a *free* bear put spread. A bear put spread is the purchase of a put at a near-the-money strike price and the sale of a put with distant strike price; such a spread offers limited risk and limited reward, and thus it is categorized as a long option strategy.

If he sells the $1,150 put, he has collected enough premium to pay for the initial cash outlay for the option of $5,000. This creates a scenario in which he is guaranteed to at least break even, but will most likely make some sort of profit. If gold rallies to any price from $1,200 to infinity, the trader essentially breaks even because both the long and short options expire worthless. This is in contrast to the futures trader who sold the put option as a buffer but was still subject to theoretically unlimited risk should gold rally significantly above $1,200. If the price of gold is below $1,150 at expiration, the trader makes $5,000. This is figured by taking the difference between the strike prices, minus the cost of entering the spread (((1,200 − 1,150) − 0) x $100) = $5,000). In this example, the trader's cost to enter the spread was nothing other than transaction costs because he was able to sell the $1,150 put for the same price he had previously purchased the $1,200 put. If the price of gold is between $1,200 and $1,150, the profit will be equivalent to the intrinsic value of the long $1,150 put.

For some lucky option buyers, this strategy works best for those who have purchased cheap options, usually deep-out-of-the money, and have found themselves on the right side of a life-changing move. In such a case, it might be possible to sell an option with a distant strike price to the one that was purchased to convert the trade into a guaranteed profit bear put spread. Imagine if the $1,200 put was purchased far before gold fell to $1,200, for $500 ($5 in premium). A plunge to $1,150 would be a windfall profit for the trader who would be netting a profit of $7,500 (assuming the option is worth $8,000 and the purchase price was $500). This trader could sell the $1,150 put for $5,000 to guarantee a profit of at least $4,500 regardless of where gold goes from there. The best-case scenario would occur if gold futures were below $1,150 at expiration; if so, the trade would result in a profit of $9,500! This accounts for the premium collected and the intrinsic value of the $1,200 put minus the intrinsic value of the $1,150, minus the original cost of the $1,200 put of $500.

((1,200 − 1,150) − 5) + 50) x $100) = $9,500 before considering transaction costs

THE SIDELINES IS A POSITION

Money in a trading account burns holes in the pockets of traders in the same way an allowance burns holes in the pockets of grade schoolers. We are all programmed to believe our money should be invested 100% of the time; anything less is a wasted

> You can't lose money on the sidelines!

opportunity. Yet, nothing could be further from the truth. In reality, funds sitting in cash such as a margin account, a savings account, or something similar are funds that can be quickly put to use when an extraordinary opportunity arises. Traders on the sidelines have a few things going for them: objectivity, and the freedom to act on excessive market moves. Those holding positions in any particular market tend to see analysis in a biased light; they also find themselves playing defense during volatile price action rather than offense. While those with positions on prior to a large move are scrambling to manage risk, traders who were previously on the sidelines are given opportunities to get comfortably bullish at discounted prices or bearish at excessive valuations.

Simply, traders aren't missing out while they sit on the sidelines; they are protecting capital and opening the door to higher-probability trading opportunities that arise in the future.

IF YOU CAN'T TAKE THE HEAT, GET OUT OF THE KITCHEN

As the cantankerous chef Gordon Ramsay once said on the TV show *Hell's Kitchen*, "I wish you'd jump in the oven. That would make my life a lot easier!" I think what he really meant was, "If you can't take the heat, get out of the [expletive] kitchen!" Trading is no different; it is a game of wits and mental stability. Similar to the medical profession in which only certain types of people are equipped to handle the sight of blood, not everyone is capable of absorbing the stresses of trading. If you are not the type of person who can stay calm and think rationally in the midst of either losses or profits, trading might not be for you (at least not on a large scale).

> "I handle losing streaks by trimming down my activity. I just wait it out. Trying to trade during a losing streak is emotionally devastating. Trying to play 'catch up' is lethal." —Ed Seykota

Trading commodities with futures or options certainly isn't for everyone. In fact, after more than a decade in the business as a commodity broker, I wake up on occasion and wonder why I do this to myself. Luckily, those days are few and far between; most of the time I absolutely love what I do but I can attest there is nothing easy about commodity speculation. It will test the patience, confidence, and pocketbooks of the most solid, intelligent, and wealthy individuals. Like an ex-spouse, the commodity markets have the ability to bring the worst out of people. If you aren't willing to accept the emotional turmoil that comes with it, don't put yourself through the agony.

Further, never trade beyond your means, or beyond your capability of rationality; doing so leads to flawed decision making and poor trading results. If you find yourself losing sleep or experiencing irrational thoughts and trading behaviors, flatten your account and walk away from the computer.

THERE IS NO BEATING AROUND THE BUSH: MARKETS ARE MEAN

I wish there were a better, softer adjective to describe the personality of the commodity markets, but I've yet to find a better description than "mean." The futures and options markets have a knack for wreaking the most havoc on the most people; this entails stop-loss running, forcing margin liquidations, and resulting stomach churning volatility. If you trade long enough...the market will make you cry. I've witnessed the most macho of men, and even very wealthy men, literally sob over a bad trade. The frustration is obviously hinged on financial losses, but it is often the pain of being wrong that delivers the emotional wallop, putting the trader over the edge. For those who are abusing leverage, trading with funds that are not truly risk capital, or simply find themselves in the wrong place at the wrong time, it is quite possible that a venture into commodity trading can ruin a marriage, personal life, and destroy life savings. It is imperative that each market participant understand what they are getting into, and structure their trading in a responsible manner. Not unlike putting money in the stock market, sports betting, or playing poker, there are various degrees of risk taking which, if unmanaged, can inflict mayhem. Trading within your means is a simple way to avoid devastation.

> "Our greatest glory is not in never failing, but in getting up every time we do." —Confucius

A way to mitigate the *mental* anguish of trading is to enter each and every trade expecting the worst, but hoping for the best. I'm not implying you throw caution to the winds to enter the market without doing your homework, but it is critical that traders realize that even the soundest fundamental and technical analysis is no match for the uncertainty of the future. Market prices are dictated by humans, who are driven by emotions; there isn't a strategy in the world that could predict with absolute conviction how traders will react to any particular event. For example, it is not uncommon for a bullish report on natural gas inventories to be met with selling, or a bearish payroll report to lure buying into stock index futures. Sometimes it is difficult to decipher the difference between good and bad news just by looking at market prices; in the end, the market does what it wants, not what the news suggests it should.

Before entering the market, traders should assess major areas of support and resistance, stop placement, option premiums, and so forth to determine a hypothetical worst-case scenario. If the thought of the worst case makes your stomach churn, the trade probably isn't for you.

DON'T CHEAT, DO YOUR HOMEWORK!

If you aren't putting in the legwork when it comes to strategy development, market opinion, and the timing of entry and exit, you are doing yourself a massive disservice when it comes to mental stability. Don't put too much faith into "market gurus," newsletter subscriptions, or signal providers. Despite hefty price tags or media popularity, they are in the same boat we are. We

> "You'll never know how good you really are until you've performed under fire." —Martin Schwartz

are *all* trying to beat the market and *everyone* is vulnerable to the possibility and inevitability of being wrong. At least if you have corroborated the opinions or recommendations of a third party, you will be prepared to make your own decisions when it comes to taking profits or cutting losses. Leaving these decisions to another party will eventually lead to frustration and eventually resentment. Thoughts such as "I know more than my broker" or "Why am I paying this advisor?" are natural, but they will affect your ability to make sound decisions. However, if you've done your homework and have come to the same conclusion or at least agree with the service you are following, it will be easier to cope when it comes down to the decision making.

Those entering trades based on the recommendations of others have a strong tendency to become overly complacent. However, their comfort in the position is often unfounded; having unrealistic faith in the ability of others can lead to massive losses. By the time you realize your favorite outspoken trader can be wrong from time to time, it might be too late for your trading account. After all, most retail traders are probably executing the trades in an account much smaller than what the recommendation service advises. Most third-party trading services assume its followers are playing with deep pockets and a higher risk tolerance than the average trader actually is. As a result, signal followers are prone to large percentage drawdowns and even blowouts even if the recommended trade eventually proves to be profitable for those with the wherewithal to stick with the trade.

Although the most common pitfall of trading via the specific recommendations of others is complacency, some traders have the opposite obstacle. They suffer from a lack of trust, which has a propensity to encourage late entry or premature liquidation by doubting traders. Either of these changes in timing are capable of being a burden on the trading results.

The bottom line is, when following the advice of a market guru, be aware that experience is an advantage but it is NOT a guarantee. Each executed trade should be confirmed by your *own* ideas and analysis. If you don't agree with the reasoning behind the trade, you shouldn't participate because even if it is a winner, you could find a way to interfere with the results.

TAKE STEPS TO KEEP YOUR FEET ON THE GROUND, AND YOUR HEAD OUT OF THE CLOUDS

Staying calm in bad times and humble in good times is a game changer. As I've attempted to mention (more than once), the difference between making and losing money is likely more dependent on the psychology of the trader than analytical techniques. Traders who lack patience or poise are prone to chasing markets into low-probability trades, or they neglect to let the chosen strategy succeed or fail on its own. The goal is to buy low and sell high, but traders who can't manage their emotions often end up doing just the opposite.

> We cannot control our emotions, or the market; but we can control our circumstances and environment.

A lucky few were born with the mental stability necessary to successfully trade commodities, but most of us are forced to develop it through experience, if at all. Many traders never develop the emotional capacity to trade futures and options because they can't, or won't, pay enough tuition to the markets to develop the skill. Unfortunately, there isn't a book or a tutorial video that teaches traders how to keep calm to make logical decisions in the direst of situations. That said, it is possible to improve the odds of developing the wherewithal to trade effectively by creating an environment conducive with stress reduction.

Although we cannot make up for a lack of experience, nor can we change our personalities, we can control our environment and exposure to stress. In my opinion, following these simple guidelines can work wonders to cut undue mental strain and mitigate the impact of emotional decision making:

 Get plenty of sleep. Fatigue weighs on our bodies physically and mentally.

 Eat proper meals and nutrition. Sipping on coffee and nibbling on a donut in front of a trading screen is a surefire way to lead to hyperactive decision making.

Exercise does both a mind and a body good. Stay active. The commodity markets are open around the clock, but that shouldn't keep you at the desk every hour of the day.

 Trade less, and don't be afraid to be on the sidelines, or even take time away from the markets.

 Trading multiple contracts multiplies the stress; less is more.

 The quickest and simplest way to manage emotion is to trade a smaller size. "Small" is relative to the trader; it might mean one lot, one mini, or even one micro contract. Remember, trading small isn't a waste of time; it only takes $50 per trading day in profits to be equal to $12,000 per year. It doesn't take multiple contracts traded to make $50; it just takes a single well-timed entry.

 If you are angry, overwhelmed, depressed, obsessed—stop trading. The markets aren't going anywhere; they will be there when you are in a better position to trade!

PLAY THE ODDS, BUT UNDERSTAND THE REALITY

Leveraged trading is a game of probabilities, but that doesn't mean having favorable odds will translate into trading success. Even the best traders on the planet, those who have diligently performed extensive market analysis to ensure attractive prospects, find themselves on the wrong side of a trade. Sometimes, speculating with the most likely outcome fails to return profits and in some scenarios can lead to massive trading losses. The market will do what it will do regardless of what seasonal tendencies, fundamentals, or technical analysis suggests it *should* do. Realizing this will help to mitigate the mental impact of losses on current and future trades. You can't control the market; you can only control how you react to it.

Successful traders typically have win/loss ratios less than 50% on average. Option sellers might experience a higher winning percentage, and trend traders might suffer a lower winning percentage, but in the end trading is a zero-sum game. For every winner, there is a loser and vice versa. Thus, any venture into the commodity markets should be done so with realistic expectations; not only will roughly half of all trades end in losses, but losses must be contained to levels conducive to trading another day.

> Don't assume favorable odds today will be the same favorable odds tomorrow. Probabilities tell us the current scenario will stand, but that reality can change tenfold before the trade is over.

In today's technologically driven world, trading software aimed at calculating the probability of success of any given trading strategy, or particular trade, is commonplace. However, despite its popularity I must question its usefulness because the results are simply derived from equations with inputs that can change in an instant. Most option probability calculators will suggest that deep-out-of-the-money options have a very low probability of success. This is obviously true; however, that conclusion is based on the market volatility and sentiment at that particular time, so it cannot possibly incorporate the impact of a news story that will hit the wires next week, or a natural disaster in the week after. The point is, today's reality isn't necessarily tomorrow's truth.

A trader selling a particular option with the assumption it has a 98% probability of success might complacently hold the position well beyond rational losses because he believes there is a mere 2% chance of loss. But the same calculator could be spitting out a completely different probability for that option in the aftermath of some game-changing fundamental stories. I've seen options in crude oil worth less than $50 and a hypothetical probability of expiring worthless in the high 90th percentile jump to several hundred dollars and a probability of expiring worthless fall into the 50th percentile in a matter of hours.

PROLONGED PAPER TRADING IS COUNTERPRODUCTIVE

There are a lot of professional paper traders out there. I have received numerous phone calls and emails from paper traders claiming they have discovered the ultimate trading method and they would be willing to trade for me, or my brokerage clients, in exchange for a "2 and 20" payout (2% management fee and 20% incentive fee, as discussed in Chapter 10). But as I begin asking questions, I generally discover the caller is not registered with the NFA, which is required to be soliciting managed trading services to anybody. Further, they are most often not trading this golden method with actual money. Instead, they would like to show me the stats from their multiyear paper trading account. I speculate that they tried executing their method in an actual trading account and failed, or they simply don't have any risk capital to apply to what they assure me is a "sure thing." In either case, such circumstances are obvious deal breakers. The former suggests their system requires a large amount of capital at risk to be successful (remember, there are no capital limits to the Monopoly money in a paper trading account). The latter suggests they haven't made proper life decisions to accumulate the small amount of wealth it takes to open an actual commodity trading account and therefore probably aren't suited to manage money for others in any capacity.

Such "career paper traders" build their virtual accounts into seven figures but never find a way to turn a profit in their live (real-money) trading account. This is because paper trading almost completely ignores the most significant factor in successful trading—emotional stability. In other words, paper trading is similar to playing a video game in that there are no real consequences in losing. In my view, paper trading for more than a few weeks is a waste of time.

Paper trading does return value to beginning traders in the short run as an introduction to commodity futures and options. Through paper trading, traders will grow familiar with market tendencies and volatility, learn about futures contract and month symbols, charting tools, order types and placement, and get a better idea of how quickly profits and losses can accumulate. Paper trading is also a great way to test out a new trading strategy, system, or theory; and it is an effective way to familiarize oneself with a new trading platform. However, the benefits end there.

Instead of paper trading beyond a handful of weeks, I believe a more beneficial manner of learning to trade comes in working with lower-risk contracts such as e-micro futures (currency/gold) or mini futures (grains, currencies), as discussed in Chapter 12. Though the risks and rewards are meager with these contract sizes, it introduces the trader into the emotional aspect of trading at a fraction of the risk of full-sized contracts. As traders gain confidence, they can graduate into larger trading instruments. Keep in mind the goal is to keep emotions in check. If that requires trading micro contracts to accomplish this, so be it.

DON'T BE AFRAID TO ADD TO A LOSING POSITION!

Most trading books focus on the mantra, "Never add to a losing position." However, perhaps that is exactly what the most logical course of action should be. Of course, if adding positions means becoming overleveraged it is a horrible idea, but for those with plenty of excess risk capital to work with, the practice of dollar cost averaging can work in favor of the trade, but the practice shouldn't be used nonchalantly.

THE BOTTOM LINE

The tips offered in this chapter certainly won't help you determine when to buy or sell, but hopefully they will help to keep you grounded. Not unlike a field goal kicker facing a 20-yard attempt with the game on the line, a task that would normally be simple can become overwhelming when pressure is applied. As much as we would like to, we cannot easily control our emotions. Instead, we must strive to put ourselves in the right scenario, under the right circumstances, to behave in a desired manner. Staying level headed in both good times and bad can be more valuable than any trading system or analysis technique ever could.

> "A good trader has to have three things: a chronic inability to accept things at face value, to feel continuously unsettled, and to have humility." — Michael Steinhardt

CHAPTER 15: UNDERSTANDING IMPLICATIONS OF TRADING COST DECISIONS.

Too often, traders choose a brokerage arrangement based on price alone. For some reason, the assumption is the service will be relatively equal across brokerage firms; after all, most traders enter their orders through an online trading platform with little intervention or contact with their brokerage firms' staff. What could go wrong? This line of thinking can come back to bite traders. Unfortunately, traders tend to spend endless hours researching the markets, but they fail to allocate the proper effort into choosing the right brokerage firm. In my opinion, aside from the mental aspects of trading, it is this single decision that might be the most critical determinant of success or failure.

Obviously, not all traders have the same trading style, experience level, account size, and so on. Thus, the optimal brokerage arrangement will vary greatly by trader. Regrettably, the only way to determine the best brokerage fit is to do the legwork and ask questions. To reiterate, the best broker for a day trader will likely not be the best broker for an option seller. In fact, if you intend to trade multiple strategies, it might require setting up commodity trading accounts at multiple firms to ensure you are providing yourself, and your strategy, with the best odds of success by implementing it in a supportive environment. Or at minimum, traders should find a broker that is well rounded and capable of effectively servicing all trader types well, as opposed to one with an intense focus on a certain type of trader. The most common type of specialized commodity brokers is the deep discount futures day trading firm. Most of these are simply not equipped to house options trading or even position trading accounts.

There is no exception to the rule that you get what you pay for. You wouldn't go to Mexico to get discount dental work without knowing the drawbacks, nor would you trust your money with a financial planner working for pennies. Hence, trusting your commodity trading funds and execution to the cheapest broker you can find probably doesn't make sense either.

Before we can get into the perils of choosing a brokerage firm solely on commission rate or convenience, it is necessary to understand the basic vocabulary and structure of the industry. First, let's discuss the primary types of brokerage firms, some of the organizational characteristics to be aware of as a consumer, and the pros and cons of each. From there, we'll discuss appropriate service levels and trading costs for various types of traders.

TYPES OF COMMODITY BROKERAGE FIRMS

Three types of brokerage firms offering commodity trading: futures trading commission merchants (FCM), introducing brokers (IB), and broker-dealers. Although the products traded are the same, the structure of the firm and the services provided will be vastly different between brokerage types, and even more so between individual brokerages, and brokers (account managers). Let's take a look at the types of brokers along with the pros and cons of placing a commodity trading account at each.

FUTURES COMMISSION MERCHANT (FCM)

A futures commission merchant (FCM) is an acronym only used in the commodity industry. Despite its widespread use in the media, I find that most individual traders lack an understanding of what exactly an FCM is and what differentiates it from other brokerage types. An FCM is an individual, or entity, that solicits or accepts orders for the execution of a commodity transaction. In short, an FCM is a commodity brokerage firm.

The primary function of an FCM is to accept margin deposits to later represent the trading interests of those that do not hold membership in the exchanges. FCMs generally have a host of individual brokers, introducing brokers (defined in the next section), and support staff to solicit and service brokerage clients.

Most FCMs also have order entry desks in which clients can call to place orders should their broker not be available, or if their order entry platform is inaccessible. Yet, most orders are submitted via online trading platforms provided by the FCM to its clients. The FCM simply routes the orders placed by its clients through the trading platform, to the exchange for execution. They later issue a statement of activity to each client depicting the transactions that had taken place in the previous trading session, the transaction costs incurred, and the associated account balance and statistics. On the surface it might seem that all FCMs should perform in a relatively similar fashion due to the fact that they are simply routing orders to the exchange for most clients, but I can assure you there are plenty of other things to consider that might prove to be imperative to success. Again, traders can opt to open an account directly with an FCM, or they can choose to open an account with an IB affiliated with particular FCMs.

Pros of trading directly with an FCM: FCMs tend to be relatively large and well-known firms; thus, some traders appreciate the comfort of trading with a recognizable name. Some popular FCMs are Gain Capital LLC, Archer Daniel Midland Investment Services (ADMIS), Rosenthal Collins Group (RCG), and Dorman.

Cons of trading directly with an FCM: Some traders find FCMs are "too big." Their large scale sometimes makes it difficult for traders to build relationships with support staff. Similarly, their clients might have difficulty accomplishing tasks or getting questions answered due to a lack of personalized service. With that said, the experience will largely be a product of the individual broker you are working with, not the FCM as a whole.

> Choosing a commodity broker is not a decision to take lightly. It could be the single most important decision you make.

A common myth is that it is cheaper to trade directly with an FCM as opposed to utilizing the services of an IB (defined next). However, in many cases that is absolutely false. I would argue that the opposite might be true because account managers at IBs often receive a larger percentage commission payout due to fewer hands being in the cookie jar. Further, I would speculate that most experienced and capable (individual) commodity brokers opt to work under an introducing broker umbrella, as opposed to working directly for an FCM because they stand to make a higher percentage payout on each commission. Thus, less experienced, and arguably less successful, brokers tend to work directly for FCMs because they receive more support in generating new clients. This is a generalized assumption, but I've found it to be overall true. If you are thinking to yourself, "I am an online trader, I don't need a broker," think again. Even if you are self-sufficient, there is a broker assigned to your account and will be the point of contact should a problem arise. Mishaps in problem solving can be expensive lessons.

INTRODUCING BROKER (IB)

An introducing broker (IB) is essentially a brokerage firm, or an individual broker. Not unlike an FCM, an IB is essentially soliciting business and accepting orders for executions of commodity transactions. To the naked eye, one might not realize there is a difference between an FCM and an IB. In fact, when I ask traders who their broker is, they rarely know whether they are with an FCM or an IB. Particularly now that technology has pushed traders toward online trading platforms, the differences are far less obvious. However, unlike an FCM, an IB is not an exchange member and cannot accept client funds for margin deposits. Instead, an introducing broker acts as an intermediary between a client and an FCM. In short, clients are trading with an IB through the services (exchange membership and trading platform technology) of an FCM.

All retail commodity traders (non-exchange members) must be associated with an FCM, either directly or through an IB to execute futures trades. Clients trading with an IB should use the IB itself, as the point of contact for any issues or questions that might arise. Yet, clients send funds to margin positions directly to the FCM. Further, the clients of IBs receive statements issued directly by the associated FCM, but with the IB's name denoted at the top.

A simple way to think about the relationship between an IB and an FCM is this. An IB is a broker, or group of brokers, working for an FCM who are paid as a contractor (on a 1099), rather than a direct employee receiving wages (W-9). Remember, the IB is acting as the middle man between the client and the FCM to perform customer service, tech support, and other client maintenance duties. However, cutting out the middle man doesn't necessarily mean cost savings to the client, but it might be sacrificing customization. In fact, a trader working with an IB is potentially receiving all the services the FCM offers in addition to those offered by the IB. In many cases, it is possible for the IB to do so at competitive or lower commission rates for a comparative service level provided by the FCM.

As always, nothing in the commodity industry is simple. Complicating the topic of brokerage types is the fact that there are two types of IBS: guaranteed introducing brokers (GIB) and independent introducing brokers (IIB). On a side note, it is rare to see the acronym *IIB*; most independent IBs simply identify as an IB without any further designation. GIBs, on the other hand, often disclose their guaranteed status; let's define the difference between these two subcategories of IBs.

GUARANTEED INTRODUCING BROKER (GIB)

A guaranteed introducing broker (GIB) is a type of introducing broker authorized to introduce commodity clients to a *single* FCM. They operate exclusively with a specific FCM in exchange for that FCM posting the NFA-required capital requirement, which is generally about $45,000, and acting as their compliance director. Because of the compliance burdens set forth by a constant stream of legislation, particularly in the wake of the financial crisis of 2008, FCMs are becoming increasingly hesitant to accept a GIB under their wing. Not only does it lock up $45,000 of their working capital, but it opens the door for compliance risk in that the associated FCM is often held responsible for any wrongdoing by its GIBs. Clearly, an FCM cannot possibly know what is going on in the office of a GIB at all times; thus, FCMs are more likely to take on IIBs because there is no financial burden and mitigated compliance responsibilities.

Pros of trading with a GIB: GIBs are often smaller firms offering a simplified approach to getting started. Clients will have fewer choices in regards to platforms, and service will be less customizable; but some beginning traders appreciate that.

Cons of trading with a GIB: Because GIBs only have the ability to clear trades via a single FCM, they have fewer options for traders when it comes to platforms. They are also at the mercy of the margin policies of that particular FCM's risk management department and the competency of the FCM support staff. In other words, a GIB has less flexibility, which could impede its ability to service clients in the manner it would like to.

Further, due to limited trade clearing options, GIBs are typically equipped to handle a single type of trader rather than offering efficient services for all types of traders. For instance, many GIBs focus on day trading services but are not prepared to deal with option traders, and vice versa. In addition, in the wake of the FCM collapses of MF Global and PFGBEST, futures traders with large trading capital tend to prefer to have multiple accounts across different FCMs to diversify their brokerage risk away from an unlikely but not necessarily impossible repeat. When trading with a GIB, it isn't possible to diversify FCMs without actually working with multiple introducing brokers (IBs), or FCMs.

In contrast, when working with an independent introducing broker, traders can clear trades through multiple FCMs while using a single IIB as the point of contact. Traders looking for flexibility are probably better off looking into the services of an independent IB as opposed to a guaranteed IB, or trading directly with an FCM.

INDEPENDENT INTRODUCING BROKER (IIB)

Unlike a GIB, which is tied to a single FCM, an independent IB is free to introduce business to multiple FCMs. In order to make this possible, they are responsible for posting a capital requirement of tens of thousands of dollars to meet National Futures Association requirements. Thus, FCMs have no financial, compliance, or operational obligations in establishing a clearing relationship with an independent IB. The IB is completely self-sufficient and is simply looking for a clearing arrangement.

> IIBs offer clients a plethora of platform and clearing choices relative to trading directly with an FCM, broker-dealer, or traditional IB.

Pros of trading with an IIB: Clients can clear trades through multiple FCMs by opening accounts with various FCMs while dealing with a single broker. An independent IB is a one-stop shop for commodity traders. They generally offer several platform choices and are organized in a manner enabling them to commendably accommodate traders of all types, sizes, and strategies in a highly specialized manner. My brokerage service, DeCarley Trading, is a branch of a long-standing IIB.

Cons of trading with an IIB: Some clients are overwhelmed by the number of choices (FCMs, platforms, and so on) offered by an IIB. They are looking for simple solutions and have little interest in stepping out of their comfort zone to find a better customized solution to their trading environment. Nonetheless, I think we can all agree that having more choices is equivalent to having the ability to customize services. Despite its complexity, this ability promotes proficiency.

BROKER-DEALER

The most familiar brokerage type is the broker-dealer. A broker-dealer is simply a stock brokerage firm; it buys and sells equity securities for its own inventory before "dealing" them to the retail trading public. Over the years, some of these traditional stock brokerage firms have slowly begun offering commodity futures products to its clients as a convenience. Many traders migrating into the commodity markets from more traditional investments have opted to take advantage of the fact that their stockbroker now offers commodity futures and options. However, in my opinion the convenience of doing all of your trading under one roof comes at a significant cost. Broker-dealers generally are not experienced in handling futures trading accounts and therefore tend to take several short cuts that could be detrimental to their clients.

Pros of trading commodities with a broker-dealer: Convenience is the primary benefit of trading with a broker-dealer; in such an arrangement, clients can trade futures, options, stocks, bonds, and sometimes even forex with a single brokerage firm.

> Trading commodities with a stockbroker is like ordering a hamburger at a Chinese restaurant; in the end, it isn't what you were hoping for.

Cons of trading commodities with a broker-dealer: Clients could be sacrificing service, and maybe even profitability, for convenience. Broker-dealers tend to be extremely inefficient in providing access to the futures, option on futures, and forex markets. After all, those products and services are not what they do; they merely offer access to the derivative markets as a side product to their primary business. As a result, their staff is typically not equipped to answer questions or facilitate trades efficiently. Those trading commodities with a broker-dealer shouldn't expect any help at all. In addition to being on their own, clients of broker-dealers are habitually charged higher margin rates and might find their broker to be heavy handed and aggressive in liquidating trades suffering losses. Many times, such liquidation is done without any regard to price and without notifying the client. Broker-dealers also limit the products, contract months, and strategies their clients can trade. In my view, if you are looking to trade commodities, you are best off doing so with a brokerage specializing in futures and options.

CHOOSING A BROKERAGE SERVICE LEVEL

> Despite advanced technology enabling commodity traders to view markets and place trades via a computerized trading platform, there is still some value in working with a full-service broker.

Now that we've discussed the various types of commodity brokers, let's take a look at the service levels offered by most, but not all, brokerage firms. Prior to opening a trading account, it is a good idea to be familiar with yourself, your support needs, and exactly what is possible at the particular broker you are interested in trading with. In addition, we will consider which makes the most sense for typical traders of differing skill and experience levels, as well as accounting for the cost of errors when considering an appropriate commission rate.

FULL SERVICE (BROKER ASSISTED)

Despite advanced technology enabling commodity traders to view markets and place trades via a computerized trading platform, or a smart phone, there is still some value in working with a full-service broker, sometimes referred to as a "broker-assisted" capacity. Technically, "broker assisted" describes a moderately lesser service than "full service," but for simplicity and brevity, we lump them together.

Full-service and broker-assisted brokers generally provide clients with a substantial amount of hand holding in regard to trade placement, market guidance, margin call management, and other hands-on tasks to improve the trading environment of clients. Perhaps the most useful service provided by such brokers is the attempt to steer clients clear of common pitfalls that often destroy new traders. It is paramount to understand that an experienced broker has seen, and maybe experienced, just about all the markets have to offer. Further, they've likely witnessed the good times and the bad times of various trading strategies. Thus, being privy to a broker with a lengthy background in the trading industry can be paramount for traders getting started in the commodity markets.

Of course, the additional service of having a living person answering questions, providing guidance, and placing orders comes at a cost. Nevertheless, the additional commission paid in hopes of sponging experience from a long-standing broker is arguably far cheaper than paying costly tuition to the markets in the form of trade placement errors and other easily avoidable mistakes. Trust me when I say, you can lose far more money in the markets in the blink of an eye than you will likely ever pay in commission.

Unlike the days of old, which involved telephones, written order tickets, and waiting several minutes for a fill price, a good full-service broker should be able to accommodate your orders instantly via telephone, email, instant message, or maybe even text message during market hours. As time goes on, I've found my brokerage clients to be increasingly in favor of communicating and even placing orders with me by electronic means. When I entered the business in early 2004, I spent the majority of my day with a clunky phone pinched between my aching shoulder and my ear, but now I spend most of my time responding to emails, text messages, and instant message communications with my clients. Many of my customers find it to be a much more efficient and effective method of handling their accounts. In the same way, electronic communications are preferred by many brokerage services because it provides an effortlessly searchable archive of communications, making it easier for compliance monitoring than listening to phone calls might be.

SELF-DIRECTED ONLINE

The majority of traders opt for a self-directed online brokerage arrangement enabling them to place orders directly into an online trading platform. On the surface, this service type appears to bypass the broker altogether, but that isn't necessarily the case. Even online traders have a broker assigned to their account. Knowing who this person is and his or her ability to properly solve issues is paramount for trading success. For example, imagine the stress of having an order to buy or sell a futures contract rejected by the trading platform. In such a scenario, you will likely scramble to determine the problem and who to call. A good broker will notice the rejected order, and contact you to help alleviate the problem. Not only would such service cut down on emotional backlash, but it could save much-needed time and money via faster trade placement.

Those choosing to trade online should have enough experience to have garnered the basic knowledge necessary to navigate a trading platform, such as commodity symbols, available trading months, and calculating risk. More so, online traders must be capable of coping with the urge to overreact, overtrade, or suffer from other types of emotional hardships. For this reason, some traders opt for a full-service brokerage account as a means of controlling their impulsive behavior. After all, it is harder to overreact, or overtrade, when picking up the phone is involved, as opposed to merely clicking a mouse.

DISCOUNT ONLINE

Discount online traders are essentially forgoing hands-on service for a lower commission rate. For those traders with ample experience, it makes sense to utilize such a service. After all, there is no need to pay for service you won't utilize. In essence, a discount online brokerage firm provides clients with access to the markets and account statements, but generally the service ends there. For some traders, this might make sense. Even so, there is a fine line between getting a good deal on commission and setting a trading experience up for failure due to inadequate support. Deep discount commission houses might seem cheap on the surface, but they might actually be very costly. Shortly, we will discuss details.

HYBRID (BROKER ASSISTED/SELF DIRECTED)

Some futures brokerages focus on a particular service type and do very little to accommodate traders interested in other service levels within the same account, or in a separate account but held at the same brokerage. In my opinion, a quality brokerage firm will not only offer its clients the choice among the aforementioned service types, but it should be capable of offering a hybrid service level. A hybrid service would include some aspects of broker-assisted trading as well as self-directed online trading. Accordingly, clients would have access to a live broker throughout the trading day in addition to the ability to place orders via an online trading platform, or even a mobile app.

This is a great option for those clients who prefer to have somebody to bounce ideas off of or don't always have computer access during market hours but would like to place most orders through a platform. This is essentially the best of both worlds: a high level of service with the convenience of online account access and moderately lower commission rates. Further, most brokerages are capable of setting up trading accounts to have different commission rates for different types of products. A trader wanting to execute futures trades on his own via a platform but wishing to trade options with the help of a broker could do so in the same account at a commission rate that makes sense for the arrangement.

BROKERAGE DECISIONS SHOULD BE BASED ON YOUR SUPPORT NEEDS, NOT COMMISSION

The primary takeaway from the discussion should be that there is no such thing as a perfect brokerage firm, but there is likely a perfect brokerage for your individual needs. Finding the appropriate brokerage relationship will take a considerable amount of work and shouldn't be overlooked; nor should the decision be made solely on the price of commission. After all, choosing a brokerage firm might just be the most important trading decision you ever make.

> "Sometimes that light at the end of the tunnel is a train." —Charles Barkley

Unfortunately, I've witnessed several traders throughout my career rush into online trading; the goal is always the same, to save money on transaction costs. This is a valid concern, since transaction costs directly affect the bottom line. However, the goal of trading is to *make* money, not *save* it. The net results experienced in a trading account are more dependent on top line factors (trading results) than they are on bottom line factors (expenses).

On countless occasions, I've seen traders choosing a discount services level to keep costs low and end up losing thousands of dollars in the market after making a rookie mistake. More than once I have observed traders enter a market order to execute a position in the domestic sugar futures (sugar #14), as opposed to the world sugar futures (sugar #11) contract, which is far more liquid. Luckily, ICE delisted sugar #14 futures, probably because the only trading activity was done by those who simply didn't know what they were getting into, and thus struggled to find someone to take the other side of their trade to exit. To a beginner, sugar is sugar—there was no need to confirm liquidity, the exchange it is traded on, the symbol used, and in some cases they failed to even confirm the price. They simply wanted to buy sugar at the market price. This was a very expensive mistake, since the sugar #14 market was a volume ghost town. As a result, it was difficult to get in and out of without losing a shirt, or more, in the process. I made many calls to colleagues on the trading floor requesting a market maker to do me a favor by "making a market" for a client of mine desperate to exit sugar #14.

This simple mistake can easily cost a trader several hundred, even thousands of dollars on a single contract. To put this avoidable mistake into perspective, world sugar futures trade 30,000 to 60,000 contracts per day, but before being delisted, domestic sugar often traded less than 10 contracts per day. In my estimation, this translates into 10 untrained commodity traders learning a difficult lesson each day. Although sugar #14 no longer trades on the ICE, they have replaced the contract with sugar #16, which is intended to be utilized for hedging. The lack of liquidity disqualifies sugar #16 for speculation, so be sure to stay away from it.

I used sugar as an example because it is a common mistake that comes with profound consequences to a trading account as well as the psychological stability of a trader. However, there are several other similar examples such as obscure energy product listings in the NYMEX division of the CME, including their "end of day" suite, which because of its low liquidity should also be avoided by most speculators.

Other common mistakes are trading the wrong year or month, buying when the intent was to sell and vice versa, not being aware of open and close times for each market, and not fully understanding the difference between stop and limit orders. Perhaps the most egregious mishaps occur due to a misunderstanding of "limit up" and "limit down." If you are unfamiliar with limit moves, they are similar to a circuit breaker in the stock market; the associated futures exchange sets a daily limit for price movement. Unlike a circuit breaker, which halts trading, once the futures price limit has been reached, prices cannot continue in the direction of the trend but traders can still enter limit orders to trade the contract. If the daily price limit for corn futures is 40 cents and the previous day's closing price was $3.95, corn can go up to $4.35, or down to $3.55 during the trading session before the limit goes into effect. If corn rallies to $4.35, the exchange prevents any trades from occurring above it. As a result, traders cannot enter market orders, but they can enter limit orders to buy or sell at any price below $4.35. Of course, those short the market needing to buy a contract to exit or those flat the market wanting to buy are free to enter orders to buy at $4.35, but unless there is a seller willing to take the other side of it, their order will go unfilled.

The justification beginning traders often use for selling into a limit-up move is that prices cannot go against them because of the price limit. They see it as a risk-free trade; however, nothing could be farther from the truth. Although the price cannot go up in the current session, the trader might not be able to exit the position until the next session. At which time prices might be considerably higher—maybe even limit up to trap them into the position with large losses until the next trading session. Selling a contract when the market is limit up puts the trader's fate in the hands of the market; he retains little control in regard to when and where he will be able to exit the trade.

Each of the mistakes discussed in this section are potentially costly but can be easily avoided with proper experience or help from somebody with market familiarity. If you are not ready to trade online, you should be willing to pay a little extra for the expertise of a full-service broker and work your way toward being an online trader. It's simple: don't suffer devastating losses fortunes trying to stretch a dollar.

Even if you are an experienced trader capable of trading online on your own, you must understand that you will always get what you pay for. Thus, I recommend resisting the temptation to trade with a highly discounted brokerage service. They keep their rates low by cutting corners and amenities. Those placing their trading accounts in such an environment are likely doing themselves, and their trading accounts, a disservice.

Regardless of the trading platform used, the quality of the broadband service or even the highest-end router will experience technical issues on occasion. Online traders experiencing technical hardships might require some additional service from their brokerage firms. In general, the firms offering highly discounted commission rates cannot afford to hire a large nor experienced staff, so you can expect long hold times, delayed service, and other obstacles should an emergency arise. The best trading in the world might not be enough to overcome such impediments. When trading leveraged futures contracts, being on hold for several minutes can be a pricey experience. Let's take a closer look at when and how a poor brokerage choice might affect trading results.

THE TRUTH ABOUT COMMISSION, AND ITS IMPACT ON TRADING RESULTS

Most people imagine commodity brokerage houses to be something like those seen in the movie *Trading Places*, which portrays futures brokers in expensive suits, working out of high-rise office buildings, and driving Bentleys. The truth, of course, is that lifestyle is a mirage existing in only the rarest of cases; most brokers struggle to make a living wage. In fact, it might surprise you to learn that many of the clerks and brokers working at deep discount futures brokerage firms are shockingly inexperienced and offer their services at minimum wage with some small opportunity for earning commission incentives. It isn't uncommon to see deep discount commodity brokerage firms place employment ads in the Chicago Craigslist website seeking "experienced salespeople." As you can imagine, the ads are not requesting experienced candidates in the industry, nor do they require any knowledge of the financial or commodity markets. This is what paying deep discount commission will get you.

> A trader's commission bill is primarily determined by his trading behavior, not the rate his brokerage is charging him.

I've been a commodity broker since 2004. Through the years, we've seen the broker/client relationship shift dramatically. At the beginning of my career, online trading platforms were still relatively new, most clients had grave reservations about using them, and most brokers opted to bypass them by calling client orders to buy or sell directly to the trading floor. Those platforms were extremely simple in nature: no charting and no streaming quote functionality, and order entry required the order placer know the commodity futures contract and month symbol before entering the trade. Considering what we take for granted now, it is hard to imagine such a world, but the truth is in the early 2000s commodity clients spoke to their brokers daily, or even dozens of times per day, because it was necessary to accomplishing simple tasks we now rely on computers for, such as market quotes and placing trades. Naturally, as the burden of phone order placement and communication has dissipated, so have transaction costs. The massive improvements to commodity trading efficiency with online trading platforms have caused commission rates to plummet.

Generally speaking, technology and easy market access have been a giant step in the right direction to leveling the playing field for the average futures market speculator. However, I believe the pendulum has swung a little too far. I argue that overly competitive commission rates have caused brokers to cut corners that shouldn't be cut. Contrary to popular assumption, the result, in my opinion, is decreased odds of trading success for the average retail trader.

Of course, the improvements in technology and market access were the primary factors enabling brokerage firms to offer low commission rates, eventually leading commodity traders to demand unreasonably low rates. However, the biggest culprit to what ultimately became a cannibalization of the futures industry is the Federal Reserve's nearly decade-long policy of holding interest rates artificially low. Prior to the prolonged period of near-zero interest rates, commodity brokerage firms thrived on a business model that allowed them to generate revenue from interest earned on the deposits of their customers, in addition to commission transaction costs. Interest earned by brokerage firms was commonly referred to as *float*. During the days of higher interest rates, brokerage firms would earn 4% to 5% annually on customer deposits, which accumulated to a significant sum. In fact, the high interest rate environment in conjunction with the expediency and adeptness of electronic trading platforms offered the perfect opportunity for discount commodity brokers to be born.

> The biggest problem online traders have with commission is they get exactly what they pay for. You can't get more for less!

Such brokers built their business model on the premise that the brokerage service could be profitable operating on very thin commission margins because the interest income earned on their brokerage book would generate enough income to keep the company profitable. As we all now know, this was not a business model built to last. Chronically low interest rates for over a decade put many of the discount brokerage firms out of business, while those that managed to survive did so by cutting costs and service. Unfortunately, now that consumers have grown accustomed to low futures commission rates, they demand access to low rates without acknowledging, or even realizing, the opportunity costs.

IS IT POSSIBLE FOR TRANSACTION COSTS TO BE TOO LOW?

Online trading has forced traders into believing that all brokers are created equal. Armed with this (arguably false) assumption, they often flock to the brokerage that happens to be offering the lowest commission rate at that moment, or at least one that is marketing in a way that creates the illusion of the lowest cost. Keep in mind that when it comes to commission there is more than meets the eye; hidden fees can add up quickly.

Commodity brokers dating back to the 1980s will tell you they enjoyed round-turn commissions in the $50 to $100 range. Fast forward to the 2010s and brokers are charging well under $10 for online trading. Some firms offer traders rates falling under $5.00 per round turn. If you are unfamiliar with the way futures commission is charged, it can be quoted on a round-turn basis that accounts for both the entering and exiting of a trade. Some brokers advertise a "per-side" commission quote to make their rates seem cheaper. Naturally, the per-side rate only accounts for entering a trade, not exiting it. Thus, commission rates quoted on a per-side basis should be doubled to compare to round-turn commission rates.

Lower transaction costs have been a fabulous transformation for retail traders, but there is such a thing as too much of a good thing. I argue a low commission encourages green commodity futures and options traders to participate in the markets without the proper assistance they need. Even worse, discounted transaction costs act as a constant temptation to trade higher lot sizes, and trade more frequently.

In addition, experienced traders who are normally highly self-sufficient are sometimes finding themselves in a precarious position due to the inadequacy of their brokerage firm. If you are new to commodity trading, you might not understand this, but if you've traded through a calamity such as the 2010 flash crash, the August 2011 debt crisis, or even the August 2015 China collapse, you've probably discovered that your brokerage firm has the potential to play a big part in determining trading success or failure.

WHERE ARE DISCOUNT BROKERS CUTTING CORNERS?

A small mishap at the brokerage level can lead to mass frustration, missed trades, and even unnecessary realized losses at the hands of temporary market moves and an irrationally risk-averse brokerage house. You might be surprised at the disregard for quality service discount commodity brokers have when it comes to cost cutting.

SKELETON CREWS

Without the float acting as a subsidy to revenue and commission rates in the gutter, all brokerage firms are far more exposed to economic cycles and industry risk than they once were. But it is the *discount futures brokers* who are really put in a vice. The first step in reducing costs is done at the personnel level. Whether it is customer service reps, tech support staff, or back office accounting, deep discount brokerage firms around the globe moved to skeleton crews.

> Not unlike any other commission-based industry, the commodity business is a brutal display of Darwinism. As a result, most brokers are new and inexperienced, and few survive beyond a year or two.

Because commodity brokers are the salesmen of a brokerage firm, they are compensated through commission and are rarely provided additional benefits such as medical insurance by their employer. Accordingly, they are rarely laid off. Instead, they are simply starved out. In a post–low interest rate and low-commission rate world, those individual commodity brokers who could no longer put food on the table to feed their families walked away from the business and were replaced with undereducated, unqualified, and underpaid brokers. From the outside, futures brokerage houses look similar to those of decades ago, but from the inside many of them are gutted. Not surprisingly, less staff and fewer experienced brokers result in a subpar trading service.

Imagine the angst you might feel if your trading platform malfunctions while you have a large position open, and you can't get your brokerage firm on the line to correct it. Or the frustration of having your futures or options position force-liquidated near the lows of a flash crash despite your account having plenty of margin on deposit, only to watch the market recover without you. These are real examples, and in many cases the unnecessary trading losses suffered at the hands of an inept brokerage service can amount to thousands of dollars. In the end, the pennies saved on commission might not mean anything relative to the damage to the trading account inflicted by a poor commodity brokerage.

RISK MANAGEMENT STAFF AND PROCEDURES

An often-overlooked fact about the commodity brokerage business is the fact that because clients are trading leveraged derivatives, a situation could be created in which they lose more money than is on deposit with the broker. In these situations, client accounts can actually go into a negative balance if losses exceed margin money on deposit. Consequently, clients pose a risk to the brokerage firm; each client a brokerage accepts represents an opportunity for commission revenue, with strings attached.

Many discount futures and options brokers are charging commission rates so low that their potential profit margin is a few pennies per trade. Accordingly, they cannot afford to accept the risk of a client losing more than he or she has on deposit. Obviously, nobody wants to owe his brokerage firm money after a stint in the commodity markets. Likewise for your broker, because collecting the debt can be challenging and costly.

> Discount futures brokerage firms are known for using a hatchet on client positions in trouble, as opposed to a scalpel. The result is often unnecessary trade liquidation and incredibly painful slippage.

The result of skimpy commission rates is a severely aggressive and overly quick risk manager leading to frequent forced liquidation of brokerage client positions. You are probably thinking that could never happen to *you*, but trust me, it can happen to anyone. If you trade commodities long enough, you will be at the wrong place at the wrong time. Surviving such a trying experience will depend on proper funding and excess margin, as well as being with a brokerage that allows clients to clean up their own mess. Poorly timed forced liquidation of positions by a brokerage firm risk manager can be an expensive lesson for a trader to learn, particularly an option trader. A risk manager's job is simple; eliminate price risk through liquidation in the quickest manner possible. This generally entails market orders without regard to price or time, and with plenty of price slippage. During times of high volatility, such as the S&P 500 mini crash that took place in late August 2015, inopportune and involuntary position liquidation might be the type of devastation a trading account can't recover from.

LIMIT MARKET ACCESS TO PRODUCTS OR STRATEGIES

> "Fast food is popular because it's convenient, it's cheap, and it tastes good. But the real cost of eating fast food never appears on the menu." — Eric Schlosser

Brokers facing skimpy profit margins at the hand of highly discounted commission rates compensate their business model by reducing the types of products and trading strategies that clients are allowed to trade. One of the most common strategy restrictions is naked option selling; few discount brokers give their clients the green light to sell naked options, and some even prohibit limited risk option spread trading. In my opinion, this is unacceptable and even ruthless. Option strategies offer traders risk management solutions and, in many cases, higher-probability strategies relative to outright futures trading.

Another restriction that deep discount brokers set on their clients is the ability to trade back-month futures contracts. In fact, such brokers frequently set the trading platforms provided to clients to reject futures orders in contracts having any expiration month other than the most liquid front month. In my opinion, trading back-month commodity contracts are often helpful in spreading risk exposure. Perhaps these brokerage firms' actions to reduce their own risk have directly increased the risk their clients are exposed to.

Even worse, discount brokers are known to restrict access to many of the less-popular commodity markets. As a result, their clients are merely allowed to trade a handful of futures contracts, as opposed to having the freedom to trade the markets they wish. For instance, my brokerage gives traders the green light to trade any market that is listed on the US futures exchanges, in addition to many popular commodities listed on foreign futures exchanges. We have clients trading obscure markets such as milk futures, cash settled cheese, the Mexican peso, and lumber. However, many commodity brokers refuse to accept orders in these markets due to questionable liquidity. Nevertheless, I see market restrictions as an unnecessary hindrance on experienced futures traders in an effort to save the inexperienced traders from harming themselves by trading markets they shouldn't. A quality brokerage firm should be able to offer the best of both worlds by opening these products up to its clients, but also offering hands-on support to ensure beginning traders are free to find quick and easy answers to questions that will guide them away from trading in products they aren't ready for.

OPTION SELLERS MUST FIND AN ACCOMMODATING BROKERAGE SERVICE

More than any other type of trader, option sellers must find an accommodative brokerage relationship. This will, without a doubt, require traders to pay more than the rock bottom rates the industry has to offer, but in the long run it will be the most conducive for profitable trading. As an experienced commodity broker specializing in hosting option selling accounts, I can assure you there is much more to the relationship between an option trader and his brokerage firm than simply transaction costs.

Regardless of whether an option seller is placing orders directly into a trading platform or through a full-service broker, the success or failure of a short option strategy will inevitably rely on the policies of the brokerage. As discussed, not all brokers allow its clients to sell options, but even those that do tend to intentionally, and aggressively, reduce the strategy to an undesirable venture.

> Concession is a synonym for discount. If you choose a discount broker, you are certainly giving up service, market access, and trading freedom.

Specifically, they charge their clients margins in excess of standard portfolio analysis of risk (SPAN), which limits the position size that clients can safely trade as well as increases the odds of an uncomfortable margin call (if you need a refresher on the definition of SPAN margin, visit Chapter 1). Another common practice of anti-option selling brokerages is to offer SPAN minimum margin under normal market conditions but implement an upcharge during times of high volatility. This is worse than upcharging short option margin from the get-go because it gives traders the benefit of SPAN when they don't need it and takes it away when they need it the most. I've seen brokers shift from SPAN minimum margin to 10 times SPAN overnight on specific clients whom the broker deems to be higher risk according to their internal risk models. To put this into perspective, a client holding 10 short grain strangles in a $25,000 account requiring $14,000 in SPAN margin might wake up the next morning to a margin call of $115,000, despite having $11,000 in excess margin based on SPAN figures because the broker decided they would require $140,000 on deposit to hold the position. Yes, this happened.

In addition, brokers who aren't comfortable with option selling clients are prone to interfering with their client's short option strategies; this might mean force-liquidating positions at the first hint of trouble, or it could be the practice of forcing clients to purchase protective options as opposed to selling naked calls and puts. The result is mandatory credit spreads potentially altering the strategy altogether. The bottom line? Traders wishing to sell options must ensure their trading account is with a broker who will let clients trade the way they want to, not the way the brokerage firm wants them to.

CONCLUSION: SOMETIMES CHEAP IS ACTUALLY EXPENSIVE

> "It costs a lot of money to look this cheap." —Dolly Parton

It is difficult to measure the intangible expenses and benefits that come with choosing the right futures broker for your circumstances. On the contrary, it is easy to see transaction costs. After all, every penny paid to your broker, to the exchange in clearing fees and the NFA in its transaction fee, are detailed on a trading account statement for traders to analyze and possibly even mourn over. Nevertheless, the transparency and obvious nature of commission costs don't make it more important than the unpredictable costs of being with the wrong commodity broker.

Choosing a broker based on commission alone might be a big mistake. A commodity broker dictating which products its clients trade, the manner in which they trade them, and in volatile markets when they exit them as a means of keeping brokerage expenses and risk low will be a huge detriment to its clients. To be direct, traders focused on finding the lowest commission rate are, in essence, picking up pennies in front of a steamroller. If you think commission is expensive, try getting what you pay for. The odds favor that your hidden expenses will far outweigh the visible ones.

WHAT YOU MUST KNOW ABOUT FUTURES AND OPTIONS DATA FEES

Since entering the business in early 2004, I have found that the cost and implications of acquiring price data has come full circle. Early on, futures and options price data was only available through pricey subscriptions offered by individual commodity exchanges, such as the Chicago Board of Trade, the Chicago Mercantile Exchange, the New York Board of Trade, the New York Mercantile Exchange, and the Commodity Exchange (better known as COMEX). Traders seeking live price data had to pay each exchange for the luxury of seeing real-time quotes, as opposed to the 15-minute delayed quotes offered for free by many websites and phone-in services (yes, I know that dates me). The price tag on data was relatively steep at about $80 per exchange, depending on the exact trading platform being used. In my opinion, the costs, although steep, were more or less justified because at the time, the exchanges paid a clerk to stand in the corner of each of the open outcry pits to record and expedite price data. This was no easy task!

As futures and options trading migrated from the now-closed trading pits to electronic execution, the need for live open outcry pit data fizzled. Instead, traders found themselves relying on the price data of electronically traded markets, which was made available to them via live and active trading accounts at no cost. Traders, brokers, and industry insiders enjoyed the newfound cost savings. What was once costing them roughly $320 per month was now relatively complimentary in the new electronic environment as long as there was active trading occurring. Keep in mind the exchanges make anywhere from $1 to $4 on every round turn that occurs on the exchange, so offering free electronic data to traders likely increased their exchange fee revenue because transparent price data makes it convenient to trade actively. In essence, it was a win/win; all the same, it didn't last. The CME Group felt as though its vast expenditures to improve technology required a subsidy from those benefiting from the service of real-time quotes on products listed on their exchanges.

CME DATA FEES

On January 1, 2015, the CME Group rolled out a new data fee program requiring all active traders to pay for access to futures and options price data. Thankfully, most retail traders are offered data subscriptions at discounted pricing. The exact cost per trader varies, but it can be as low as $3 per month for top line data on all CME Group exchanges, or as much as $15 monthly for access to multi-tier data on all CME Group exchanges. Multi-tier data displays the 10 best bids and asks, but single-tier data provides traders with the current bid/ask quote without offering any information on proximal working limit orders beneath or above the market price.

Keep in mind, these rates are per platform, not per person. Thus, a trader utilizing a mobile platform as well as a downloaded platform might be subject to multiple sets of fees. Likewise, a trader using one platform for options trading and another for futures might be forced to pay data subscription fees for both platforms. Whether the trader is charged for both platforms depends on the FCM associated with the platform, and whether the order entry server and data service provider are the same. As you can tell, it gets complicated; accordingly, it is imperative to consult with a broker to ensure against making a mistake and causing unnecessary data fee expenses.

At these rates ($3 to $15), the data costs for using one or two platforms are more of an annoyance than a game changer; most traders simply absorb the new costs and carry on as they always have. I hate to admit it, but these low fees are actually good business by the CME because it doesn't hinder anybody's ability to trade while offering the CME a handsome monthly revenue it didn't previously enjoy. Further, the burden of collecting fees from active traders lies in the hands of the brokerage firms themselves, so implementation of this policy enabled the CME to pass administrative costs on to brokers while padding their own bottom line. As an entrepreneur, I respect the ingenuity. However, the CME charges substantially more to anyone categorized as a "professional trader," according to the exchange's definition and stipulations.

NON-PROFESSIONAL CME DATA FEES

According to the CME Group, a non-professional trader is either an individual or natural person, or certain small business entity (limited liability companies, partnerships, trusts, or corporations) that receive and use price data on electronically traded futures and options in a manner consistent with the following capacities:

1. The subscriber must have an active futures trading account.
2. The subscriber must not be a member of a CME Group exchange (or hold a lease).
3. The subscriber does not have a primary business purpose that involves trading.
4. The subscriber must not be registered or qualified as a professional trader or investment advisor with any stock, commodities, or futures exchange or contract market, or with any regulatory authority, professional association, or recognized professional body.
5. The subscriber must not be affiliated with any entity that is or may be considered a professional user.
6. The subscriber use of price information must be solely for the subscriber's personal, non-business use.

7. The subscriber's use of price data information must be limited to managing the subscriber's own property and, for the avoidance of doubt, not in connection with the management of any property of any third party in any capacity, whether as a principal, officer, partner, employee, or agent of any business or on behalf of any other individual, and whether the subscriber receives any remuneration therefore.

8. The subscriber must not be acting on behalf of an institution that engages in brokerage, banking, investment, or financial activities.

9. The subscriber has no more than two means for accessing information from each distributor.

10. The subscriber must view the information only on a device that is capable of routing orders to the CME's electronic GLOBEX exchange.

Any data subscriber who does not meet the aforementioned conditions is categorized as a *professional trader*. This might sound like an inconsequential designation, and maybe even flattering, but I assure you it is highly undesirable.

PROFESSIONAL DATA FEES

Unfortunately, there is a caveat to the CME Group's data policy that has had a substantial negative impact on the commodity industry. In the previous paragraph, I mentioned the discounted data fees that most individual retail traders enjoy. The CME refers to this group of traders as "non-professionals"; yet, for those falling within the CME's distinction of a professional trader, the cost of data access skyrockets. Professional traders don't have the ability to choose top line or bottom line data; instead, they face a single fee of $85 per exchange per platform. For those wishing to access all four of the CME Group exchanges, the total monthly cost is $340. Once again, this is per platform; a commodity broker wishing to assist clients on more than one platform and FCM must pay $340 for each platform. Prior to the data fee policy being employed by the CME, many brokers under an IIB relationship were working with five to 10 trading platforms. If you've done the math, you are aware the monthly cost for price data might range somewhere between $1,700 and $3,400. Despite the implications of high earnings among commodity brokers, I can assure you that is not reality for the majority. Similar to any other sales jobs, 20% of the brokers make "all" of the money and the other 80% would be better off waiting tables at the neighborhood café. Many commodity brokers simply couldn't absorb this new cost of doing business. Soon, we'll discuss the impact this has had on the industry.

AVOID BEING INCORRECTLY CATEGORIZED AS A PROFESSIONAL TRADER

The implications of being categorized by the CME as a professional trader are profound. It is important to understand the steps that should be taken to avoid incorrectly being designated as such. Anybody registered as a member or directly affiliated with a member of the NFA, CFTC, SEC, or any other global financial industry is considered a professional trader for data fee purposes. In addition, any person who makes a living in any other capacity related to the commodity or financial markets will be tagged as a pro trader. However, in some instances an "average Joe" trader with a day job can unexpectedly trigger professional classification, which is unfortunate.

Generally speaking, aside from a spouse trading an account for a spouse, anytime a trader takes power of attorney trading privileges over an account in which there are funds other than their own, the trader is considered a professional trader. To clarify, if a trader decides to trade an account for his friend or even family members, he will be subject to the CME's professional data fees at a rate of $340 per month. Don't forget, if the trader wishes to have access to live data for ICE products as well, he will be charged another set of data fees. We'll discuss ICE fees later on.

HOW THE CME PROFESSIONAL DATA FEES HAVE CHANGED THE FUTURES INDUSTRY

Facing massive data fees at the hands of the CME Group's new policies, the commodity brokerage industry made momentous changes to accommodate the new reality. For starters, the commodity brokerage profession has been thinned out. Most individual brokers are expected to pay their platform and data costs; prior to the CME Group's data fee policy, many had managed to keep costs extremely low to ensure survival in the business. Yet in a post–data fee policy world, many commodity brokers made the difficult decision to undergo a career change. Suddenly, decade-long colleagues of mine were dropping like flies because of the implications of higher costs combined with falling commissions, burdensome regulations, and a shrinking client pool. Many had a foot out the door anyway, but high data fees were commonly described as the straw that broke the camel's back. Similarly, those brokerage firms paying the technology costs for each of its brokers simply stopped hiring new brokers and laid off those who weren't producing enough revenue to justify the increased costs.

As a commodity broker, I likely have a bias, but in my opinion we are the lifeline of the futures and options industry. Futures brokers are the front line in servicing traders, and they are responsible for attracting mass liquidity into the marketplace. Thus, although it was probably necessary to weed out the brokers who were simply taking up space, as opposed to being productive members of the industry, there has likely been a detriment to the level of service clients will receive. After all, if there are fewer brokers servicing accounts, the client experience will suffer.

Another detriment to retail traders is a reduction in platform choices at brokerage firms. Brokers don't offer as many platform choices to clients. This is because each individual broker must pay $340 for each platform he would like to access to place orders for clients, or at least view client accounts for risk management purposes. In addition, there is a lack of freedom to trade on multiple platforms. In the past, it was fairly common for traders of all types and sizes to utilize multiple trading platforms, but now, facing a penalty in the form of data fees, most opt to use a single platform.

Aside from the hardships that brokerage firms themselves have suffered as a result of increased costs of doing business, which aren't limited to price data fees, the new fee structure has deterred many clients from participating in the futures and options markets. As touched upon in the previous section, those who discover the data fee hardships that come with futures trading for friends and family opt to participate in leveraged ETFs or forex as an alternative. Nevertheless, most traders will easily fall within the confines of the non-professional designation and, therefore, are seeing little impact to their trading at the hands of the cost of price data.

ICE PRICE DATA FEES

A little over a year after the CME Group implemented their controversial data fee policy, the Intercontinental Exchange rolled out their own set of hefty fees levied on commodity traders. Before we talk about the magnitude and implications of the ICE data fee policy, I'll first remind you which markets are traded on the exchange—the softs (sugar, cocoa, coffee, cotton, and orange juice), along with the dollar index and the Russell 2000 (at least until it moves to the CME Group in August 2017).

NEW DATA FEE POLICY BEGINNING APRIL 1, 2016

As of April 1, 2016, the ICE charges each trader, broker, risk manager, and market watcher $110 per month for access to live market data per exchange. This fee will be levied to each user and each platform, and per each ICE exchange, making it extremely cumbersome for traders and industry insiders. To illustrate, a trader accessing live ICE US data while trading in the softs, who also subscribes to ICE Europe data, would be subject to a bill of $220 per month. This isn't necessarily a far-fetched setup because one of the most popular ICE products is Brent crude oil, which trades on the ICE Europe division. If the same trader wished to have access to a mobile platform, depending on the arrangement and platform chosen, he would most likely have to pay another $220 for such access. You've probably done the math in your head; this is equivalent to $440 per month! Prior to April 2016, most traders were provided with real-time streaming data for ICE futures and options products at no cost. Thus, there was mass sticker shock across the industry.

HOW THIS DIFFERS FROM THE CME'S DATA FEE POLICY

The distinguishing factor between ICE and CME Group data fees is the CME policy differentiates professional traders from non-professional traders. The CME's data fees are a negligible burden to retail traders and a heavy burden to industry professionals utilizing multiple platforms or wanting access to all four CME exchanges at a cost of $340 per month. On the other hand, the ICE policy treats all market participants the same and charges unfathomable data costs to the average retail trader. The ICE policy is likely closing the door to their products for most retail traders—$110 per month, or more, is a deal breaker to the majority of small speculators.

WHAT ICE PRICE DATA FEES MEAN FOR TRADERS AND THE INDUSTRY

We won't know the full effect of the ICE data fee policy for quite some time. Nonetheless, there are consequences to retail traders, the ICE, and the industry as a whole. I can't imagine very many retail traders paying $110 per month, or more, for a data subscription fee, particularly because ICE products are such a small part of most commodity traders' portfolios. Judging by my own brokerage clients, the majority of retail traders will simply stop trading ICE products. Consequently, trading volume in the softs is set to decline significantly. This leaves the door open for competing exchanges, such as the CME to either buy out the ICE operations, individual products, or lobby the CFTC to list competing contracts in an attempt to steal market share.

With that said, the ICE might have come to the conclusion that because they make the lion's share of their revenue from commercial hedgers and large institutional traders, it isn't worth their resources to accommodate individual, small traders. In this case, they will probably get what they are asking for.

CHAPTER 16: RISK MANAGEMENT: UNDERSTAND, PROPERLY UTILIZE, AND HEDGE COMMODITY MARKET LEVERAGE

O utside the world of finance, the term *leverage* is used to describe the practice of utilizing one object to maximize the mechanical advantage of exertion being used to accomplish a goal. It can also be used to describe the influence a person, or entity, has on the decisions and behaviors of others. Within the financial realm, the same overall premise of leverage applies, but it focuses on the use of a small amount of capital to reap the potential of a much bigger financial endeavor. In nearly all examples, leverage involves the borrowing of funds, or more specifically the use of trading margin to exploit the advantage of a speculative undertaking. Ironically, the practice intended to maximize return is more often the culprit responsible for minimizing trading capital.

> "The most important rule of trading is to play great defense, not great offense."
> —Paul Tudor Jones

A prominent example of investing on leverage is the purchase of a home with a minimal down payment. Although the buyer of the home is entitled to any price appreciation of the home, he is also subject to the pain of declining home values. Yet his profits and losses in regard to the home value are exaggerated on a percentage basis because of a lack of true equity in the home. Simply, if a home buyer puts $20,000 toward a down payment for a $200,000 home, a 10% increase in the value of the home to $220,000 results in a 100% return to the homeowner, but a decline to $180,000 results in a 100% loss of principal! It is easy to see how leverage can be either an expensive, or lucrative, venture. Despite the casual approach to leverage in the commodity markets, it is even more treacherous than that of real estate. After all, even after the 2006 downturn, real estate volatility pales in comparison to most commodities.

The purpose of this discussion certainly isn't to deter you from trading commodities. Instead, I aim to help readers understand the difference between responsible leveraged speculation and treating the futures markets as a roulette wheel. Hopefully, with the proper expectations and mindset, it will be possible to bypass some of the painful leverage-induced lessons many traders learn the hard way.

UNDERSTAND THE MAGNITUDE OF FUTURES MARKET LEVERAGE

Because leverage in the futures market is so casually granted to nearly everyone who completes an account application, it is easy to get sucked into the naïve mindset that commodity market leverage is reasonable, but I can

> "Derivatives are financial weapons of mass destruction." —Warren Buffett

assure you it isn't. Have you ever tried trading with your stockbroker on leverage? He will likely require that you have at least $50,000 to $100,000 in your trading account. Further, he will charge you interest for the privilege of borrowing brokerage firm shares to short. To reiterate, because stock exchanges are facilitating buys and sales of actual assets, rather than agreements to trade an underlying asset as futures contracts do, there is no natural leverage in trading equity shares. Any leverage enjoyed by a stock trader is granted solely by his brokerage firm—with multiple strings attached. Stock brokerages intentionally make trading shares on margin expensive and inconvenient due to the risks involve to the investor as well as the broker. You might have seen the viral story of stock trader Joe Campbell on social media; at the hands of a short bet on KaloBios Pharmaceuticals gone awry, he owed his broker (E-Trade) about $106,000. The entire loss occurred in aftermarket trade and was realized when E-Trade stepped in to liquidate the position. Feeling victimized, the trader set up a GoFundMe campaign in which he received a little over $5,000 from donors to go toward his brokerage debt. Most members of the trading community, however, showed little sympathy. The inexperienced trader placed a large short position on a low-priced stock, which offered dismal profit potential; in short, it was a foolish trade to begin with.

On the contrary to stock brokerage houses, futures brokers operate with a differing mindset. Not only do futures traders have access to interest-free margin accounts, they can trade on unreasonably high levels of leverage with few restrictions, or even minimum account sizes.

The luxury of cheap and easy leverage is primarily extended to commodity traders via the exchanges because it is essentially built into market structure requiring traders to deposit minimal margin, rather than the actual contract value to trade a given commodity. Nonetheless, brokers have a say in how much leverage their day trading clients are granted and often exacerbates leverage abuse. Naturally, propensity to promote high-volume trading, which translates into higher commission revenue, encourages brokers to lower required margin rates to day traders. This exponentially increases trading leverage to a point that it is nearly impossible to make money. Of course, they don't tell clients this, but they know. That said, having access to convenient leverage is a privilege, not a right; don't abuse it. Traders often assume leverage is owed to them, but it is something that can only be earned. Just like a bank vets a borrower before granting a loan, a commodity broker won't grant access to extreme day trading futures market leverage before confirming the client is good for it.

I often hear traders casually mention their intention to buy or sell 10 e-mini NASDAQ futures as if it is a minor undertaking. Many consistently downplay the leverage and risk of such a position, but I wonder if they have ever taken the time to do the math to determine just how much exposure such a trade comes with. Let's

> "People who look for easy money invariably pay for the privilege of proving conclusively that it cannot be found on this earth." —Jesse Livermore

assume the e-mini NASDAQ is valued at 4,400; each point is worth $20, so the notional value of the contract is $88,000 (4,400 x $20). Accordingly, a trader who enters an order to buy or sell 10 e-mini NASDAQ futures contracts is subject to the profits and losses of roughly $880,000 worth of tech stocks. The exchange requires about $5,000 to hold a single e-mini NASDAQ contract overnight, which is the equivalent of about 6% of the underlying asset. Thus, a futures trader needs only $50,000 in a trading account to buy and hold $880,000 worth of NASDAQ stocks.

Even more astounding, some brokerage firms offer day trading margin in the e-mini NASDAQ as low as $500, which translates into a margin down payment equivalent to half of a percent. We all know what happened to homeowners who put a down payment of less than 1% toward their mortgage. There are day traders out there who think little of trading 10 e-mini NASDAQ futures in a $5,000 account simply because their brokerage firm allows them. Nevertheless, some quick math reveals that the odds of success when trading $880,000 worth of securities in a $5,000 futures trading account are dire. As we were all reminded of in the early 2000s, even a nonleveraged tech stock portfolio, or some similar ETF or mutual fund, can see large drawdowns. Further, risk and leverage is just as treacherous using the more popular, and arguably better balanced, S&P 500 e-mini futures contract. Adding leverage to already volatile assets such as stock index futures and commodities can be challenging to manage for those who aren't properly prepared to give the market the respect it deserves.

The commodity trading industry is a massive for-profit endeavor thriving off of speculator trading volume. Exchanges and brokerage firms generate revenue each time a futures contract or option trade is executed. As a reminder, for this reason, as well as others, they extend low margin rates with high levels of leverage to encourage trading volume.

As much as I hate to admit it, although most commodity brokers operate with high levels of integrity, not all brokers, firms, and even futures exchanges care whether traders make money. They simply desire transactions to be made knowing that some traders will walk away winners, while others could very well be devastated. In fact, there are several discount future brokerage firms simply playing a numbers game. Their goal is to open as many accounts as possible in hopes they will be able to, at least, open an account for every client they lose due to account devastating losses. Although the consequences are more severe, it isn't unlike a casino decorating their buffet with wild patterns and colors to promote visitors to eat quickly, increasing the turnover of guests and therefore revenue. Before you fall into the trap of conforming to the behaviors that the industry, and your brokerage firm, are indirectly encouraging, take responsibility for your actions by being aware of these tactics and utilizing strategies such as those outlined below to counteract the temptation of biting off more than you can chew.

Just because such leverage is available doesn't mean it is appropriate to utilize; in fact, less is more. It is possible to greatly reduce leverage in the following ways:

$ **Overfund the trading account.** The most effective way to lower leverage and increase the odds of trading success is by simply holding more money in the account than is required in margin. For instance, if the initial margin to trade gold is $4,125 and the contract value is $110,000 (with gold valued at $1,100), a trader can completely eliminate leverage by trading a one lot in a $110,000 account. Similarly, the same trader could reduce the leverage from the exchanges roughly 26 to 1, to a more comfortable 13 to 1 by trading a one-lot gold futures contract in a $55,000 account, and so on. Eliminating the leverage, or at least mitigating it, sharply improves the likelihood of a successful speculation because it increases the room for error and reduces emotional consequences of less than perfect timing.

$ **Trade smaller contracts.** If you don't have the funds available to fully fund a futures trading account, you are not alone. Further, a full funding isn't necessary; most commodity traders are prepared to take reasonable risk and utilize moderate amounts of leverage. Thus, the goal should simply be to get to an emotionally comfortable level of leverage. It is possible to do this efficiently, particularly in relatively small trading accounts, with e-micro currencies and metals (as described in Chapter 12). To clarify, the contract size of an e-micro euro currency futures contract is approximately $13,750 when the euro is trading near $1.10; thus, the leverage can be completely eliminated by trading a single e-micro in an account funded with $13,750. Naturally, for most traders it is reasonable to trade two to five contracts in an account that size, but the point is it is the trader who determines the leverage, not the exchange or brokerage firm. All traders must learn to manage their trading risk via appropriate leverage management.

$ **Sell antagonistic options.** Many stock traders love the added income provided by a covered call strategy, but for some reason the practice isn't as popular in futures trading; perhaps it should be. Even so, the leverage that comes with futures trading makes selling deep out-of-the-money calls against a long futures strategy a relatively dangerous strategy. This is because a price decline will result in much bigger futures contract losses than short call option gains. Accordingly, in futures it makes more sense to sell closer-to-the-money calls against a long futures contract, or maybe even sell two call options for every one long futures contracts held. The same strategy can be applied to a short futures contract, but the trader would be selling a nearby put option. The practice brings in a healthy amount of premium to cushion the blow of any adverse futures market move, and does wonders for taking the stress away from trading because it favorably shifts the profit zone of the trade. This topic is discussed further in Chapter 17.

$ **Buy antagonistic options.** In my opinion, the practice of selling antagonistic options is preferable, but purchasing a put as insurance against a long futures contract, or buying a call against a short futures contract, can be an attractive form of hedging. Further, the purchase of the option acts as absolute insurance, which limits the risk of the trade to a specified amount regardless of how horribly wrong the trade goes. This is referred to as a synthetic strategy, because if constructed in a particular way, it mimics the payout of a long option. Later in the chapter, we'll cover this idea in detail as a substitute for placing stop-loss orders

$ **Establish a commodity collar.** This is a strategy in which a trader goes long a futures contract, purchases a put for insurance, then sells a call to pay for the put. Similarly, a trader might go short a futures contract, buy a call option for protection, then sell a put option to finance the position. In other words, a collar is the strategy of combining the benefits of buying and selling antagonistic options against a primary futures position. Depending on the strike price placement, there may or may not be any real profit potential, but the risks are limited and generally low. However, placing the strike prices of the short options distant from the current market price could create a scenario in which the risk, although limited, could become rather deep. A collar is among the most conservative methods of achieving a directional speculation with limited risk.

Keep in mind that a collar, or trading antagonistic options around a futures position, will work best in a market in which either the calls or puts are priced higher than the other. For instance, in grains the calls are normally valued slightly higher, and in the e-mini S&P the puts tend to have higher values to traders. Thus, the grains might be a better candidate to buy puts and sell calls against a long futures contract, but the S&P is a more attractive arena to buy calls and sell puts against a short futures contract.

> "As a trader you should have no opinion. The more opinion you have, the harder it gets to get out of a losing position." —Paul Rotter

DON'T UNDERESTIMATE LEVERAGE

I know leverage abuse and risk aren't popular topics among traders because most of them overdo it. It is human nature to indulge when we can, knowing we shouldn't. If you ever want a reminder of this very powerful human nature, go to a high-quality Las Vegas buffet. Even knowing better, we still can't seem to avoid pushing our capacity beyond the limits of reason.

Take for example a trader who is willing to risk 10% of his account, valued at $100,000, on any particular trade. Should he employ a strategy that involves a single gold futures contract, his trading rules would allow for a loss of $10,000, which is equal to a $100 price change in gold. To illustrate, if a gold futures contract is purchased at $1,100, the trader might place a stop-loss order at $1,000, or $100 below the current market price, to attempt to prevent the loss on the trade from exceeding 10% of the account value. Yet a trader who is more comfortable with leverage might opt to purchase three gold futures contracts instead of one. This decision requires the trader place a stop-loss order at about $1,067 to limit losses to 10% of the account value. Assuming the speculation calling for higher gold prices is accurate, the first version of the trade allows for 9% decline in gold prices, but the second version of the trade requires the trader to have chosen the bottom in the gold market within 3%. Anybody who has followed financial assets knows that any particular asset can appreciate or depreciate 3% in the blink of an eye.

Yet a 10% price change is far less frequent. Although the profit potential of the second trade is far more attractive, the chances of those profits materializing are greatly reduced. Acknowledging that market timing will never be perfect can go a long way toward trading success and should be incentive to mitigate leverage.

USING STOP-LOSS ORDERS FOR RISK MANAGEMENT

Nearly all trading publications, trading courses, and forums list the number one rule of trading as "Always use stops." This is because a stop-loss order is a quick and easy way to ensure losses don't get out of hand. Further, each trading venture comes with defined risk, ignoring the possibility of slippage or a price gap through the stop price. As we've learned, a stop-loss order is an order placed to buy a futures contract should the market reach a specified price above the current market price or to sell a futures contract should the price reach a specified price below the current market price. In either case, the market price must get "worse" for the order to be elected; thus, buy-stop orders are getting filled on upswings and sell-stop orders on down swings.

ADVANTAGES OF STOP-LOSS ORDERS

The assumed advantage to using stop-loss orders is risk reduction. As the name implies, this order type is used to "stop the loss" of a trade as the futures price moves adversely. In some cases, stop-loss orders do just that; they liquidate a trade if the futures price has reached a predetermined pain threshold. If triggered, the stop-loss order might actually incur a trading loss, but it might also be a stop order that has been trailed by the trader to lock in profits. In either case, if a stop order is elected and filled, it is certain the futures price has moved unfavorably to trigger execution.

As previously mentioned, the most glaring benefit of using a stop-loss order for risk management is to reduce the odds of a runaway trade. There are times when commodity markets experience extreme volatility mitigating, or even eliminating, the ability of a trader to manually exit his position before significant damage is inflicted. Stop-loss orders are proficient at preventing unpleasant surprises. For instance, I've had traders tell me horror stories of a day trade that was breaking even before they walked to the coffee machine to pour a cup of joe, which had turned into a several-thousand-dollar loss by the time they made it back to their desk. These types of quick and unexpected market moves are rare, yet possible at any time. They are generally the result of a surprise news story but can be caused by something as inconsequential as an inaccurate tweet. Ignoring the possibility of price slippage, having a set stop order provides some comfort to the trader in knowing the worst-case scenario in advance.

For some, stop-loss orders are used to reduce the psychological stress that comes with deciding when to pull the plug on a trade gone badly. A trader who enters a market and subsequently places a stop order has already predefined his pain tolerance and simply lets the market and his strategy determine his fate. A trader who enters a market without a stop-loss order, or any other alternative risk management technique, is leaving his exit point up to a strenuous decision process. Human nature leads us to be optimistic; when a trade is going badly, we have the tendency to refuse to admit we are wrong. An intense belief that the trade will improve, or stubbornly refusing to acknowledge a loss, can lead to a situation in which a trader has stopped being a "player" and started being a "prayer." Not only is this detrimental to the financial health of a trading account, but the agony often stays with the trader long afterward, leading to continued poor decision making down the road.

DISADVANTAGES OF STOP-LOSS ORDERS

Trading with stop-loss orders has its advantages, but there are some glaring disadvantages. In fact, I believe that stop-loss orders often cause more harm than good. The most prominent disadvantage to using stop-loss orders is the finite nature of the trade exit. Once a stop-loss order is executed to offset an open position, the trader has no chance of recovering losses, even if the market does. Further, although stop-loss orders limit the risk of a particular trade, they are highly prone to being triggered. As a result, traders are often prematurely stopped out of what would have eventually been a winner. The unfortunate stop-loss trigger could be at the hands of temporary market volatility, or it could simply be that the trader placed the stop order too close to the market. In any case, watching a market move in the intended direction after a stop-loss offset the trade is a painful experience, both financially and psychologically.

Imagine having a catastrophic stop-loss order in the e-mini S&P 500 on May 6, 2010, the day of the infamous flash crash. A plethora of traders were stopped out with massive losses on what turned out to be a quick intraday blip in prices that mostly recovered by the end of the trading day. That unfortunate day was as much as a nightmare for futures brokers as it was for traders caught on the wrong side of the trade. As you know, futures traders can lose more than they have on deposit; thus, a 150 plunge in the e-mini S&P 500, which is equivalent to $7,500 per contract, littered the industry with negative account balances in a matter of minutes. In case you are wondering, if a trader allows his account to go into a negative balance, he is expected to immediately wire funds to his brokerage account to alleviate the shortfall. If he is unable to do so, the individual broker handling the account must forfeit his commission to cover the deficit until the client pays the owed balance. In extreme cases, the broker might take legal action against the client in an attempt to recover lost commissions. Regretfully, I've experienced this to the tune of six figures. It is an uncomfortable situation on both sides.

Getting back to stop-loss orders, I often remind traders that limited risk is not the same thing as low risk. Placing a stop-loss order is effective at limiting the risk to the desired tolerance; for some traders that might be several thousand dollars and for others it might be less than $100. On the surface, risking less than $100 on a futures trade with theoretically unlimited profit potential seems preferable but that isn't necessarily true, because a stop-loss placed to risk $100 will almost certainly get triggered. Simply put, a trader might lose money on 95% of trades entered with a $100 stop-loss. Assuming this is true, as my experience has led me to "guesstimate," after 50 trades and a lot of blood, sweat, and tears, he would have lost roughly 48 out of 50 with a total loss of $4,800 before transaction costs. In theory, two out of 50 winning trades could have made up for the losses, but it is highly unlikely that they would have been profitable by $2,400. After all, to achieve such success the trade would have to catch a $24 per ounce move in gold, a $2.40 move in crude oil, or a 48-point run in the e-mini S&P 500 to recoup losses on the estimated 48 trades that would have likely been stopped out. Thus, a trader placing tight stop-loss orders for the sake of risk management is most likely accomplishing the exact opposite; ironically, his aggressive tactics to cut losses is ensuring he loses money in the markets.

On the other hand, a trader taking the opposite approach by placing deep stop-loss orders to simply protect his trade from catastrophic losses might experience similar frustration. The odds of a deeply placed stop-loss order being triggered are far less than that of a tight stop; accordingly, the trader is giving himself a much better chance of triumph. Nevertheless, deep stop-loss orders are not immune to the possibility of a premature stop out and when they do occur, the stakes are high.

Those opting to use stop-loss orders as a means of risk management must be realistic in their expectations; price slippage can, and will, occur. *Slippage* is a term used by trading professionals to describe the difference in the stated stop-loss price and the actual fill price. As previously discussed, stop-loss orders become market orders once the stop price is reached. Accordingly, the market price might, or might not, be the stated stop price. In thinly traded or unusually volatile markets, the slippage can be astounding. Further, if a commodity market experiences a price gap higher, or lower, on the open of a trading session, it is possible the market gaps through the stated stop-loss price. In this situation, a stop order becomes a market order as usual, but the fill price can be highly unfavorable.

In an even more extreme situation, a commodity market might go limit up or down. In a locked limit environment, there is no trading allowed beyond the daily price limits; thus, stop orders often go unfilled and offer absolutely no protection to the trader. In today's electronic markets, stop slippage, limit up or down price moves, and markets gapping through stop-loss orders have become relatively less frequent, but it is imperative that traders understand stop orders are not guarantees, and therefore, don't always limit losses to the intended amount.

STOP-LOSS ORDER PLACEMENT

There are as many rules for stop-loss order placement as there are traders. The truth is, there isn't an exact science determining where a stop order should be placed. Instead, it should first be determined by risk tolerance and trading strategy. From there, traders should look to areas of support and resistance for guidance.

As a guideline, if the trading strategy is to trend trade, the stops should be placed deep (a substantial distance from the market), yet a swing trader will likely want to keep the stop-loss order at a relatively shallow level. With that said, "shallow" doesn't mean so tight that normal ebb and flow will be sure to trigger the stop-loss order. Due to the ambiguity of stop-loss placement techniques and the dire consequences that come with being stopped out, this is a major source of frustration for futures traders. This is true unless, of course, the less common occurrence of a stop-loss order successfully saving the trader the heartache of massive losses actually plays out.

In my opinion, if a trader is going to use stop-loss orders, it is important to place them beyond obvious support and resistance areas. This is because most traders simply look at the most recent high or low price and place their stop-loss orders near those levels. The problem with this is, if most traders are placing their stop orders in the same general area, once that price range is hit, the stop-loss triggers will push the market in the direction of the trend to consistently climax at unsustainable levels (Figure 53). This is a common occurrence, frequently referred to as *stop running*, or running of the stops. Once most of the stop-loss orders are elected, the market is free to trade according to more normal supply and demand assessments; therefore, prices repeatedly reverse course.

Figure 53: Stop running is a big problem for traders, particularly day traders. Markets are prone to electing the majority of stop orders before reversing, leaving those whose stops were hit in the dust.

SHOULD TRADERS USE STOPS AT ALL?

In conclusion, it is my opinion the drawbacks of using stop-loss orders might outweigh the benefits.   The reality is, markets need room to breathe and trades need slack in the rope to work. Stop-loss orders mitigate the ability of traders to ride out trades whose timing could have been better, but the overall premise of the trade was sound. Obviously, this point of view differs dramatically from most of the literature available to traders, but as a futures broker I've had the luxury of witnessing several trading strategies and approaches to risk management. In the long run, it has been my observation that the traditional use of stop orders is detrimental to trading strategies.

Instead, I believe traders should use either long options to protect futures trades or short options to hedge the risk of a futures trade. Similarly, if it isn't possible to trade futures without stop-loss orders due to risk tolerance, account size, or failure to watch the market, a viable alternative is to trade smaller size by using e-micro currencies and metals, or the mini grains. These smaller-sized commodity futures contracts enable even smaller traders to facilitate a comfortable buy and hold approach without the need for stop orders, and therefore avoiding the risk of inopportune premature liquidation. For those who need predefined risk, perhaps the practice of using long options in place of stop orders is a reasonable approach.

USE LONG AND SHORT OPTIONS TO MANAGE RISK

It is inevitable, regardless of your strategy, time frame, experience level, or account funding, if you have ever traded futures, you have almost certainly experienced the agony of watching a market move without you following an untimely market exit. Perhaps you are stopped out prematurely, ran out of margin money, or simply couldn't take the pain any longer; being hastily forced out of a trade prior to the desired movement in the futures market price is a common, yet painful, reality.

> "You are going to be wrong a lot. If that's the case, you better make sure your losses are as small as they can be, and that your winners are bigger." — Steve Cohen

The problem with involuntary liquidation at the hands of stop-loss order, or manual panic liquidation, is the impossibility of recovery. Once a trader is on the sidelines, it is impossible to mend a trading account from a poorly timed speculation. Ironically, traders are prone to exiting their losing trades at precisely the worst time. After all, stop-loss orders are placed at the absolute pain threshold, and manual liquidation generally leads to traders "puking" up their holdings with the herd to stop the pain.

Nevertheless, when the masses are throwing in the towel, the end of the trend is usually near. In my experience, as long as the fundamental, seasonal, and technical analysis still coincides with the trade, it is typically easier to recover from large losses by waiting until other market participants have given up hope. Markets under severe price pressure rarely sustain extreme pricing; instead, they make a dramatic reversal back toward more equilibrium prices. Of course, if at all possible it is preferable to avoid taking part in such costly lessons, but if you find yourself in the middle of a violent and irrational price move beyond your risk tolerance, simply waiting a day or two for the dust to clear can make a significant difference in your bottom line. Remember, most traders lose money—so if you are following the masses to the exits, trampling others on your way, it is probably the wrong move. In disparity, finding a way to hedge your bet is generally a better idea.

As a reminder, traders using stop-loss orders are exposed to the risk of prices gapping through their stated price, excessive fill slippage, and even limit up or limit down moves. Regrettably, there are no mulligans in trading, but there is a way traders can enter the market with lasting power, absolute risk management (even during limit moves), and peace of mind: buying options as insurance against a futures speculation. This market tactic is known as a *synthetic strategy*.

SYNTHETIC STRATEGIES

A synthetic strategy is one in which a traders uses the combination of at least two financial products to mimic the payout of another. In my view, the simplest and most useful synthetic strategies are synthetic calls and synthetic puts. Specifically, a synthetic call is a strategy in which a trader goes long a futures contract and simultaneously buys a put option for protection. It is not a coincidence the strategy has been coined a synthetic call; the combination of a long futures contract and a long at-the-money put option mimics the risk and reward of a long at-the-money call option. However, by opting to purchase an out-of-the-money option, as opposed to an at-the-money option, the trade becomes increasingly less like a long call option and more like a long futures contract with a hedge. Hopefully, the ambiguity of trading is becoming obvious; each speculation can be designed to fit the account size, personality, and desires of each individual trader. The markets, and its instruments, are one size fits all, assuming traders are savvy enough to properly construct a market approach to fit their needs.

ADVANTAGES OF SYNTHETIC STRATEGIES

In contrast to a synthetic call, a trader executing a synthetic put would go short a futures contract and purchase a call option as an absolute hedge. In both cases, similar to a more traditional stop-loss order, the purchased option acts as an insurance policy to limit the risk of adverse price moves. The result is a trade that enjoys unlimited profit potential with the comfort of limited risk. However, unlike a stop-loss order, synthetic calls and puts don't run the risk of premature liquidation at the hands of a temporary price spike, the margin clerk, or an emotional fury.

Because a synthetic call or put strategy involves limited risk, like a long option position, it is a nearly margin-free strategy if the protective option purchased has an at-the-money strike price. With that said, even if an at-the-money option is purchased against a futures contract, some brokerage firms will require a minor margin deposit. The moderate margin charge is to account for the possibility of temporary volatility before option expiration in which gains on the purchased option don't keep up with losses on the futures contract, but for all intents and purposes we'll assume the trade requires no margin. Don't make the mistake of believing because there isn't a margin requirement, you can execute the strategy in an account with little to no money. To put the trade on a speculator will need at least the cash on hand needed to purchase the protective option, and preferably a bit more.

Synthetic calls and puts can be executed in any market, but because the strategy involves the liability of costly insurance, it is a good idea to avoid markets that have high-priced options. Conversely, markets that offer cheap options are perfect candidates. Some commodities we've found to be optimal for this strategy are the Treasury notes, the dollar index, soybean oil, corn and, in certain situations, maybe even the e-mini NASDAQ.

> "Logic will get you from A to B. Imagination will take you everywhere."
> —Albert Einstein

Shorter-term traders, such as those looking to swing or day trade a particular market, might find opportunities using the short-dated options such as weekly e-mini S&P, grain, Treasury, or currency, options. With weekly options it is possible to buy insurance against a futures trade for a lower out-of-pocket expense.

MODIFY A SYNTHETIC STRATEGY INTO A COLLAR STRATEGY

> In the worst-case scenario for a synthetic strategy trader, the position cannot get any worse, but it can always get better. This is preferable to being stopped out with a loss, and no possibility of recovery.

For traders interested constructing synthetic strategies in markets that tend to have higher-priced options, such as crude oil, gold, or the e-mini S&P, a better play is usually some sort of collar strategy in which an antagonistic option is sold to pay for the insurance. To illustrate, a trader who is bullish in gold might consider going long a futures contract, buying a put to limit the downside risk, and sell a call to pay for the cost of protecting the trade. The burden of the cash outlay for the long option can be partially offset by the sale of an antagonistic option. Collar trades have small risks and small rewards, but the trader determines how much risk and reward the position is exposed to by choosing appropriate strike prices.

DISADVANTAGES OF SYNTHETIC STRATEGIES

Of course, neither insurance nor peace of mind is ever free; the purchase of the option creates a scenario in which the trader must first overcome the burden of the insurance before the trade becomes profitable. Accordingly, synthetic strategies are not always appropriate if the cost of establishing the trade is such that it undermines profitability to the point that rendering success is highly unlikely. Nonetheless, the luxury of having the opportunity to hold the trade with no additional risk and without the jeopardy of being prematurely forced out of the trade regardless of how fast or far the futures market moves adversely is substantial. Let's take a look at a hands-on example to demonstrate the premise of a synthetic strategy.

Example

A trader who is bullish corn could buy a futures contract and place a stop order to protect from runaway losses, but he runs the risk of getting stopped out of the trade at an unfortunate price and poor timing. Trading without a stop-loss order, on the other hand, comes with its own demons, leaving the trader vulnerable to unknown, and unlimited, risk in addition to the urge to manually liquidate the trade in a sea of panic. I speak from experience when I say it is common for traders to hastily exit a losing trade, only to see the market turn on a dime and subsequently move in the intended direction while they watch, frustrated, from the sidelines.

Using a synthetic call option prevents either of these scenarios from playing out. Even if corn futures drop to zero, the trader will be suffering the maximum allowable loss by the strategy but still have a foot in the door. Should prices sharply reverse, the trade is still active and capable of possibly turning a profit. This is a case of "You have to be in it to win it"—a trade that is stopped out at a loss has no hope of recovering without re-entering the market, adding risk and frustration to the trade, not to mention increasing the probability of poor decision making under emotional duress. On the other hand, a trader holding a synthetic call is in a situation in which the damage has been done, but things can only get better.

> Synthetic calls and puts offer traders the safety of limited risk, with the benefit of flexibility.

For instance, with corn futures trading near $3.60 per bushel (Figure 54), a bullish trader might have opted to purchase a March corn futures contract on a dip to $3.50. To ensure the position against runaway losses, the same trader could have bought a $3.50 put expiring in about 50 days for $0.08 (8 cents). Each penny in corn is worth $50 to the trader, so the purchase of this put option to provide insurance against a long futures trade would have cost a total of $400 ($50 x 8 cents) before considering transaction costs such as commission. The result is a long futures position with limited risk, and more lasting power than a traditional stop order. The position is a limited risk venture, not unlike buying a call option, thus the name *synthetic call*. However, unlike trading a call option in which a trader is essentially either "all in" or "all out," trading a synthetic call (long futures contract and long put) enables the trader to make quick and easy adjustments such as peeling one leg off and holding the other. In addition, options aren't always liquid in the overnight session but futures contracts are, so a synthetic strategy gives a trader the ability to offset the futures contract, which is the money maker leg of the trade, nearly 24 hours per day at sufficient market liquidity. Should the trader opt to offset the futures contract in the overnight trading session, it might be necessary to offset the option during the following day session when liquidity returns to the option market. However, in this situation the option value would likely have eroded to an inconsequential amount. Hopefully, the futures profits more than made up for it!

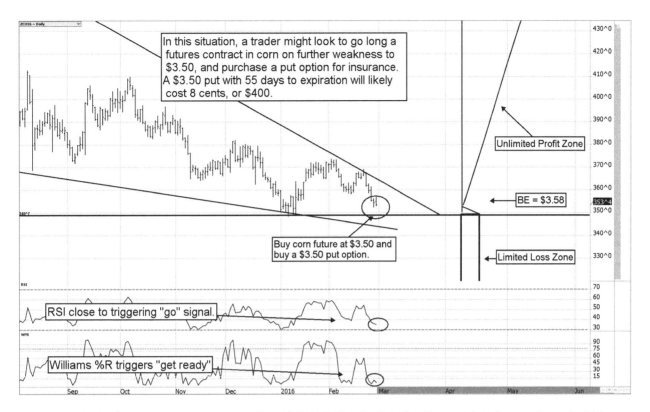

In this situation, a trader might look to go long a futures contract in corn on further weakness to $3.50, and purchase a put option for insurance. A $3.50 put with 55 days to expiration will likely cost 8 cents, or $400.

Unlimited Profit Zone

BE = $3.58

Buy corn future at $3.50 and buy a $3.50 put option.

Limited Loss Zone

RSI close to triggering "go" signal.

Williams %R triggers "get ready".

Figure 54: Synthetic calls are a great way to enter a market with limited risk and unlimited profit potential. In the case of corn, the risk is often very little.

In this example, the trader faces a total risk in the amount of the cash outlay to establish the strategy because the strike price of the option is equivalent to the entry price of the futures contract. However, had the trader opted to purchase the $3.45 put instead for 6 cents, the total risk would have been 11 cents because there would be risk exposure from the entry of the futures contract at $3.50 to the strike price of the put option at $3.45. Thus, the risk is equivalent to the premium paid for the put, plus the additional futures contract risk exposure between the strike price of the option and the entry price of the futures contract. So why would anybody take the higher risk trade to save a mere 2 cents in premium? A trader who is highly confident in the trade might do this knowing a recovery in corn prices will render the long put option nearly worthless rather quickly. Thus, in some scenarios the savings on the purchase of an out-of-the-money vs. an at-the-money put option might be worthwhile for accepting moderately higher risk.

The worst-case scenario for a synthetic call trader, which represents the maximum possible loss, occurs if the futures price is trading beneath the strike price of the long put at expiration. Because the CME Group automatically exercises any option that is in-the-money at expiration, the long put becomes a short futures contract from $3.50. In turn, the newly assigned short futures contract offsets the long futures position that was established at the onset of the strategy. Although the long put protects the trade beneath $3.50, the traders must also account for the premium paid for the long put when figuring the profit and loss. Hence, should the futures price be lower than the strike price of the long put at expiration, the total loss would be the premium paid for the put option, plus transaction costs. In this example, it is 8 cents, or $400 plus commissions and exchange fees.

Of course, the trader could have gone another route. He could have simply entered a stop order to protect his long corn futures from runaway losses. However, doing so would have forced the trader to face a difficult decision of placing a tight stop-loss to keep risk low, or to place a deeper stop-loss to keep the probability of a premature stopout at bay. A trader opting to place a distant stop-loss at a level that clears the swing low support would mean a stop price of $3.35, which is moderately below trendline support, and a total risk of 15 cents, or $750. Clearly, the purchase of the put offers lower risk and more lasting power in this scenario.

Ideally, the price of corn will rally to provide the trader with the prospect of theoretically unlimited gains. Obviously, most traders would be willing to take a quick profit; few would stick around for the possibility of windfall profits if they presented themselves, but in theory anything can happen. As we all know, a bird in the hand is worth several in the bush.

Naturally, insurance is never free. If you want to enjoy the luxury of price protection with the wherewithal to withstand price fluctuations, you have to give something up. With this strategy, the opportunity cost is the burden of recovering the cost of the protective put option in the form of futures gains before a profit is possible. Specifically, corn would need to rally to $3.58 ($3.50 + 0.08) before the trade would be profitable at expiration because the cost of the $3.50 put was 8 cents. Likewise, should the market rally to the previous swing high, allowing the trader to exit the futures contract at $3.70, the futures portion of the trade would be profitable by 20 cents, or $1,000 ($50 x 20 cents). Yet, after accounting for the money lost on the long put option, which would likely be worthless at that point, the total profit would be 12 cents, or $600 ($50 x (20 – 8)). I doubt many traders would complain about such an outcome, particularly because the stress level and risk is muted. Let's take the synthetic call strategy one step farther by converting the position into a market collar.

Figure 55: A collar trader has limited risk and limited reward, but he or she would get plenty of peaceful nights' sleep. In this example, the breakeven point is shifted favorably to $3.53, from the original $3.58.

The trader in the previous example might have opted to sell a call option to pay for his put option (Figure 55). Generally speaking, calls and puts are priced relatively equally, so collecting enough premium to pay for the put would require selling a close-to-the-money call option. Which is also counterproductive, because the net result of selling an at-the-money call could be a position that is nearly guaranteed *not* to make money. On the bright side, it would also be guaranteed not to lose money either. Accordingly, the trader would want to sell an out-of-the-money call option, or hope for a rally to occur before selling the call option, creating a collar. Knowing resistance lies at $3.70, the trader might decide to sell a $3.70 call at the time he entered the long futures contract and put option; he would probably only collect about 5 cents, or $250. Nevertheless, this essentially cuts the cost of the put insurance to 3 cents, or $150. On the flip side, it limits the profit potential to 17 cents, or $850. This trade wouldn't get anybody rich, but for a risk of $150 plus transaction costs, it might not be a bad idea.

In the end, synthetic strategies and collars are a particularly attractive method of trading for those with low risk tolerance and the virtue of patience. Overactive traders have the propensity to eliminate the advantages of such strategies by breaking the trade apart at inopportune times, or simply fail to exercise the patience necessary to enable the strategy to work. Some might say synthetic and collar strategies are akin to watching paint dry.

USING STANDARD PORTFOLIO ANALYSIS OF RISK MARGIN (SPAN) TO YOUR ADVANTAGE

To understand the premise of margin adjustment, it is necessary to be familiar with the mechanics of margining in a futures and options account. Futures margin is straightforward in that there are concrete initial and maintenance margin requirements, and although the requirements are adjusted from time to time, they are relatively static. If you are still unsure of the difference

> Understanding margin management and adjustments magnifies the lasting power of traders in a predicament.

between maintenance margin, initial margin, and the basics of portfolio margin, it might be worthwhile to revisit Chapter 1, "Commodity Refresher," in the section "What is margin?"

CONTROLLING FUTURES MARGIN WITH NET DELTA

The most common question I receive from beginning traders is, "What do I do if I receive a margin call?" The answer is simple: Don't panic! In most situations, there is usually an easy fix to alleviate a margin problem that doesn't involve wiring funds or offsetting trades at unfavorable prices.

Ideally, margin call avoidance is the best policy. However, even the most responsible traders will encounter the predicament sooner or later. Rather than simply throwing in the towel and liquidating positions or adding additional funds to what might become equivalent of a money pit, there are an unlimited number of ways to influence the exchange-required margin in your favor via risk reduction, or at least the perception of such. Naturally, lower risk equates to lower margin and, in most cases, lower profit potential, but for those who find themselves in a dire margin situation, beggars can't be choosers.

As we learned in Chapter 1, futures traders face an exceptionally uncomplicated margining process of stated initial and maintenance margins, but option traders are dealing with much more ambiguity. Those trading option spreads, or a combination of futures and options, are levied margins based on a software system known as standardized portfolio analysis of risk (SPAN). SPAN in commodities is similar to portfolio margining in equities. However, equity traders must typically have $100,000 or more on deposit to enjoy the benefits of such a margining system, yet futures traders of all types and sizes are automatically granted the privilege. For these traders, margin requirements are dynamic and changing constantly as the market ebbs and flows.

The specific parameters used by SPAN is a relatively closely held secret by its developer, the Chicago Mercantile Exchange. Understanding the basic premise, at least, will help you determine how certain adjustments will affect your margin requirement. SPAN margin fluctuates with market volatility, proximity of the risk (in other words, how close the short options are to the futures price), event risk, and other factors the CME believes will affect the price exposure of holding any particular option position. The exchange generally requires a margin amount equivalent to their calculations of the losses that a maximum adverse daily move might produce.

One of the most critical aspects of portfolio margining, and more important adjusting a position to eliminate a margin call, is figuring the account's net position.

KNOWING YOUR NET POSITION VIA DELTA

Being conscious of the net position simply means knowing the aggregate long or short exposure in a particular market in terms of equivalent futures contract risk exposure. For someone trading futures contracts, it is as simple as adding the longs or shorts; a trader who has purchased 10 July corn futures throughout the day is net long 10 contracts, regardless of fill prices. On the other hand, a trader holding a combination of futures and options, or a combination of long and short options, will have to take a few extra steps to arrive at a net position.

Most brokerage firms provide a net position figure on client statements, but if you want to compute it intraday, you are left to your math skills or finding software that will do it for you. Because technology isn't always available or trustworthy, I'll show you how to do it manually using delta.

Option delta is one of the commonly referred to suite of option greeks used by traders to assess the risk and reward of a particular option or strategy. *Delta* is a mathematical representation of the *pace* of risk exposure in terms of a ratio. By definition, it is the degree of change in an option value relative to a price change in the underlying futures contract. A futures contract has a delta of 1 because for every point of price movement the market makes, the trader is making or losing a point. But option traders are typically dealing with incremental deltas. For instance, an option with a delta of 0.25 will appreciate or depreciate a quarter of a point for every point that the futures market moves. Thus, a person holding a short put option with a delta of 0.25 is essentially net long a quarter of a futures contract. Conversely, a trader who is long that put is net short the market by a quarter of a futures contract. To clarify, the short put trader is bullish with a position equivalent to being long 0.25 futures contracts, and the put buyer is bearish to the tune of 0.25 futures contracts.

In the case of call options, the net position is inverse; a trader long a call option with a delta of 0.40 is net long four-tenths of a futures contract, but the trader short that call option is net short four-tenths of a futures contract.

Armed with this knowledge, you will find that figuring position delta is as simple as adding the sum of each instrument delta, and this is the key to adjusting your way out of a margin call. We'll briefly demonstrate this in the next section.

It seems obvious that a trader should always be aware of his net position in each market; yet many short option or spread traders fail to realize the magnitude of their positions until it is too late. This is particularly true for traders partaking in a strategy involving selling deep-out-of-the-money options. For instance, on the surface, selling a quantity of 50 crude oil $25 puts with two weeks to expiration for 5 cents in premium at a time when oil is valued in the high $30s seems like a virtual profit printing press. The odds of oil dipping $10 per barrel, or roughly 25%, in a few short weeks are rather slim. Even so, such a trade can quickly get out of hand if the price of crude drops sharply. Whether or not it ever reaches $25 is irrelevant; if the option prices explode, the trader's net position and margin requirement will as well—along with a large paper loss.

For instance, in the heat of volatility it is not uncommon to see options priced at a nickel quickly double, triple, or quadruple in value. A trader holding 50 puts valued at 5 cents, or $2,500 (($10 x 5 cents) x 50), could easily see a paper loss of several thousand dollars in short order if circumstances change. Imagine the option increasing in value to 20 cents; this would create a loss of 15 cents, or $150 per lot traded. A trader holding 50 of them would be sitting in a loss of $7,500 ($150 x $50). Even more concerning, the net long position could go from a fraction of a contract to multiple contracts rather quickly. In this example, the trader started out with a net long position of about five contracts because each of the $25 puts had an individual delta of 0.10, but he likely ended up with a net long position of 15 to 20 futures contracts due to a spike in delta toward 0.35. In short, although he didn't change the quantity of his position, his net position actually quadrupled!

ADJUSTING DELTA TO ADJUST MARGIN AND RISK

A trader's delta is essentially a gauge of risk. Obviously, a trader holding a net long delta of 1.5 is taking on more risk than a trader with a net long delta of 0.5. In either case, the speculator is hoping for higher prices, but the former will make or lose money more quickly.

> "To hell with circumstances; I create opportunities." —Bruce Lee

Because the delta of a futures contract is 1, a trader holding a single long July natural gas futures is net long one July natural gas. The same trader could lower his risk and margin requirement by reducing the overall delta of his position. There are several ways to adjust position delta, so being creative is a virtue; nevertheless, all methods of lowering the position delta of a position would involve taking a position with the opposite directional bias, with a related instrument.

For instance, the purchase of a put acts as an antagonist to a long futures contract because it stands to profit in a declining market while the futures will profit when prices increase. Thus, buying a put against a long futures contract lowers the delta of the position, as well as the required initial margin. As we've also learned, the long put option acts as insurance against losses; accordingly, the purchase of a put is a powerful tactic. The strike price of the long put, and more important, its delta, determines how beneficial the margin break, and risk reduction, will be.

Traders long a futures contract and long a put option with a delta of 0.25 would face a position delta of 0.75 (1-.25). In short, this hedged trader is exposed to 75% of the delta and volatility risk than a trader simply long a futures contract would be. Of course, as the futures price approached the strike price of the option, the hedge would become more powerful because the delta of the option would increase, and the advantages of having an insurance policy beneath the strike price of the option becomes more valuable.

An alternative to purchasing a put to lower the delta of a long futures trade is to sell a call option. A short call is antagonistic to a long futures contract because it benefits from lower futures contract pricing, whereas the long futures position must have higher prices to thrive. In this scenario, the trader doesn't have the benefit of absolute insurance, as is the case with a long put, but there is some comfort in knowing that the short call acts as a hedge to the existing speculative position. A trader who is long an e-mini S&P futures and short a call option with a delta of 0.4 is maintaining a position delta of 0.6. In other words, the position is equivalent to being long 0.6 futures contracts. This type of delta manipulation can be looked at as a way to decrease leverage and essentially create a smaller contract size than is offered organically by the commodity exchange.

On a side note, a popular strategy in the ES is to sell an at-the-money call option against a long futures contract for what is often a hefty premium. This generally carries a delta of 0.50 and can offer traders a higher probability venture relative to buying a futures contract outright because the premium collected acts as a buffer against a down draft. The premium collected represents the maximum potential on the trade, but if employed under the right circumstances, it can be an attractive proposition.

The key takeaway from this is that position delta and margin are closely related; adjusting the delta using long and short antagonistic options is essentially manipulating the margin and risk of a particular speculation. Such a strategy can effectively lower the initial margin of a new venture, or it can be used to alleviate a triggered margin call. Let's look at an example to demonstrate the point.

Assuming the current margin to hold a single crude oil futures contract is $4,000, a trader would need at least $4,000 in his trading account to initiate a position. I would argue that it would be desirable to have far more in the account to speculate in crude oil futures ($10,000 or more), but if the goal is to use the maximum allowable leverage, it would be possible to begin a position with the minimum initial margin. That said, oil margin fluctuates periodically but generally ranges between $3,000 and $5,000. A trader with $4,000 in his trading account would likely trigger a margin call if the price of oil went against his position to the tune of about $400, or a $0.40 cent change in the price of oil (remember, maintenance margin is typically 10% beneath the initial margin). If you have followed crude oil at all, you realize the market can move 40 cents in a matter of seconds; thus, a margin call is likely.

A trader who started with $4,000 in his trading account and purchased a crude oil futures contract at $35.00 would trigger a margin call on a closing price in crude oil below $34.60, which results in a drawdown of $400. In Figure 56, this is exactly what occurred. The trader could opt to send a wire for at least $400, preferably more, to bring the account back to the initial margin requirement, or he could simply exit the position at a loss. Another option, so to speak, would be to mitigate the exchange's margin requirement by selling a call option against his long futures contract, and maybe even buying a put option. In either case, the trader is not only lowering his margin requirement, but he is decreasing the delta, and therefore, risk of the trade.

The same trader could sell a $40.00 crude oil call expiring in approximately 40 days for $1.00 in premium, or $1,000. Doing so reduces the margin of the position from $4,000 to $3,200. This alone meets the margin call because after the $0.40 loss on the futures contract, his account balance is $3,600 before considering transaction costs. The trader could take it a step farther by purchasing a $29.00 put option for $0.35 cents, or $350. Doing so shaves off another $800 from the initial margin, bringing it to a more comfortable $2,400. The trader now has about $1,200 in excess margin and has collected a total of $650, or $0.65 in option premium. The $650 option premium collected in excess of the premium paid is known as the net credit. This is figured by subtracting the $350 spent on the long $29.00 put from the $1,000 collected for the sold $40 call. You might recognize this strategy as a market collar. Most collar traders use closer-to-the-money options, but this strategy is in fact identical to a collar.

Figure 56: Traders can lower margin, and even meet a margin call, by purchasing and selling antagonistic options.

In the end, the trader is long a crude oil futures contract from $35.00 with a $0.65 downside buffer from losses, compliments of the net credit received. He is also protected from runaway losses under $29.00. However, if the futures price is below $29.00 at expiration, the trader will lose $5,350 on the trade; $6,000 on the futures contract entered at $35, with a loss limited under $29. This is because $6.00 in oil is equivalent to $6,000 to a futures trader, but the loss is reduced by the net credit of $650 from the option trades.

The drawback of this adjustment to lower margin is the forfeiture of unlimited profit potential above $40.00. If oil is above $40.00 at expiration, the trader's profit is maxed out at $5,650, which accounts for the profit in the futures contract from $35.00 to the strike price of the short $40.00 call option, or $5,000 ($1,000 x $5.00), plus the net credit (((40.00 – 35.00) x $1,000)) + ((1.00 – 0.35) x $1,000))).

USING DELTA TO ADJUST OPTION MARGIN

Until this point, we've addressed buying and selling options against futures contract to mitigate the initial margin requirement of a futures position, but we've failed to address the idea of doing so to provide similar benefits to a naked option seller. The concept of lowering delta of a short option position is generally the same as doing so for a futures position, but the instruments involved will all have a delta lower than 1 and there are cash inflows and outflows to be aware of.

HOW SHORT OPTIONS ARE MARGINED

Before we can discuss the manipulation of SPAN margin via option adjustments, we need to understand the basics of short option margining. Of course, long options come with limited risk so they do not have a margin requirement. As long as your trading account has enough money to purchase the option, there is no additional funding requirement. Not only that, as discussed, long options can be an efficient means of reducing margin requirements. Nevertheless, don't

> Options purchased decrease available cash for margin, but lower the margin requirement when purchased against an antagonistic position.

forget that the cash used to purchase options is cash that is no longer available to use toward margin. Specifically, because options are an eroding asset, they are not accepted as a means of meeting margin. Thus, if the margin requirement for a particular trade is $2,000, the trader must have at least $2,000 in cold hard cash on deposit with his broker. Simply having $2,000 worth of option securities doesn't cut it.

Short options, on the other hand, expose the trader to unlimited risk and therefore carry a margin requirement that can be mitigated through the purchase or sale of combative options, or even futures contracts.

What many don't realize is selling an option immediately increases the cash in a trading account in the amount of premium collected minus transaction costs. The premium collected represents the maximum profit potential, but it also represents cash added to the margin coffer. Although the short option itself is a liability, the cash collected enhances the equity in which the margin is measured against. Accordingly, each dollar collected in premium increases the marginable funds available. This is an extremely important aspect of short option margining because it opens the door for selling antagonistic options to decrease margin while increasing profit potential.

That said, option selling isn't a risk-free monetary printing press; short option premium acts as a cushion toward losses at expiration but also leaves the door open to theoretically unlimited risk of loss.

Let's take a look at some hands-on examples of managing short option margin deficits through the purchase and sale of antagonistic futures contracts and options.

A trader short five natural gas puts with a strike price of $1.50 at a premium of $0.030, or $300 per lot, might have run into margin trouble in early 2016. Gluttonous supply forced gas prices down to levels not seen in over a decade, and likely caught speculators by surprise.

> Short options immediately increase the cash available to use toward margin, and if used antagonistically can sometimes reduce margin requirements.

Assume, if you will, that the margin on the aforementioned short put position in natural gas is $4,300. Should the trader need to take action to eliminate a margin call, or to lower margin in an attempt to avoid a margin call, he might look to add money to the account via bank wire, sell futures against his short puts, sell some calls, or possibly buy puts as a means of getting the margin shortage in check. Assuming the delta of the $1.50 puts is 20%, the net delta of five contracts is 1.00. This happens to be the same delta of a futures contract. Thus, selling a single futures contract against the five short $1.50 puts would put the trader into a delta neutral position and cut the margin by $2,000 to $2,300. However, the resulting position might be uncomfortable to a trader who is clearly bullish natural gas. After all, he wouldn't be holding five short puts in a market unless he believed prices would rise. It might make more sense to sell calls against the short puts instead of selling a futures contract. Doing so brings in additional premium, directly increasing the profit potential, reducing the margin requirement, and increasing the funds available to use toward margin. Of course, short calls will get into trouble should natural gas prices reverse sharply, but this approach gives the market more room to breathe and causes less stress than simply selling a futures contract would.

Figure 57: Option sellers can reduce margin and possibly eliminate margin calls by converting directional trades into strangles, and purchasing a few long options for insurance.

Selling the $2.10 natural gas calls for $0.040, or $400 per lot, would leave the trader relatively delta neutral. It would also bring in an additional $2,000 in profit potential ($400 x 5 lots) (Figure 57). Selling the $2.10 calls would reduce the margin requirement in our hypothetical trade to $3,300, which is $1,000 less than the original requirement. If further margin cuts are necessary, the trader could buy two of the 1.40 puts for about $200 per contract to cut the margin by about $1,200. The net result would be a margin requirement near $2,100, down from $4,300. Also, the trader collected an additional $1,600 (($2,000 – ($200 x 2)) in net option premium and provided a healthy hedge to downside risk in exchange for shifting the position risk to the upside of the market. The long put quantity of two wasn't a typo. The trader certainly could have purchased five puts to match the quantity of short puts, but doing so requires spending precious trading capital on options likely to expire worthless. If the trader can reduce margin to a desired level by only partially protecting his risk, it is a viable solution for anybody willing to accept the associated exposure.

MARGIN-TO-EQUITY RATIO

As we've already discussed, increased leverage supercharges the profits and losses in a trading account, habitually causing overzealous traders to prematurely liquidate positions. A good way to reduce the odds of such ill-timed liquidation is to keep a margin to equity ratio that allows for plenty of market volatility without interfering with the traders' capacity to hold positions.

Specifically, the margin to equity ratio of a particular account is simply the margin being used relative to the account balance. If a trader has $50,000 on deposit with his commodity brokerage and is holding positions that carry an initial margin requirement of $40,000, he is utilizing 80% ($40,000/$50,000) of his account toward margin. Such a trader is said to have a margin-to-equity ratio of 80%. Similarly, a trader with open positions requiring $30,000 in initial margin in a trading account valued at $50,000 is operating at a 60% ($30,000/$50,000) margin-to-equity ratio.

The appropriate margin-to-equity-ratio varies based on the experience and comfort level of the trader, as well as the strategy being employed. For instance, a futures trader faces static margin requirements and is therefore less likely to be shocked by exploding margin requirements relative to an option trader; consequently, a futures trader can typically get away with a higher margin-to-equity-ratio. Remember, sometimes the changes in SPAN option margin can be dramatic and unexpected; thus, an option seller, or option spread trader with open-ended risk, should maintain a relatively lower margin-to-equity ratio. Just how low depends on the trader, but as a rule of thumb the goal should be to keep it under 50%. Some of the more experienced option sellers believe the ratio should be closer to 30% to decrease the odds of being unwillingly forced out of short option positions. Futures traders are probably best off keeping their margin-to-equity ratio around 50%. Of course, these are simply suggestions. Those with higher risk tolerance and a propensity for gambling might choose to run their account at a higher ratio, and those with low risk tolerance might trade more conservatively. I can attest to the likelihood of an aggressive trader getting into margin trouble, which eventually takes over the trading decisions in an account. As a trader, you want to do everything in your power to ensure you are buying or selling futures and options based on your trading method or market analysis, not at the hands of a margin call, or panic. The first step in maintaining the right to make educated decisions in your trading account, as opposed to margin-induced verdicts, is keeping the margin-to-equity ratio low.

Naturally, long option traders facing limited risk and a lack of margin requirement don't need to worry about being forced out of trades prematurely at the hands of a margin shortage. Thus, the concept of a minimal margin-to-equity ratio does not apply to option buyers.

CHAPTER 17: USE COMMODITY MARKET VOLATILITY TO YOUR ADVANTAGE — MEAN REVERSION AND DELTA NEUTRAL TRADING

Anybody who has been around the commodity markets for any length of time knows volatility can work for you, but when it works against you, the damage is profound. Thus, regardless of the path chosen, a key to successful commodity trading will be finding a way to use volatility to your advantage. Even the best of traders will fail at this task on occasion, or maybe even frequently, but the consequences that volatility has on any particular trading effort cannot be ignored.

Market volatility generally increases the value of options, making it a prime time to be an option seller and an inopportune time to be buyer of calls and puts. It is also a time in which futures traders face higher odds of getting stopped out of a trade prematurely, while encountering massive swings of profit and loss.

The highest volatility is generally experienced at major market highs and lows because these are areas of escalated fear and greed emotions. In such market environments, the risks *and* rewards are exaggerated. Paul Tudor Jones once said, "I believe the very best money is made at the market turns. Everyone says you get killed trying to pick tops and bottoms and you make all your money by playing the trend in the middle. Well, for 12 years I have been missing the meat in the middle but I have made a lot of money at tops and bottoms." Reading between the lines, this statement says a lot about markets in that there are vast differences in experience among various market participants in the same market situations, due to different approaches to trading. Again, there isn't a legitimate or illegitimate way to trade as long as the strategy is congruent with the trader's personality, offering as much peace of mind as can be expected when money is involved.

Back to volatility. Actions speak louder than words; it isn't enough to say, "I want to be an option buyer when volatility is low and a seller when volatility is high." Most traders recognize this simple and fundamental rule of options trading, but when it comes down to acting accordingly, it is very difficult. This is because markets can stay quiet for several months, or even years, which lures those preferring option selling strategies to sell premium in a relatively low-volatility market. Additionally, during times of low-market volatility, it is extremely comfortable to sell options; after all, if the market isn't moving much on a daily basis, the thought of selling an option seems like easy money. However, I assure you such a scenario is exactly when it will be the hardest money to make. Low volatility generally shifts to high volatility in the blink of an eye. Anybody with open short options at the time is already facing substantial losses, and stress. It is only a matter of time before these same traders are forced to buy their options back at large losses after an unexpected spike in volatility.

Similarly, when volatility is high, it can be downright scary to establish a short option position facing unlimited risk, despite doing so being in line with conventional wisdom. Even those utilizing limited risk premium collection strategies, such as credit spreads, are facing deep risks for establishing a trade at precisely the moment it feels the least comfortable. In summary, those who fail to exercise patience will find themselves behaving in the exact opposite way they should according to the well-known, and accepted, relationship between option prices and volatility.

Futures traders aren't off the hook when it comes to poor judgment during volatile market conditions. Regardless of the chosen strategy, a trading plan always runs the risk of being compromised due to human nature and emotions. Everyone knows the goal of trading is to buy low and sell high. It doesn't get any fundamentally simpler than that. Nevertheless, when the market starts moving, the majority of traders find themselves selling a market near a low, and buying it near highs. Once again, most of us are wired to be comfortable selling a market that is going down and buying a market that is going up. However, in normal market conditions, this is a challenged approach. Although the one-way commodity markets of 2014 and 2015 didn't conform to traditional school of thought, it is widely accepted that markets spend about 80% of the time trading sideways in a range and 20% of the time redefining that range. I believe in the long run this is an accurate portrayal of the futures markets. With that said, traders might be best served looking for price anomalies made possible by overly volatile trade to buy into sharp dips, and sell sharp rips.

MEAN REVERSION TRADING

Although mean reversion trading strategies aren't always categorized as volatility plays, in my opinion that is exactly what they are. The theory of mean revision suggests that once markets become overextended in one direction or the other, they will inevitably return to the mean, or average price. Therefore, the goal of a mean reversion trading strategy is to identify a commodity valued at a potentially unsustainable price, then implement a countertrend speculative play in hopes of a quick reversion to some sort of equilibrium price. Obviously, this approach to trading involves taking a position in the opposite direction of a market trend and defies the comfort level of most. Nevertheless, I've found this approach to trading to be favorable for those with the capital to provide ample leeway for inaccuracy, and the emotional steadiness necessary to let the strategy work as intended. Believe me when I say, it is easier said than done.

> In short, mean reversion trading is counterherd trading. Sell signals are triggered as the masses are buying, and vice versa.

As great as mean reversion strategies look on paper, they come with anxiety. Sometimes market extremes become even more extravagant before finally exhausting the trend; as a result, mean reversion traders must temporarily endure painful losses, or if they opt to abort the trade in desperation, the losses could be permanent. Simply put, this strategy is not for the faint of heart, but I do believe it is attractive in regards to the percentage of winners. This approach is not only countertrend, but it is counterherd; while the masses are selling into new lows, the mean reversion trader is buying against the grain.

There are several technical tools that mean reversion traders use to identify a market due for a reversion; among the most popular are RSI and Bollinger bands. Each indicator, in its own way, signals a market extension has likely gone too far too fast, and is, therefore, assumed to inevitably reverse. In summation, these indicators are mathematical representations of whether the last of the buyers have entered a bull market, or the sellers have fired their ammo in a bear market. Of course, these indicators aren't perfect; nor are any others. Nevertheless, they provide a good guide for traders to begin establishing a countertrend position that stands to profit from a mean reversion.

As is the case with any trading-related topic, there is plenty of ambiguity in mean reversion trading. For example, which time frame and data set is the assumed average price based on? Which indicators should the strategy use to assess unsustainable price spikes? As prices rise or fall to extreme levels, when and how should the trade be triggered? What are the appropriate manners of risk management to avoid being a victim of temporary volatility? Each of these questions are valid in relation to any market approach but are even more dire when employing a trading tactic based on a premise of going against the grain, or catching the proverbial knife.

> "Price is what you pay. Value is what you get." —Warren Buffett

Mispriced commodity markets occur rather frequently; in some cases, it is a story of stop orders being run, or it might be a mass exodus from a popular commodity trade due to margin call liquidation. Once margin calls begin to take hold of market pricing, there are few limits to the insanity because market participants are buying and selling on necessity of capital preservation, not market fundamentals. Unfortunately, the net result for some is being forced out of a long position at a significant market low or squeezed out of short positions at a meaningful high. These types of experiences can be difficult to come back from, both financially and mentally. Nevertheless, for those lucky enough to be on the sidelines and mentally prepared to employ a mean reversion strategy, someone else's pain can be another trader's good fortune.

Soon we will take a look at an example of a commodity market that fell to the depths of despair, to trade at prices that shouldn't have been seen had market participants acted according to realistic market fundamentals as opposed to being forced to trade for margin, or discomfort, reasons.

Naturally, mean reversion trading can come in many forms—buying or selling futures outright, buying or selling options outright, and complex strategies such as option spreads and covered calls. Years of market watching leads me to believe either selling countertrend options, or establishing covered calls, to be optimal ways of playing potential reversions, but regardless of the path chosen, there is certainly a fair amount of stress accompanying the trade. The challenge of this strategy, aside from the difficulty in accurately pinpointing a potential turning point, is giving the trade enough breathing room to work. Tight stop-loss orders, or overly sensitive risk management, will convert this relatively high-probability technique into a guaranteed loser.

CHARTING AND TRADING MEAN REVERSION

The purest and simplest method of reversion trading is purchasing an outright futures contract. However, this is also the most dangerous and mentally taxing way to proceed. Many mean reversion traders might find the use of e-micros and mini contracts to be a great alternative to facing the large and volatile risks of trading full-sized contracts in this strategy.

In Figure 58, it is clear that a futures trader might have done very well using a mean reversion strategy using soybean futures in late 2015 and early 2016. Of course, it doesn't always work this well, but this is a great example of what mean reversion traders hope for. It is also a fair representation of the turmoil one might suffer as a mean reversion trader. Although Figure 57 makes trading the ebbs and flows around the mean look like a cake walk, in real time with real money on the line, it is a different story. For example, in late October, a mean reversion trader would have likely been early to enter a short futures contract. Most strategies would have called for a short near $9.10 per bushel, but selling there would have resulted in an almost immediate loss of 20 cents, or $1,000 per contract, as prices soared to $9.30 (each cent in soybeans results in a profit or loss of $50 to traders). The price of soybeans subsequently collapsed to $8.55. Had a trader stayed the course, he would have made 55 cents, or $2,750 (55 cents x $50). Yet most mean reversion strategies would have taken profits once prices approached the mean price near $9.00, a mere profit of $500. This probably seems like a lot of work and risk for $500, and it is, but mean reversion trades generally go a little smoother. In late November, a buy signal at $8.55 immediately yields a profit of 20 cents, or $1,000 on a run to $8.75 (20 cents x $50). In fact, nearly identical setups and successful mean reversions occur four more times in Figure 58; that is what the reversion trader lives for.

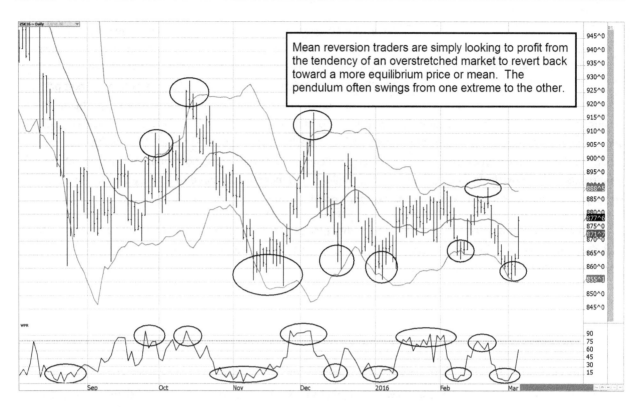

Mean reversion traders are simply looking to profit from the tendency of an overstretched market to revert back toward a more equilibrium price or mean. The pendulum often swings from one extreme to the other.

Figure 58: A futures trader might try to buy into extended lows and sell into extended highs in hopes the market reverts back toward the mean, or average price; it habitually does just that.

COUNTERTREND OPTION SELLING

Thus far we've pointed out that most brokerage firms detest, and therefore deter, their clients from option selling due to prospects of unlimited risk and complicated valuation during high-volatility market conditions. But we're also pointing out it can be a high-probability strategy for those willing to finance, and stomach, the occasional tumultuous trade. That said, selling options with little regard to volatility will (*not* could) eventually end in account draining devastation.

We already know that options should be sold when it is least comfortable to do so—specifically, when volatility is high. But unfortunately, market volatility is a function of human emotion, which has no limits. Sometimes, selling option premium in elevated volatility eventually results in buying that premium back at even higher-volatility levels. It is imperative to be patient and keep the big picture in mind when choosing a commodity market to sell options in and when to execute the trade. In my opinion, selling options against the trend, or at least on a big countertrend day, yields the maximum premium collection, optimal potential profit, and highest chances of turning a profit.

One will never know exactly when volatility is peaking, or when and where to sell a particular option to avoid an initial drawdown. In fact, when selling countertrend options it is almost a guarantee the position will be under water before it ever returns a profit. This is because selling an instrument that derives its value from panic is a messy endeavor. Nevertheless, the strategy opens the door for favorable odds of success. To demonstrate the magnitude in which probabilities shift in favor of an option seller during spikes of volatility, let's take a look at an example.

In January 2016, the S&P 500 was on the skids. Chatter in trading forums, social media, and of course business news stations was clouded with fear. What eventually proved to be a temporary rocky patch resulted in high levels of volatility and, therefore, overpriced option premiums.

Utilizing some of the concepts discussed in earlier chapters, a trader might have deemed it appropriate to sell a put against the e-mini S&P 500 decline. Implied volatility was at an elevated level and the Williams %R indicator, which I like to use as the "get set" trigger, had dipped below 20, suggesting prices were oversold. Further, the RSI, which I like to consider the "take action" trigger, fell below 30,

> Sell options like Warren Buffett trades stocks; hoard cash to take advantage of higher-probability ventures when they materialize.

implying the downside was likely limited from there (Figure 59). At the inflection point, the ES dipped to 1,800, causing the March 1600 put with roughly 50 days to expiration to reach a premium of 24.00, or $1,200 (remember, each point in the e-mini S&P is worth $50 to a trader).

> Countertrend option selling works well in normal market conditions, but during times of mass hysteria the strategy painfully fails.

It isn't reasonable to assume a trader would have sold the option at precisely the best time, but even an early trader might have collected $15.00 in premium, or $750. That isn't a bad trade, given the ES hadn't been to 1,600 in three years; the likelihood of it doing so in the allotted 50-day time frame was slim, despite the option market temporarily giving the event a rather high probability. Don't forget, if held to expiration, the only way a trader can lose on a short option is if the futures price is beyond the strike price of the option. In this particular case, the e-mini S&P would have had to fall another 200 points in 50 days before the trader gets into trouble. In a moment, we'll revisit the reality that this concept is a little more complicated than meets the eye because options can gain in value at any time prior to expiration, regardless of whether or not the future price ever reaches the strike price.

A month later, the same option was worth a mere 1.00, or $50. The buyer of that option likely suffered a great deal of remorse, but the seller would have come out smelling like a rose. Assuming an entry of $750, or 15.00 in premium, the trade would be profitable by $700 per contract before transaction costs. Those lucky enough to sell the exact high price of that particular option of 24.00 ($1,200) would be netting $1,150! As my friend and colleague Jim Cramer likes to say, "You can't make money panicking." This particular strategy of mean reversion option selling is attempting to exploit market panics in hopes they are merely temporary. Not only is this strategy an attempt to profit from the panic of others, but it will test the mental capacity of the trader implementing countertrend option selling. This approach will miserably fail if the trader employing the strategy cannot overcome the desire to execute panic liquidation of his own position.

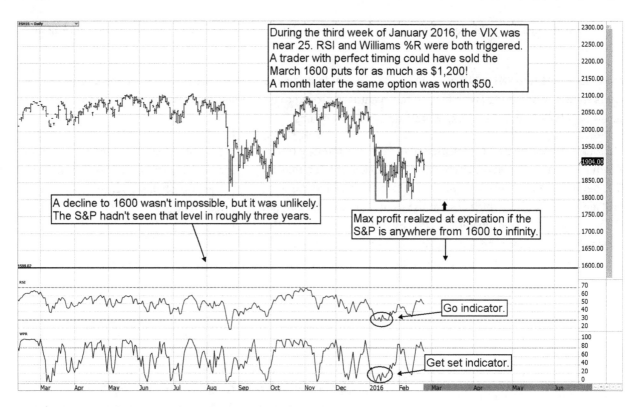

During the third week of January 2016, the VIX was near 25. RSI and Williams %R were both triggered. A trader with perfect timing could have sold the March 1600 puts for as much as $1,200! A month later the same option was worth $50.

A decline to 1600 wasn't impossible, but it was unlikely. The S&P hadn't seen that level in roughly three years.

Max profit realized at expiration if the S&P is anywhere from 1600 to infinity.

Go indicator.

Get set indicator.

Figure 59: An option seller willing to sell options against the trend, and into high levels of implied volatility, might be able to construct a trade with abnormally high probabilities of success in normal market conditions.

Of course, participating in such a trade is easier from a hypothetical standpoint than reality. For starters, before a trader could consider executing a trade such as the one used in this example, it would be necessary to either be flat the market or at least have a substantial amount of cash on the sidelines, providing the opportunity to take advantage of price anomalies. In other words, option sellers might be best off treating their commodity account in the same manner that Warren Buffett treats his stock account, by always keeping plenty of cash on hand. You never know when or where volatility will strike, but you know it eventually will.

To illustrate just how important timing and volatility are to an option seller, Figure 60 displays the fluctuations in value of the same 1600 e-mini S&P put used in the previous example, during late 2015 and early 2016. It is clear the option is continuously eroding, as we've discussed options tend to do. However, this chart also offers the not-so-obvious path the option takes during bouts of market volatility. Although most traders want to sell put options in a quiet or uptrending S&P 500 market, it might mean suffering massive paper losses as the price of put options balloon in value along with market volatility. Imagine selling a 1600 put in the e-mini S&P in late December 2015 for a mere $250 under the premise that a move to 1,600 was extremely unlikely; at the time the S&P 500 was at 2,100. A few weeks later, as the S&P approached 1,800, a plunge to 1,600 was similarly unlikely in reality, but the market had convinced itself it was a real possibility. Option buyers were willing to bid the price of the 1600 put up to $1,200. The trader who sold the 1600 put for what amounted to chump change would have had to endure a paper loss of $950 per contract before eventually seeing the option lose most of its value. On the other hand, the option seller executing his strategy in the midst of an emotional market might have quickly made several hundred dollars without suffering a massive drawdown. It is obvious which option seller we would all prefer to be; but in practice, it takes a considerable amount of patience and discipline to be the ideal option seller.

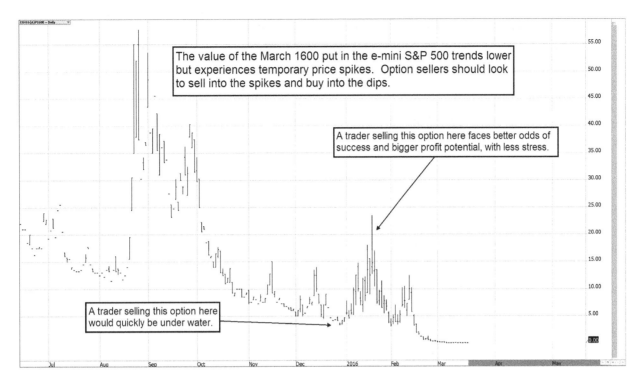

The value of the March 1600 put in the e-mini S&P 500 trends lower but experiences temporary price spikes. Option sellers should look to sell into the spikes and buy into the dips.

A trader selling this option here faces better odds of success and bigger profit potential, with less stress.

A trader selling this option here would quickly be under water.

Figure 60: Too many option sellers ignore timing and volatility. They simply assume if the strike price of the option goes untouched, the trade makes money, but this attitude could lead to unnecessary paper losses and stress.

RATIO OPTION SPREADS

A different version of mean reversion with a countertrend option strategy is a one-by-two ratio spread. This entails a trader purchase a relatively close-to-the-money put option, then sell two options with distant strike prices. If constructed correctly, the result is a credit to the trader and the potential to make a substantial amount of money in a declining market, or a moderate profit in an inclining market. Of course, the same concept can be used in a sharp rally using a call option ratio spread.

This strategy, known as a *ratio spread*, can be implemented in any market condition but poses the least risk with the most profit potential in a highly volatile market. Unfortunately, for those who have tried and learned the hard way (guilty), executing a ratio spread in a quiet market can quickly turn into a disaster if volatility rears its ugly head. Let's take a look.

Around the same time as the previous example, a trader could have gone about things a little differently by purchasing the March e-mini S&P 1800 put for 30.00 points, and then selling two of the March 1700 puts for a total of 45.00 points (22.50 each) (Figure 61). The net credit to the trader would be 15.00, or $750. The resulting trade returns $750 to the trader if the price of the e-mini S&P at expiration is above 1,800. However, the beauty of this strategy is that it stands to make money even if prices decline moderately. Specifically, if the price of the e-mini S&P falls below 1,800, the long put option begins to work in favor of the trader. In fact, if the market is trading at 1,700 (the strike price of the two short options), the trader earns the maximum profit of 115 points, equivalent to $5,750 (115 x $50) before considering transaction costs. This is because at that price, the short options expire worthless, the long 1,800 put option is intrinsically worth 100 points, and the trader keeps the 15 points originally collected. If prices fall below 1,700, the trader is essentially giving back profits until running out of money at 1,585. This is because the long 1,800 put offsets losses on one of the short 1,700 puts, but the other is naked.   At 1,600 all of the gains from the long 1800 put are eaten up by losses on the short 1700 puts, and at 1,585 the premium collected is negated. Thus, at this price the trader is the equivalent of being long a futures contract outright. As we've already touched upon, although anything is possible, a selloff in the S&P below 1,600 was highly improbable.

Figure 61: In a high-volatility environment, it is possible to construct unusually attractive put spreads in the e-mini S&P 500.

I feel it necessary to point out that regardless of how high volatility is at any given time, it can always go higher. Once again, there is no limit to human emotion and the power of panic. Even a ratio spread as promising as the aforementioned example can get hairy in the short run. If prices in the e-mini S&P continued to fall, it is quite possible the two short 1700 puts would outpace gains on the long 1800 put. Because of the volatility smile, options with distant strike prices can be far more volatile relative to close-to-the-money options.

COVERED CALLS AND COVERED PUTS IN SEARCH OF MEAN REVERSION

There is nothing scarier than buying a futures contract in a sharply declining market, except for maybe selling a futures contract in a runaway market. Nevertheless, sometimes taking Warren Buffett's advice, "Get greedy when others are fearful, and fearful when others are greedy," pays off. Yet entering such a venture without a hedge, or any reasonable means of risk protection, is asking for trouble. As we've discussed, the use of stop-loss orders often conclude with the despair of premature liquidation, yet buying call options in a sharply higher market, or put options in a plummeting market, for insurance purposes would mean paying top dollar, shifting the probability of profit unfavorably. Alternatively, however, there are advantageous opportunities to implement a covered call or covered put position.

We initially introduced covered calls and covered puts in Chapter 9. As a refresher, it is a strategy in which a trader takes a long or short position in the underlying futures market, and an antagonistic short option position. In the case of a covered call, the trader is going long the futures contract and selling a call option, bringing in premium to cushion the downside risk. Covered put traders are selling a futures contract and then selling a put option to hedge the upside risk of the futures contact. In my opinion, applying this strategy to a mean reversion trade makes a lot of sense because it generally offers relatively attractive profit potential, using a strategy containing a built-in hedge against adverse price movement at a time it is imperative to have a buffer. Remember, market tops and bottoms are messy; if you are going to try to play them, you had better give yourself room for error.

It might seem odd that I would suggest the idea of selling a call option in a declining market to protect a long futures contract. After all, selling calls in a down market is doing so at discounted pricing. We've just spent entire chapters of this book arguing that call options should be sold when futures prices are in an upswing, not a downswing. However, in the case of covered calls or covered puts, the sold option is not the primary position; rather, it is merely an antagonistic position taken to hedge the portion of the trade intended to be the money maker. Further, believe it or not, when markets get to ridiculously unsustainable extremes, options in the opposite direction tend to hold value better than would be reasonably expected. This is because a market trading at extreme lows attracts speculators wishing to buy calls options in hopes of a recovery. Likewise, a market trading at lofty levels attracts countertrend put buyers, which can sometimes help to drive put prices above their expected theoretical value. If pricing is extreme enough, the options sold in a covered call or covered put strategy might be executed at attractive prices in spite of everything suggesting otherwise.

In my view, the best covered call or covered put strategy going against the grain of the market is designed to collect a substantial amount of premium. Although the primary position is the long or short futures contract, the premium sold as a hedge should be done so using a strike price that is relatively close-to-the-money. This seems to provide a healthy mix of optimal profit potential and diversified risk. To illustrate, in the case of a covered call, as the futures market goes down, a close-to-the-money short call will lose significant value to offset a considerable portion of losses on a long futures contract. If the market goes higher, losses on the short call option generally don't keep up with the gains on the futures contract; even more intriguing, if held to expiration the trader gets to keep all of the premium collected! This is because if the call option is in-the-money at the time of expiration, the exchange will automatically exercise it. As a result, the long futures contract will be offset by the short futures contract assigned at the strike price of the option by the exchange's exercise. In the end, the profit and loss on both the original futures contract and the assigned futures contract equal each other, but the original option premium collected by the trader can be added to the win column. Let's take a look at an example of how such as trade might be constructed.

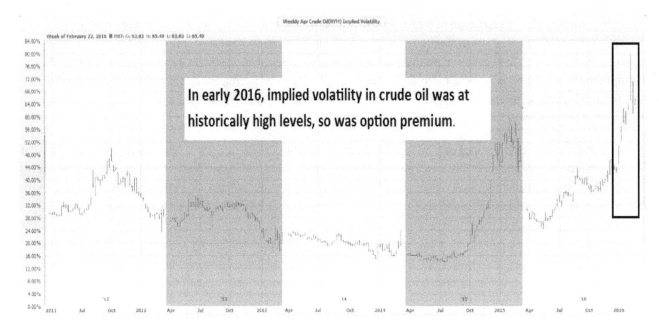

In early 2016, implied volatility in crude oil was at historically high levels, so was option premium.

Figure 62: Extreme implied volatility in crude oil options created opportunities for premium collection despite relatively tame futures market pricing.

In February 2016, crude oil futures were on the decline at a time in which implied volatility was historically high. Figure 62 portrays the extreme option pricing; during this time, the oil market was coping with the reality of oversupply while compensating for the possibility of OPEC production cuts, and the fact that US shale producers were dropping like flies. Although oil futures were contained in a reasonable trading range between $38 and $30 per barrel, option traders were bidding option values higher, speculating on a change in the fundamental landscape.

Compliments of extreme implied volatility, it was possible for a crude oil futures trader to construct a bullish position with relatively tapered risk and position fluctuation through the sale of option premium. A trader might have recognized on February 11 that crude futures prices being slightly oversold and approaching lows that were posted roughly a month earlier, were at the lowest price in nearly a decade. Weighing the various strategies available, he could simply buy a call option, but with implied volatility at elevated levels, it would have resulted in a low-probability undertaking. Alternatively, he could have purchased a futures contract, but with option premium so high, the purchase of a protective put would have been outrageously expensive and trading without a hedge could be an expensive lesson in risk management. Further, simply placing a stop-loss order poses the risk of premature liquidation. This leaves the trader contemplating either selling a put option, or buying a futures contract and selling a call option as a hedge. Either would be appropriate, but a trader willing to get somewhat aggressive might opt for the covered call option simply because a commodity near a decade low likely doesn't have a tremendous amount of downside risk.

As depicted in Figure 63, hypothetically, a trader could have gone long a May crude oil futures contract at $32.00 per barrel and simultaneously sold a $32 call option for about $3.50 in premium, or $3,500 (remember, each dollar in crude oil is worth $1,000 to the trader). This particular version of the strategy provides a hedge on the futures contract down to $28.50. At expiration, if the futures price is exactly $28.50, the trade breaks even before consideration of transaction costs and possible slippage. This is figured by subtracting the premium collected of

$3.50 from the entry price of the futures contract; the premium collected acts as a buffer to losses should crude oil decline. Below this price, the trader is essentially long a naked futures contract without any additional protection, but with the futures prices of oil on the day of expiration at any point above the breakeven point of $28.50, the trader makes *something*. If the futures price is above the entry price of $32.00 at expiration, the trader keeps the entire $3,500 in premium.

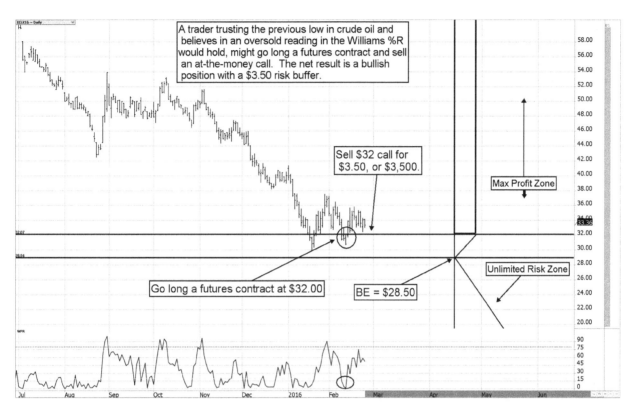

Figure 63: Going long a futures contract and selling an at-the-money call option creates a scenario in which the trader keeps all of the premium if the market is higher than his futures entry at expiration because gains in the futures contract offset intrinsic losses in the short call.

The drawback of this approach to trading is the opportunity cost of unlimited profits. In short, the trader is sacrificing the unlimited profit potential of being long the futures contract for a more certain payout. Regardless of how far above $32.00 the futures market travels, the trader's maximum profit will always equate to the premium collected—in this example, $3,500. Nevertheless, I can assure you the reduction in position volatility and, therefore, anxiety, makes this a much more comfortable method of trading. Further, the trade stands to make money even if the original speculation is moderately inaccurate, and I doubt many would complain about a profit of $3,500 even after transaction costs are deducted.

DELTA NEUTRAL TRADING IN HIGH VOLATILITY

Not all traders are confident in picking a top or bottom in a commodity market, nor should they be. Picking the precise reversal area of any market has almost as much to do with luck as it does skill. Some traders might be more comfortable speculating on changes in volatility, rather than attempting to predict the direction of price. For these traders, taking a delta neutral approach to the market is likely a better fit.

> Trading options is an art, not a science. It requires creativity and an open mind.

You might recall the introduction of delta in Chapter 16 in relation to risk management, but as a reminder, delta is simply the pace of change in an option strategy relative to the rate of change in the underlying futures price. A delta neutral position is one constructed in a manner that absorbs price change but experiences profit and loss at the hand of volatility and time value erosion in options.

RATIO COVERED CALLS AND PUTS

Delta neutral strategies come in all shapes and sizes. In fact, in the previous example using the crude oil covered call, a trader could have sold two at-the-money call options against a single long futures contract to create a delta neutral position (Figure 64). This is because the delta of a futures contract is equal to 1.0, and the delta of an at-the-money option is roughly 0.50. Thus, the new delta neutral version of the trade would no longer be seeking higher crude oil prices. Instead, the trader would be anticipating relatively sideways action.

The trader would have collected $7.00 in premium, or $7,000. This $7,000 would cushion losses on the futures contract all the way down to $25.00 ($32.00 - $7.00), but unlike the original version of selling one call option for every futures contract purchased, there is upside risk. Initially, the futures contract will make or lose approximately the same amount of money the two options do, but as time goes on, if the futures price is increasing, the option losses will outpace the gains in the futures contract. The premium collected when the options were initially sold act as a buffer on the upside, just as they do on the downside, but once the benefit of the collected premium runs out the trader is left with what is theoretically a naked short call option. This occurs at the breakeven point of $39.00 ($32.00 + $7.00). Once again, the long futures contract offsets any intrinsic value for one short call option as the price of crude oil increases. The other short call option, on the other hand, is essentially naked. As a result, the premium collected of $7.00 cushions losses on the second short call option until running out of premium at $39.00. Above this price, the trader is exposed to unlimited risk, equivalent to being long a single futures contract.

A delta neutral trader might sell 2 at-the-money call options against each bought futures contract. The result is a directionless trade that profits from sideways price action and/or a decrease in volatility.

Sell 2 $32.00 calls for $3.50 each, or $7,000.

Unlimited Loss Zone

BE = $39.00

Max Profit at $32

Go long a futures contract at $32.00.

BE = $25.00

Unlimited Risk Zone

Figure 64: A covered call can be converted to a delta neutral position by selling an additional call option. The new version of the trade has no directional bias and is intended to profit from lower implied volatility, or at least time erosion in a sideways market.

SHORT OPTION STRANGLES

Another delta neutral strategy that is appealing during times of excessive implied volatility is to sell a simple short strangle. If constructed in a relatively balanced manner, a short option strangle is delta neutral because as prices ebb and flow, the trader is profiting on one side of the strangle and losing on the other. However, ideally over time, the erosion of extrinsic value and decline in volatility will leave the trader with a profitable position as the options lose value. Going back to the early 2016 crude oil example in which implied volatility was elevated, we saw short option strangle traders facing unprecedented opportunities. Overpriced option premiums enabled traders to sell strangles using deep-out-of-the-money strike prices for relatively high premium. For instance, around the same time of the previous examples, a trader could have sold a May crude oil strangle, expiring roughly two months from the date of entry, using the $44.00 call option and the $22.00 put (Figure 65). Based on historical data available (to me), the total premium collected might have been roughly $1.00, or $1,000. For this example, we'll assume the fill prices were exactly $0.50 for the call and the put, and we'll ignore the implications of transaction costs, which obviously reduce the profit, and increase the loss, of any given trade.

At the time, crude oil was at about $32.00 per barrel, which means the strike price of the put option was exactly $10.00 under the current market price. However, the call option strike price was $12.00 above the current price of crude oil. The imbalance causing call options with more distant strike prices to have equivalent value to a closer-to-the-money put is a reflection of implied volatility. Option market participants were expecting a crude oil recovery; therefore, they are willing to pay more for calls. In effect, they are actively bidding the price of call options higher.

The resulting position is rather impressive in regards to odds of success. Although things could get hairy before expiration, causing angst and large paper losses, at expiration the trader keeps all of the premium collected, ignoring transaction costs, as long as oil is trading somewhere between $44.00 and $22.00. Even better, because the trader collected $1.00 in premium, there is a buffer against losses in the amount of $1.00 beyond each of the strike prices. Thus, if crude oil is above $44.00 but below $45.00 at expiration, the trade still pays off something less than $1,000, but still in the green. The same can be said about the put side of the trade; if prices are below $22.00 but above $21.00, the trader makes something. For clarity, if crude oil is at $21.50, the trader would make $500. This is because the premium collected of $1,000 covers the intrinsic loss on the $22.00 put, at least until the collected premium runs out at $21.00. At $21.50, the intrinsic value of the put is $0.50, meaning it has only eaten half of the premium collected.

Figure 65: In this example, the trade yields the maximum profit as long as crude oil prices are above $22.00 and below $44.00 at expiration.

Under most circumstances, it is fair to say a trade standing to yield $1,000 if held to expiration while carrying a margin requirement of about $1,000, as this type of trade generally does, giving crude oil the ability to roam within a $22.00 range, is highly attractive. Under normal market conditions, expecting crude oil to trade within the parameters of this trade are realistic. It would require oil to rally more than 37.5%, or decline more than 31.25%, in two months to cause a problem to the trader.

CHAPTER 18: IN CONCLUSION, COMMODITY TRADING IS MENTAL; DON'T BE

Despite the lengths taken to explain commodity market analysis and trading techniques in this book, I believe becoming a successful futures and options trader comes down to instinct and the ability to control emotion. If you have ever been involved in athletics, you have probably heard the

> "When anger rises, think of the consequences." —Confucius

adage that performance is 95% mental and only 5% physical. I have found this to be true in trading as well, although instead of being physical, trading is technical. Quite simply, it isn't which oscillators or indicators you use, nor is it your analytical techniques that determines trading success. There are millions of people deciphering the same information and receiving the same signals from technical oscillators; yet few of them make money in the markets. What matters is what the trader does with his findings, and perhaps more important, how he deals with fear and greed as he charts and implements his trading plan.

Although we cannot control the market, we can control the environment and the circumstances we choose to put ourselves in. The best way to keep your mental demons in check is to avoid compromising situations. For traders, this achievement is certainly impossible, but if you can merely minimize the exposure to stressful endeavors, it will go a long way toward trading success.

It can be difficult for many to wrap their heads around, but the reality is, trading is an ambiguous game without right or wrong answers. The best trading strategy is one that fits the personality of the trader in such a way that emotional stress is mitigated. For some, this might mean identifying a confirmed market trend and jumping on for the ride, or it might mean seeking abnormally cheap or expensive markets in hopes of profiting from the turn in prices. Further, some trading strategies are designed to profit in directionless markets with decreasing volatility, while others require a massive one-directional move to become profitable. Regardless of the approach taken, there will also be decisions to make in regards to

> Trading is a zero-sum game. If few traders are making money, those who are in the green stand to make substantial profits.

time horizon, risk, timing, and execution. As you can imagine, it is an overwhelming task for those seeking black or white solutions.

MAKE SURE YOUR STRATEGY FITS YOUR PERSONALITY

The approach you take in the markets should be dependent on your personality and risk tolerances, not necessarily what has worked for somebody else. Let's face it—there are only about 20 to 30 commonly used technical oscillators, and most market participants have access to the same news sources, business newspapers, and government supply and demand data. If there were absolute magic to any of these resources, more people would have discovered the holy grail of commodity speculation by now.

Rather than expecting an indicator or an oscillator, a market guru, or *The Wall Street Journal*, to do the work for you, I believe it to be more productive to properly educate oneself to the risks and rewards of the markets and mentally prepare for the task of making sound decisions on your own. This process begins with choosing a trading method that ruffles the fewest feathers possible.

For example, if you are a hyperactive decision maker prone to ill-advised trade entries and exits, it will be worth your while to choose technical indicators that have the ability to smooth out results by offering traders relatively slower triggered signals. Such indicators might include the MACD or the RSI (Chapter 2). Ideally, using slow trigger oscillators will work against your tendency to overreact. You might even want to consider placing trades by phone with a broker or trade desk. This sounds archaic, but it is an effective way to temper the urge to trade recklessly. Too many traders find themselves enamored by the flashing lights of a trading platform to the point of massively overtrading. Your broker will love you for being a quick-fingered online trader, but your spouse will not.

Know your tendencies and be honest with yourself when constructing a trading strategy. If you have a hard time pulling the trigger on a trade you've spent countless hours dissecting, then you should consider some sort of automatically programmed trading strategy based on the desired parameters. Another way around this mental obstacle is to place limit, or stop, orders in advance to employ the trading strategy in your absence. To illustrate, if your trading strategy calls for buying a gold future should the price break above technical resistance, you can instruct your broker, or your trading platform, to purchase a contract should it get to the desired level via a stop order. You can even instruct the broker or platform to exit the trade on your behalf if the trade moves adversely to a specified price. This too would be a stop order. If the strategy is to purchase crude oil at the bottom of a trading range, you could enter a limit order to go long at the specified price should it be reached, then leave for work knowing your strategy in play, but your emotions won't sway the results. Of course, if you aren't watching the market, a stop-loss exit order or some other type of risk management technique would be a good idea.

PATIENCE GOES FARTHER THAN STRATEGY

Regardless of the strategy you choose, waiting for the highest-probability setups is imperative. Unfortunately, it is also challenging. It is easy to fall into the mindset that suggests being on the sidelines is equivalent to missing out on profits. However, the best advice I can give to traders is that it is better to be on the sidelines wishing you were in, than in the market wishing you were on the sidelines. If you pass on a signal that turns out to be accurate, don't fret; there will be another opportunity around the corner. Executing commodity trades based on mediocre signals will work occasionally, but the risk of getting caught off guard by a false signal is far greater than the potential reward might be.

THE ONLY THING WE KNOW FOR SURE IS THAT WE DON'T KNOW

"Success is a pile of failure that you are standing on." —Dave Ramsay

Some of the sharpest minds in the trading industry have expressed sentiment proposing that they enter each trade with the inkling they are probably wrong. This gives them the proper mindset to avoid crippling losses, keeps them humble, and allows them to be willing to take profits at reasonable levels when things go in their favor. If the best of the best understand their analytical efforts could produce less than perfect trading signals, there isn't any reason for each of us to believe we are somehow smarter or savvier than they are.

Each and every day, market prices are influenced by a theoretically unlimited number of factors. More so, even if a trader's market analysis is tireless and flawless, he cannot possibly know what the future will bring. At any given time, an unexpected news event or piece of economic data could change the focus, and direction, of the market. It shouldn't be surprising that predicting the direction, magnitude, and timing of price changes is an exceedingly difficult task. After all, the tools we are using to gauge market direction are all the result of historical pricing; technical oscillators simply tell us what the market has already done, and fundamental stats give us insight into the supply and demand picture at some point in history (usually several months prior). As we've been reminded throughout our trading lives, "Past performance is not indicative of future results."

> "Time is your friend; impulse is your enemy." —John Bogle

Some might view my comments as being pessimistic in regard to trading futures and options, while others might go as far as to suggest this book is an anti-trading piece. My intention isn't to dissuade you from participating in the commodity markets. In fact, I have the opposite motive! I make my living through commission paid by my brokerage clients, but I've made it a personal undertaking to ensure that the general public is privy to the hardships of trading futures and options. There is a lot of money to be made in the commodity markets, but there is absolutely *no easy money.*

The media, and even Congress, would have one believe that all speculators make money. You might recall the Congressional hearings to discuss the greedy speculators profiting from $150 per barrel oil, while the consumer suffered. However, the truth is most speculators lost money in the ordeal. Much of the rally that brought oil to all-time highs before crashing back into the $30s was short covering by bearish traders losing substantial amounts of money. Not many could have imagined $150 crude oil; as a result, not everyone was on the right side of the move despite the widespread perception that commodity traders were enjoying life-changing profits at the expense of the American public. On the flip side, those who did make money on the largest crude oil rally in history probably gave most, or all, of it back as the market fell (in fact, crashed) from grace.

The reality is, there is no effortless money in the markets. Most who venture into commodities will leave with less than they started with. Yet, for those who do find the path to consistently profitable trading, the compensation on risk is enough to keep less fortunate market participants coming back for more.

I hope I have managed to provide readers with straightforward and positive guidance in commodity market analysis, strategy development, and market logistics to put them at better odds with the market.

INDEX

CPSIA information can be obtained
at www.ICGtesting.com
Printed in the USA
LVHW102109010720
659499LV00024B/460